Natural Law and Practical Rationality

Natural law theory has recently been undergoing a revival, especially in political philosophy and jurisprudence. Yet, most fundamentally, natural law theory is not a political theory but a moral theory, or more accurately a theory of practical rationality.

The theory of practical rationality aims to identify and characterize reasons for action and to explain how choice between actions worth performing can be appropriately governed by rational standards. The natural law view holds that the basic reasons for action are intrinsic goods that are grounded in the nature of human beings. It also holds that the rational standards that govern choice are justified by reference to features of the human goods that are fundamental reasons for action.

Natural Law and Practical Rationality is a defense of a contemporary natural law theory of practical rationality, exhibiting its inherent plausibility and engaging systematically with rival egoist, consequentialist, Kantian, and virtue accounts. It will be of interest to professionals and students of moral philosophy, the philosophy of law, and political theory.

Mark C. Murphy is Associate Professor of Philosophy at Georgetown University. He is coeditor of *What Is Justice?* (2nd ed. 2000) and editor of *Alasdair MacIntyre* (Cambridge University Press, forthcoming).

Cambridge Studies in Philosophy and Law

Some other books in the series:

Natural Law and Practical Rationality

Mark C. Murphy

Georgetown University

PUBLISHED BY THE PRESS SYNDICATE OF THE UNIVERSITY OF CAMBRIDGE
The Pitt Building, Trumpington Street, Cambridge, United Kingdom

CAMBRIDGE UNIVERSITY PRESS
The Edinburgh Building, Cambridge CB2 2RU, UK
40 West 20th Street, New York, NY 10011-4211, USA
10 Stamford Road, Oakleigh, VIC 3166, Australia
Ruiz de Alarcón 13, 28014 Madrid, Spain
Dock House, The Waterfront, Cape Town 8001, South Africa

http://www.cambridge.org

First published 2001

Printed in the United States of America

Typeface Times Roman 10/12 pt.   *System* QuarkXPress 4.04 [AG]

A catalog record for this book is available from the British Library.

Library of Congress Cataloging in Publication Data
Murphy, Mark C.
Natural law and practical rationality / Mark C. Murphy.
p.   cm. – (Cambridge studies in philosophy and law)
Includes bibliographical references and index.
ISBN 0-521-80229-6
1. Natural law. 2. Reason. 3. Rationalism. I. Title II. Series.

K474.M87   A36   2001
340′.112 – dc21   00-045551

ISBN 0 521 80229 6 hardback

for
Ryan Elizabeth
a divine gift

Contents

Acknowledgments

I owe a number of debts to people who read and offered comments on all or part of the manuscript of this book. I am especially indebted to Henry Richardson, Terence Cuneo, Paul Weithman, and two referees at Cambridge University Press for commenting in close detail on the entire manuscript. I thank also Richard Arneson, Melissa Barry, Ron Bontekoe, Denis Bradley, Jeff Brower, Christoph Fehige, Alfonso Gomez-Lobo, Lenn Goodman, Christopher Gowans, Germain Griscz, John Hare, Sean Kelsey, Jeremy Koons, Steve Kuhn, Tony Lisska, Trenton Merricks, Elijah Millgram, John O'Callaghan, Madison Powers, Connie Rosati, Jim Tiles, Linda Wetzel, Heath White, and Thomas Williams for their criticisms of portions of the text. Early versions of some of the arguments here were presented at the Georgetown/Maryland Moral Psychology Discussion Group; at philosophy department colloquia at Georgetown, Virginia Commonwealth University, and Virginia Tech; at the 1995 APA Central Division meeting (where my commentator was Larry May); at the 1996 APA Central Division meeting (where my commentator was Michael Gorr); at the 1996 Thomistic Institute at the University of Notre Dame; at the 1997 ISUS meeting (where my commentator was Richard Arneson); and at the 1999 ACPA meeting (where my commentator was Tony Lisska). I found the critical comments of those present at these gatherings most helpful.

My work on this book spanned residence at three different institutions. I began work on it during my first academic appointment, at the University of Hawaii at Manoa. The senior faculty there kept my service burdens light, giving me lots of time to devote to research; I am grateful especially to them for their mentorship and *aloha*. The bulk of the work on the manuscript was done at my home institution, Georgetown University, which has been extraordinarily generous in its support, providing summer grants in 1996, 1997, and 1998, as well as a junior faculty leave for the spring semester of 1999. This book was substantially completed while I was in residence as a fellow at the Erasmus Institute at the University of Notre Dame; I am very grateful to that Institute for generously offering fellowship support for a year of full-time research.

I thank also the following parties for permission to use material from these previously published articles: "Self-Evidence, Human Nature, and Natural Law," *American Catholic Philosophical Quarterly* 69 (1995), pp. 471–484, used by permission of that journal; "Natural Law, Impartialism, and Others' Good," *Thomist* 60 (1996), pp. 53–80, used by permission of that journal; "Natural Law and the Moral Absolute against Lying," *American Journal of Jurisprudence* 41 (1996), pp. 81–101, used by permission of that journal; "The Conscience Principle," *Journal of Philosophical Research* 22 (1997), pp. 387–407, used by permission of the Philosophy Documentation Center; "Natural Law Reconstructed," *Review of Politics* 60 (1998), pp. 189–192, used by permission of that journal; "The Simple Desire-Fulfillment Theory," *Noûs* 33 (1999), pp. 247–272, used by permission of Basil Blackwell; and "Functioning and Flourishing," *Proceedings of the American Catholic Philosophical Association* 73 (2000), pp. 193–206, used by permission of the American Catholic Philosophical Association.

Finally, my wife, Jeanette, has been unfailingly supportive and encouraging. I am often irritable about moral philosophy, and her constancy in the face of my surliness is an estimable feat.

M.C.M.
Herndon, Virginia
December 2000

Introduction

Natural Law and the Theory of Practical Rationality

0.1 Natural Law Theory as an Account of Practical Rationality

The theory of practical rationality is fundamentally concerned with two types of evaluations with respect to action: that of *intelligibility* and that of *rationality,* or *reasonableness.*[1] This book is a formulation and defense of a natural law account of practical rationality. We may begin, then, by considering briefly the notions of intelligible and rational action, and noting what theses concerning intelligible and rational action are essential to the defense of a natural law account of practical rationality.

For something to be intelligible is for it to make sense, to be something that can be understood. But an item can be considered in different ways, and thus may be intelligible in one respect while lacking intelligibility in a different respect. There are different ways to consider human action, and correspondingly different senses in which human action can be intelligible. It is thus crucial to be clear about the sense of intelligibility that is central to the theory of practical rationality. The performance of an action can be considered simply as behavior, and can be intelligible merely as such: it might be understandable as the outcome of the conjunction of a determinate set of antecedent conditions with the totality of psychological laws. But even if all human actions were intelligible in this way, in that they could be understood as behaviors, there would still be a sense of intelligibility in which some human actions might yet fail to be intelligible.

Consider, for example, a person who is stabbing himself in the leg with a fork at regular intervals. When asked about this – is this some extreme form of acupuncture, enabling the relief of a nagging injury? is this an experiment to determine to what extent the human can withstand pain? is this a sacrificial religious ritual of some sort? – the agent rejects all of these suggestions; he is aiming simply to stab himself in the leg. I take it that there is a clear sense in which we would find this behavior unintelligible, even if we were able to diagnose precisely what is the case with respect to this agent's physical condition that gives rise to this peculiar behavior. Even if intelligible with respect to its etiology – the behavior might be locatable within a true, comprehensive descriptive theory of the springs of human action – it would not be, as I shall say, *practically* intelligible: we cannot understand what the agent is *up to,* we cannot see a *point* to his actions, we cannot see that what he is doing is in any way *worth doing.*

For an action to be practically intelligible is, I propose, for it to be an action that is worth performing under the description under which it is performed; it must be possible to offer what Anscombe calls a "desirability-characterization" with respect to which the action is a choiceworthy one (Anscombe 1957, p. 71; see also Norman 1971, pp. 53–55, 63). For an action to be practically intelligible is for it to have a worthwhile point, something that makes the action worth doing. The first task of a theory of practical rationality is, then, to provide an account of what makes actions practically intelligible. What the theory of practical rationality must provide, that is, is an account of *reasons for action:* for a reason for action just is whatever it is that confers intelligibility on action. Such a theory must identify what reasons for action there are and must characterize as fully as possible the nature of those reasons.

The theory of practical rationality presupposes the applicability of the idea of practical intelligibility; its search for an account of the identity and nature of reasons for action is a search for a clear understanding of that which underwrites whatever practical intelligibility that actions possess. Now, the theory of practical rationality also presupposes that the possibilities of intelligible action outrun the capacity of agents to act on them. There are, that is, cases of *practically significant choice,* cases where an agent may φ intelligibly or may ψ intelligibly, but it is impossible for the agent both to φ and to ψ (see also Finnis, Boyle, and Grisez 1987, pp. 254–260). The second fundamental task of a theory of practical rationality is to provide, in light of its theory of reasons for action, an account of how agents can act in conditions of practically significant choice in a way that is insusceptible to rational criticism. For an action to be insusceptible to rational criticism is for that action to be rational, or reasonable (see also Parfit 1984, p. 119).

A theory of practical rationality aims, then, to identify and characterize reasons for action and to explain how choice between actions worth performing can be appropriately governed by rational standards. A natural law theory of practical rationality is a theory that aims to accomplish these two tasks in the following distinctive way. First, a natural law theory asserts that the fundamental reasons for action are certain goods that are grounded in the nature of human beings. Thus, natural law theory provides a catalog of goods in its identification of the fundamental reasons for action, and offers a characterization of those goods by connecting them to human nature. Secondly, a natural law theory asserts that the requirements of practical reasonableness, those standards the following of which makes action fully rational, are justified by reference to features of the goods that are the fundamental reasons for action. Thus, natural law theory explains how it is reasonable to deliberate in cases of practically significant choice by appealing to principles that have their warrant from the nature of the fundamental reasons for action themselves.

This book is a defense of a particular natural law account of practical rationality. The first three chapters constitute a defense of the natural law theorist's claim that the fundamental reasons for action are goods that are grounded in the nature of human beings. In Chapter 1, I provide an interpretation of the claim that the basic goods are grounded in human nature, an interpretation that I call the 'real identity thesis': this thesis both makes an assertion about the metaphysics of human goods and suggests a method for defending a catalog of human goods. In Chapter 2, I introduce the idea that the natural law theorist should understand the basic goods as aspects of human well-being. Since the present philosophical orthodoxy concerning well-being is that it is best understood along subjectivist lines, an understanding that is inconsistent with this natural law view's objectivist account of the nature of the good, I devote most of this chapter to indicating the severe difficulties that accompany subjectivist accounts of well-being. In Chapter 3 I provide a catalog of goods, justified by appeal to the method of knowing the basic goods elaborated in Chapter 1; the plausibility of this catalog of goods completes the case against subjectivist accounts of well-being begun in Chapter 2.

Chapters 4 through 6 are devoted to the defense and elaboration of the second natural law thesis, that concerning the natural law theorist's understanding of how principles of practical reasonableness are to be formulated and justified. Since this natural law account of practical rationality is welfarist – it holds that the fundamental reasons for action are aspects of agents' well being – it is subject to all of the criticisms that have been leveled against welfarist conceptions of practical rationality as such. In Chapter 4, I consider these criticisms, and hold that they are best understood not as criticisms of welfarism as such but as criticisms of welfarism in conjunction with some other distinct theses about practical rationality – theses that this natural law view rejects. In Chapter 5, I offer an account of natural law principles for situations of practically significant choice, defending them in terms of the nature of the fundamental reasons for action against rival egoist, consequentialist, Kantian, and virtue accounts. And finally, in Chapter 6 I explore the issue of whether a plausible account of morality can be constructed within the natural law view.

0.2 The Ways in Which This Work Is Incomplete

There are at least two major ways in which this work is incomplete as an account of natural law theory. The first way in which this work is incomplete is that the title 'natural law theory' names more than a theory of practical rationality. 'Natural law theory' names also a certain type of theory of politics, a theory that provides an account of the value, source, form, and limits of political authority. Moreover, it names a certain type of theory of religious morality, that is to say, an account of how we are to make intelligible the moral claims of some specific religious tradition or other. And 'natural law theory' is also a label applied to certain accounts of how practical rationality fits within the scheme of divine providence. It is this last usage of the term 'natural law' that makes sense of the very name: for, on such a view, the natural law by which human agents may reasonably guide their own conduct is, as Aquinas puts it, a participation in the eternal law by which God governs all creation (for the eternal law, see *Summa Theologiae* IaIIae 91, 1; for natural law as a participation in the eternal law, see IaIIae 91, 2; for God's providence, see Ia 22, 1–2). Clearly, these uses of the term 'natural law theory' are not merely equivocal: rather, natural law theories of politics and religious morality are outgrowths or applications of the natural law theory of practical rationality; and the natural law account of the relationship between rational action and divine providence is a way of adding a new dimension of explanation to the theory of rational action (see, e.g., Finnis 1980, pp. 371–410, esp. 403–410, and Lisska 1996, pp. 128–131).

The original plan for this book included both a discussion of the natural law account of practical rationality and additional chapters on political and divine authority. But these additional chapters turned out underdeveloped and unsatisfactory, and it soon became clear that they could not be developed satisfactorily without the book's becoming unreasonably long. My failure to treat these issues here is not, then, an indication that I think them unimportant in the development of a natural law view, or that I think that somehow political and theological issues historically bound up with natural law theory are mere accretions to be cast off by a contemporary, 'purified' version of the view. Rather, I think these issues still to be central to the development of an adequate natural law account and, thus, to be too important to be dealt with in a slipshod way. The present book thus concludes with an account of why a natural law account of authority is needed, that is, how the incompleteness of the natural law theory of practical rationality indicates a need for a natural law theory of authority (and, in particular, political authority), but it does not take any steps toward providing such an account. I hope to return in the future to the issue of natural law and political authority and that of natural law and divine authority. (For a developed natural law account of political authority, which I, however, do not affirm, see Finnis 1984 and Finnis 1989; for a sketchy attempt at my own natural law take on political authority, see Murphy 2001.)

The second major incompleteness of this book is that it does not on its surface give much indication of the way that the history of natural law thought contributed to its conclusions. This is not to say merely that it is not a history of natural law theorizing: it is obviously not a broad work on the natural law tradition (such as, e.g., Crowe 1977 and Haakonssen 1996), and it is just as obviously not an attempt to describe finely, or to recast, the work of any of the great natural law theorists (such as, e.g., Lisska 1996 and Bradley 1997). It is to say, rather, that little space is devoted to formulating and considering the arguments of past natural law thinkers, even for the sake of furthering my own argument. Aquinas, of course, makes several appearances; and, of course, there are a number of themes and debates central to the natural law tradition that are central to the working out of my view. But my concern in this book is not to recapitulate the history of natural law thought as culminating in my own, partially developed view – that would be the most extreme hubris – but rather to show how positions definitive of or consonant with the tradition of natural law thought about practical rationality can emerge as serious contenders within contemporary analytic ethics.

'Naturalism,' 'objectivism,' 'cognitivism,' 'welfarism,' 'anti-particularism,' 'anti-consequentialism' – all of these name views that are, individually, now taken seriously within analytic ethics, even if not as dominant positions. What I want to do in this book is to make a case for a particular naturalist, objectivist, cognitivist, welfarist, anti-particularist, anti-consequentialist view – which, it turns out, is a version of natural law theory as traditionally understood.

1

The Real Identity Thesis

1.1 Rival Views of How Goods Are Known

The natural law theorist aims to fulfill the first task of a theory of practical reasoning (to provide an account of the reasons that make action intelligible; see 0.1) by offering a catalog of basic goods. These basic goods are the fundamental reasons for action. This chapter is primarily devoted to the issue of the justification of the most basic natural law principles, that is, to an account of how these basic goods are known to be such. But it will turn out that the disputed question of how basic goods are to be known cannot be treated except by reference to another of the central theses of natural law theory, the claim that the basic goods are grounded in human nature. So, by the end of this chapter, I will have offered both an account of how the basic goods can be known (to be put to work in Chapter 3 to provide the catalog of fundamental reasons for action) and an interpretation of the thesis that the natural law is grounded in human nature, an interpretation that I call the 'real identity thesis.'

Inclinationist and Derivationist Accounts of Fundamental
Practical Knowledge

Standard natural law accounts of how the basic goods are known fall into two classes. One type of view, which I shall call 'inclinationism,' holds that no practical judgments regarding which objects are goods to be pursued can be derived from any set of nonpractical judgments; rather, knowledge of such goods is immediate and underived, occasioned by an inclination toward those goods. The other type of view, which I shall call 'derivationism,' holds that practical judgments regarding goods to be sought are not self-evident; rather, they must be derived from theoretical judgments regarding human nature.[1]

Let us consider first the derivationist view, which is the popular image of natural law theory. According to derivationism, the first principles of the natural law, which specify the basic goods to be pursued, are derived from claims about human nature knowable by speculative reason. Even apart from worries about how this task is to be accomplished, this may seem a strange claim: how could the principles of the natural law be *first* principles if they are to be *derived* from other propositions? The answer is, however, that while the principles of the natural law are, on the derivationist view, derived from premises drawn from the speculative order, they are first in the practical order. As such, they are the principles from which practical reason proper takes its guidance concerning how one ought to act.

Part of the attractiveness of derivationism comes from widely shared assumptions about the capacities of practical reason. A widely shared view of practical reason can be summed up by the slogan: practical reasoning is deliberation. To reason well in the practical domain is to deliberate well. A widely shared view of deliberation can be summed up by the slogan: deliberation is from ends, not about ends. (But see Schmidtz 1994 and Richardson 1994.) Now, in the contemporary philosophical climate, the conjunction of these slogans often leads writers in the philosophy of action to use objects of desire or preference as the ends from which deliberation operates. If one were to reject, though, the view that the starting points for practical reason-as-deliberation are nonrational, it seems clear that one would have to find those starting points in a product of theoretical reason.

This sort of picture of practical reason provides support of a negative kind for the derivationist claim: it cannot be practical reason that grasps the first principles of the natural law, and so it must be theoretical reason. But we yet have no account of that to which theoretical reason can appeal in order to derive the first principles of the natural law. Typically, though, one who is interested in defending a natural law theory of practical reason will want to appeal to some feature or other of human nature in order to determine what those first principles are: the derivationist generally holds that theoretical reflection on the nature of human beings enables us to characterize what the human good consists in, with the result that this conception of the human good can be employed by practical reason in determining how agents are to act.

Consider as an example of this kind of derivationist reasoning Aristotle's function argument in the *Nicomachean Ethics* (1097b24–1098a3), or at least a common understanding of that argument. While I would not claim that Aristotle was himself a natural law theorist, the function argument had a great influence on later natural law thinkers; and, indeed, it seems as if it is the derivationist elements of Aristotle's view that lead many to classify him as a proto–natural law thinker.[2] The function argument appears to be an argument carried out in theoretical terms, starting with a conceptual connection between the idea of 'good' and 'kind,' followed by an examination into what the human's kind is, and concluding with an at least partial statement of the human good, rational activity carried out well. On this derivationist interpretation of Aristotle, the conclusion of the theoretical function argument serves as a starting point for deliberation about how to act – what we ought to do can be determined by reference to our theoretically discovered good, rational activity. (I will return to the function argument for a more detailed treatment in 1.2.)

Or consider the derivationist interpretation of Aquinas recently offered by Anthony Lisska. On his view, Aquinas characterizes human nature in terms of essential properties that are dispositional – that is, that explain the human being's tending to develop a certain way. It is the complete and harmonious attainment of the objects of these dispositions that constitutes the human end (Lisska 1996, p. 103). But Aquinas defines goodness in terms of ends: it is analytically true that such ends are good (Lisska 1996, pp. 198–199). This understanding of goods as the ends to which we tend by nature yields an account of the epistemology of practical knowledge: such knowledge takes its first principles from our speculative understanding of human nature, and thus we come to know the natural law by grasping the character of the dispositional properties that are essential to us.

Derivationism is often quickly dismissed, due to the widely held – and, in my view, eminently plausible – view that its presupposition that practical judgments can be deduced from nonpractical judgments alone is simply logically untenable. But it does have its rationale within a natural law theory of practical reasoning: if one accepts common doctrines concerning the limited capacities of practical reasoning, it seems that one must either reject natural law theory or affirm a derivationist account of how the goods are known.

Let us now turn to the 'inclinationist' account of how basic goods are to be known, and begin by considering a particular version of the inclinationist picture, that offered by John Finnis. Finnis rejects derivationism's account of the relationship between judgments about human nature and the principles of the natural law:

> The first principles of the natural law, which specify the basic forms of good and evil and which can be adequately grasped by anyone of the age of reason (and not just metaphysicians), are *per se nota* (self-evident) and indemonstrable. They are not inferred from speculative principles. They are not inferred from facts. They are not inferred from metaphysical propositions about human nature, or about the nature of good and evil, or about 'the function of a human being', nor are they inferred from a teleological conception of nature or any other conception of nature. They are not inferred or derived from anything. They are underived. (Finnis 1980, p. 34)

Given that no derivations from theoretical considerations are allowed in the defense of one's account of these principles of practical reason, how does practical reason grasp the correctness of these principles? On Finnis's view, one's grasp of these goods must be wholly internal to practical reason: one becomes aware "by a simple act of non-inferential understanding" that certain objects are goods to be sought (Finnis 1980, p. 34). Thus, Finnis rejects one of the slogans about practical reason that underwrites the derivationist view: the claim that practical reasoning is deliberation. On his view, practical reason is capable of grasping first principles, which is an act distinct from deliberating.

Finnis describes the process by which one comes to grasp the character of the basic goods as such as a twofold movement: a movement from inclination to awareness of value and from the specific to the general. Essential to the process of grasping a basic good to be pursued is the agent's having at some point a felt want, desire, inclination for a particular object. Finnis illustrates this point with regard to knowledge, which is on his view a basic good. The seed of one's awareness that knowledge is a basic good is curiosity, "the desire or inclination or felt want that we have when, just for the sake of knowing, we want to find out about something. One wants to know the answer to a particular question" (Finnis 1980, p. 60). But since "[c]ommonly one's interest in knowledge . . . is not bounded by the particular questions that first aroused one's desire to find out, . . . it becomes clear that knowledge is a good thing to have" (Finnis 1980, p. 61). It is important to note here that, on Finnis's view, one does not *derive* the conclusion "Knowledge is a good" from such propositions as "I have an inclination toward knowing" or "Everyone has an inclination toward knowing." A view that held that practical principles are derived from statements about what inclinations we have would be a version of derivationism, since it derives practical claims from purely descriptive claims about human nature. Rather, the presence of these inclinations is simply a condition that occasions reason's consideration of and grasp of the good of knowledge. (Thus: if in some person the inclination of curiosity is lacking, that person will have difficulty recognizing knowledge as a good at all.)

I take to be essential to inclinationism both the affirmation of the indemonstrability of the first practical principles of the natural law and the reliance on inclinations as providing the impetus toward knowledge of the good. While it seems to me that Finnis is right to to emphasize the relationship between the particular object of inclination and the general form of good that that object instantiates (that is, that the inclination toward the particular is the occasion for the grasp of a general form of good), the best version of inclinationism would portray the relevant inclinations in a slightly different way than Finnis presents them and would move away from the 'flash of insight' picture that Finnis's remarks suggest. Let us examine first the issue of what is the nature of the inclinations that are the preconditions for knowledge of the basic goods. Consider, as a foil for Finnis's inclinationist picture, the account offered by Aquinas:

The precepts of the natural law bear the same relation to practical reason that the first principles of demonstration bear to speculative reason, for both are self-evident [*per se nota*] principles. . . .

The first principle of practical reason is that which is based on the nature of good: "The good is that which all things desire." The primary precept of the law, therefore, is that good is to be done and pursued, and evil is to be avoided. On this precept all the other precepts of the natural law are based, so that all things to be done or avoided pertain to the precepts of the natural law that practical reason naturally apprehends as human goods [or evils]. Because, however, good has the nature of an end, whereas evil has the nature of its contrary, thus it is the case that reason apprehends all things to which the human has a natural *inclinatio* as good, and consequently as objects to be pursued, and their contraries as evil and to be avoided. Therefore, the order of the natural *inclinationes* corresponds to the order of the precepts of the natural law. (*Summa Theologiae,* IaIIae 94, 2)

Like Finnis, Aquinas emphasizes the self-evidence of the principles of the natural law, and also indicates that practical reason's grasp of those principles is tied closely to inclinations toward those goods. But the notion of *inclinatio* as it appears in Aquinas differs from the notion of inclination as it appears in Finnis. For Finnis, inclination is paradigmatically something felt, a sort of urge – even if in particular cases this urge can be fairly colorless. But Aquinas's notion of *inclinatio* is different – it is better translated as 'directedness,' denoting an agent's tendency to act purposively to secure certain objects. (For this translation, and discussion of this point, see MacIntyre 1988, pp. 173–174.)

I think that the best inclinationist view would rely on Aquinas's notion of inclination, rather than on Finnis's. On Finnis's view, the precondition for recognizing a good as such is an urge; on Aquinas's, the precondition is a tendency to act. Now, the reason that Aquinas's account seems better suited is that the basic goods are held to be reasons for action, ways in which action can be made intelligible. Thus, there seems to be a tighter connection between Aquinas's view of how goods are known and the role that a theory of basic goods is supposed to play in the natural law theory of practical rationality, that is, of conferring intelligibility on action (0.1).

The notion of intelligibility is also central to the rejection of Finnis's account of how reason moves from inclination to grasp of value. Finnis denies that his view can correctly be called intuitionistic, because the act of insight by which one becomes aware of the status of a basic good as such cannot take place without data – one's felt inclinations toward objects as understood (Finnis 1983, p. 51). Theoretical reason thus plays a subsidiary role in Finnis's account, as providing *descriptions* of objects; practical reason then makes its judgments upon these objects as described by theoretical reason (Finnis 1980, p. 66). Now, I do not think that it is a sufficient criticism of Finnis's account that it requires at some point a simple insight into the truth of a principle; at some point, we must stop with insights of this sort. What gives Finnis's view the appearance of intuitionism, though, is the absence of any explanation of how the transition from inclination to grasp of value takes place. Even if one's grasp of the first principles is unmediated by deductive proof, can we say nothing about how one moves from inclination to judgments of goodness?

Perhaps we should keep in mind that first principles are often affirmed because their affirmation is necessary to make intelligible other claims that one affirms. (The premier case of this is Aristotle's defense of the principle of noncontradiction, the first of all first principles: its affirmation is necessary to make intelligible *any* other claim that one makes. See the *Metaphysics,* 1005b6–1006a29.) The question that one asks in deciding whether to affirm propositions of this sort is not "Is this proposition deducible from other claims?" or "Does it have the force of a Cartesian or Sidgwickian intuition?" but rather "Does this proposition make these other claims that I affirm intelligible? Is it necessary to make these other claims intelligible? Are these other claims intelligible in the first place, so that first principles are needed to explain their status as intelligible?"

Now, it is of course not only affirmations that can be intelligible or unintelligible; actions can possess or fail to possess intelligibility (0.1). And this is why the notion of intelligibility plays a key role in seeing how we move from inclination – viewed as a tendency to act – to grasp of value. One might say that the attempt to formulate explicitly the principles of the natural law is the attempt to explain what makes intelligible the actions that human agents have a tendency to perform. When Aquinas writes that the first principle of practical reason is that good is to be pursued – and note his insistence on a tight analogy between that first principle and the first principle of all reasoning, the principle of noncontradiction – what he is offering is the supreme principle of intelligibility for actions: that human actions are intelligible only insofar as they are for the sake of some good, only insofar as they are performed *sub ratione boni* (see also Grisez 1965). If this is what Aquinas has in mind, then he must also be claiming that the more specific principles of the natural law, which state which objects are goods to be pursued, are to be affirmed because affirmation of such principles is necessary to make intelligible the actions that humans tend to perform for the sake of these objects.

If this view is correct, then the following are the questions that we have to ask with regard to the formulation of the first principles of the natural law: "What sorts of actions do we tend to perform? What sorts of objects are these actions aimed at? What is the set of practical principles the affirmation of which would best render intelligible intelligible acts (and leave unintelligible unintelligible acts)?" Ultimately, we may agree, the answers to these questions will be simply grasped as correct, or will not be at all. We see this sort of procedure, as we might expect, in Aquinas's work. In prosecuting his Aristotelian investigation into the good, considering and criticizing a number of answers that have been offered, he is asking what sorts of objects must be affirmed as good to make our acts intelligible.[3]

Now, to all of this a straightforward objection can be raised. The aim of presenting an account of how the first principles of the natural law are justified, even one as crude as the underelaborated derivationism and inclinationism, is to provide a defensible account of the basic goods. And a catalog of the basic

goods is wanted because it is the natural law theorist's account of the fundamental reasons for action, of what makes action intelligible. But according to
the inclinationist view, it seems that we have to know *already* what makes actions intelligible; we don't have here a method for coming up with new information about how action is rendered intelligible. This objection is basically correct in saying that this emended inclinationism provides no new information
about goods, but it misunderstands the aims and presuppositions of the inclinationist method. The inclinationist does not see the method being so much a
way of unearthing fresh, new information about what makes action intelligible
as it is a way to move from implicit knowledge of the good to fully explicit
knowledge of the good. All of us, on this view, have some implicit knowledge
of what the basic goods are, and this implicit knowledge is manifested in our
tendency to pursue certain objects. Regardless of whether some disavow such
knowledge, or even deny particular natural law principles, the natural law theorist ascribes such implicit knowledge to them; for to fail to ascribe to them this
knowledge would be to render their actions unintelligible (just as we have to
ascribe to everyone at least implicit knowledge of noncontradiction if their as-
sertions are to be intelligible). It is by asking the sorts of questions discussed in
the previous paragraph that one can make explicit one's implicit knowledge of
the basic goods, and thus provide oneself with a general account of those goods
that make action intelligible.

The process of making explicit our awareness of the basic goods is, of
course, prone to error in a number of ways, some having to do merely with difficulties inherent in formulating general principles, some having to do with the
way that the peculiar characteristics of some of the goods might themselves
mask the status of these goods as such. When asking what principles are needed
to make action intelligible, there may be a tendency to overgeneralize, to provide too broad a theory of the good, and as a result to include acts as intelligible that really are not.[4] Sometimes, due to an over-affection for parsimony, one
will undergeneralize, and exclude from the class of intelligibility acts that are
clearly intelligible. The character of the goods themselves could be responsible
for undergeneralization problems like this. If there were some good that makes
action intelligible, yet whose status as a good is difficult to see because in most
cases action in pursuit of it can be made intelligible in relation to some other
good, we would be likely to fail to recognize its status as a basic good. (I suggest in 3.3 that the goods of life, inner peace, and community have this sort of
problem.) If there were some good that often 'comes to us,' as it were, without
having to act for the sake of it, it would be more difficult to perceive its character as an independent good. (I suggest in 3.3 that the good of aesthetic experience is sometimes difficult to recognize for this reason.) In these cases, what
is needed is either a more direct insight into their status as goods or the sort of
careful analysis that can reveal the structure of action as requiring the affirmation of these goods in order for that action to be intelligible.

These, then, are the derivationist and inclinationist accounts of knowledge of the basic goods. Note that, as I have characterized them, each of these accounts imposes a constraint on how practical judgments regarding goods to be pursued are to be justified. Inclinationism blocks any fundamental appeal to facts about human nature, or indeed to any facts grasped by theoretical reason. There is a very close analogy on this point between Finnis's view and Hume's view. While Finnis rejects Hume's assimilation of value to sentiment and fact to reason – Finnis places the grasp of values and the grasp of facts as simply different functions of one reason – Finnis's account of how theoretical reason is involved in the grasp of value is strictly isomorphic to Hume's account of how reason is involved in evaluation. On Hume's view, all that reason can do with regard to things that are valued for their own sakes is to describe them as accurately as possible so that feeling can place a stamp of approval or disapproval on them: reason "excites a passion by informing us of the existence of something which is a proper object of it" (*Treatise,* III, 1).[5] On Finnis's inclinationist view, all that theoretical reason can do is to describe objects more accurately so that practical reason can judge them worthy of or unworthy of pursuit. On both Hume's sentimentalism and Finnis's inclinationism, practical evaluation is one-sided, as it were. On the derivationist view, on the other hand, practical reason is, with regard to the most fundamental practical claims, not competent to evaluate; the most basic forms of evaluation are the outcome of reasoning performed wholly by speculative reason.

Inclinationism and derivationism are thus alike in their one-sidedness. It is thus an important task to determine whether the catalog of basic goods to be presented will be justified in an inclinationist or derivationist manner, or whether there is perhaps a third way of justifying a catalog of goods that is superior both to inclinationism as stated and to derivationism as stated.

Difficulties with Derivationism and Inclinationism

The central difficulty with derivationism is, unsurprisingly, its presupposition that practical judgments can be logically derived from nonpractical judgments, a violation of the 'no ought from is' principle. Given the drastic differences between the concepts employed in practical and nonpractical judgments, it is not surprising that it is impossible to deduce judgments of the former sort from judgments of the latter sort alone. Now, while the advocate of derivationism is obviously committed to denying that 'Hume's law' is a principle of logic, it is up to the derivationist to show how such a deduction is possible.

Lisska, for example, argues that on a metaethics like Aquinas's, one can derive the natural law from facts about human nature because of the dynamic character of the properties in terms of which Aquinas characterizes human nature. "There is no fact/value dichotomy because the 'value' . . . is the result of the normal development of the 'fact.' . . . The value as fact is a state of completion of the disposition as fact" (Lisska 1996, p. 199). The dynamism of the dispositional properties, which underlies and explains the human tendency toward particular ends, is supposed to prevent us from seeing the value as a sheer add-on that we are not warranted in positing on the basis of the given facts. But it seems to me that Aquinas as interpreted by Lisska does not achieve this result. After all, if it is to be considered an analytic truth that ends are goods, then the claim "such and such are goods" says no more than the claim "such and such are the ends of natural human dispositions" says. But the truth in open-question type arguments is that it seems clear that the former *does* say something more than the latter does; if it does not, then the sense of 'good' employed is not the 'good' of practical reasoning with which the is/ought issue is concerned. We can put the point in a slightly different way. Lisska's explication of dispositional properties employs terms that are unqualifiedly nonevaluative, nonprescriptive, nonnormative. If, after the discussion of such properties, the only transition to the idea of goodness is through the claim "ends are goods," we can be sure either that the goods in question are not the goods of practical reasoning or that the claim that ends are goods is not analytic. But if either of these is true, then Lisska's Aquinas does not provide a solution to the is/ought problem.

There is a second crucial objection to derivationism, which results from derivationism's insistence that fundamental practical truths are known by deriving them from truths about human nature known by theoretical reason. The difficulty with this position is that it seems to have the implication that very few persons would have access even to rudimentary practical knowledge. As Finnis bluntly asserts in his defense of inclinationism, the basic principles of the natural law are such that they can be grasped by everyone, "not just metaphysicians" (Finnis 1980, p. 34); elsewhere he remarks that they are *"per se* (not *per metaphysicam) nota"* (Finnis 1981, p. 275). To hold that the principles of the natural law are derived from judgments knowable by speculative reason, as derivationism does, would seem to imply that even the most basic principles of the natural law, those regarding goods worth pursuing, can be known only by those who have studied human nature.[6] This seems to be an unacceptable, indeed an absurd, result. (For further discussion of this difficulty for derivationist natural law views, see MacIntyre 1997, p. 98.)

Now, inclinationism, which does not hold that fundamental practical truths need be derived from any other set of propositions, is not subject to the same sorts of worry that befall derivationism. But inclinationism has its own worries. The strength of derivationism is its straightforward account of how the natural law is grounded in human nature. The inclinationists agree that the natural law is grounded in human nature; this is, after all, a defining thesis of natural law theory. There is, however, a long line of contemporary defenders of natural law theory who hold that Finnis and other inclinationists reject this defining natural law thesis (see, e.g., Veatch 1981, p. 252; McInerny 1982, pp. 54–55; Weinreb 1987, pp. 97–101; Hittinger 1987, p. 8; Hall 1994, pp. 16–19; and Lisska

1996, pp. 157–158). But Finnis wholly disowns this characterization of his natural law view: he denies the claims that "ethical principles can have no grounding in fact and in nature" and that there is "an absolute independence of ethics as over against metaphysics, or of morals with respect to a knowledge of nature" (Finnis 1981, p. 266). Rather, he holds that one's understanding of the self-evident, underivable first principles of the natural law "can be integrated into a general account of human nature, i.e. of human potentialities and their various forms of fulfilment" (Finnis 1983, p. 12).

Finnis's inclinationist view cannot be faulted as a natural law account for failing to affirm the thesis that the natural law is grounded in human nature. Nor can his view be faulted by claiming that the joint affirmation of the thesis that the principles of the natural law are self-evident and the thesis that the natural law is grounded in human nature is inconsistent. There is, however, a strong case to be made that one cannot *justifiably* affirm both of these theses; call this state of affairs 'non-co-assertibility.' If the self-evidence and grounding theses are non-co-assertible, those who wish to defend inclinationist natural law theories face a serious difficulty. For if one's justified affirmation of inclinationism would imply that one cannot justifiably assert that the natural law is grounded in human nature, one who affirms inclinationism cannot justifiably assert a central, defining thesis of natural law theory.

The argument for the non-co-assertibility of the self-evidence and grounding theses is the following. There seem to be two plausible interpretations of the grounding thesis. A weak version of this thesis is co-assertible with the self-evidence thesis, but it is not a strong enough interpretation of the grounding thesis to make natural law theory a distinctive theory. A stronger version of this thesis, on the other hand, is sufficiently distinctive for natural law theory, but seems not to be co-assertible with the self-evidence thesis.

The basic goods are, on the inclinationist account, grasped as potential objects of worthwhile pursuit. By fixing on the notion of possibility, the inclinationist might support the *weak grounding thesis,* the claim that it is human nature that determines what sorts of goods are genuine possibilities for humans to achieve. On this reading of the grounding thesis, what is asserted is that if human nature were sufficiently different, certain goods would no longer be available to humans; they would be inaccessible to us. This thesis is eminently plausible: for if one is to participate in a human good, there must be some feature of human nature that enables one to do so; the possibilities for human fulfillment extend only as far as the given capacities of human nature permit.[7]

Now, there seems to be nothing objectionable about the weak grounding thesis. There is excellent confirming evidence for the claim that if humans were structured differently, certain goods would be unavailable, for we have observed cases in which changes in human structure have made participation in certain goods impossible. There is a high statistical correlation, for example, between having massive brain damage and lacking the ability to participate in the good of knowledge. (I am assuming here that knowledge is a basic good; I defend this claim in 1.3 and 3.3.) And one can affirm that knowledge is a good for all human persons, and therefore for this person with a damaged brain; unfortunately, such people are unable to participate in that good. What would be objectionable, on the other hand, would be the refusal of a natural law theorist to assert anything more than the weak grounding thesis regarding the relationship between human nature and the first principles of the natural law. For if one declines to assert that there is anything more to the grounding of natural law in human nature than (e.g.) the fact that if our brains were structured differently, we could not participate in the good of knowledge, then one is no longer entitled to the claim that what one is advocating is a *natural law* theory of practical reason.

One might ask, of course, what criteria one needs to employ to determine whether any given theory's version of the grounding thesis is strong enough for natural law theory; and I admit that such criteria are hard to come by. We need not have a set of necessary and sufficient conditions in hand, though, to recognize that the weak grounding thesis is too weak for natural law theory, for a natural law theory that asserts only the weak version of the grounding thesis is indistinguishable in relevant respects from any other normative theory (such as that proposed by G. E. Moore, for example)[8] that asserts the existence of objective goods. For *no* moral theorist could reasonably deny that if human nature were sufficiently different, certain goods would be inaccessible to us. Hence, if the inclinationist were to hold that natural law is grounded in human nature only in the weak sense of the grounding thesis, we would have a good deal of reason to doubt that what he or she is presenting is a distinctively natural law theory of practical reason.

If an inclinationist is to defend a natural law theory, he or she must affirm a more contentious version of the grounding thesis. What could this more contentious version be? It might be the *strong grounding* thesis, the claim that facts about human nature *explain* why that which is a human good is a human good. Note the crucial difference between the weak and the strong grounding interpretations. On the weak grounding interpretation, if human nature were different, certain goods would no longer be available for participation by us; it is consistent with the affirmation of the weak ground thesis, though, to hold that if human nature were different, those unavailable goods would nonetheless be genuine goods. On the strong grounding interpretation, though, if human nature were different, certain goods would not simply be unavailable; they would no longer be goods at all.[9]

The strong grounding reading does seem to assert a connection between human nature and principles of practical reason that is strong enough for a natural law theory of practical reason. But how could any inclinationist be justified in making this sort of explanatory claim while also affirming the self-evidence thesis, the thesis that practical principles such as 'Life is a good' and 'Knowledge is a good' are self-evident and underivable? There are, no doubt, some senses of 'explanation' that do not depend on derivability. Statistical explanations do not: one's lung cancer, for example, can be explained by one's smoking, even if there is no derivability relationship between smoking and cancer. The explanations that we provide for free actions may not depend on derivability, either: one's performing a certain action might be explained by the reasons for action one has, even if the having of such reasons does not imply even *ceteris paribus* the performance of the action. But neither of these sorts of explanation is the sort of explanation that would be relevant in the case of the relationship between human nature and natural law.

The most familiar models of explanation endorse the following thesis: the set of facts consisting of p, q, and r is a possible explanation for s only if under some describable set of circumstances s is derivable from the conjunction of p, q, and r. But on the inclinationist view, the principles of the natural law are self-evident, underivable. Hence, no facts about human nature could explain the principles of the natural law. If the only relevant notions of 'explanation' depend on derivability, it follows that one cannot justifiably assert that natural law is strongly grounded in human nature if the principles of the natural law are in no sense derivable from human nature; the inclinationist can assert the self-evidence thesis, or the strong grounding thesis, but not both. It may seem, then, that one cannot justifiably endorse inclinationism while remaining a natural law theorist.[10]

What, then, are we to make of these arguments against derivationism and inclinationism as natural law theories of fundamental practical knowledge? While the invocation of Hume's law decisively rules out derivationist conceptions of practical knowledge, in my view, the argument that I have just presented against inclinationism as part of a natural law view provides a challenge to inclinationism, rather than a complete basis for rejecting it. The challenge is to provide an interpretation of the grounding thesis that is strong enough for natural law theory without relying on a claim that is both untenable and inconsistent with inclinationism – that fundamental practical truths are deducible from nonpractical truths alone. (It may be the belief that there is no sufficiently strong version of the grounding thesis that does not rely on the notion of derivability, which has led critics of inclinationism – like Lisska (1996, pp. 157–161), and myself in earlier work (1995a, pp. 472–477) – to hold that Finnis and other inclinationists reject natural law theory by implication.) Let us now turn to the task of trying to meet this challenge.

The Real Identity Thesis Stated

The inclinationist and derivationist models of practical knowledge are mirror images of each other with respect to their virtues and vices. While the inclinationist has no need to worry either about the possibility of deriving practical from nonpractical truths or about the difficulties involved in explaining how plain persons come to know the basic principles of the natural law, his or her account of practical knowledge is in tension with natural law theory's essential thesis that the natural law is rooted in human nature. While the derivationist provides a straightforward interpretation of the claim that the natural law is grounded in human nature, this straightforwardness is gained through logically dubious means and at the cost of denying even the most rudimentary practical knowledge to the vast majority of agents.

What would be ideal for natural law theory, of course, would be a view that preserves the accessibility of at least the most basic practical principles while offering an account of a tight and distinctive connection between human nature and natural law. We can see what a model of such an account might look like, I suggest, if we attend to a case that is (at least with regard to its most basic features) less controversial and more familiar. Consider the relationship between indexical and nonindexical judgments. Now, there is no denying that this relationship has been the occasion of a tremendous amount of philosophical dispute. But there are a number of claims that we can make about the relationship between certain of these judgments that are comparatively uncontroversial, and it is only to such claims that I will appeal in suggesting a similar view of the relationship between certain nonpractical and certain practical judgments.

Consider the following judgments, held by me: 'I am in my office' and 'Murphy is in his office.' The following points are worth noting about the relationship between these two judgments. First, it is possible for me – under admittedly unusual circumstances that involve loss of knowledge of my own identity – to form the third-person judgment without forming the first-person judgment. Secondly, not only is it possible to form the third-person judgment without forming the first-person judgment, but it is also not possible to deduce the first-person judgment from the third-person judgment, or from the third-person judgment in conjunction with any set of wholly nonindexical judgments. There is no way to deduce logically 'I am in my office' from 'Murphy is in his office,' or from 'Murphy is in his office' along with any other set of wholly third-person judgments. In the absence of what John Perry calls "locating beliefs" – beliefs about who I am, where I am, etc. – I would not be able to deduce from any impersonally formulated judgments about the world any knowledge about my own place in that world (Perry 1993b, p. 35). But, thirdly and importantly, no one would hold, on the basis of the fact that indexical judgments cannot be deduced from wholly nonindexical judgments, that there are not extremely tight connections between these judgments. It is not just that, necessarily, my judgments of the form 'I am P' are true if and only if my judgments of the form 'Murphy is P' would also be true. It is that what would make these judgments true is one and the same thing – the obtaining of the very same state of affairs is what would make both of these judgments true, and the failing to obtain of that very same state of affairs would make both of these judgments false.

The connection between my judgments 'I am in my office' and 'Murphy is in his office,' one might suppose, could not be tighter without improperly conflating the two undeniably distinct judgments into one. What such judgments present to us is a fairly clear case in which judgments of one type cannot be deduced solely from judgments of another type, yet in which there is little doubt that the correctness of the judgments of one type displays, upon inspection, a deep connection with judgments of the other type. It is worth exploring the possibility that the relationship between the principles of the natural law and certain judgments concerning human nature is similar to the relationship between first- and third-person judgments. There is no reason to suppose that we can deduce the practical principles of natural law from any set of theoretical judgments about human nature: these types of judgment are so conceptually different that any putative derivation seems bound to be fallacious. But as the case of indexical and nonindexical judgments illustrates, this tremendous conceptual difference does not in itself give us reason to suppose that there could not be an extremely tight connection between these judgments. It could be the case, as it clearly seems to be with respect to certain first- and third-person judgments, that the principles of the natural law and some judgments about human nature refer to the same states of affairs, and are made true by the obtaining of the same states of affairs; these judgments differ because the former are formulated by practical reason and the latter by theoretical reason, which function in very different ways. Furthermore, just as in the case of personal and impersonal judgments, once we become aware of the existence and precise nature of the connection between these types of judgments, we may be able to use this information to argue in a justifiable way from judgments of one type to judgments of the other type.[11]

What is necessary, then, to show that this model of the relationship between human nature and natural law is not only coherent but also correct? We need both to identify the particular class of judgments about human nature that we propose to connect with the principles of the natural law and to give some grounds for supposing that the corresponding theoretical and practical judgments are made true by the same states of affairs. The theses that I am concerned to defend are these: first, that there is a set of truths, knowable by theoretical reason, that both affirm the existence of such a thing as human flourishing and state what aspects of human flourishing there are; and second, that there are strong reasons to suppose that any state of affairs that theoretical reason correctly grasps as 'x is an aspect of human flourishing' would be correctly grasped by practical reason as 'x is a good worth having,' and vice versa. This position – that states of affairs understood by theoretical reason as aspects of flourishing are really identical with states of affairs understood by practical reason as goods worth having – is the interpretation of the grounding thesis that I call the 'real identity thesis.'

In 1.2 I defend the idea that there is such a thing as human flourishing that is discoverable by human reason functioning in a speculative mode; in 1.3 I provide an account of how we come to know what the particular aspects of human flourishing are; and in 1.4 I explain how this information about human flourishing provides evidence that points toward the truth of the real identity thesis. But before I turn to the task of making good the claim that the real identity thesis is the best natural law account of the relationship between basic practical principles and human nature, I want to consider what relevance the truth of the real identity thesis would have to our understanding of how an account of basic goods is to be justified.

I noted above that the inclinationist and derivationist accounts of practical knowledge are alike in their one-sidedness: inclinationism denies a fundamental place for practical evaluation to speculative reason, and derivationism denies a fundamental place for practical evaluation to practical reason. It is worth pointing out that if the real identity thesis is a recognizably correct account of the relationship between aspects of human flourishing and goods to be pursued, we can find a place for both practical and theoretical reason in defending an account of the principles of the natural law. We can affirm an inclinationist model of how fundamental practical truths are known, holding that practical reason formulates such judgments in order to made intelligible our tendency to pursue certain objects. But we can also affirm that our grasp of fundamental practical truths concerning goods worth having can be informed in a particularly deep way by theoretical reason, even if the way that it is informed by theoretical reason is not what the derivationist had envisioned. We do not directly derive practical truths from factual claims about the human function, or about human dispositions. Rather, given independent, theoretical access to the nature of human flourishing, *and* the affirmation of the real identity thesis, we can conclude that those states of affairs that are grasped as aspects of human flourishing are, in truth, goods worth having. (This works the other way around as well: our speculative grasp of human nature can be enlightened, by way of the real identity thesis, by our practical judgments concerning goods to be pursued.)

Now, one might ask, what would be the point of trying to inform practical judgment with speculative knowledge about human nature? If the first principles of the natural law regarding basic goods are self-evident to practical reason, how could anything discovered by speculative reason inform practical judgment, rather than simply being an after-the-fact account of the relationship between goods and human nature? Two responses are to the point here.

The first is that the judgments of practical reason that specify what are goods to be pursued are highly general and sometimes seem remote from particular cases. A general practical judgment about a form of good may seem suspect in a particular case, so that while we may recognize, in general terms, the correctness of a practical judgment about the form of good, one does not fully understand the state of affairs referred to in that judgment; or one's practical judgment can on occasion be clouded by emotion, so that one becomes in some sense unaware of what one really knows (see MacIntyre 1988, p. 173).[12]

The second is that, as was noted earlier in our discussion of inclinationism's account of how basic goods are known, the fact that these principles are self-evident does not imply that we know them as clear intuitions. We work toward these first principles in attempting to account for the intelligibility of the actions that we have a tendency to perform. But (to use an overworked analogy) just as an infinite number of equations can fit a set of data points, so it is the case that an infinite number of principles could be posited to account for the intelligibility of those actions. Many of these candidate principles will be discarded on the basis of their overcomplexity, their initial implausibility, or other such criteria. But there may be more than one set of candidates remaining, and it may seem a residue – though no more than that – of intuitionism if we were to have no standard at all with which to adjudicate between these candidate sets.

With regard to both of these considerations, speculative reason might have an important role to play. For it might be possible that in some cases one can have an easier time recognizing that something is an aspect of human flourishing when one takes the point of view of the theorist; and this sort of judgment can guide our interpretations of general practical judgments and can help us become aware of what we knew all along but was obscured from our vision by emotion. And it might also be possible for speculative reason to suggest, or adjudicate between, candidate sets of first principles of practical reasoning. I will employ this method – we might call it a 'dialectical' approach, since it moves between practical judgments occasioned by inclination and judgments of speculative reason, thus avoiding the one-sidedness shared by inclinationism and derivationism – in Chapter 3 in our attempt to provide a catalog of the basic goods.

1.2 Functioning and Flourishing

The real identity thesis presupposes that there is such a thing as flourishing, which condition is identifiable by theoretical reason. I shall defend the existence of flourishing in nature and, in particular, human flourishing, by taking as a starting point Aristotle's 'function argument' in the *Nicomachean Ethics,* an argument the status of which in Aristotelian ethics is, of course, quite controversial.[13] The function argument aims to give insight into the nature of the human good by showing that the human has a function and by identifying that function:

> Well, perhaps we shall find the best good if we first find the function of a human being. For just as the good, i.e. [doing] well, for a flautist, a sculptor, and every craftsman, and, in general, for whatever has a function and [characteristic] action, seems to depend on its function, the same seems to be true for a human being, if a human being has some function.
> Then do the carpenter and the leatherworker have their functions and actions, while a human being has none, and is by nature idle, without any function? Or, just as eye,

hand, foot, and, in general, every [bodily] part apparently has its functions, may we likewise ascribe to a human being some function besides all of theirs?

What, then, could this be? For living is apparently shared with plants, but what we
are looking for is the special function of a human being; hence we should set aside the
life of nutrition and growth. The life next in order is some sort of life of sense-percep-
tion; but this too is apparently shared with horse, ox, and every animal. The remaining
possibility, then, is some sort of life of action of the [part of the soul] that has reason.
(*Nicomachean Ethics,* 1097b24–1098a3)

Thus, Aristotle concludes that "the human function is the soul's activity that expresses reason or requires reason" (*Nicomachean Ethics,* 1098a7).

A number of neo-Aristotelians have been reluctant to rely on this sort of argument in holding that there is such a thing as human flourishing the existence
and nature of which can be grasped by theoretical reason. MacIntyre holds that
the function argument depends for its success on Aristotle's "metaphysical biology," and at one point made it a desideratum for a successful Aristotelianism
that it not depend on such a thoroughly discredited view (1981, pp. 148, 162;
but see 1990a). In defending the function argument against Bernard Williams's
criticisms, Martha Nussbaum has argued that it would be a mistake to view the
function argument as depending on some speculative awareness of the human
function; rather, that argument is thoroughly practical, relying at all points on
an evaluative awareness of what is worth pursuing that can only be had within
a human life, rather than from some scientific, outsider's perspective (1995, pp.
87–131). And Finnis has held simply that the function argument is an "erratic
boulder" in Aristotelian ethics (1983, p. 17). The main source of this reluctance
seems to be that even if one sees merit in the idea of "a function-based naturalism for various evaluative uses of 'good,'" one might "still resist extending such
an account to a good human life – perhaps because one cannot see one's way
to a view about what a human life (as opposed to a pitch pipe or even a dentist)
is *for*" (Darwall, Gibbard, and Railton 1992, p. 168). I aim, though, to defend
an account of flourishing understood in this functionalist way: it will make clear
how one might see one's way to a view about what a human life is for, while
keeping at bay the central objections that have been leveled against accounts of
the human good that are grounded in functional concepts.

Aristotle's argument has three parts. In the first part, he connects the concept of a thing's function to the concept of a thing's good. In the second, he
shows that the human being must have a function. In the third, he argues that
the function of the human is rational activity. Now, for the moment, I want to
put the third part of this argument to the side, since my aim is not at present to
put forward or to reject any particular conception of human flourishing. Rather,
I want to examine what reasons there are for thinking that the human being has
a function and for thinking that its functioning well is to be identified with its
good.

That the Human Has a Function: The Functional-Composition Thesis

Aristotle seems to claim that the fact that the eyes, ears, heart, etc. have functions gives us reason to affirm the thesis that the human has a function. What is not so clear is what the relationship is supposed to be between the claims about the parts' having functions and the whole's having a function, and one might feel a pull either toward overstating the strength of the alleged connection or understating it. One might, as some introductory logic texts do, overstate the argument by turning it into a deductive proof that is then criticized as a gross fallacy of composition: if all of the parts of the human have functions, then the human must have a function, because if all of the parts of x have property P, then x must have property P. But even aside from invocations of the principle of charity, this could not be what Aristotle had in mind: for in the early going in the *Ethics,* where the function argument appears, we are on our way to first principles, not drawing conclusions from them (*Nicomachean Ethics,* 1098b2); so the function argument cannot be meant to be deductive. One might attempt to avoid this extreme by understating the argument, by portraying it merely as a set of considerations that will 'point the mind in the right direction,' as it were, so that one will intuitively grasp the fact that the human being has a function. While correctly rejecting the alleged deductive character of the function argument, this interpretation offers no insight into what it is about these particular examples that is supposed to help us see that the human has a function.

Perhaps the following might serve as a clue, though: often when Aristotle argues for particular first principles, the argument seems to be that the affirmation of those first principles is necessary in order to make a certain set of phenomena intelligible. (The premier example, as I noted above [1.1], is the argument for the noncontradiction principle [*Metaphysics,* 1005b6–1006a29]; the argument for it is that its truth is necessary to make any assertion whatever intelligible.) We might think, then, that what Aristotle is asserting is that it is only by holding that the human being has a function that the fact that the parts of the human have functions becomes intelligible. Their status as possessing functions is intelligible only if the human as a whole has a function.

I think that Aristotle had in mind an argument of this sort, but the argument that I will present claims no fidelity to the particulars of Aristotle's position, only to the strategy that Aristotle seems to be relying on. I shall argue, that is, that considerations involving the status of human organs, both as having functions and as being parts of the human in virtue of that function, can be made intelligible only by ascribing a function to the human being as a whole.

Suppose for a moment, as Aristotle does, that the eyes, ears, heart, etc. have functions. This is fairly uncontroversial;[14] the only controversy – to be discussed later in this section – concerns how the idea of 'function' is to be analyzed. Suppose for a moment also that the eyes, ears, heart, etc. are parts of the human being, that is, in normal circumstances, any particular eye is part of a human, and so forth. This is also uncontroversial. Suppose also that the following slightly more controversial yet plausible claim is true: that of any particular eye, ear, heart, etc. that is part of a human, its parthood is due to something about that part's functioning. It is, that is, some feature of the part's activity, that activity which constitutes its functioning, that makes it a part of the human. It seems, though, that if these three claims are true, one could exploit them in the argument for the thesis that the human being has a function. One might claim, that is, that it is only by ascribing a function to the human being as a whole that we can intelligibly view its organs as having their parthood by way of their functions. Or, to put it another way: if we do not ascribe a function to the human being, then we would have a hard time explaining how there is a human being present, rather than simply a bunch of objects that happen to be active in the same general location. The unifying notion is that of contribution: the organ is a part of the human because the organ's function contributes to one of the human's functions.

Any such claim should not, of course, be restricted to the special case of human beings, or even (I imagine) of living things; we should, rather, formulate a general principle of which the human is simply an instance. Call it the *functional-composition* principle: if x is a part of y on account of x's function f, then there is a function g which is a function of y's and to which x's f-ing contributes. This is not meant to be an empirical principle, for it is neither empirically verifiable nor falsifiable. Rather, it is a conceptual principle that (partially) governs our ascriptions of *having a function* and *is a part of* to objects. As such, it is not open to empirical confirmation, but only to conceptual confirmation: does this principle divide things into the appropriate categories? does it faithfully reflect how the notions of function and being a part of are related to one another? can it be used in novel cases to extend our beliefs about what objects are parts of others, why they are parts of others, or what objects have functions?

There are a number of cases in which the functional-composition principle seems correct. Consider, for example, how automobiles and their parts are related to one another. It seems that a transmission assembly is a part of a car due to its function: it is neither the mere location of that assembly in relation to the other parts of the car, nor its being in contact with those other parts, that makes it a part; rather, the location and the contact are merely conditions sine qua non for the functioning of that transmission assembly as such. It also seems plausible, though, that if we want to know why it has its parthood from its function, the answer is that the function of the transmission assembly contributes to the function of the entire automobile. It seems to me that this sort of reasoning can be carried out with regard to those clearest examples of functioning things, that is, artifacts; and it is not obvious why the same sort of reasoning cannot be carried out with regard to living things whose parts clearly seem to possess functions.

If the functional-composition principle is true, and it is the case that there are parts of the human that have their parthood in virtue of their functions, then it, of course, follows that the human being as a whole has a function. (I ask the reader to put to the side, for the moment, doubts about the success of this argument that derive from worries about the plausibility of the conclusion of the argument: these worries are, it seems, typically the result of some presupposed view on what it is to have a function. But I will argue that the most plausible analysis of the concept of a function does not make the idea that the human has a function suspicious or mysterious.) Strictly speaking, that is all that is needed at this stage in the argument; I set out to show why it might be reasonable to hold that the human has a function, and I have done so. But I want to suggest that a stronger principle relating functions of parts and wholes is true as well, one that yields a stronger conclusion about the nature of the human function.

The functional-composition principle concerns the relationship between a given functioning part and the functioning whole of which it is a part. But it would be useful to say something concerning how several functioning parts are related to the whole of which they are parts. Now, we can, employing nothing but the functional-composition principle, assert the following about the relationship between several functioning parts and the whole to which they belong. Consider a set of parts $\{x_1, x_2, \ldots x_n\}$ all of which are parts of y in virtue of their functions. The functional-composition principle implies the following: if x_1 is a part of y in virtue of its function f_1, x_2 is a part of y in virtue of its function f_2, $\ldots$ and x_n is a part of y in virtue of its function f_n, then there is a *set* of functions F such that y has all of the functions belonging to F, and x_1's f_1-ing contributes to some member of F, x_2's f_2-ing contributes to some member of F, $\ldots$ and x_n's f_n-ing contributes to some member of F. Or, less annoyingly: everything that is a part of y on account of its function contributes to some function of y. This does *not* mean that there is some function of y to which all of those parts of y must contribute. It means only that a condition of their all being parts of the same object on account of their functions is that each of them contributes to at least one of the functions of that object.

I want to suggest, however, that while the stronger claim is not implied by the functional-composition principle, it is a claim that we ought to affirm nonetheless. For suppose that several parts of y $x_1, x_2, \ldots x_n$ are unified inasmuch as they contribute to functions of y, but they contribute to diverse functions. x_1 contributes to g_1, x_2 to g_2, and so on. The question at this point becomes, I think, why we should think that y itself is a unity, if there is not some function that unifies its diverse functions. It is possible that what unifies its diverse functions will be a distinct function to which all other functions contribute – we might call this a 'dominant function.' But I want to leave open the possibility that this unifying function could be nothing more than a compound of diverse functions – call this an 'inclusive function.' If, for example, we have a hard time seeing why we should say that it is a single object y that has diverse functions g_1, g_2, and g_3, we might say that what unifies these functions is that y has an inclusive function $(g_1 \& g_2 \& g_3)$.[15]

Consider, for example, a combination corkscrew–bottle opener. Now, I will not here utter any authoritative pronouncement on whether combination corkscrew–bottle openers are one object or two. But I will make the following conditional claim. If one gives up the idea (as one ought) that what would decide this issue is simply that the corkscrew part and the bottle opener part are stuck together (or could be pulled apart), what might be decisive in this matter is whether the corkscrew–bottle opener should be viewed as simply possessing two distinct functions (in which case one might say that there are two objects present) or as possessing a single complex function (in which case one might say that there is but one object present).

I will, then, affirm this stronger version of the functional-composition principle. If x_1 is a part of y on account of function f_1, x_2 is a part of y on account of function f_2, . . . and x_n is a part of y on account of function f_n, then there is a function g such that x_1's f_1-ing contributes to g, x_2's f_2-ing contributes to g, . . . and x_n's f_n-ing contributes to g. If this principle is true, then not only is it true that the human being has a function; it is also true that there is a single function that the human has. This function may itself be compound, an inclusive function. But holding it to be a single complex function, rather than a variety of distinct functions, might be necessary for accounting for the unity of the human being.[16]

An Analysis of 'Function'

The first stage of the reconstruction of an Aristotelian function argument is complete. If what I have said so far is correct, then the human has a function, which may be either a dominant or an inclusive function. What remains to be done is to connect the concept of functioning with the concept of flourishing, and to show, in particular, that the human's functioning is to be identified with its flourishing. I shall first briefly discuss the analysis of propositions of the form 'A B-s in order to C' (e.g., 'the heart pumps in order to circulate the blood') offered by Mark Bedau, and show how it can easily be transformed into an analysis of propositions of the form 'a function of A is to B.' By relying on this analysis of the concept of a function, I will show that affirming the existence of a human function makes it reasonable to affirm the existence of such a thing as human flourishing.

What makes Bedau's account of 'A B-s in order to C' propositions important for our purposes is that he argues that no analysis of such judgments that fails to include some sort of evaluative condition can succeed. Consider the following two constraints that many would want to place on propositions of this sort: the *goal-productivity* condition that A's B-ing tends to promote the obtaining of C, and the *etiological* condition that A B-s because A's B-ing promotes the obtaining of C. (See, for defenses of views that make these conditions jointly sufficient, Wright 1973, Millikan 1984, and Neander 1991.) It may seem that these constraints are sufficient for an analysis of 'in order to' judgments, for consider how successful they are in capturing the relevant features of a paradigm case of teleology in nature:

[T]he heart pumps blood only because the creature possessing it is alive, and the creature is alive only because blood is being circulated throughout its body. If the heart stopped circulating the blood, the creature would die and its heart would stop pumping. In this way, part of the explanation of why the heart pumps at all is that the heart's pumping contributes to circulating the blood. (Bedau 1992a, p. 786; see also Bedau 1992b, pp. 34–51)

However, Bedau continues, the goal-productivity and etiological conditions are not jointly sufficient to mark out the realm of teleology in nature. For

[c]onsider a stick floating down a stream that brushes against a rock and comes to be pinned there by the backwash it creates. The stick is creating the backwash because of a number of considerations, including the flow of the water, the shape and mass of the stick, etc., but part of the explanation of why it creates the backwash is that the stick is pinned in a certain way on the rock by the water. . . . Once pinned, part of the reason why the stick creates the backwash is that the backwash keeps it pinned there and being pinned there causes the backwash. (Bedau 1992a, p. 786)

The stick generates backwash because the stick's backwash contributes to its being pinned to the rock. But it is obvious that the stick does not create backwash in order to be pinned to the rock.

What is the relevant difference between the heart's pumping blood and the stick's generating the backwash? Why is the former part of a true in-order-to statement while the latter is not? Bedau notes that "One clear difference between the two cases is that the heart's pumping is good for the creature, but the stick's backwash is not good for anything" (Bedau 1992a, p. 787). On Bedau's view, the appeal to goodness is a necessary condition for the truth of in-order-to statements; such statements are correct only within "value-centered systems."[17]

It is also worth noting that for Bedau, the inclusion of both etiological and value conditions makes possible distinctions between grades of teleology, from radically diminished to full-blown forms. On the most meager form of teleology, which Bedau labels Grade 1, the goal-productivity and value constraints are met, but the etiological condition is absent: Bedau imagines a swimmer whose swimming keeps him fit, but whose swimming is not brought about by its keeping him fit. On a Grade 2 analysis, the goal-productivity, etiological, and value conditions are all met, but the goodness of C is not causally effective in bringing about A's B-ing; on a Grade 3 analysis, by contrast, the goal-productivity, etiological, and value conditions are all satisfied, and the goodness of C is causally effective in bringing about A's B-ing. Grade 3 is clearly the central case of teleology: examples of it include what are taken to be paradigms of

teleology, intentional actions (John's going to the store) and the activities of artifacts (the thermostat's turning on the heat).

What of teleology in nature, though, such as the pumping of the heart? What
grade of teleology appears here? Consider the explanation of the heart's pumping: while the heart's circulating the blood is good for the creature, the goodness itself is not part of the explanation for the heart's pumping. Assuming that
natural selection is in fact responsible for the heart's characteristics, the heart
does not respond as it does because of the goodness of anything; natural selection responds not to goodness but to survival (even if survival is a good thing).
So while teleology in nature moves beyond Grade 1, it does not reach full-
blooded Grade 3 teleology; biological teleology is Grade 2.

This assessment of teleology in nature is particularly important. While there
are powerful objections to the standard Aristotelian teleological account of nature, these objections focus on the fact that Aristotelian teleology is Grade 3, not
Grade 2 (see, e.g., Ayala 1972, p. 7). By weakening the claim that nature exhibits
teleology, Bedau avoids the force of anti-teleology objections designed with
Aristotelian views in mind. There is nothing in Bedau's account that should of-
fend anti-Aristotelian sensibilities generated by the successes of modern biology.

If Bedau is right, then if there is a close connection between the notion of
'in order to' and the notion of function, then we should be able to rely on Bedau's analysis in formulating an account of what it is for something to have a
particular function. And it seems clear that there is such a connection. As a first
approximation, we might say that a function of A is to B only if there is a state
of affairs C such that A B-s in order that C obtain. For example: a function of
the heart is to pump blood if and only if there is a state of affairs (the blood's
circulating) such that the heart pumps the blood in order that this state of affairs
might obtain.

Unfortunately, this first approximation falls short. The reason for this is that
it is possible for A to have the function of B-ing yet to fail to B. One noteworthy feature of things with functions is that they can malfunction, that is, they
can fail to do what it is their function to do. It is a function of my heart to pump
blood; yet I may have a heart attack. The heart does not lose its function the moment I have a heart attack; rather, it is failing to perform its function. Whatever
else is necessary for a successful account of what it is to have a function, it
should not logically exclude the possibility of malfunction.

The only way that I can see to remedy this difficulty is to include within the
analysis the notion of a kind. A function of A is to B if and only if there is a state
of affairs C such that A is the kind of thing that B-s in order that C might obtain. Even when I have a heart attack, my heart does not cease to be the kind of
thing that pumps in order that my blood might be circulated. We can thus see
why we need to introduce the notion of 'kind' into the definition. Of course, one
might immediately insist on an account of what it means for an object to be a
member of a certain kind; and, slightly embarrassingly, for the sort of object we

are dealing with, it is usually the case that accounts of those kind terms employ the notion of function. Thus: if one attempts to define what a heart or eye or ear is, the definition will invoke functional notions. While we might be slightly embarrassed by this, I don't think that we should be humiliated by it. It is widely held that certain concepts are interdefinable, and that one cannot 'break the loop' in defining them; consider, for example, the concepts of necessity and possibility. 'Function' and 'kind' seem to be such concepts as well.

Suppose, then, that we accept this analysis of function. If we do, then we can apply Bedau's analysis of '*A B*-s in order to *C*' to cash out what it is to have a function; and we can see that there are also grades of evaluative involvement in functioning that correspond to the grades of evaluative involvement in in-order-to statements. *A*'s Grade 1 function is to *B* if and only if *A* is the kind of thing that *B*-s, *B*-ing contributes to *C,* and *C*'s obtaining is good. *A*'s Grade 2 function is to *B* if and only if *A* is the kind of thing that *B*-s, *A B*-s because *A*'s *B*-ing contributes to *C,* and *C*'s obtaining is good. *A*'s Grade 3 function is to *B* if and only if *A* is the kind of thing that *B*-s, *A B*-s both because *A*'s *B*-ing contributes to *C,* and *C*'s obtaining is good.

That the Human's Functioning Is to Be Identified with Its Flourishing

Now, we saw earlier that so long as we hold that the eye, ear, etc. of humans are parts of the human in virtue of their functions, we are also committed to the view that the human being as a whole has a function. Call this function of a human being 'to *H*.' To say of any given human that its function is to *H* is to say, on this proposed analysis, that there is some state of affairs *C* such that the human is the kind of thing that *H*-s in order that *C* might obtain. Since we admitted that teleology in nature is Grade 2, any functions in nature – including the human function – is Grade 2 also. Thus, given the analysis of Grade 2 functions, the human is the kind if thing that *H*-s because *H*-ing contributes to the obtaining of some state of affairs *C* and *C*'s obtaining is good. Given this application of the analysis of 'function' to the case of the human, what reason is there to assert that the functioning of the human constitutes its flourishing?

It seems to me that if some state of affairs is held to constitute a being's flourishing, it must fulfill the following desiderata. First, that activity must be good in some way: flourishing is a value notion. Secondly, the goodness of that state of affairs must not be of a merely instrumental variety: the state of affairs that constitutes flourishing must have its value – or at least some of its value – in itself, not merely by reference to its contribution to some other good state of affairs. And, thirdly, the goodness of that state of affairs must not be of the sort that is grasped only by practical reason. This last criterion must seem slightly strange, but there are reasons for insisting on it: in particular, that the concept of flourishing should be the sort of thing that we can apply not just to ourselves but to other creatures. Yet surely we do not want to say that the goodness of the flourishing of other creatures is something grasped by our practical reason – after all, we often recognize that a plant's or animal's flourishing is inimical to us, that we have reason to prevent it. Suppose, then, that these desiderata are correct. Does the human's function fulfill these criteria such that we could reasonably identify it with the human's flourishing?

Notice first that nothing in our analysis of 'function' implies that the activity of an object that has a function and the state of affairs that it functions to realize cannot be one and the same. Nothing that has been said so far, that is, precludes the state of affairs C from being identical to H-ing: it could be, that is, that the human H-s because H-ing contributes to H-ing. If this were the case, though, then our first two desiderata for an account of flourishing would be satisfied. The activity of H-ing would not be for the sake of something distinct from itself, and so the activity involved in the human function would not be merely an instrument for the bringing about of some other state of affairs. And, of course, since the analysis of a function requires that the state of affairs C be good, if H-ing is identical to C it follows that H-ing is good. Thus, two of the desiderata that would have to be met for the human's functioning to be identified with its flourishing – that its function be good, and not merely instrumentally so – would be satisfied. Further, it seems that the identity of C and H-ing in the human case would dispel a central worry about ascribing a function to the human being: what drives that worry is, at least in part, the assumption that if a human has a function, then that function is to contribute to some distinct good state of affairs; when one wonders about what a human's activity could possibly be for, one characteristically is thinking about some distinct aim to which the human's activity contributes. The identity of the activity that constitutes the human function with the end to which it contributes would both justify identifying functioning well with flourishing and put to rest a serious obstacle to functionalist understandings of the human good.

Is the human being such that the activity that constitutes its function (H-ing) is identical with the good state of affairs (C) to which it contributes? I don't know of any way to argue for this claim other than to raise a few intuitive considerations in favor of the plausibility of this claim and to show that the identity of H-ing with C is not repugnant to anything else we have said about functions. The intuitive considerations I have in mind are simply these: (1) the human's functioning does not seem to need some other state of affairs to account for it; (2) even if one were to want some other state of affairs to account for the human function, there is no other object (a) to the functioning of which the human's functioning seems directed in the way that the heart's function is directed to the functioning of the human or (b) which lacks a function but which the human's function is to promote (e.g., the existence of pyramids); and (3) even if through a remarkable special revelation humans were informed that one of their functions is to promote some state of affairs independent of their own activity, such a revelation would not seem to tell the whole story about the goodness of the activity that constitutes human functioning.

Even if these intuitive considerations have some force, it might be asked whether there is anything unseemly about holding that the activity of H-ing that is the human function is identical to the state of affairs C, which is the point of that activity. After all, one of the conditions on in-order-to and function statements is etiological: A B-s because A's B-ing contributes to C. But it seems to me that nothing unseemly happens to this etiological condition by affirming the identity of B-ing and C. Given this supposed identity, A B-s because A's B-ing contributes to A's B-ing. There are at least two ways of reading this claim, neither of which calls the possibility of this identity into question.

One way of reading this claim is to say that B-ing is self-perpetuating by way of some feedback loop. Consider an analogy: Stephen skips class because skipping class contributes to skipping class. In other words, Stephen is caught in a 'vicious cycle' – perhaps he skips class because he is behind on his work, and he is behind on his work because he skips class, and so forth. The feedback loop operates by way of the fact that skipping class contributes to being behind on work, a condition in which it is undesirable to show up to class. Now, this interpretation can be applied to the human function: the human's function is an activity that is self-perpetuated, at least in part, in well-functioning humans. But that is not the only possible interpretation. Consider Stephen again. There is another way of understanding the statement that Stephen skips class because skipping class contributes to skipping class: it is to say simply that that is the sort of person that Stephen is; he is a class skipper. This is, of course, not an explanation, but rather the end of the line of explanations: that is just the sort of person Stephen is. This way of interpreting A B-s because A's B-ing contributes to A's B-ing can be applied to the human case: if we want a further explanation of why humans H, there is none to be found; humans are just the kind of thing that H.

If we hold that in humans H-ing is identical with the state of affairs C, which construal of the 'humans are the kind of thing that H because H-ing contributes to H-ing' claim ought we to affirm? It might seem that we should affirm the former: its emphasis on feedback loops offers an explanatory dimension that is missing in the latter. And this view does not seem obviously false: if the human's functioning well is good, and it turns out that part of the human's function is to recognize the good and pursue it, then if a human is functioning well, there would be just this sort of feedback relationship. But nevertheless I want to suggest that we have nothing to be ashamed of by affirming the latter construal, that the human is the kind of thing that H-s: perhaps the etiological account comes to an end at this point.

Thus, there is reason to believe that the activity that constitutes the human's function fulfills two of the characteristics of flourishing, that it possess goodness and that its goodness be not merely instrumental. What of the third criterion, that its goodness be theoretically graspable as such, rather than practically graspable as such? It seems clear that the goodness of the human's function must be of this sort. After all, the entire argument given so far – from the first remarks on parts' having functions to the present lines – could have been carried out with regard to the claim that rats have functions, or that begonias have functions. Yet surely we don't want to say that the goodness of the begonias' functioning, or the rat's, resides in something known by human practical reason: after all, such practical reason often grasps the rat's flourishing as something downright bad. Thus, the grasp of the goodness of the human function must be a product of speculative, rather than practical, reason. Since the human has a function such that its functioning is good, not (merely) for the sake of another being's functioning, and is knowable by speculative reason, it seems reasonable to identify its functioning with its flourishing.[18]

A Superfluous Concept?

My aim has been to provide a defense of the existence of flourishing in nature and, in particular, of the existence of human flourishing, and to do so in a way that is inoffensive to any well-entrenched anti-Aristotelian scientific theses. Beginning with the notion that parts of humans have their status as parts from their functions, and relying on claims both about the relationship between functioning parts and the wholes of which they form a part and about the proper analysis of function claims, I concluded that there must be such a thing as human flourishing. Now, it is clear that this argument will be devoid of force against any who deny that the parts of the human have functions, for the argument in my view really is just an unpacking of the presuppositions of the affirmation of that claim. On its own, such a denial seems unmotivated: for it seems that the main source of suspicion about functions in nature is fear of creeping Aristotelian teleology, and the view proposed here, while clearly Aristotelian in some respects, does not assert any thesis of Aristotelian teleology that any well-established scientific theory has pronounced false.[19]

There is a deeper worry that might be voiced here, though. The worry is that while no part of my argument is repugnant to any well-established claims of modern science, the price that the argument pays for its inoffensiveness is the violation of a methodological canon analogous to Occam's razor. Old-style Aristotelian teleology held that the flourishing of a creature, its final cause, was an explanatory principle – the development of a creature could be explained by the fact that such-and-such is its good. The teleological theses asserted were Grade 3, where the goodness of C as such played a part in explaining why A B-s. Now, modern science dispenses with final causes, holding that the only true causes are efficient causes; and, assuming this view to be correct, Aristotelian teleology is false. But while Aristotle's teleology is mistaken, it is at least a candidate as an explanatory scheme. On the other hand, new-style biological tele-ology, Grade 2, does not hold that the creature's flourishing qua flourishing ex-plains why *A B*-s, and so it cannot be held false in the same way that Aristotelian teleology is false. But it might be claimed that new-style teleology should be rejected because it contains a concept that is explanatorily otiose – that of flour-ishing. Even if Grade 2 teleology does not contradict any claims of modern bi-ology, it contains a concept that has no explanatory value, and so Grade 2 tele-ology is deficient in that respect.

Even granting the success of the argument that the concept of flourishing lacks explanatory power – to be made good, the argument has to assume both that causation is efficient causation and that the relevant notion of explanation is causal – it is far from clear that a view should contain no concepts such that the objects that answer to those concepts lack causal power. Consider, for ex-ample, the epiphenomenalist account of mental states. (See, for example, Jack-son 1982.) On this view, mental states are caused by physical states, but they are themselves causal dead ends. Now, if the methodological principle that no entities without causal power and thus (since *explanatory* is considered exten-sionally equivalent to *causal* in this context) no explanatory power are to be al-lowed into one's theory, then epiphenomenalism is not just a possibly false the-ory but one that is radically wrongheaded. But epiphenomenalism, while undoubtedly burdened by its own problems, is not radically wrongheaded. Why? It seems simply that epiphenomenalism is engaged in the task of fitting together a set of commonsense beliefs about mental states with an account, not repugnant to theses of modern neuroscience, of how these commonsense be-liefs could be true. What epiphenomenalism as theory attempts to do is to al-low for the possible truth of a set of relatively uncontroversial judgments. The same sort of aim is the motivation for affirming Grade 2 teleology. We possess a set of relatively uncontroversial biological beliefs of the form '*A*'s function is to *B*.' While it is true that in all cases in which we ascribe such a function *A B*-s because *A*'s *B*-ing contributes to some state of affairs *C,* we are not tempted to ascribe a function whenever there is this sort of contribution; we need to introduce some value notions in order to mark this distinction. This in-troduction of value notions makes applicable the concept of flourishing in na-ture. Thus, there is reason to allow that concept into our account.

I do not think this eliminates the worry completely; after all, there are still questions regarding the extent to which we should be permitted causally su-perfluous concepts in our philosophical or scientific views in order to account for pre- or nonphilosophical judgments. But I shall leave this question unan-swered. It is difficult not to think in terms of functions when considering the activity of the parts of the human. In the absence of compelling philosophical reasons to the contrary, I shall continue to assume that we are justified in think-ing of these things as possessing functions. And if we are justified in these be-liefs, then we ought to affirm the existence of human flourishing.

1.3 Knowledge of Human Flourishing

Suppose that the account so far is correct, that the fact that human organs are parts of the human on account of their functions indicates that we should ascribe a function to the human as a whole. We have not yet considered, though, how we might come to know what the flourishing of humans, or any other being, consists in. This question concerns us at this point for at least two reasons. First, recall that the aim of engaging in this enquiry concerning human flourishing was to defend a certain account of how natural law is grounded in human nature, that is, the 'real identity thesis': that certain states of affairs understood by practical reason as 'this is a good worth having' are really identical with certain states of affairs understood by theoretical reason as 'this is an aspect of human flourishing.' It would seem that at least part of the evidence for this real identity thesis must come from some correspondence relationship between the goods to be pursued knowable by practical reason and the aspects of flourishing knowable by theoretical reason. It is thus crucial that we have some way of knowing what the aspects of human flourishing are. Secondly, the absence of an account of how flourishing could be known might generate skepticism regarding the existence of such a thing, thus calling into doubt the results of the argument to this point. If, for example, we were to take a very restrictive view of the sort of knowledge of which we are capable, we might be led to adopt a skeptical stance on our capacity to recognize flourishing; and in such cases, the philosophical pull is often toward offering explanations as to why we would ever think there to be such a thing as flourishing, rather than toward expanding our conception of what speculative reason is capable of accomplishing. How, then, could we come to know what the flourishing of a creature consists in?

Mentalism

One implausible position that one can find oneself taking in the face of the skeptical challenge is a mentalist stance toward knowledge of flourishing in nature. On the mentalist view, what counts as a creature's flourishing is ultimately dependent on some introspectively accessible state of the observer. If biological teleology has an ineliminable reference to flourishing, one is confident that one can make correct teleological judgments, yet one is suspicious about one's ability to make judgments regarding what constitutes the creature's ultimate flourishing, one might be tempted to turn one's gaze inward, so to speak, rather than outward. One might be led, that is, to suspect that what counts as a creature's flourishing is merely its meeting human purposes, satisfying human desires, being what humans want it to be. The assumption is that we know our own desires in a relatively straightforward fashion, and so knowledge of what constitutes a creature's flourishing shouldn't be too much of a problem: the goodness of the activity that is the creature's flourishing consists in its satisfying a human desire. This position has the implication that if it were a common human desire to have dogs as paperweights, then it would be an aspect of a dog's flourishing to have no legs, and a dog that had four legs would be degenerate, not flourishing, in poor condition. This position strikes me as absurd. Better to deny that there is flourishing in nature than to affirm that flourishing in nature is a function of human wants.[20]

As far as I can tell, the only attractiveness of the mentalist picture derives from its being clearly true that function is often the product of human intention and design and from the difficulty involved in understanding how we could come to know what the flourishing of a natural creature is. But it implies conclusions so bizarre that only one in the grips of a bad theory could affirm it.

Statistical Normalcy

To hold that knowledge of our own desires can enable us to identify flourishing in nature is only one version of a more general mistake, that of rushing to a more certain form of knowledge that can serve as a surrogate for knowledge of the seemingly more occult quality of flourishing. Another version of this error is to try to make knowledge of flourishing into some sort of statistical matter. One might hold that one comes to know what constitutes a creature's flourishing by experiencing a number of samples of that kind of thing and determining what is normal, statistically speaking, for that sort of thing. This norm can then serve as a standard for flourishing. Once more, a more straightforward way of knowing – gathering a sample, looking for general features held in common – is supposed to tell us what counts as aspects of a creature's flourishing.

This 'normalcy' method is, however, also inadequate. Grant for a moment that one can grasp, completely independently of any explicit or implicit understanding of what a thing's flourishing is, the kind to which that thing belongs. There still remain serious problems. It is clearly possible that all of the members of the sample group – or even all of the members of that kind in existence – are degenerate cases. Consider as an analogy the obvious fact that, given a kind of functionally defined artifact, it is possible that all of the members of that kind are degenerate, that all of them are nonfunctioning or malfunctioning. Suppose, for example, that the automobile industry is in dire straits. The cars that it produces are of horrendous quality. Clearly, it is possible that all of those instances of the kind automobile are degenerate, and it would be the height of absurdity to try to determine what the automobile's function is by looking to the statistical norm with regard to existing automobiles. But if such is the case for automobiles, then it seems as if it would be the case for natural objects with functions, such as begonias, rats, and humans.

If this analogy does not hold, it must be due to the fact that there is a designer for the automobile, whose intention can fix its function independently of what is statistically the norm among actually existing cars, and that there is not (we shall assume for the moment) a designer for natural objects. But even if there is a difference between these cases, it seems false that this would matter with regard to the relevance of this example to the viability of using a statistical norm as a way of determining what the flourishing of a creature is. For the automobile case does not have its force, it seems to me, by any appeal to a contrast between the designer's intention as such and the statistical norm; it works simply by appealing to the fact that we know that the car has a particular function and that it is possible for all cars in existence to fail to perform this function. (To assert that the existence of a designing intelligence *must* make the difference seems to be no more than a retreat into a mentalistic account of functions.)

Even if the analogy were not convincing, we could always appeal directly to cases in nature in which the statistical norm seems obviously not to be a correct guide to our intuitive grasp of a creature's flourishing. Plantinga mentions, for example, that very few baby tortoises live to adulthood. Surely the fact that it is statistically normal for a baby tortoise to die before adulthood does not indicate that this is part of its flourishing, and that one that lives to a ripe old age is in any way failing to flourish (1993, pp. 200–201).[21]

There is something right about the normalcy view: if there were not sufficient regularity, then there would be no occasion to form concepts like *function* and *flourishing* with regard to nature. But that some regularity is a necessary condition for the formation of these concepts does not show that these concepts are reducible to the concept of statistical normalcy, or that normalcy is a necessary or sufficient condition for something's being the function or flourishing of any given creature.

Knowledge of Flourishing as Implicit in Particular Function Judgments

How, then, do we come to know a creature's flourishing? I suggest that we will inevitably fall into error if we employ any reductionist strategy to try to discover what the aspects of any creature's flourishing are. Rather, the correct account of how one can come to know a creature's flourishing will involve simply making our implicit, immediate grasp of the content of a creature's flourishing explicit. On the mentalist and statistical normalcy accounts, there is a set of facts to which we have unproblematic access, access that does not depend on any prior explicit or implicit grasp of the creature's flourishing. On the view that I propose, our starting points are judgments that already presuppose particular judgments about creaturely flourishing, so that our aim is to uncover the presuppositions of judgments we already hold. Thus there is a marked similarity between the sort of argument that I presented for the existing of flourishing in nature and the method that I propose for coming to know what a creature's flourishing consists in.

We might put it this way: just as the fact that the general judgment that parts of a creature are such in virtue of their functions presupposes that the creature as a whole has a function, the particular judgments about what functions the parts of creatures have presuppose particular judgments about what the function of the creature as a whole is (and thus, since the creature's functioning is identified with its flourishing, our particular judgments about functioning parts presuppose judgments about the flourishing of the whole). So, the suggestion is that in virtue of the fact that we do grasp that the parts of the creature have particular functions, we must have some grasp of the flourishing of the whole. Thus, what we find ourselves doing is making explicit a vague and unformed grasp of what constitutes a given creature's flourishing.[22] The question to which our attention must be turned, therefore, becomes: what is the function of the *human* that makes the subsidiary functions of the parts of humans intelligible? What is it, that is, that explains their status as having the particular functions that they have?

To this question there is an obvious response: living, or perhaps living and reproducing. The functions of the parts of humans can be made intelligible as contributors to one or another of these functions. And one might suspect that these are the *only* aspects of human flourishing that there are, or at least the only ones that we are entitled to affirm if the suggested account of knowing flourishing is correct. For one might hold that all of the functions of the parts of the human are understandable by reference to these functions, so that no other aspect of flourishing is grasped by speculative reason.

I am going to concede that living or living-and-reproducing is one aspect of human flourishing, for it seems clear that at least one of these would result from the application of the method that I have described. The question that is more pressing is whether, given this method, there are any other aspects of human flourishing the status of which as such is presupposed in our particular function judgments. (These other aspects would be what Sorabji aptly calls "luxury functions"; see his 1964, p. 294.) In providing some reason to think that we have a grasp on aspects of human flourishing other than living, or living-and-reproducing, I shall not make the obviously false claim that in normal conditions it is not the case that the performance of the functions of the parts of the human contribute to these functions. What I shall try to show is that there is an overdetermination inasmuch as the functions of the human's parts are also made intelligible as functions by aspects of flourishing other than life and reproduction.

The argument that I am going to present focuses, in a way that is admittedly naive about physiological details, on the activity of the brain. It relies in part on thought experiments, and what we would say if certain sorts of changes in brain activity were to occur. I think that changes similar to the type I describe could occur, and that in mentally ill persons sometimes do occur. At any rate, if there is something wrong with the argument, it is unlikely to be in the fact that it appeals to a thought experiment. If there is an error, it occurs either in what I think the result of the thought experiment is, or in a general principle to which I appeal in using the thought experiment to reach specific conclusions regarding aspects of human flourishing.

Suppose that x has a function f which is to contribute to g, a function of y. When x functions properly (and other circumstances that I will ignore from now on are right), then x's f-ing contributes to y's g-ing, and y g-s. Now, suppose that when x is properly performing function f, then in performing that function, x also contributes to a distinct activity of y – call it h. Thus, when x is f-ing, x contributes to two activities, y's g-ing and y's h-ing. I want to claim that we have evidence that it is also x's function to contribute to y's h-ing if the following conditions hold: (i) x is not seriously malfunctioning with regard to y's g-ing; (ii) x's activity is not contributing to h-ing; and (iii) x is seriously malfunctioning. Intuitively, the idea is that if we want to say that x is seriously malfunctioning, but not with regard to one activity that it contributes to, then we have evidence that it is seriously malfunctioning with regard to another activity that it contributes to. If the change in its normal operation is that it is now failing to contribute to a certain activity, then we have reason to think that contributing to that activity is another one of its functions, or another part of its complex function.

Consider an example of this. Suppose that you believe that living is a function of the human being to which the functioning of its parts contributes; living makes intelligible the status of the parts as having the functions that they have. Now, call 'unhelpful propositions' true propositions knowledge of which is not instrumentally valuable for keeping one alive. Most people think that the set of unhelpful propositions is nonempty, and that humans can know some of these propositions; I shall make both of these assumptions. Now, one's brain is, we may concede, such that its proper functioning contributes to the survival of the person whose brain it is. I shall assume that it is a function of the brain to keep the human of which it is a part alive. Further, when one's brain is functioning properly, it has the capacity to understand and evaluate the truth of unhelpful propositions. Now, suppose that one's brain is functioning properly up to a certain time. At that time, its activity changes: it becomes incapable of knowing unhelpful propositions. Any piece of information that is useful for survival gets processed; any piece of information that is not useful for survival goes unprocessed.

In certain respects, this case undeniably fits the model described. The brain has a function, which is to contribute to the human's living. When the brain functions properly, then the brain's functioning contributes to the human's living. Now, when the brain is properly performing that function, it also contributes to a distinct activity of the human – that is, processing unhelpful propositions. Thus, when the brain is functioning, it contributes to two activities, the human's living and the human's knowing unhelpful bits of knowledge. Now, the question is whether the activity of grasping the truth or falsity of unhelpful propositions is also an aspect of human flourishing, or simply a side effect of it – as the clock's making a ticking sound is a mere side effect of the clock's proper functioning. That the capacity to grasp the truth is part of the human function is suggested by reflection on what we would think if the change in activity described previously were to occur. I have described the case so that (ii) holds: the brain is not contributing to the knowing of unhelpful propositions. I imagine that most of us would agree that in this case (iii) the brain is seriously malfunctioning. This leaves us with the following conditional: if it is the case that the brain could be in a condition in which it is not seriously malfunctioning with regard to the human's living in such a case, then the brain's function is also that of contributing to the human's knowing unhelpful propositions. And if the antecedent is true, then given the method for making explicit one's grasp of aspects of flourishing discussed earlier, it follows that there are other aspects of flourishing besides living – at least that of speculative knowledge.

If one is to be skeptical about the status of speculative knowledge as an aspect of one's flourishing, then one will have to hold that in any case in which the brain fails to contribute to the human's capacity to know speculatively, it is also the case that the brain is seriously malfunctioning with regard to the function of living. One might think that this is obviously not the case: for if the brain's activity is contributing to the function of living, then it is not seriously malfunctioning with regard to life; and so, if it is seriously malfunctioning, it must be that part of its function is to contribute to speculative knowing. But this is too quick. The principle that this argument relies on – if x's function is to contribute to y's functioning, then in any case in which x's activity contributes to y's functioning x is not seriously malfunctioning – is false. The reason is that there is more than one way to malfunction seriously: x can malfunction seriously vis-à-vis y's functioning either by failing to contribute to it or by contributing to it in a way that is drastically different from its design plan. And one might say that in any case in which the human's brain functions in a way that does not contribute to knowing speculatively, its activity differs sufficiently from how it is designed to act, such that even if it continues to contribute to the good of life, it is seriously malfunctioning in doing so.

This is the view that the opponent of the claim that speculative knowledge is an aspect of flourishing must take; the difficulty is in understanding why this response is not completely ad hoc. Suppose that the premise of the thought experiment is true, that the process by which the brain's function contributes to the human's living is isolable, so that the brain's activity doesn't contribute to speculative knowing. The branch has been cut off of the tree, so to speak. What grounds are there for calling this a serious malfunction vis-à-vis the activity of life? The causal connections between brain function and the human function of living are, ex hypothesi, intact. Everything relevant to sustaining life seems to have remained the same; all that has occurred is that the contribution to the knowledge of unhelpful propositions has been prevented. What grounds would there be for asserting that this is a serious malfunction, if the only function relevant is that of living?

It seems that the brain is seriously malfunctioning in this case, and its malfunction cannot be due to the brain's function of contributing to the human's living. Since by stipulation the effect on the brain was that of cutting off its capacity to know speculatively, and it seems to be the activity of speculative knowing in terms of which the change in brain activity is called a malfunction, I suggest that one of the functions of the human is to know speculatively. This would give us reason to think that speculative knowing is an aspect of human flourishing – that in addition to life, it is part of the human function to know.

The strategy is, I hope, clear. One way to come to understand what aspects of flourishing there are is to attempt to isolate them by way of imagined malfunctions. This enables one to render explicit what is known in some implicit way. This process is, of course, far from infallible; it is not a recipe for generating aspects of flourishing but a starting point for speculative reflection. And it does seem that many of the activities that are included in accounts of human flourishing can be plausibly viewed as such through the application of this method: imagine what we would say about the seriousness of the malfunctions in the brain that would prevent us from entering into friendships or any social relationships; or from appreciating beauty in any form; or in making practical judgments; and so forth. Some of these conditions are not merely possible but actual. It seems that since we recognize, or would recognize on due reflection, that these inabilities would count as serious malfunctions of the brain, we should allow that these activities of friendship, aesthetic experience, and excellent agency are aspects of the human being's flourishing.[23]

1.4 The Real Identity Thesis

We need now to consider what the argument so far – that there is such a thing as human flourishing, and that we can grasp by way of speculative reason what aspects of human flourishing there are – can contribute to a distinctively natural law theory of practical rationality, one that holds that the practical principles specifying forms of good to be sought are grounded in human nature. The account of this grounding relationship that I have been aiming toward is the 'real identity' thesis: that the states of affairs grasped by practical reason as 'x is a good to be pursued' are identical with those states of affairs grasped by theoretical reason as 'x is an aspect of human flourishing.' On the real identity view, these judgments refer to the same states of affairs, and are made true by the same states of affairs.

Reasons to Affirm the Real Identity Thesis

Affirmation of the real identity thesis appears to be a coherent position, but the question remains – even given a defense of the existence of flourishing in nature – why one would think that there is a real identity between aspects of flourishing and goods to be pursued. We cannot, after all, take the states of affairs grasped as aspects of flourishing and the states of affairs grasped as goods worth having out of their respective theoretical and practical 'wrappers' in order to see if the same item is inside. Why, then, should we not simply think that there is one set of entities understood by theoretical reason, another grasped by practical reason, not identical to each other? Why assert their identity?

One reason, upon which I will not place much weight, is that the real identity thesis offers a coherent account that possesses terrific unifying power. It is a view on which there is a tight connection between the normative and non-normative orders; indeed, it is hard to see how any theory of goods to be pursued could connect practical and theoretical reason so tightly together. It is of course true, though, that regardless of the attractiveness of this theoretical benefit, we need additional good reasons to think the view correct. Short of intuitive obviousness, which is *not* present in this case, the best evidence for their identity would be a list of similarities of salient features between goods to be pursued and aspects of flourishing for which the best available explanation is the real identity of the two: similarities in the categories to which aspects of flourishing and goods to be pursued belong, in the way that they are structured, in the way that they are known, and in the lists of the particular states of affairs that are grasped as aspects of flourishing and goods to be pursued. In these respects, it seems to me that the similarities between aspects of flourishing and goods to be pursued are telling.

Consider first that both the states of affairs that are grasped as aspects of flourishing and the states of affairs that are grasped as goods to be pursued are characterized by judgments that rely on evaluative concepts. (While practical judgments form a class of evaluative judgments, 'evaluative' and 'practical' are not synonymous or coextensive: 'this plant is in good condition' is an evaluative judgment, but it is not a practical judgment.) We cannot understand something as an aspect of human flourishing except by understanding it as good, as perfective of the sorts of being that we are; similarly, we cannot understand something as a basic good without understanding it as worth pursuing and having. Now it would be – as some critics of a particular interpretation of Aristotle's *ergon* argument have pointed out – fallacious to assume that by understanding what the good (that is, perfected) human is we thereby understand what is good for the human (that is, what is worth pursuing and having by humans). But it does seem plausible that if we are to hold that a certain set of states of affairs grasped by theoretical reason are to be identified with a certain set of states of affairs grasped by practical reason, the most likely candidates for identification on the theoretical side of the equation are states of affairs characterized by judgments that employ evaluative concepts.[24]

Consider next the similarity between the structural features of aspects of flourishing (and functions generally) and goods to be pursued. Note, for example, the following structural similarity: some functions are for the sake of other functions, and so have their character as functions in virtue of the functions to which they contribute, just as some goods are for the sake of other goods, and have their character as goods in virtue of the goods to which they contribute. Functions that are the 'end of the line,' at least in creatures to which the concept of 'flourishing' applies, are aspects of flourishing; goods that are the 'end of the line' are intrinsic goods. Consider also the concepts of inclusive and dominant functions (1.2). The argument that a being that seems to have a number of distinct functions has instead a single dominant or inclusive function proceeds by suggesting that only by positing such a function can the being be seen as a unity. One could argue, with similar plausibility, that there must be an inclusive or dominant good to which all of one's other goods contribute, for only by positing such a good can the agent be viewed as a unity, a single agent. The concepts of *for the sake of, in order to, instrumental, inclusive, dominant,* then, are equally at home in the world of functions and goods to be pursued. In short, the concepts that sort out different sorts of function and place them into certain relationships with other functions – including functions that constitute a thing's flourishing – are also applicable to the realm of goods to be pursued. This is a remarkable fact. One way to explain this remarkable fact is that the goods to be pursued that practical reason grasps are really identical with states of affairs involving the function that constitutes human flourishing.

Also suggestive is the way that flourishing and goods to be pursued are grasped. If the inclinationist method is defensible, practical reason can grasp the intrinsic goodness of certain states of affairs by examining the particular things that one is inclined to pursue and asking what goods ultimately make those things worth seeking. This method bears a striking resemblance to the method for determining what a creature's flourishing is by looking at what makes the functions of its parts intelligible. Here, as in the case of goods to be pursued, there is no question of derivation. In both cases, one is trying to make explicit that of which one already has an implicit grasp.

While these broad similarities in structural features are suggestive, they do not seem sufficient evidence for the real identity thesis. There would also have to be similarity in *content* between what is understood as aspects of flourishing and what is grasped as goods to be pursued. We seem to find ourselves in a bind here, though, since the point of defending the real identity thesis was to support the use of the dialectical method for justifying an account of the goods to be pursued that provide the fundamental reasons for action. Suppose we were to hold that we need to provide a one-to-one correspondence between aspects of flourishing and fundamental reasons for action, where the status of each of these is determined independently by theoretical and practical reason, in order reasonably to affirm the real identity thesis. If we were to insist on this strict evidential constraint, then we would not need a dialectical method, having already established what the fundamental reasons for action are in the course of defending the real identity thesis. It seems unreasonable, though, to say that we have to provide for a complete correspondence between aspects of flourishing and fundamental reasons before we are justified in placing some reliance on the real identity thesis. We can say that there are some aspects of flourishing and some goods to be pursued that can be established independently and that display the requisite correspondence, so that there is some rational motivation for holding the real identity thesis. Once this *prima facie* evidence in favor of the real identity thesis is accepted, that theory can be used to justify, at least tentatively, the dialectical method of generating a catalog of fundamental reasons for action. The defense of the real identity thesis cannot be completed, then, until we turn to the task of providing a catalog of basic goods in Chapter 3 (3.3).

Aquinas's Natural Law Theory and the Real Identity Thesis

We began our discussion of natural law theory's view of fundamental practical knowledge by examining inclinationist and derivationist accounts. Writers have found both of these views in the work of the paradigmatic natural law theorist, Aquinas: Finnis emphasizes Aquinas's insistence that the first principles of the natural law are *per se nota,* whereas Lisska emphasizes the way that goodness is tied to aspects of human nature within the Thomistic scheme. I want to conclude this chapter by arguing for the continuity of the view that I have defended with Aquinas's account of nature and ethics; indeed, the similarities between Aquinas's account and the view that I have defended would help to explain why writers have alternately conceived Aquinas's natural law theory as endorsing inclinationism and derivationism.

There are close similarities between the philosophy of nature within which the existence of flourishing in nature is defended in my own account and the philosophy of nature defended by Aquinas. My view is, of course, un-Thomistic, precisely because it is un-Aristotelian, in its unwillingness to affirm the presence of Grade 3 teleology in nature (1.2). But it clearly is akin to Aquinas's view in a number of respects. First, it insists, as Aquinas does, that whether a being is flourishing is a natural fact discoverable by human reason. On Aquinas's view, theoretical reason grasps that natural objects move from potency to actuality; complete actuality is the final cause of a creature's existence, what makes it good, perfect (*Summa Theologiae,* Ia 5, 1).[25] Secondly, I follow Aquinas in connecting the notion of flourishing to the notion of kind: I suggested that the activity that constitutes a thing's flourishing is simply the activity that this kind of being performs (1.2), just as on Aquinas's view, what determines the perfection of a being is the same as what determines the kind that it belongs to, that is, its form. Thirdly, the account proposed here can be placed neatly within a more general Thomistic account of goodness. On the Thomistic account, goodness is fullness of being in accordance with one's kind. A creature is good to the extent to which it is in act, that is, to the extent to which it displays the activities characteristic of the sort of being that it is. Badness, in contrast, is a lack, a failing to be; it is not a positive existence, but an absence. It is thus clear that the account of flourishing proposed here, on which flourishing consists of functioning in certain ways, fits readily into a Thomistic account of goodness.

The philosophy of nature in terms of which I have offered a preliminary defense of the real identity thesis is developed, then, roughly along Thomistic lines. With respect to the issue of fundamental practical knowledge, we have already considered evidence (1.1) that Aquinas holds a form of inclinationist view, on which practical reason formulates the principles of the natural law in an attempt to make intelligible those acts that one has a tendency to perform; and I have affirmed the capacity of practical reason to grasp truths about basic goods in this way. What, then, shall we say about Aquinas's view on the relationship between the principles of the natural law, grasped self-evidently by practical reason, and truths about human perfection, knowable by speculative reason? Is there any reason to suppose that Aquinas held a view akin to the real identity thesis?

There is some evidence that this was Aquinas's view. Early in the *Summa,* he writes, "Goodness and being are really the same, and differ only in idea" (*Summa Theologiae,* Ia 5, 1). One natural way to read that claim is that the state of affairs grasped as 'such-and-such is an aspect of flourishing' (fullness of being in accordance with one's kind) is identical with the state of affairs grasped as 'such-and-such is a good to be pursued.' Also suggestive is his account of the relationship between speculative and practical reason (*Summa Theologiae,* Ia 14, 16).[26] 'Speculative' and 'practical,' Aquinas holds, can be applied to three aspects of the act of knowledge: first, with regard to the object of the act of knowledge; secondly, with regard to the manner of knowing; and thirdly, with regard to the aim of the act of knowledge.[27] If the object of knowledge is something that can be done or made by human action, then the knowledge is practical with respect to its object; if the object cannot be done or made, then the knowledge is speculative with respect to its object. If the object is known qua something that can be made or done, then the knowledge is practical with respect to the manner of knowing; if it is not known qua something that can be made or done, then the knowledge is speculative with respect to the manner of knowing. If the knowledge is for the sake of action, then the knowledge is practical with respect to its end; if the knowledge is not for the sake of action, then the knowledge is speculative with respect to its end.[28]

What is important about this classification for our purposes is that in the case of knowledge that is either speculative or practical with respect to the aim, it is one and the same piece of information that can be grasped either by speculative or practical reason, information that will, of course, receive different formulations depending on whether it is speculative or practical reason that is doing the formulating. It might, then, be the case that the state of affairs that is grasped by speculative reason as an aspect of human perfection would be grasped by practical reason as a good to be pursued.

I am uncertain as to whether the view that Aquinas held the real identity thesis in the version presented here is ultimately defensible, but it certainly seems to flow naturally from his views on nature, reason, and ethics. And, furthermore, because a theory of fundamental practical knowledge underwritten by the real identity thesis confirms the legitimacy of both inclinationist and derivationist accounts of practical knowledge, ascription of the real identity thesis to Aquinas would go some way toward explaining why able scholars would interpret Aquinas as affirming both of these views. There is, thus, strong reason to ascribe something like the real identity account to Aquinas, and therefore to hold that the view of the relationship between nature and ethics defended in this chapter is closely continuous with Aquinas's position.[29]

2

Well-Being

2.1 Natural Law Theory as Welfarist and Objectivist

Natural law theory, or at least that strand of it that has its philosophical roots in Aristotle, is welfarist:[1] it asserts, that is, that the fundamental reasons for action are aspects of agents' well-being.[2] Natural law theory, or at least that strand of it that has its philosophical roots in Aristotle, is also objectivist:[3] it holds that the well-being of an agent is not fundamentally a matter of the agent's attitudes or preferences. Yet the prevailing philosophical orthodoxy concerning welfare is that it should be given some kind of subjectivist interpretation. In this chapter, I want to take up some of the difficulties that arise from the conjunction of a welfarist theory of practical reasonableness with an objectivist theory of the good.

The very usefulness of this subjectivism/objectivism distinction with respect to theories of well-being has been called into question (by Griffin: see his 1986, p. 33), but it seems to me to be a helpful one, at least so long as we keep in mind that there are various dimensions along which a theory of well-being might be classified as subjectivist or objectivist, and that a theory of well-being might be subjectivist (or objectivist) with respect to one dimension and not with respect to others. We can distinguish at least three areas in which the subjectivism/objectivism distinction is relevant: with respect to the *concept, nature,* and *content* of well-being.

Consider propositions of the form 'x is an aspect of A's well-being,' where x is a state of affairs and A is a welfare subject. One dimension along which theories of well-being might be classified as subjectivist or objectivist is conceptual. One might hold that it is a conceptual truth that 'x is an aspect of A's well-being' is correct only if A has some subjective response to x (liking x, being pleased by x, desiring x, having a pro-attitude toward x, or the like). One might hold, by contrast, that it is a conceptual truth that the correctness of 'x is an aspect of A's well-being' is not constituted by A's having any subjective response to x. The former of these views we may call subjectivism about the concept of well-being, or *conceptual subjectivism;* the latter of these views we may call objectivism about the concept of well-being, or *conceptual objectivism.* One might reject both of these positions, holding that the concept of well-being allows for both the possibility of a subjectivist or an objectivist interpretation: call this position neutralism about the concept of well-being, or *conceptual neutralism.*

Another dimension along which views on well-being can vary concerns the truth-conditions for the claim '*x* is an aspect of *A*'s well-being.' On some views, the truth-maker for '*x* is an aspect of *A*'s well-being' always includes some mental state of *A*'s. On some views, the truth-maker for '*x* is an aspect of *A*'s well-being' does not include some mental state of *A*'s. Views of the former type are varieties of subjectivism about the nature of well-being, or (for lack of a better term) *formal subjectivism;* views of the latter type are varieties of objectivism about the nature of well-being, or *formal objectivism.* We can make a further important distinction between types of subjectivism about the nature of well-being. One might hold that *A*'s having a certain mental state with respect to *x* is both necessary and sufficient for *x*'s being an aspect of *A*'s well-being: we can call this position *strong subjectivism* about the nature of well-being. One might hold, by contrast, that *A*'s having a certain mental state with respect to *x* is necessary for *x*'s being an aspect of *A*'s well-being: we can call this position *weak subjectivism* about the nature of well-being. It is possible to hold that some propositions of the form '*x* is an aspect of *A*'s well-being' have as part of their truth-conditions some mental state of *A*'s while others do not: this would be a *hybrid* view on the nature of well-being.

We can, further, employ the subjectivist/objectivist distinction with respect to the content of well-being. We may call the thesis that for any true proposition '*x* is an aspect of *A*'s well-being' *x* includes some mental state of *A*'s *subjectivism about the content of well-being,* or *substantive subjectivism;* we may call the thesis that for no true proposition '*x* is an aspect of *A*'s well-being' does *x* include some mental state of *A*'s *objectivism about the content of well-being,* or *substantive objectivism.* One that holds that some aspects of well-being include the subject's mental states, while some do not, affirms a *mixed* view on the content of well-being.

What, then, is the form or forms of objectivism that this natural law view affirms? My concern is to defend only formal objectivism, objectivism about the nature of well-being. Such a view clearly places this natural law theory at odds with both the strong and weak versions of formal subjectivism, as well as with the hybrid view on the nature of well-being. It also places it at odds with conceptual subjectivism: while formal objectivism is compatible with either conceptual objectivism or neutralism, the truth of conceptual subjectivism would rule out the possibility of a formally objectivist account of well-being. On the other hand, the formal objectivism of the natural law view commits the natural law theorist to no stand whatsoever on the content of well-being: the natural law theorist could coherently affirm formal objectivism while offering a substantially subjectivist (or, more plausibly, a mixed) theory of well-being. The natural law theorist that defends formal objectivism about well-being, therefore, has no reason to be worried about substantive subjectivisms; even though (as I will argue in Chapter 3) such views are false, they pose no threat to its central objectivist thesis.

I will treat, in turn, the subjectivisms with which this natural law theory's formal objectivism are incompatible: subjectivism about the concept of well-being (2.2) and both strong and weak subjectivism about the nature of well-being (2.3–2.4, 2.5). The hybrid view on the nature of well-being, which is also incompatible with natural law theory's pure objectivism, will be considered briefly at the conclusion of 2.5 and, for reasons discussed there, will be revisited in Chapter 3.

2.2 The Refutation of Conceptual Subjectivism

While the claim that both subjectivist and objectivist interpretations of well-being are possible might seem an obvious truth, it has recently been denied by Thomas Hurka, whose perfectionist theory of morality bears some similarities to the view presented in this book. On his view, the notions of 'being good for' and 'well-being' are inevitably connected to subjectivist theories of the good, and thus are unsuitable for any theory that affirms an objectivist account of the good.

The [perfectionist] ideal is not about what is "good for" agents. . . . "Good for" is tied to concepts of well-being or welfare and interests: Something is "good for" a person if it increases his well-being or furthers his interests. Well-being itself is often characterized subjectively, in terms of actual or hypothetical desires. Given this subjective characterization, perfectionism cannot concern well-being. Its ideal cannot define the "good for" a human because the ideal is one he ought to pursue regardless of his desires. In my view, perfectionism should never be expressed in terms of well-being. (Hurka 1993, p. 17)

Now, since both Hurka and I affirm an objectivist account of the good, if Hurka provides good reasons for declining to identify his account of the good as an account of well-being, I too should decline to identify the two. But there is clearly nothing in this passage to show that the concept of well-being is inevitably tied to subjectivism; all that it says is that theories of well-being are typically subjectivist. Only later does Hurka offer an argument that there is no "conceptual room" for an objectivist account of well-being:

Could there not be an objective or perfectionist account of well-being, which characterized well-being not in terms of desires, but in terms of developing human nature? I do not believe there is conceptual room for such an account, for I do not believe that "well-being" has any meaning independent both of particular accounts of well-being and of the moral predicate "good." I do not see that "developing human nature constitutes well-being and is therefore good" says anything over and above "developing human nature is good." (Hurka 1993, p. 194, n. 17)

This argument against the possibility of an objectivist account of well-being has little to recommend it.[4] All that one needs to do in order to disarm it is to provide an intelligible notion of 'good for' that is independent both of objectivist and subjectivist interpretations. We are aided in providing such a notion by the recent attempts to characterize the difference between agent-relative and agent-neutral reasons for action; for, after all, the notion of 'good for' is just an agent-relative conception of goodness, and if one can formally define what makes something an agent-relative reason, it seems as if one should also be able to state what makes something an agent-relative good, a good *for an agent.*

Consider, for example, Nagel's account (1970, pp. 89–92, where he uses the terms 'subjective' and 'objective' rather than 'agent-relative' and 'agent-neutral,' respectively). On his view, reasons can be characterized as predicates. Suppose that the variable x ranges over agents and the variable y ranges over events. The generic form of statement that R is a reason for action is $(x)(y)(Ry\rightarrow$ there is a reason for x to promote y). Given this generic form of reason-statement, we can define agent-relative reasons for action as those in which there is a free occurrence of x in $R;$ agent-neutral reasons are those in which there is no free occurrence of x in R. (Thus, the predicate 'provides x with knowledge' could be only an agent-relative reason for action, while the predicate 'provides someone with knowledge' could be only an agent-neutral reason for action.) But, given the adequacy of this characterization of agent-relativity, we can characterize the notion of 'goodness for.' Suppose that A ranges over agents and x ranges over states of affairs. We can say that G is a goodness-predicate when $(A)(x)(Gx\rightarrow$ with regard to $A,$ x is good). A goodness-predicate G is agent-relative if there is a free occurrence of A in $G;$ otherwise, it is agent-neutral. Thus 'is an instance of A's enjoying friendship' is an agent-relative goodness predicate; 'is an instance of Murphy's enjoying friendship' or 'is an instance of someone's enjoying friendship' is an agent-neutral goodness predicate. Using this definition, we can distinguish between those states of affairs that are held to be good for some agent and those that are supposed to be good *simpliciter.*

Now, this notion of 'goodness for' can be used in offering a preliminary account of the concept of well-being. The aspects of an agent's well-being, we might say, are those states of affairs that are good for an agent, but not merely in the instrumental sense of goodness. In other words, a state of affairs is an aspect of an agent's well-being if that state of affairs is good for that agent and the goodness of that state of affairs for the agent is not due solely to its capacity to bring about some other state of affairs that is good for the agent.

Two things should be immediately noted regarding these accounts of 'goodness for' and well-being. First, these accounts are in their present form conceptually neutral between objectivist and subjectivist interpretations: it thus appears to be an open question whether an objectivist or subjectivist theory of well-being is the correct one. Secondly, on these accounts, Hurka seems wrong to say that "developing human nature constitutes well-being and is therefore good," says nothing over and above "developing human nature is good." For the notion of goodness involved in saying that "developing human nature is good" seems to be quite different from that involved in saying that "developing human nature is good for people." In asserting that "developing human nature constitutes well-being and is therefore good" what one is asserting is a connection between prudential and moral goodness: one is claiming that since a state of affairs promotes an agent's well-being, there are moral grounds for ensuring that that state of affairs obtains. (How this transition is made is problematic, but that there is a transition is not the least in doubt.)

Even though Hurka is wrong to say that accounts of well-being are inevitably subjectivist,[5] he is right to say that the current orthodoxy about the nature of well-being is some variety of subjectivism. Let us turn, then, to reasons for rejecting this orthodoxy.

2.3 The Simple Desire-Fulfillment Theory as the Best Version of Strong Subjectivism

According to strong subjectivism about the nature of well-being – a view that often goes by the name of the *desire-fulfillment theory* (Parfit 1984, p. 493) – the obtaining of a state of affairs x makes an agent better off if and only if the agent desires that x obtain, or would, under certain formally described conditions, desire that x obtain.[6] But any such theory must be false, for it would generate false implications about the reasons for action that an agent has.

Or so I will argue (2.4). But while it might be conceded that such an argument might succeed against certain naive versions of strong subjectivism, it might be held that it is doomed to fail against more sophisticated versions, those in which one's desires are, consistently with the main thrust of strong subjectivism, in some way improved. Now, I think that this sort of reply is mistaken, and that the argument will succeed against any genuine version of strong subjectivism. But as an additional defense against this line of reply, I want to consider what the best, most principled formulation of strong subjectivism is. I want to argue that the best version of strong subjectivism is a simple view that appeals only to an agent's actual desires, rather than a more complex view that appeals to desires that an agent would have under some idealized set of circumstances. (Those readers already convinced that desire-fulfillment theories of well-being are not improved in any essential, non–ad-hoc way by appealing to idealized over actual desires can skip to 2.4 without losing the thread of argument.)

While all desire-fulfillment, or 'DF,' theorists affirm that what makes an agent well off must ultimately refer to desire, there now appears to be a consensus among those defending DF theories that it is not the satisfaction of the agent's actual desires that constitutes an agent's well-being, but rather the satisfaction of those desires that the agent would have in what I will call a 'hypothetical desire situation.' Just as Rawls holds that the principles of right are those that would be unanimously chosen in a hypothetical choice situation, that is, a setting optimal for choosing such principles (1971, p. 12), defenders of DF theory hold that an agent's well-being is what he or she would desire in a hypothetical desire situation, that is, a setting optimal for desiring.

While the precise nature of the hypothetical desire situation is a matter of debate among DF theorists, all of them seem to agree that any adequate DF theory will incorporate a strong information condition into the hypothetical desire situation. In treating of the concept of an individual's good, Sidgwick writes:

It would seem . . . that if we interpret the notion 'good' in relation to 'desire,' we must identify it not with the actually desired, but rather with the desirable: – meaning by 'desirable' not necessarily 'what ought to be desired' but what would be desired . . . if it were judged attainable by voluntary action, supposing the desirer to possess a perfect forecast, emotional as well as intellectual, of the state of attainment or fruition. (*Methods,* pp. 110–111)

Brandt writes that a state of affairs belongs to an agent's welfare only if it is such that "that person would want it if he were fully rational" (1979, p. 268); an agent's desire is rational, on Brandt's view,

if it would survive or be produced by careful 'cognitive psychotherapy' [where cognitive psychotherapy is the 'whole process of confronting desires with relevant information']. . . . I shall call a desire 'irrational' if it cannot survive compatibly with clear and repeated judgments about established facts. What this means is that rational desire . . . can confront, or will even be produced by, awareness of the truth. (1979, p. 113)

And Railton has argued that we should consider an agent's good to be "what he would want himself to want . . . were he to contemplate his present situation from a standpoint fully and vividly informed about himself and his circumstances, and entirely free of cognitive error or lapses of instrumental rationality" (1986a, p. 16).

Now, it is clear even from these brief quotations from a small sample of DF theories that DF theorists differ in their accounts of the relevant hypothetical desire situation. Only Railton appeals to a hypothetical desire situation in which second-order desires are at stake. Sidgwick and Railton appeal to "perfect" or "full" information, whereas on Brandt's view, only knowledge of "established facts" need be included in the hypothetical desire situation. But these differences should not distract from the remarkable consensus reached among DF theorists, both that DF theory should appeal not to actual desires but to desires had in a hypothetical desire situation and that the idealization of the information available to the agent will be a feature of that hypothetical desire situation. Call all such theories of well-being 'Knowledge-Modified' DF theories: a DF theory is Knowledge-Modified if it affirms either that the satisfaction of certain of an agent's desires fails to contribute to that agent's well-being because that agent would lack those desires in some hypothetical desire situation in which he or she is better informed, or that the satisfaction of certain desires that an agent has in some hypothetical desire situation (yet actually lacks) contributes to that agent's well-being.

Against this consensus I want to defend the 'Simple' DF theory as the best version of strong subjectivism. According to the Simple theory, only the satisfaction of an agent's actual desires contributes to that agent's well-being, and no actual desire is to be excluded from relevance to an agent's well-being because the agent would lack that desire in a hypothetical desire situation. Now, the Simple DF theory asserts a view stronger than merely the denial of the Knowledge-Modified DF theory: it asserts not only the irrelevance to well-being of hypothetical desire situations involving improved information, but also the irrelevance to well-being of *any* hypothetical desire situation. A DF theorist might, therefore, reject both, opting for some sort of Modified view where the hypothetical desire situation does not include the agent's being better informed. Nevertheless, a successful argument against the Knowledge-Modified DF theory is a good argument for the view that if one is a DF theorist, one should affirm the Simple view. Of all the conditions that DF theorists have incorporated within their hypothetical desire situations, the information condition has been the most common and has been thought to be the weakest and most in the spirit of DF theory. A successful argument against the Knowledge-Modified form of DF theory is thus an excellent, if still prima facie, case against all Modified versions of DF theory, and, in turn, a strong case in favor of the Simple account – if, that is, one is to affirm DF theory at all.

My argument is this. If one is a DF theorist, holding that there is a tight connection between an agent's desires and that agent's good, one should prefer the Simple view, which appeals only to an agent's actual desires, unless there is a good reason for moving to a Knowledge-Modified view. But there are two possible reasons that the DF theorist could have for moving to the Knowledge-Modified view: either that possessing inaccurate information can lead agents to have desires the satisfaction of which is irrelevant to well-being or that lacking accurate information can cause agents to lack desires the satisfaction of which would be relevant to well-being. The introduction of a hypothetical desire situation incorporating an information condition is supposed to be justified by its role in remedying these deficiencies. But, as I will show, neither of these grounds, in fact, gives the DF theorist reason to affirm a Knowledge-Modified view. Thus, the DF theorist should affirm the Simple view.

Against the Simple View: That Desires Can Be Based on False Beliefs

One rationale that might be offered for moving from a Simple DF view to a Knowledge-Modified DF view is that an agent might have desires the satisfaction of which is irrelevant to that agent's well-being because those desires are based on false beliefs. If it is true that a Knowledge-Modified view has the resources to explain why such desires are irrelevant to the agent's well-being whereas a Simple view has not, then there would be grounds for moving from a Simple to a Knowledge-Modified view.

I will consider two senses in which a desire can be based on a false belief. In one sense in which a desire can be based on a false belief, it is true that the desire is irrelevant to the content of the agent's well-being, but the Knowledge-Modified view does not possess an account of the irrelevance of that desire superior to the account that the Simple DF theorist can provide. In another sense in which a desire can be based on a false belief, it is true that the Knowledge-Modified view implies the irrelevance of that desire to the agent's well-being while the Simple view allows its relevance. But in this case, the differences in implication favor the Simple view, for in this sense of 'based on,' there is nothing objectionable about the idea that one's well-being is determined by desires that are based on his or her false beliefs. Since these are the only two ways, I shall argue, that desires can be based on false beliefs, it follows that the existence of desires based on false beliefs provides no rationale for moving from a Simple to a Knowledge-Modified DF view.

Suppose that I have a desire to own this particular baseball that is based on a false belief that it was autographed by Will Clark.[7] One way in which I may be said to have a desire for this baseball because of my false belief that Will Clark has signed it is the following: I desire a baseball with 'WC' signed on it; I falsely believe that this baseball has WC signed on it; thus, because of my false belief that this baseball satisfies the description of the object that I desire, I am motivated to obtain that baseball; in virtue of my being motivated to obtain this baseball, it is the case that I have a desire for this baseball. Now, there is a way to construct an argument for the superiority of a Knowledge-Modified view on the basis of desires of this sort. Since it is obvious that my obtaining this particular baseball would not contribute to my well-being, the DF theorist wants to say that we need some way to rule out the desire's relevance to well-being. One way to fulfill this task is by appeal to a Knowledge-Modified view: since I would not desire this particular baseball were I to lack the false belief that it was signed by Will Clark, the Knowledge-Modified DF theory does not imply that the satisfaction of this desire contributes to my well-being. But it seems, by contrast, that the unmodified, Simple DF theory has the implausible implication that my owning this baseball as such makes me better off. Thus, one might hold that there are grounds to prefer the Knowledge-Modified DF theory to the Simple view.

Even those writers who affirm some version of Knowledge-Modified DF theory are not likely to find this a very persuasive argument on behalf of that view. That a Knowledge-Modified DF theory implies that my desire for this baseball is not relevant to my well-being counts in favor of that view only if there is not some other, at least equally plausible explanation for the irrelevance of this desire available to the Simple DF theorist. But there is, according to many DF theorists, such an alternative explanation available: call it the 'basic desires' response. According to this view, DF theory should claim that only desires that have a certain place in the agent's motivational structure should count in determining that agent's good; it is only the satisfaction of an agent's *fundamental* or *basic* desires that makes that agent well off.

While I do not know precisely how to spell out what defenders of this view mean by 'basic,' we might offer the following examples of the sorts of desires that they mean to rule out as nonbasic: those states of affairs desired by an agent merely because they are believed to be either *instances* of states of affairs already desired by the agent or *instruments* to the promotion of states of affairs already desired by the agent are not to be counted constituents of an agent's good. (I will call these desires, and the beliefs on which they are based, 'specificatory' and 'instrumental,' respectively.) Given the appropriateness of the basic-desires response, it is clear that the Simple DF theory would have a way to explain why my desire for this baseball, which is based on my false belief that this ball was signed by Will Clark, is not relevant to the constitution of my well-being: it is that no desires that are based in this way on *any* beliefs, true or false, are relevant to the constitution of my well-being. Thus, the Simple DF theorist can account for the irrelevance of such desires without requiring the machinery of a hypothetical desire situation.

Since my aim is to argue that there is no need to move from the naively Simple to the sophisticated Knowledge-Modified DF theory, it may seem overscrupulous to worry about a response that is so uniformly endorsed and which provides a means of explaining why desires based in a certain way on false beliefs can be denied relevance to well-being in the absence of an appeal to the agent's hypothetical desires. But it does not seem that the propriety of the basic desires response is self-evident: why, precisely, is it that only basic desires count? Suppose an agent to have a basic desire that x obtain and to have a specificatory or instrumental desire that y obtain, where y's obtaining is believed by that agent to be either an instance of or an instrument to x's obtaining. What justification can the DF theorist give for holding that it is only the agent's desire for x the fulfillment of which makes him or her better off? Why isn't the fulfillment of the desire for y a constituent of the agent's well-being also?

One argument that is clearly unsuccessful appeals to the idea of dependence: the reason that the desire for x is relevant and the desire for y is not is that the desire for y is dependent on the desire for x; the agent would not want y unless that agent wanted x, and if the agent ceased to want x, the agent would no longer want y. But the mere fact of counterfactual dependence is surely not enough to warrant the normative conclusion that the satisfaction of one desire makes the agent better off while the satisfaction of the other does not. For, after all, this counterfactual dependence might be exhibited in the case of two unquestionably basic desires, where brute natural law might determine in the case of a particular agent that there is this sort of dependence of one desire upon the other.

Sometimes it is said that the source of the difference is that the agent wants x 'for its own sake' whereas the agent wants y only for the sake of x. While there is no further 'in order to' explanation for the agent's wanting x, there is a further in-order-to explanation for the agent's wanting y: the agent wants y in order to bring about x. But even if we were to grant the success of this argument with respect to instrumental desires, the argument is far less powerful with respect to specificatory desires: for in the most natural sense of 'wanting something for its own sake,' states of affairs that are the objects of specificatory desires are usually thought to be wanted for their own sakes, for such desires are not for states of affairs that are sought only in order to bring about further, distinct ends. It thus seems that this sort of argument fails to explain why the DF theorist should hold that specificatory desires are not relevant to agents' well-being.

We still lack a reason to think that the basic-desires response provides a justifiable way for the Simple DF theorist to account for the irrelevance of my desire for this baseball, given that it is a specificatory desire based on a false belief. But, to press the point a bit further, it still seems to me to be far from clear why even instrumental desires are to be denied relevance. Given that a desire for x and an instrumental desire for y are both desires, that for an agent x's obtaining and y's obtaining both matter to that agent, that the agent is motivated both to promote x and to promote y, why is the obtaining of x a part of the agent's well-being while the obtaining of y is not?

One might say, as Parfit does in dealing with a desire-based theory of rationality, that

[w]e should ignore *derived* desires. These are desires for what are mere means to the fulfilment of other desires. Suppose that I want to go to some library merely so that I can meet some beautiful librarian. If you introduce me to the librarian, I have no desire that is unfulfilled. It is irrelevant that you have not fulfilled my desire to join this library. (Parfit 1984, p. 117)

Parfit seems to be suggesting the following. If one has a basic desire and an instrumental desire, then the satisfaction of the basic desire – even if it is achieved in a way that does not involve the obtaining of the state of affairs desired instrumentally – will leave that agent with no unsatisfied desires. Thus, the satisfaction of the instrumental desire is not itself worthy of consideration merely as such. But this argument also fails. Once again, it could be true with respect to two of an agent's basic desires that, as a matter of sheer, brute natural fact, if one of these desires were satisfied, the other would be extinguished. But this sort of dependence alone is surely not enough to call into question the place of the counterfactually dependent desire with respect to my well-being.

If one is tempted by the view that this sort of dependence is relevant, the likely source is a mistake about what DF theories of well-being claim: they do not claim that being well off consists in being a person with no unsatisfied desires, but rather that being well off consists in the satisfaction of the desires that one has. Perhaps one might claim that once the desire to join the library is extinguished, joining the library is not an aspect of the agent's well-being. But the mere fact that this desire will be extinguished if one meets the librarian by some other means cannot be sufficient to call the relevance of that desire into question.

Here is another argument. One might appeal to the idea that to allow the relevance of instrumental desires in the consideration of an agent's well-being is to engage in illegitimate *double counting* of desires. But this is clearly incomplete: what needs explaining is why this double counting is illegitimate. If what fundamentally matters with respect to an agent's well-being is the satisfaction of his or her desires, and there are two distinct desires – one basic, one instrumental – present, why shouldn't both be counted in determining what makes that agent well off?

Even if the basic-desires response yields intuitively correct implications with respect to the constitution of an agent's well-being, what is missing is a principled account of why the DF theorist is entitled to this response. One way of providing such an account is to take literally a common manner of speaking: one that wants y solely in order to satisfy his or her desire for x doesn't *really* want $y;$ all that agent *really* wants is x. To take this turn of phrase literally is, of course, just to hold that there are, in fact, no specificatory or instrumental desires; the only desires that exist are basic desires. If this thesis can be defended, then it is obvious why the DF theorist's basic-desires response is appropriate: if there exist nothing but basic desires, then surely only basic desires are relevant to an agent's well-being.

The rationale for holding that the only desires that exist are basic desires derives from a certain plausible view on what the best principle of individuation for desires would entail about the possibility of specificatory or instrumental desires. It seems to me that a principle of individuation for desires must fulfill the following desiderata. First, it must be adequately responsive to the fact that desires are ascribed to an agent as explaining why an agent acts as he or she does. Secondly, it should be parsimonious: it should allow one to ascribe two desires to an agent, rather than one, only if the ascription of more than one desire will make a difference in the capacity to explain an agent's actions. Given these desiderata, I suggest the following principle of individuation for desires: for all putative desires A and B, A and B are distinct if and only if A and B together would have motivational force in addition to that which either of them alone would have.[8]

While this principle may lack the self-evidence of a Sidgwickian intuition, it is extremely plausible, at least once the following clarifications are made. First, with regard to the idea of 'additional motivational force': what I have in mind, roughly, is that the presence of both desires, rather than one or the other alone, would add to either the *scope* or the *power* of the agent's motivation, where the scope of motivation is the set of states of affairs toward which the agent is motivated, and the power of motivation is the degree to which the agent is motivated to promote some state of affairs. So, with respect to scope: if there is a single state of affairs toward which A and B together motivate, yet toward which A alone does not, and a single state of affairs toward which A and B together motivate, yet toward which B alone does not, then we will know that we are dealing with distinct desires. With respect to power: if there is a single state of affairs toward which A and B motivate the agent to a greater degree than A alone does, and there is a single state of affairs toward which A and B motivate to a greater degree than B alone does, then we will know that we are dealing with distinct desires. If A and B together would motivate the agent with the same scope and power as A alone would, then B is superfluous, and should not be ascribed to the agent along with A; if A and B together would motivate the agent with the same scope and power as B alone would, then A is superfluous, and should not be ascribed to the agent along with B.

Secondly, when one attempts to compare the motivational force of these desires and sets of desires, the background conditions that might affect the scope and power of the agent's motivation must be kept constant. Such background conditions include, most prominently, the agent's belief set.

Given these clarifications, this principle for individuating desires seems prima facie plausible. After all, desires are ascribed to agents as explaining why they act as they do. If a putative desire does not add at all to the motivational force of another desire, either by extending to further states of affairs or more powerfully moving the agent to a particular state of affairs, then it is hard to see what sense there is in the ascription of that additional, distinct desire to the agent, given the aim of explaining agents' actions.

Now, consider the case of my desiring a particular baseball because of my false belief that Will Clark has signed it. Given the principle of individuation for desires that I have suggested, it is clear what the DF theorist should say: the DF theorist should deny that in this case I have a desire for this particular baseball. The reason is that my desire for a baseball with WC signed on it and my alleged desire for this particular baseball fail the plausible test for individuating desires. As this case is described, the desire for a baseball with WC on it and the desire for this particular baseball together have no motivational force beyond that which the desire for a baseball with 'WC' on it has on its own. The positing of this additional desire neither adds to the extent that I am motivated to promote any particular state of affairs nor adds to the set of states of affairs that I am motivated to pursue.

Why is this? Consider two sets of background conditions: one in which I believe that this particular baseball has WC on it, and one in which I lack this belief. In the former case, my desire for a baseball with WC on it along with my belief that this baseball has WC on it explains my seeking to own this baseball; nothing is added by positing an additional desire for this particular baseball. (Surely I am not motivated more strongly to have *this* ball than to have *a* ball with WC on it?) In the latter case, one might think that these desires pass the test for individuating desires; for, lacking the belief that this ball has WC on it, my desire to own a baseball with WC on it will not motivate me toward the state of affairs of my owning this particular baseball, but my alleged desire to own this baseball must motivate me toward the obtaining of that state of affairs. The problem, though, is that the existence of my desire for that particular baseball is inconsistent with the situation as described: as the situation is characterized, the existence of my desire for that particular baseball depends on my having the belief that this particular baseball answers to the description 'is signed by Will Clark.' Thus, there are not distinct desires present: while I have a desire for a baseball with Will Clark's signature on it, I have no desire for this particular baseball.

One might be tempted to reject this conclusion on the basis of the sheer obviousness of the fact that I do desire this baseball. After all, I'm trying to get it; I'm motivated to obtain it. But what should be rejected is the inference from *being motivated to get X* to *having a desire for X*. Being motivated to get X is an event; the desire for X is a certain functional state. One's desire enters into an explanation for one's being motivated to act a certain way. While it is true (we may grant) that one's being motivated to get X implies that there is *some* desire that gives rise to that motivation, it does not imply that the desire responsible is a desire *to get X*. While I am motivated to get this baseball, then, it does not follow from my being thus motivated that I have a desire for this baseball. All that follows is that I have some desire that gives rise to this motivation. That desire is the desire for a baseball with Will Clark's signature on it, which motivates me to try to get this baseball in conjunction with, and only because of, the fact that I believe that this baseball was signed by Will Clark.

This account of the individuation of desires, and its implications with respect to those putative desires based on specificatory or instrumental beliefs, provides the DF theorist with the sought, principled rationale for the basic-desires response. Consider the case of putative specificatory desires. The rationale for rejecting the relevance of any specificatory desire is clear from the treatment of the case in which I seem to desire a baseball because of my false belief that it was signed by Will Clark. For there is nothing in that argument that relied on the belief's being *false;* rather, the argument relied only on that belief's being *specificatory.* If, therefore, that argument was successful in establishing that there are no desires based in this way on false beliefs, then it was successful in establishing that there are no desires based in this way on true beliefs, either.

This principle of individuation underwrites the same sort of explanation for why the satisfaction of instrumental desires is not constitutive of an agent's good. Consider, by way of example, one's desire to pass a test, and a (putative) desire to study that is had as a result of the instrumental belief that studying is a means to doing well on tests. I claim that there cannot be these two distinct desires. According to the principle of individuation for desires, they are distinct only if these two desires in tandem have motivational force in addition to that which either of them alone has. For these two desires in tandem to have additional motivational force, one of the following must be true: either the desire to pass and the desire to study together motivate the agent toward states of affairs beyond those that the desire to pass alone does, or the desire to pass and the desire to study together motivate the agent more powerfully to some state of affairs than the desire to pass alone does. But it seems that neither of these is the case. The desire to pass the test, together with the belief that studying is a means to passing tests, is sufficient to explain the agent's motivation to study. And if the motivation toward passing the test extends to the act of studying, it would be strange if there were more motivation to perform an act of studying than that provided by the desire to pass the test: after all, in the case as described, the whole point of studying is to pass the test. Thus, it follows that the desire to study is not distinct from the desire to pass the test. In the case as described, the agent has no desire to study.

Since this argument is obviously generalizable to any instance of a putative instrumental desire, its success would show that there are no instrumental desires. Apart from the principle of individuation for desires upon which the argument relies, the most controversial premise is its claim that the desire to pass the test together with the belief that studying is a means to passing the test is sufficient to explain the agent's motivation to study. This is not so hard to see in the case of specificatory beliefs: if one wants an *x,* it seems sufficient to explain that person's motivation for this particular object that he or she believes this particular object to be an *x.* Perhaps what occasions doubt in the case of instrumental beliefs is that the motivation extends to a state of affairs that is at a distance from the state of affairs originally desired, where there is no such distance in the case of specificatory beliefs. But it seems to me that to insist on the positing of a distinct desire to fill this gap is a mistake. Think of desires as pushing agents from the presently obtaining state of affairs toward the obtaining of another state of affairs. It seems that there is already present in desires thus conceived a latent motivation to employ some means believed to transform the present situation into one in which the desired state of affairs is realized. All that is necessary to make that motivation manifest is a belief about those means that will effect that transformation. No ascription of an additional, distinct desire to promote the means to the desired end is necessary.

There are, of course, some cases in which a putative desire based on a false belief does pass the test for individuating desires. In such cases, the motivation to acquire the object does not depend, as in the previously described case, on the agent's being motivated to pursue the object qua satisfying some other desire. Rather, the false belief simply occasions a basic desire for that object. My false belief that this baseball has WC signed on it might, in conjunction with other features of my psychological constitution and the natural laws governing desire formation, generate a desire in me for this particular baseball. Given the special features of my psychological makeup, this desire could depend on the false belief in either of the following ways. It could remain dependent on it, in that if I were to lose the false belief I would no longer desire the object. It could, on the other hand, be the case that while the desire was brought about by the false belief, it does not depend for its persistence on my continuing to hold the false belief.

Now, it seems perfectly likely that there could be desires of this sort, and that they could pass the test for individuating desires that I have offered. The Simple DF theorist could not hold that the satisfaction of such a desire does not contribute to my well-being on the grounds that it is not really a desire of mine at all. But this seems to me to be no problem for the Simple DF theory: in this sense of 'being based on a false belief,' it does not seem objectionable that one might have a desire the satisfaction of which contributes to one's well-being, yet part of the causal history of which includes one's believing something false. Why would one find a desire of this sort problematic? Why would the mere fact that the set of causal origins of a desire includes a false belief call into question the contribution of the satisfaction of that desire to one's well-being?

That DF theories should not be concerned with ruling out desires generated by false beliefs in this sense is clearest in those cases where the desire persists even once the falsity of one's belief comes to light. Suppose that just as a matter of the laws of nature, my falsely believing that Will Clark has signed this baseball generates in me a desire to own this baseball – or that any other state of affairs obtain (that I get a drink, that I write a philosophy paper, etc.). Later I come to hold the true belief that Clark did not sign this ball, but I continue to desire to own this ball (or to take a drink, or to write a paper, etc.). Is it not clear that the DF theorist lacks grounds for denying that owning that ball would contribute to my well-being? And while this may not be as clear in the case where my desire is a matter of natural fact conditional on my holding the false belief – in part, I think, because these cases exhibit the same counterfactual dependence of desire on belief that holds when one desires something qua fitting a certain description – it seems that the DF theorist lacks any reason for holding that there is anything intrinsically disreputable about this sort of desire.

The defender of the Knowledge-Modified view owes the defender of the Simple view an explanation of why the fact that a false belief figures causally in the generation of a desire is sufficient to call that desire's relevance to well-being into question. Suppose that my previous arguments were mistaken, and that where I am motivated to seek this baseball qua signed by Will Clark due to my false belief that it was signed by Will Clark, there is a genuine desire for this baseball present. If such were the case, then there would be a natural explanation available for why the DF theorist holds that the satisfaction of my desire for this baseball does not contribute to my well-being. If I had a desire to own a baseball signed by Will Clark, and I formed a desire for this particular baseball qua *signed by Will Clark,* I would justify my having this latter desire on the basis of there being a logical relationship between the contents of those desires: 'my owning a baseball signed by Will Clark,' I would say, is an existential generalization of 'my owning this baseball.' But my assertion of this logical relationship between the contents of my desires has its warrant only from the truth of my belief that this baseball was signed by Will Clark. Thus, it is clearly important to the justification of my desire to own this particular baseball that my belief that it is signed by Will Clark be true; and so, if my belief is false, the DF theorist has grounds for denying that the satisfaction of this desire contributes to my well-being.

This sort of account is clearly unavailable, though, in cases where false beliefs play a merely causal, and not also a justificatory, role in the generation of desires. Where a desire is justified by appeal to a prior desire and a belief that there is some logical relationship between the content of the two desires, it is apparent why the truth or falsity of the belief that played a role in generating the desire would be relevant. In the absence of such an attempt at justification, though, it is unclear why the fact that a desire was occasioned by a false belief would provide any reason to discount the place of that desire in an agent's well-being. After all, on a DF theory of an agent's good, what is good for an agent boils down, ultimately, to what that agent just wants. And on any DF theory, Modified or not, what agents want depends on all sorts of quirky facts about them – their physical constitution, their environments, the (apparently, anyway) whimsical arbitrariness of the content of the laws of nature. What is special about desires that have false beliefs as part of their causal history? Since these are not cases in which justification of the desire is called for by appeal to some other desire, it appears that the role of a false belief in the generation of the desire has no normative relevance above and beyond that of any other contingent fact in the absence of which the agent would lack that particular want.

Consider, for example, Brandt's attempt to rule out desires based on false beliefs where the sense of 'based on' is merely causal. Brandt, who holds that one's good consists in what one would desire for oneself if one were to undergo 'cognitive psychotherapy,' suggests that it is a matter of psychological law that some desires caused by false beliefs will fade away if placed in the light of truth. He offers an example of a person who decided to work in an academic profession because he believed that such a life is what his parents wished of him; but, as it turned out, they didn't wish such a life for him. Nevertheless, he has now come to desire an academic life for its own sake. Brandt claims that this desire will be extinguished if "the person repeats to himself the fact that he will not achieve the goals involved in instituting the desire [e.g., pleasing his parents] by doing a certain thing [e.g., becoming an academic]"; thus, the satisfaction of this desire is not to be accounted part of his good, for it would not survive cognitive psychotherapy (Brandt 1979, p. 116).

It seems unlikely that a DF theorist can provide an adequate rationale for holding that the satisfaction of this desire does not constitute part of the academic's good. I do not deny that such a rationale could be found during the time in which he wanted an academic life only because he believed that such a life fit the description 'doing what my parents want me to do': during that time, the academic would justify that desire by appeal to his belief that his parents wanted such a life for him, and the falsity of that belief would provide grounds for denying that the satisfaction of the desire for a scholarly career has a place in the academic's well-being. But once the academic desires that life for its own sake, the place of the false belief in the generation of the desire is merely causal; and it is unclear why the truth or falsity of the belief would have any bearing on whether the satisfaction of the desire would make the academic well off. Why would the fact that, as a matter of brute psychological law, the repeating of 'I first sought an academic career to please my parents, but I was wrong to think it the way to please my parents' would extinguish the intrinsic desire for an academic career give us any reason to doubt that the satisfaction of that desire contributes to that agent's well-being? (For a more detailed critical discussion of Brandt's views, see Velleman 1988.)

I thus conclude that the Knowledge-Modified DF theory lacks a rationale for its hypothetical desire machinery in dealing with desires based on false beliefs. With regard to one way that desires are said to be based on false beliefs, there are, in fact, no such desires, and thus no reason to try to rule out such desires by invoking a hypothetical desire situation. With regard to the other way that desires can be based on false beliefs, there are such desires, but the DF theorist offers no grounds for doubting that the satisfaction of such desires does contribute to the agent's well-being.

Against the Simple View: That Desires Can Be Absent due to a Lack of True Beliefs

It is sometimes suggested, though, that since agents often fail to have certain desires because they lack important pieces of information, some kind of idealization is necessary: the states of affairs the obtaining of which constitutes one's well-being are those that satisfy the desires that one would have if one possessed a more adequate stock of true beliefs. Suppose that I lack a desire to own this particular baseball, but if I possessed the true belief that this baseball has Will Clark's signature on it, I would desire it. One might reject Simple DF views on the basis that idealization of desires in a hypothetical desire situation is necessary to capture the fact that possessing this baseball would contribute to my well-being. The Simple DF theorist can reject the necessity of this idealization by using only slightly altered formulations of the arguments used against the first rationale for the Knowledge-Modified view. For, once again, there are two sorts of cases that fit the description of the situation that I have described. In one sort of case, there is no need to appeal to idealization to capture the plausibility of the view that owning that baseball contributes to my well-being; in the other sort, it is not implausible that owning that baseball is, in this situation, not relevant to my well-being at all.

Consider the most straightforward version of the case that I describe. Suppose that I have a desire for a baseball with 'WC' on it, and this particular baseball has WC on it. Since I do not believe that this ball has WC signed on it, however, I lack a desire for this particular ball. But it might be thought that since I lack a desire for this ball, the contribution to my well-being of my owning that ball cannot be explained unless my desire-set is idealized to what I would desire if I had true beliefs, including the belief that this ball has WC signed on it. This line of reasoning is mistaken, though. First, this argument supposes that, in the hypothetical desire situation of more complete information, I would have a distinct desire for this particular baseball. But, once again, since the desire for a baseball with WC on it and the alleged desire for that particular baseball would together have no more explanatory power with respect to my motivation than the desire for a baseball with WC on it alone, these desires could not be distinct. Secondly, there is no need to appeal to idealized desires in this type of case. If one wishes to explain the contribution of owning this baseball to my well-being, one need appeal only to the facts that I have a desire for a baseball with WC on it and that this baseball really does have WC on it. Reliance on a desire formed only in a hypothetical desire situation is completely otiose.

There is another sense, though, in which lacking certain information might be said to cause one to lack a certain desire. In the case just described, what is missing is information about what will, in fact, satisfy one's desires; one is lacking true specificatory beliefs. In a different sort of case, possessing additional true beliefs would transform the desires that one has. Just as holding false beliefs might causally contribute to the possession of a certain distinct, basic desire, having true beliefs might do the same. It might be the case that even though I at present have no desire for a baseball with WC on it, or a desire for this baseball, it is a matter of sheer psychological fact that if I were to come to believe that this baseball has WC on it, I would come to desire this baseball. It seems obvious that in this type of case, the Simple DF theorist has no way to explain how owning this baseball would contribute to my well-being in the absence of my actually coming to have that desire. But it also seems implausible that the Simple DF theorist needs to explain this contribution, for it does not seem that owning this baseball contributes to my well-being at all. Why is it relevant to my well-being that, as a matter of sheer psychological fact, if I were to form this true belief, then I would desire that ball?

Even though it is a mistake to think that, in the case in which one lacks such a belief, an appeal to a hypothetical desire situation of better information is needed (or even useful), the rationale behind that maneuver is clear. Just as one who affirms p, where p entails q, is committed to affirming q, it seems that one who desires x, where y is an instance of x, is (in some analogous sense) committed to desiring y. But no such rationale is available in the case of desires that are formed as a matter of brute causal fact upon coming to hold true beliefs. The Knowledge-Modified DF theorist, in my view, can offer no account of why the Simple DF theorist should be at all concerned to accommodate such hypothetical desires as relevant to anyone's good. Thus, the upshot is clear: just as the Knowledge-Modified DF theorist provides no rationale to reject the Simple DF view on account of desires possessed due to false beliefs, that theorist also provides no rationale to reject the Simple DF view on account of desires lacked due to an absence of true beliefs.

Against the Simple View: That Second-Order Desires Must Be Taken into Account

The two rationales for the Knowledge-Modified view that we have discussed thus far – that desires irrelevant to well-being can be present due to false beliefs, and that desires relevant to well-being can be absent due to a lack of true beliefs – would provide, if successful, the most straightforward account of why the Simple view must be rejected. But even if these two rationales are ultimately shown to be empty, there are other available routes to the conclusion that a Knowledge-Modified view is the most defensible version of DF theory. It might be claimed, for example, that I have not paid sufficient attention to the sort of Modified DF view presented by Railton, who defends a DF theory on which an agent's good depends on what that agent would, from a fully informed standpoint, want him- or herself to want.[9] This view is doubly Modified, for it involves appeal to two hypothetical desire situations. The first is that an agent's good is determined not by the agent's actual desires, but by the desires that the agent would have if he or she were to desire in accordance with his or her second-order desires. The second is that the relevant second-order desires are not the agent's actual second-order desires, but those that the agent would have "from a standpoint fully and vividly informed about himself and his circumstances, and entirely free of cognitive error or lapses of instrumental rationality" (Railton 1986a, p. 16). But it seems to me that the earlier argument against the employment of knowledge conditions in DF theory turns out to be sufficient to undercut Railton's appeal to second-order desires in determining the content of an agent's good.

Consider Warren Quinn's remarks criticizing those subjectivist views that hold that while an agent's desires generate reasons for action, it is only those desires that are approved, or at least not disapproved, by second-order desires that should count as reasons. He imagines a pyromaniac who looks upon his own fire-setting tendencies with distaste. Does the subjectivist have an adequate rationale to hold that the pyromaniac's disapproval of his desires to burn things precludes those desires from constituting reasons to act?

I think that it is very doubtful that a subjectivist can legitimately attach this significance to the existence or nonexistence of opposing higher-level attitudes. Here, as elsewhere, he is presupposing a significance that depends not on level but on content. . . . The subjectivist . . . can see nothing in the higher-level disapproval except more complexly structured psychological opposition, and such opposition would seem to leave the lower-level attitude securely in place with its own proper force. (Quinn 1993b, pp. 238–239)

Now, Quinn's criticism concerns subjectivism about reasons for action, but it is clearly applicable – or at least transformable – into a concern about those DF theories that appeal to second-order desires. Why is it, we might ask, that in the case of the imagined pyromaniac, we should say that the pyromaniac's good does not include setting fires? What grounds can the DF theorist offer for saying anything more than that there is just a tension in the imagined pyro's motivational structure, so that while he is made better off by setting things afire, he is made worse off by continuing to desire to set things afire? Quinn's charge against subjectivists that appeal to higher-order desires is that they are covertly appealing to content, looking for some way to exclude the pyromaniac's first-order desire from constituting a reason for action on the basis of its unsavory object. But even if we refrain from ascribing this motive to the DF theorist that appeals to second-order desires, Quinn's concern remains: how is the DF theorist to explain "the *authority* of the higher-level attitudes" (1993b, p. 239)?

It seems to me that a second order desire view like Railton's will not be able to explain this, if the arguments that I have already made against Knowledge-Modified views are sound. Railton's case for the authority of the second-order desires depends on those desires' being more subject to influence by the nature of our beliefs, so that they can have a claim to be better justified than the particular first-order desires that are their objects (Railton 1986a, p. 16). What guarantees that the second-order desires that determine the content of the agent's good will not be merely *potentially* more authoritative, but *actually* so, is his appeal to a hypothetical desire situation of full and vivid information in which the agent's second-order desires are formed. But if my earlier arguments against the Knowledge-Modified view were correct, then no differences between an agent's actual second-order desires and an agent's second-order desires in a hypothetical desire situation would be of any normative importance. At the risk of being tedious: the only roles for a hypothetical desire situation involving improved information would be either to rule out desires based on false beliefs or to bring into play desires that the agent would have if he or she possessed additional true beliefs. But neither role calls for the use of a hypothetical desire situation.

Suppose that a pyromaniac has a second-order desire to desire to set fires, which is based on a false belief. On one hand, this desire might be possessed qua satisfying some other desire: one might desire to have desires whose satisfaction doesn't endanger others, and one might possess the false belief that setting fires doesn't endanger others. In this case, there really is no desire to desire to set fires present: the principle of individuation for desires implies that there is only one desire, a desire to have desires whose satisfaction does not endanger others. Thus, there is no need to appeal to a hypothetical desire situation to rule out this second-order desire, for this putative desire does not even exist. On the other hand, if the second-order desire were merely occasioned by some false belief, that would not seem to be sufficient grounds to rule it out: just as many of our first-order desires have strange causal histories, so too do many of our second-order desires. Again, there is no need to appeal to a hypothetical desire situation to rule out this second-order desire, for there are no principled grounds within DF theory for denying it a role in determining the content of the agent's well-being.

Suppose that a pyromaniac lacks a second-order desire not to want to set fires, but would have that desire if fully informed. If, on one hand, the agent already has a desire not to engage in activities that endanger others, and thus would desire not to want to set fires if he or she possessed the true belief that setting fires endangers others, we can say both that appeal to a hypothetical desire situation is unnecessary, because the agent already has a second-order desire that would condemn setting fires, and that this appeal is unhelpful, because there is in reality no additional desire generated by that true belief. If, on the other hand, some new true belief simply occasions a second-order desire not to want to set fires, it is unclear why we would think that what the agent would want in a situation in which he or she possesses this true belief would have any bearing on the agent's good while he or she lacks this true belief. Thus, the same considerations that render otiose appeal to a hypothetical desire situation to improve the agent's first-order desires render otiose appeal to a hypothetical desire situation to improve the agent's second-order desires.

How, though, does showing there to be no need to appeal to a hypothetical desire situation of improved information render dubious Railton's Modified DF theory? After all, one might still claim that only those first-order desires that would be held by an agent if he or she were to desire in accordance with his or her second-order desires determine the nature of the agent's well-being. But this leaves unanswered Quinn's question of the authority of those second-order desires. Without the higher level of justification of the second-order desires that is supposed to come with a greater responsiveness to information and a hypothetical desire situation of full information to which those desires can respond, it appears that all that is left is two different sorts of desires, without any grounds for asserting the preeminence of one over the other in determining the content of an agent's good.

Does this mean that there is a stalemate between the defender of the Simple theory and the defender of a view like Railton's? No. The Simple DF theory has the fundamental idea of DF theory on its side: that what makes people better off is the satisfaction of their desires; what makes them worse off is their desires' being frustrated. Since the defender of the second-order desires view wants to rule out the relevance of some desires to the content of agents' good, it is up to them to provide an account of why the DF theorist should follow that path. Without such an account, the Simple DF theory is the superior version of DF theory.

Against the Simple View: That It Is Unable to Capture the Critical Character of the Good

Railton writes that the Simple DF theory "has many virtues: it is uncomplicated, nonpaternalistic, and epistemically as straightforward as the idea of desire." Unfortunately, he says, "this theory is deeply unsatisfactory, since it seems incapable of capturing important elements of the critical and self-critical character of value judgments" (Railton 1986a, p. 11). And James Griffin has written that the Simple DF view is doomed because

we mistake our own interests. It is depressingly common that when even some of our strongest and most central desires are fulfilled, we are no better, even worse, off. Since the notion we are after is the ordinary notion of 'well-being', what must matter for utility will have to be, not persons' actual desires, but their desires in some way improved. The objection to the actual-desire account is overwhelming. (Griffin 1986, p. 10)

These are distinct concerns. Railton's appeals primarily to a formal constraint on theories of the nature of well-being: such theories must be able to capture the fact that the notion of well-being is used to criticize one's passing desires. Griffin's, on the other hand, appeals to particular beliefs that each of us has: that on some occasions we have mistaken our own interests, and on some occasions the satisfaction of our desires has made us worse rather than better off. But in both cases, the form of response that the defender of the Simple DF theory should offer is the same: that the Knowledge-Modified view does no better in fulfilling these desiderata than a Simple view does. Given that the default setting of DF theory is the Simple view, it will suffice as a defense against these criticisms of the Simple view if it can be shown that the Knowledge-Modified view succeeds in providing an account of the critical character of the good no further than the Simple view does.

Consider, first, Railton's criticism: that while the standard of well-being is employed to criticize agents' particular desires, the Simple view does not explain how this could be so. Since the Simple view understands the agent's well-being to be constituted by the obtaining of the states of affairs actually desired by that agent, well-being cannot serve to criticize those actual desires. Now, there is clearly a sense in which the Knowledge-Modified view provides a standard independent of actual desire where the Simple view does not: since it is possible for the agent's desires under conditions of full information to differ from the agent's actual desires, the Knowledge-Modified view satisfies the necessary condition for critical standards that they be possibly distinct from what they are used to criticize. But it is pretty obvious that it is not sufficient for the Knowledge-Modified view to be superior to the Simple view that it satisfies this necessary condition. It is surely not a sufficient justification for finding the Simple view inferior to the *Height-Modified* DF theory – an agent's good is determined by what the agent would want if he or she were of average height – that the Height-Modified view satisfies this necessary condition, merely on the basis that one's desires might be different if one were of average height. It is not sufficient for any Modified view to be superior to a Simple view merely that it provides a standard distinct from actual desire so that actual desires can be criticized: rather, it must provide a standard that is a plausible one, one that we have a reasonable basis to believe to be a better reflection, or description, of the agent's well-being than the agent's actual desires are.

But if the earlier arguments against the rationales for invoking an information condition were sound, then we have strong reasons to doubt the plausibility of the standard invoked by the defenders of the Knowledge-Modified position. I argued earlier that the desires allegedly formed or banished in a hypothetical desire situation of full information are of one of two kinds: either they are 'nonbasic,' that is, instrumental or specificatory desires, or they are merely the causal result of the agent's beliefs and the particular features of the agent's psychological constitution. In the former case, since there really are no nonbasic desires, the appearance that the Knowledge-Modified DF theory offers an independent standard for one's actual desires is a false one: no changes in desires occur as the result of the adjustment of specificatory or instrumental beliefs. In the latter case, the Knowledge-Modified view really does offer a distinct standard that can be used to criticize one's actual desires, but it is far from clear that it is a plausible one. Since the beliefs in question play a merely causal, and not a justificatory, role in the generation of these desires, we lack a basis for affirming that the desires that would be caused to exist in the presence of these beliefs are a reasonable standard by which to criticize actual desires.

Perhaps the defender of the Modified view will appeal only to the claim that, as a matter of fact, it appears that the results of adjusting desires by way of idealization of information matches up with our considered judgments about agents' well-being better than the Simple view does, and thus we are justified in holding this Modified view to be superior to the Simple view on account of the Modified view's critical capacities. If this were true, I suppose that it would provide at least a prima facie basis for moving to a Modified view – even if we would still want to know *why* exactly it turned out to be that the implications of a Knowledge-Modified view happen to cohere so well with our considered judgments. But I just don't see that we have evidence to believe that this is true. Once we move beyond the relatively facile cases of alleged changes in desires that occur as a result of improvement of instrumental or specificatory beliefs – cases that the Simple and Knowledge-Modified views handle equally well – I do not see that we have any evidence that the Knowledge-Modified view yields the right results with greater frequency than the Simple view does. (For a detailed discussion of the extent to which the Knowledge-Modified view generates counterintuitive implications, see Loeb 1995.)

The defender of the Simple view can also point out that this view is not completely lacking in the capacity to serve as a kind of critical standard. We might put it this way. What seems to call most for criticism are the various passing, particular desires that grip us during the course of our everyday lives. But once we have distinguished between desires and occasions of being motivated toward particular states of affairs (e.g., between my desire for a baseball with Will Clark's signature on it and my being motivated to obtain this particular baseball), it seems likely that many events that have been loosely called 'passing desires' are, in fact, better characterized as occasions of being motivated toward some particular states of affairs, which motivation occurs in virtue of some belief-desire complex.[10] These occasions of being motivated toward some particular states of affairs are, however, subject to criticism on the Simple DF theory. My being motivated to get x can be criticized, on the Simple DF view, by way of the claim that my desires are such that in conjunction with true beliefs I would not be motivated to get x (e.g., my being motivated to obtain this baseball – what is misleadingly sometimes called my desire for this baseball – can be criticized in virtue of the fact that my desires are such that if I did not falsely believe it to be signed by Will Clark, I would not be motivated to obtain it). What does lie beyond criticism in terms of well-being, on the Simple theory, is our deep, actual desires – whatever those happen to be. But once the appropriate distinctions are in place, it is not as clear how powerful the objection is against the Simple view and in favor of the Knowledge-Modified view that the Simple view cannot subject the agent's desires to rational criticism in terms of well-being.

It seems to me, then, that the distinction between desires and particular occasions of motivation blunts some of the force of Railton's objection; and even if that objection is granted force, it does not appear that the Knowledge-Modified view succeeds in providing a sufficiently plausible standard to constitute a rationale for the move from the Simple to the Knowledge-Modified version of DF theory. Let us turn, then, to Griffin's worry about the Simple view: that it seems unable to account for the fact that we can mistake our own interests.

Now, the defender of the Simple view can note that his or her view allows at least one sense in which we can easily mistake our interests: even if each of us correctly believes that well-being is a matter of the satisfaction of actual desires,

since what each of us desires is not transparent to us but is knowable only by a
fallible process of investigation, it is possible for our false beliefs about what
we want to translate into false beliefs about what our good consists in. Griffin
is clearly more concerned, though, about a different sense in which one can mistake one's interests: one can desire x, yet when x obtains one can feel that one
is no better off.

To some extent, the Simple DF theorist can respond to this objection by offering both a model of how such could occur within the constraints set by the
Simple view and challenges to our intuitions about these cases. The Simple DF
view surely allows that one might have a desire satisfied, yet end up no better
or even worse off: such could occur if the obtaining of an object of desire precludes the satisfaction of some other desire. In other cases, the Simple DF theorist will be inclined to challenge the intuitions that ground the objection. In
some cases, the challenge will concern the judgment that the agent's desires
have really been satisfied: a more careful analysis of the agent's motivational
structure, an analysis that will include employment of the appropriate principle
for individuation of desires, might yield the result that the agent's desires were
not in fact satisfied. In some cases, the challenge will concern the judgment that
the agent is no better off by having the desire satisfied: even if the aim of an account of well-being is to capture the ordinary notion of an agent's good, we
should not be surprised if our account of well-being calls into question some of
our intuitions about the extent to which an agent is well-off. Surely, those that
press the view that Simple DF theories are insufficiently critical of our present
particular desires would be in a strange position to hold that a theory of well-
being should not be critical of our present particular intuitions about how well-
off some agent is.

The mention of these strategies for dealing with the sorts of cases that Griffin has in mind does not show, of course, that these strategies will satisfactorily
put to rest all such instances that might be urged against the Simple DF view.
The Simple DF theorist might remain content with the response that until a
writer sympathetic to Griffin's view brings forward a case that is not susceptible to these strategies, the status of the Simple DF theory, being the default version of DF theory, is not imperiled. But the Simple DF theorist can further point
out that even if some of these cases did cause trouble for the Simple version of
the theory, that would constitute a basis for preferring the Knowledge-Modified
to the Simple view only if the Knowledge-Modified view were free from these
troubles, or subject to them to a lesser extent. And, again, this is a claim that we
have much reason to doubt.

What generates Griffin's worry is not entirely a matter of the information
available to the agent – if so, we would likely be able to handle the worry by
employment of the same sorts of arguments used previously against the rationales offered for the Knowledge-Modified view – but, rather, a result of the
sheer fact that the desires that Griffin has in mind are *prospective*. As Sumner

has recently argued, the gap between our ex ante expectation and our ex post experience creates difficulties for DF theory even under conditions of fuller information: even if we have a clear vision of what we want and how things will go, the obtaining of the objects of our desires can feel disappointing and unrewarding (Sumner 1996, pp. 130–133). Since the worries raised by Griffin arise for both the Simple and the Knowledge-Modified view, they cannot constitute an adequate rationale for moving from a Simple to a Knowledge-Modified DF theory.

2.4 The Refutation of Strong Subjectivism

It seems to me, then, that the version of strong subjectivism about the nature of well-being that is most faithful to DF theory's guiding idea and least tolerant of ad hoc emendations is a Simple view that appeals only to the agent's actual desires. I want to argue now that any version of strong subjectivism, but most obviously the Simple DF theory, must fail, for all such views generate false implications about the reasons for action that an agent has. My argument against strong subjectivist theories of well-being requires the following relatively uncontroversial assumption concerning the relationship between well-being and reasons for action: if x is an aspect of A's well-being, then A has a reason to secure x (see also Scanlon 1993, p. 191). One clarification regarding this assumption needs to be noted immediately. The sense of 'reason' employed in the assumption has, as a necessary condition for its application, the capacity to confer intelligibility on action: reasons are, at least in part, what make actions intelligible (0.1). The important contrast to be highlighted here is that between the sense of reason in which reasons make action intelligible and the sense of reason in which whatever motivates action is the reason for that action. No matter how closely motivational power is tied into the notion of a reason, mere motivational power is not enough to make a reason for action in the sense of reason employed in the assumption; the power to confer intelligibility must be present as well.

Given this assumption about the connection between aspects of well-being and reasons for action, we can offer a preliminary statement of the argument against desire-fulfillment theories of well-being. From the assumption that aspects of well-being generate reasons for action, it follows that if an agent does not have a reason to promote a state of affairs, then that state of affairs is not an aspect of the agent's well-being. But, as I shall argue, a desire for some state of affairs does not imply the existence of a reason to promote that state of affairs. Since a desire for x does not imply a reason to secure x, the fact that the obtaining of a state of affairs would fulfill an agent's desires does not imply that the obtaining of that state of affairs is an aspect of the agent's well-being. To affirm this claim, though, is just to deny the truth of strong subjectivism.

My argument against the thesis that a desire for x implies a reason to promote x depends on two claims. One of these claims is that a reason to ϕ or to ψ neither is identical with nor entails a reason to ϕ. The other is that a desire for x as such entails no more than a reason either to promote x or to rid oneself of the desire for x. If both of these claims are true, then a desire for x does not imply a reason to promote x.

How Desires Entail Reasons

It may appear that the former claim is very easy to prove. Just as 'p or q implies p' is obviously invalid, it might be thought that 'A has a reason either to ϕ or to ψ implies that A has a reason to ϕ' is just as obviously invalid. But these cases are not analogous. The proper analogy to 'p or q does not imply p' is 'having a reason to ϕ or having a reason to ψ does not entail having a reason to ϕ.' In neither case is there an entailment from the former state of affairs to the latter. But it seems clearly false that 'having a reason either to ϕ or to ψ' is equivalent to 'having a reason to ϕ or having a reason to ψ.' I have a reason to feed the poor, and by addition I have a reason to feed the poor or I have a reason to kill the poor. Does this mean that I have a reason to feed the poor or to kill the poor? Surely not.

Even if the putative analogy between 'p or q implies p' and 'A has a reason either to ϕ or to ψ implies that A has a reason to ϕ' fails to show that the latter is invalid, it might be thought that it is just *obvious* that having a reason to ϕ or to ψ does not imply having a reason to ϕ. Surprisingly, though, a plausible argument can be made that would support the validity of the implication. Suppose that I have a reason to get a soda from a machine, and the machine requires twenty-five cents in order to get a soda from it. I have a quarter in my left pocket and a quarter in my right pocket. For simplicity, we might say that I have a reason either to put the coin in my left pocket into the machine or to put the coin in my right pocket into the machine. This is a reason either to ϕ or to ψ. But many would intuitively say that I have a reason to put the coin in my left pocket into the machine, as well as a reason to put the coin in my right pocket into the machine. The explanation for this intuition, which provides the motivation for the claim that a reason to ϕ or to ψ implies a reason to ϕ, is this. When one has a reason to ϕ or to ψ, either ϕ-ing or ψ-ing will satisfy that reason. But if ϕ-ing will satisfy a reason, it seems that one has a reason to ϕ. In the example, I have a reason either to put the coin in my left pocket into the machine or to put the coin in my right pocket into the machine. But since putting the coin in my left pocket into the machine will satisfy the reason, doesn't that mean that I have a reason to put the coin in my left pocket into the machine? If this general pattern of argument is correct, then contrary to appearances, a reason to ϕ or to ψ *does* imply a reason to ϕ.

This line of reasoning is initially plausible but ultimately unsuccessful, for the alleged reason to ϕ implied by the reason either to ϕ or to ψ cannot be either identical to or distinct from the reason either to ϕ or to ψ. Since it cannot be identical to or distinct from the reason either to ϕ or to ψ, there must not be any such reason.

The reason either to ϕ or to ψ and the putative reason to ϕ cannot be identical, for they exhibit inconsistent properties. Necessarily, an act of ψ-ing would satisfy a reason either to ϕ or to ψ. But it is possible that an act of ψ-ing would not satisfy a reason to ϕ. To return to our example: a reason either to place the coin in my left pocket into the machine or to place the coin in my right pocket into the machine cannot be identical with a reason to place the coin in my left pocket into the machine. For placing the coin in my right pocket into the machine must satisfy the former reason, while placing the coin in my right pocket into the machine does not satisfy the latter reason. Thus the two reasons cannot be identical.

But neither, though, can these two reasons be distinct, for they fail the most plausible test for individuating reasons for action that we possess. Recall the rationale behind the principle of individuation for desires discussed earlier (2.3): any adequate principle for individuating desires must be parsimonious, and it must be responsive to the fact that desires are ascribed to agents as explaining what those agents are motivated to do. Analogously, we might say that any adequate principle of individuation for reasons for action must be similarly parsimonious while being adequately responsive to the fact that reasons are ascribed to agents in virtue of their making choiceworthy the performance of certain actions. We might say, then, that there exist two distinct reasons for action only if in conjunction, those reasons possess greater capacity to explain the choiceworthiness for an agent of the actions that he or she might perform than either of those reasons alone does.

Again following our previous discussion of the individuation of desires, we might gloss this requirement by saying that reasons R_1 and R_2 have greater capacity to explain the choiceworthiness of actions than either R_1 or R_2 alone does if either (a) R_1 and R_2 in tandem better explain the extent to which some action is worth performing than either of them alone does, or (b) R_1 and R_2 in tandem better explain the scope of actions worth choosing than R_1 or R_2 alone does. Given these clarifications, this principle for individuating reasons for action is extremely plausible. For since reasons for action are ascribed to agents in virtue of their making choiceworthy the performance of certain actions, it is hard to see what point there would be to the ascription of an additional, distinct reason for action to an agent unless that reason adds to our ability to explain the range of choiceworthy actions and the extent to which each action is worth choosing.

If this principle of individuation for reasons is correct, though, then a reason to ϕ or to ψ cannot imply a reason to ϕ, for the reason to ϕ would not add any explanatory power above that which is already possessed by the reason either to ϕ or to ψ. It is the failure to meet this condition that shows that there cannot be a reason to put the quarter in my left pocket into the machine in addition to the reason either to put the quarter in my left pocket or the quarter in my right pocket into the machine. The reason to put the quarter in my left pocket into the machine obviously does not extend to the performance of any action that the reason either to put the quarter in my left pocket or the quarter in my right pocket into the machine does not extend to. Neither, though, does this alleged reason to place the quarter in my left pocket into the machine place any additional normative weight on the performance of that action: all of the choice-worthiness possessed by the act of putting the quarter in my left pocket into the machine comes from the reason just to put a quarter into the machine. (It seems there could not be a distinct reason to put the quarter in my left pocket into the machine unless there were some purpose, beyond that of getting a soda, that putting *that particular quarter* into the machine would serve.)

The mistake in the plausible line of reasoning that aimed to show that a reason to φ or to ψ implies a reason to φ must be the assumption that if φ-ing is an action that satisfies a reason, then φ-ing is an action that one has a reason to perform. I think that this is false. In the case of a reason to φ or to ψ, it is possible that while φ-ing satisfies that reason, there is no reason to φ.[11] One explanation for this state of affairs is that in some cases in which one has a reason either to φ or to ψ, that reason extends to φ-ing and ψ-ing under a certain description (e.g., the reason extends both to 'an act of placing the quarter in my left pocket into the machine' and to 'an act of placing the quarter in my right pocket into the machine' under the description 'an act of placing twenty-five cents into the machine'). Such reasons may extend to φ-ing and ψ-ing indifferently: performing either action would satisfy the reason, and neither of these actions is picked out in any special way by the reason. The existence of a reason either to φ or to ψ does not, then, imply the existence of a reason to φ.

The next part of the argument aims to establish that the existence of a desire for *x* does not as such generate a reason to promote *x,* but at most is able to generate a reason either to promote *x* or to rid oneself of the desire for *x*. (See also Lomasky 1987, p. 23.) Consider the following example. Suppose that I have a desire not to touch brown boxes.[12] Now, the claim that a desire for *x* implies a reason to promote *x* entails that my desire not to touch brown boxes implies that I have a reason not to touch brown boxes. But it seems that my having a desire not to touch brown boxes does not give me a reason not to touch brown boxes, but rather only a reason either not to touch brown boxes or to rid myself of the desire not to touch brown boxes. But a reason either not to touch brown boxes or to rid myself of the desire not to touch brown boxes (that is, a reason to φ or to ψ) neither is identical with nor entails a reason not to touch brown boxes (that is, a reason to φ). Thus, considered only insofar as it is a desire for *x,* a desire for *x* does not imply a reason to promote *x*.

The crucial premise of this argument as yet undefended is that a desire to *x* as such generates only a reason to promote *x* or to rid oneself of the desire for *x*. Consider the following thought experiment. Imagine that the desires that humans have are controlled by a huge number of tiny switches on their left wrists. Each switch is labeled with the description of an action or state of affairs ('not to be dead,' 'to defend a plausible objectivist theory of well-being,' 'that the United States win the World Cup in my lifetime,' etc.). Each switch has two settings, ON and OFF, and when a switch is set to ON, the agent has the desire to perform the corresponding action or to have realized the corresponding state of affairs, and when a switch is set to OFF, the agent lacks the corresponding desire. Now, suppose that one of the switches on your wrist is labeled 'to avoid touching brown boxes.' This switch is set to ON, and you thus have the corresponding desire not to touch brown boxes. Now, it seems that in such a circumstance, you have no reason not to touch brown boxes. Rather, you have a reason either not to touch brown boxes *or* to turn the switch on your wrist from ON to OFF. Either of these actions is perfectly intelligible, given the desire not to touch brown boxes.[13]

My argument against strong subjectivist theories of well-being, then, is this. If an agent has a desire for x, then (on account of that desire) the agent has only a reason to secure x or to rid him- or herself of the desire for x. Having a reason to secure x or to rid oneself of the desire for x does not imply having a reason to secure x (because a reason either to ϕ or to ψ does not imply a reason to ϕ). But if having a desire for x does not imply having a reason to secure x, then the desire-fulfillment theory of well-being is false. For that x is an aspect of one's well-being always provides a reason for one to act to secure x, but one does not always have a reason to fulfill one's desires for x. Thus, strong subjectivist theories of well-being are false.

As I mentioned earlier, this argument might be criticized for its failure to take into account the fact that most DF theorists have held that only informed desires, or desires meeting some other standard, count in determining the content of one's well-being. Thus, the fact that desires to avoid brown boxes would not count as reasons not to avoid brown boxes does not call into question views that would weed out this type of desire. In response to this potential line of criticism, I have argued that a Simple version of strong subjectivism, which appeals only to actual desires and does not rule out any desires because they would be absent in a hypothetical desire situation, is the best version of strong subjectivism. My argument, if successful, refutes the best version of strong subjectivism. But even if it is supposed that my argument for the superiority of the Simple DF theory among varieties of strong subjectivism is unsuccessful, it still seems to me that this argument would succeed against Modified DF views. For since all genuine strong subjectivist theories do not discriminate among desires on the basis of content, it will be possible for bizarre and pointless desires, like a fundamental desire to avoid touching brown boxes, to persist or even to be made present for the first time in one's preferred hypothetical desire situation. But these are desires that one has no reason to try to satisfy, no matter how well informed the agent that has them; the most one might have reason to do is either to satisfy them or to rid oneself of those desires. This would be enough to show that strong subjectivism is a false view.

A Question Left Open

The success of this argument against strong subjectivism may yet depend on an unanswered question. I suggest that when an agent has a desire for x, that agent has a reason either to promote x or to rid him- or herself of the desire for x. But this is a funny disjunctive reason, and the strangeness of its structure calls for explanation. In the absence of an explanation as to why desires underlie reasons with that sort of structure, we might doubt that this is a correct account of the reason-giving status of desires, even if the account is initially plausible. Since the account of fundamental reasons for action will not be developed until Chapter 3, however, the resolution of this issue must be postponed. But we can get some preliminary idea of what this account will have to look like. I suggested earlier that when a reason to ϕ or to ψ is generated, the explanation is that under a certain description, the reason extends indifferently to ϕ-ing and to ψ-ing (i.e., there is an act that one has reason to perform and of which ϕ-ing and ψ-ing are both instantiations), and by its nature that reason cannot extend to ϕ-ing and ψ-ing individually. By considering both what we know so far of natural law theories of practical reasoning and this view of how desires translate into reasons, we may say the following: that there is a certain basic good that is such that, when one has a desire for x, one can participate in that good either by securing x or by ridding oneself of the desire for x. I shall argue later (3.3) that the good in question is that of inner peace.

2.5 The Refutation of Weak Subjectivism

Even if strong subjectivist theories of the nature of well-being are as a class inadequate, formal subjectivism remains a live possibility: the weak subjectivist, after all, claims only that 'x is an aspect of A's well-being' has among its truth-conditions the presence of some mental state of A's vis-à-vis x. Such accounts would be immune to the argument put forward in 2.4, for that argument challenged only the notion that x's being desired by A is a sufficient condition for x's being an aspect of A's well-being. What grounds might one offer, though, for holding that any successful account of welfare must have a subjective component?

The Subject-Relativity of Well-Being

One weak subjectivist view is that recently advanced by Sumner. He argues that by attending carefully to what a theory of welfare must accomplish, we can see that no objectivist theory of the nature of well-being can possibly be successful, and that weak subjectivist theories of well-being are as a class superior to objectivist theories.

A theory of well-being, says Sumner, is a theory of its nature; and such theories must be formal. If one is providing a theory of the nature of *X*, one must take into account those properties that are uncontroversially attributed to *X*, regardless of what particular theory of *X* one is attracted to. (Those who provide a theory of knowledge must do justice to its having positive epistemic status; those who provide a theory of numbers must do justice to their being used for counting.) Now, apart from the formal feature of being a variety of goodness, well-being is marked by its displaying *subject-relativity:* well-being is not goodness "from the point of view . . . of the Universe" (to use Sidgwick's phrase; see *Methods,* p. 382) but rather goodness *for* some subject. (See 2.2 for the characterization of well-being in terms of an agent-relative conception of goodness.) Sumner argues, though, that while subjectivist accounts of well-being – those that hold that well-being is constituted by the obtaining of certain states of affairs toward which a subject has some sort of pro-attitude – are able to capture the subject-relativity of welfare, objectivist theories of well-being are unable to do so. Since an adequate theory of well-being has to be able to explain its subject-relativity, objectivist theories of well-being are, as a class, inferior to subjectivist theories of well-being.

It might be immediately objected that an account of well-being built upon the view put forward in Chapter 1 would be a clear counterexample to Sumner's thesis that objectivist theories of well-being cannot capture subject-relativity. Since on that theory the agent's good consists in its flourishing in accordance with the type of being that it is, certain states of affairs can be good for an agent irrespective of the attitudes that the subject has toward those states of affairs: for example, knowing important scientific truths, on this view, is an aspect of a human subject's well-being, even if that subject has no desire for or pro-attitude toward the possession of that knowledge. Interestingly, Sumner admits that theories of this sort, which he labels as a class "teleological" theories of well-being, are objective and do display subject-relativity. How, then, can Sumner condemn all objectivist theories of well-being on the ground that they do not do justice to subject-relativity? The answer is that, on Sumner's view, if we examine teleological theories closely, we will discover that they are not theories of well-being at all: "the teleological theory is fundamentally misconceived as a theory about the nature of welfare; it is really about something quite different" (Sumner 1996, p. 80). Since for Sumner the teleological theory is not a theory of well-being, it cannot be put forward as a counterexample to Sumner's thesis that all objectivist theories of well-being are unable to do justice to the subject-relativity of welfare.

Because of its centrality to Sumner's argument, the claim that the teleological theory is not a theory of well-being needs to be examined closely. Sumner wants to say that the teleological theory is not a theory of prudential value but, instead, a theory of what Sumner calls "perfectionist" value:

A theory of welfare must be about the nature of prudential value. A thing has perfectionist value if it displays the excellences appropriate to its kind. . . . But then [teleological accounts] conflate prudential and perfectionist value: they are really theories about the latter rather than the former. (Sumner 1996, p. 78)

The success of Sumner's attack on objectivism thus depends on his earlier defense of the claim that prudential value is distinct from perfectionist value. This is the premise of Sumner's argument that I would resist: on my view, prudential value just is perfectionist value;[14] this is, after all, merely another way of formulating the real identity thesis. It is, thus, crucial that Sumner have a good argument against the identification of prudential and perfectionist value. When we examine the main argument offered by Sumner against this identification, though, its question-begging character becomes apparent.

"The best way," Sumner writes, "to provide a preliminary sense of what [subject-relativity] is about is to contrast prudential value with some of the other standpoints from which lives can be evaluated" (Sumner 1996, p. 21). One of these other standpoints is that of perfectionist value:

The distinction between prudential and perfectionist value is clear enough. . . . You can easily imagine yourself, at the end of your life, taking pride in your high level of self-development but none the less wishing you had gotten more out of life, that it had been more rewarding or fulfilling, and thinking it might have gone better for you had you devoted less energy to perfecting your talents and more to just hanging out or diversifying your interests. Whatever we are to count as excellences for creatures of our nature, they will raise the perfectionist value of our lives regardless of the extent of their payoff for us. . . . The perfectionist value of a life is independent of how well it is going for its owner. (Sumner 1996, p. 24)

Sumner's argument seems to amount to this. For any perfectionist account, it is possible for a person to examine his or her life, a life that ex hypothesi ranks very highly on that perfectionist scale of value, and wish that he or she had done things differently because doing things differently would have produced greater well-being. From this possibility, we can see that perfectionist value must be distinct from prudential value. But this argument is, it seems to me, straightforwardly question begging. In order to evaluate one's life as not possessing great prudential value in spite of its perfectionist value, on the basis that it was not "rewarding" or "fulfilling," one must presuppose the truth of some version of subjectivism about well-being. The fact that subjectivists about well-being can look at a life high in perfectionist value, and declare that life bad for the person whose life it is, is as unhelpful in resolving the dispute between subjectivism and objectivism as it is unsurprising.

The extent to which Sumner's argument begs the question can be made clear by considering that an argument exactly like Sumner's could be put forward by a defender of a teleological theory of well-being who wishes to show that subjectivism about well-being is a complete nonstarter. This defender might begin (following Sumner; see his 1996, pp. 20–21) by explaining that any adequate conception of well-being must display subject-relativity, and by showing (following Sumner; see his 1996, p. 71) that teleological theories fulfill this desideratum and, thus, are a promising candidate for a successful account of prudential value. In order to explain prudential value, it might be deemed helpful to contrast it with other sorts of value, among which would be included (this is where the writer finally diverges from Sumner) "subjectivist value." A state of affairs has subjectivist value for a subject, this writer might explain, if the obtaining of that state of affairs is something toward which the subject has a pro-attitude. But, this author might continue, it is clear that prudential value differs from subjectivist value, and he or she might offer the following argument in defense of this claim:

> The distinction between prudential and subjectivist value is clear enough. You can easily imagine yourself, at the end of your life, thinking that throughout life you possessed con-attitudes toward a great deal of what happened to you, and pro-attitudes toward little, but realizing that, contrary to those attitudes, your life had gone fairly well for you, as it had been a life with a great deal of self-development and cultivation of excellence. The subjectivist value of a life is thus independent of how well it has gone for its owner.

If this writer were later to rely on this argument to show that even if subjectivist theories of well-being satisfy the criterion that accounts of well-being preserve subject-relativity, they are inadequate because "subjectivist theories are really theories about subjectivist value, not about prudential value," it would be obvious that the argument begs the question in favor of objectivism. And if the argument that I have attributed to this imaginary writer is question begging, then surely Sumner's argument is question begging as well.[15]

For the claim that perfectionist value is distinct from prudential value, there is but one other line of argument suggested by Sumner's remarks, and it is based on the fact that the relationship between the concepts of prudential and perfectionist value is a "logically open question" (1996, p. 79): "There is . . . no logical guarantee that the best human specimens will also be the best off" (1996, p. 24). Sumner seems to be suggesting that since the relationship between the concepts of prudential and perfectionist value is logically open, perfectionist and prudential value must be distinct. But this is an unpromising line for Sumner to endorse, for two reasons. First, from the fact that two concepts are different, and the relationship between them logically open, it does not follow that two different items answer to that concept, or even that it is metaphysically possible that two different items answer to that concept. (The classic discussion of this point is Kripke 1972, p. 140.) It would be a bad idea for Sumner to be committed to holding that the line of reasoning that ensures a split between prudential and perfectionist value also shows that water is not H_2O and that heat is not molecular motion. It is, after all, the fact that the relationship between these concepts *is* logically open that makes the statements "Water is H_2O" and "Heat is molecular motion" interesting, informative, worth mentioning; after all, it is this logical openness that makes the real identity thesis interesting, informative, worth mentioning (see also Sobel 1997, pp. 507–508). Secondly, even if this "open question" type argument were to succeed, it would not show that subjectivist conceptions of well-being are superior to objectivist conceptions. For, after all, the concept of *being an object of a subject's pro-attitudes* is distinct from the concept of *being an aspect of a subject's well-being,* and it is a logically open question what the relationship between these concepts is.

If, then, this line of argument were to preclude the possibility of identifying prudential and perfectionist value, it would also preclude the possibility of identifying well-being with subjectivist value, or even with holding that subjectivist value is a necessary component of well-being. Indeed, if we were to press this sort of argument, we might end up reaching the same conclusion about well-being that Moore reached about good in general: that being well-off, like being good, is a simple, indefinable property. (For Moore's argument, see *Principia,* §13.)

Internalist Constraints

Sumner's question-begging argument does not exhaust the resources of weak subjectivism. Another attack on formal objectivism about well-being might be based on the thesis of *internalism:* one might claim, that is, that formally objectivist theories of the nature of well-being run afoul of internalist constraints on the notion of a reason for action. The success of such an attack would be a particular embarrassment for the objectivist; after all, the natural law objectivist relied upon the connection between well-being and reasons to show that strong subjectivism is in error.

The internalist argument is as follows. As the refutation of strong subjectivism assumed, aspects of well-being are reasons for action: if x is an aspect of A's well-being, then A has a reason to promote x. But nothing can be a reason for action for an agent that lacks motivational force for that agent, and objectivist theories of well-being seem to be such that one can fail to be at all motivated by what these theories posit as aspects of well-being. Thus, objectivist theories of well-being fail to satisfy plausible internalist constraints on what can possibly count as reasons for action.

Sumner's question-begging attempt to distinguish perfectionist and prudential value might be recast in terms of an appeal to internalist constraints: his argument might, that is, be reformulated to assert that prudential value is distinct from perfectionist value in that prudential value must satisfy the internalist constraint, whereas perfectionist value clearly need not. And there are other attempts to defend a broadly subjectivist account of well-being that rely even more directly on internalism. When Railton claims that any plausible account of an agent's good must not allow one to be alienated from it, what he is affirming is an internalist constraint on the notion of one's good (1986a, p. 9). I think that a great deal of the hesitation to affirm a formally objectivist account of well-being stems not from the attractiveness of strongly subjectivist theories but from the apparent inability of objectivist theories to satisfy internalist constraints.

What leaves an opening for the objectivist to proceed dialectically against the threat posed by the internalist thesis is that the only plausible forms of internalism are those on which a state of affairs is ruled out as providing a reason for action only if it fails to motivate *rational* agents. In his famous paper denying the existence of external reasons, Bernard Williams writes that an agent has a reason to ϕ only if that agent, upon undergoing informed, rational deliberation, would be motivated to ϕ (1981b, p. 109); and when Railton expresses worries about any account of the good on which an agent's good can fail to motivate him or her, he adds the proviso that such accounts are suspect only if the agent that is "rational and aware" is unmoved by what is, according to that account, his or her good (1986a, p. 9). But this clarification of the internalist constraint leaves an opening for an obvious rejoinder from the defender of an objectivist account of well-being: the defender of that view can deny that one who is completely rational can be unmoved by the fact that such-and-such is an aspect of well-being. After all, the objectivist about well-being might reply, what is it to be practically rational other than to respond appropriately to reasons, and where part of responding appropriately to them is to be motivated by them?

It is perfectly clear that the internalist would not want to allow the propriety of such a response. The preferred notion of rationality employed in the formulation of the internalist thesis is a thin, formal one: Railton characterizes the rationality at stake as "instrumental" (1986a, p. 16), while Williams proceeds mostly by example, allowing that the conception of rationality invoked by the internalist allows for means/end thinking, temporally ordering the satisfaction of desires, determining which objects one is most interested in procuring, and deciding what specifications of the desired object are possible (1981b, p. 104; 1995b, p. 38). To allow a thicker, more substantive account of rationality into the formulation of internalism would result in the destruction of the distinction between externalism and internalism about reasons: on such a view, Williams writes, "there would be no significant difference between internalist and externalist accounts" (1995b, p. 36).[16] But the fact that the internalist thesis loses interest when coupled with a substantive theory of rationality is no basis for employing a formal conception of rationality in the formulation of that thesis, of course: it could be that the only formulation of internalism that is plausible is weak and uninteresting. So what the defender of the formally objectivist theory of well-being, or any externalist, will want to know is why the insistence on a more limited account of rationality in the characterization of internalism is not merely to beg the question. If the internalist is not claiming that reasons for action must motivate the agent as he or she is in fact, but rather that they would motivate the agent if he or she were rational, what warrants the internalist in rejecting out of hand the thick conception of rationality as part of the characterization of the internalist constraint?

Now, the answer might be that every substantive theory of rationality turns out to be flawed; as Railton writes in a different paper, one of the background assumptions that he is working with is that "no substantive theory of rationality can be made to work" (1989, p. 151, n. 1). This would provide a rationale for formulating the internalist thesis with reference to a more formal account of rationality, but not of the sort that we are presently interested in: we want to know whether there is any *independent* reason to reject formal objectivism that derives from the internalist thesis. If there were some other problem with natural law theory's account of reasons for action, then we could appeal directly to that problem in showing what is wrong with the view; we would not need to take a detour through internalism to expose its difficulties.

Williams does offer rationales of the requisite sort, but it seems to me that they fail to cast any doubt on a formally objectivist account of well-being. One such rationale appeals to the fact that the internalist can provide an articulation of what is meant by, or what makes true, the statement that there exists a reason for action; externalists, by contrast, fail to "offer any content for external reasons statements" (1995c, p. 191), and thus "the sense of external reasons statements is [not] in the least clear" (1995b, p. 40). This charge appears to be intended to support the claim not that externalism is false, but that it does not constitute a clear alternative to the internalist position.

There is a rather quick dialectical point that the externalist can make here against this 'no content' charge. What raises the question about the content of external reasons statements, and what is supposed to make the same question inapplicable to the internalist, is that the internalist can provide a partial spelling out of the notion of a reason in terms of the agent's rationality. This route seems unavailable to the externalist, because it is likely that the externalist will affirm a substantive conception of rationality that would define practical rationality at least partially in terms of reasons, rather than the other way around. But if that is the case, then the internalist can be asked to provide content for the claim that such-and-such is a *rational* deliberative procedure. (It will not do, of course, to provide lists of such procedures, for the defender of a substantive view may well be able to provide a list of external reasons.) Unless that challenge is answered by the internalist, the externalist should be unbothered by the suggestion that there is no content to external reasons claims.

Parfit has argued that the externalist should hold that what is expressed in an external reasons statement is an irreducibly normative truth, and thus cannot be explained in more fundamental (nonnormative) terms:

Reasons for acting, we might say, are facts that count in favour of some act. But 'counting in favour of' means 'giving a reason for'. Or we might say that, if we have most reason to act in some way, that is what we ought rationally to do, or – more colloquially – what we should do. But we could not understand this use of 'should' unless we had the concept of a reason.

These two concepts – that of a normative reason, and the concept that is expressed by this use of 'should' – cannot I believe be helpfully explained, since they cannot be explained in non-normative terms. This fact is not surprising. Normative concepts form a fundamental category – like, say, temporal or logical concepts. We should not expect to explain time, or logic, in non-temporal or non-logical terms. Similarly, normative truths are of a distinctive kind, which we should not expect to be like ordinary, empirical truths. (1997, p. 121)[17]

Now, Parfit's view seems to me to be correct. But I think that it should also be noted that if the internalist charge against the externalist is to have force, it will go beyond establishing internalism as a thesis about a necessary condition for the existence of a reason for action, and further establish internalism as a thesis about sufficient conditions for the existence of a reason for action. Since internalism as a thesis about sufficient conditions for the existence of reasons is far less plausible than as a thesis about necessary conditions, the charge against the externalist to provide a content for external reasons claims has much less force.

Here is why the success of this charge – that externalist reason claims are devoid of content – would imply the correctness of internalism as both a necessary and sufficient condition for the existence of a reason for action. Suppose that one affirms internalism only as a thesis about a necessary condition for a reason but denies it as a sufficient condition. This internalist holds that A has a reason to ϕ if and only if (i)A would be motivated to ϕ if informed and procedurally rational and (ii) Condition X obtains. Condition X is that which, whatever it is, is sufficient to transform a merely motivating reason, which exists if (i) obtains, into a full-fledged intelligibility-conferring reason. It might be a single condition, or a conjunction of conditions, or even possibly a wildly long disjunction. But it can be immediately asked of the defender of this brand of internalism whether he or she can give any content to Condition X. Whatever he or she answers with respect to the content of Condition X – whether the state of affairs it describes is irreducibly normative, or whether it expresses a 'naturalistic' reduction to empirically ascertainable facts, or whether we have no clue as to how to state it, only that there must be *something* in addition to the satisfaction of the internalist constraint to make an intelligibility-conferring reason – the externalist can appropriate the very same answer with respect to the request for the content of external reasons statements.

The dilemma, then, is this: to affirm internalism as an account of the sufficient conditions for reasons for action or to give up the view that the absence of content in external reasons claims is a basis for preferring externalism to internalism. Why not, as Williams allows that he is prone to do (1995b, pp. 35–36), affirm it as an account of the sufficient conditions for the existence of a reason for action? Because the fact that an agent's subjective motivational set is such that full information and procedural rationality would result in the agent's being motivated to φ does not imply that the agent has an intelligibility-conferring reason to φ; this was, after all, the basis for rejecting strong subjectivism about the nature of well-being (2.4). The fact that I have a desire not to touch brown boxes, a desire that would survive full information and procedurally rational deliberation, does not imply that I have a reason not to touch brown boxes, but only (perhaps) a reason not to touch brown boxes or to rid myself of that desire. To act intelligibly in not touching brown boxes is not to act simply under the description 'not touching brown boxes' but under the description 'fulfilling the desire not to touch brown boxes or ridding myself of the desire not to touch brown boxes.' Since the fact that φ-ing's being an instance of not touching brown boxes does not make intelligible, or choiceworthy, one's action, does not justify or rationalize it, there is no reason to φ.

If that is the case, then internalism as a theory of the sufficient conditions for the existence of reasons is false. Given the dilemma – to affirm internalism as an account of the sufficient conditions for reasons for action or to give up the view that the absence of content in external reasons claims is a basis for preferring externalism to internalism – the rejection of this former alternative requires us to conclude that the alleged contentless character of external reasons claims is no basis for preferring internalism to externalism.

Now, Williams might respond that this is all too quick: that even if the externalist can appeal to Condition X as the content of the external reasons statement, the externalist is not out of the woods yet. He might argue that even if the externalist can supply content to such claims, the content thus supplied makes external reasons statements superfluous. He has us imagine a man who is rather mean to his wife, yet whose subjective motivational set is not such that he can be brought to care about being nicer to her:

There are many things I can say about or to this man: that he is ungrateful, inconsiderate, hard, sexist, nasty, selfish, brutal, and many other disadvantageous things. I shall presumably say, whatever else I say, that it would be better if he were nicer to her. There is one specific thing the external reasons theorist wants me to say, that the man has a reason to be nicer. . . . But if it is thought to be appropriate [to say that he has a reason to be nicer], what is supposed to make it appropriate, as opposed to (or in addition to) all those other things that may be said? The question is: what is the difference supposed to be between saying that the agent has a reason to act more considerately, and saying one of the many things we can say to people whose behaviour does not accord with what we think it should be? (1995b, pp. 39–40)

It seems to me that the externalist should not be concerned about this sort of retort: the claim that the husband has a reason to treat his wife better differs from any of these other particular remarks on the basis of its generality; to say that he has a reason to be nicer is not to indicate precisely in what way being nicer is worth doing. (I take it that the fact that we can describe an object as being of some particular shade of blue does not make 'is blue' superfluous, and that the fact that we can describe an object as being some particular color does not make 'is colored' superfluous.) Now, if asked why we would say of the husband that he has a reason to be nicer, rather than appeal to one of these particular grounds for acting differently, we might reply in one of a number of ways. If Condition *X* is just a long disjunction, then perhaps saying that the husband has a reason, instead of making these other remarks, is appropriate when we want to indicate merely that the husband is unreasonable in some way, but do not feel like specifying how, or when, we are sure that there is some way in which the husband is unreasonable, but we are not certain which. If Condition *X* names some property or conjunction of properties, whether normative or non-normative, perhaps we want the person we are addressing to focus on what all reasons have in common, rather than the particular way that being nicer is something that is worth doing by the husband. Either way, there is no basis here to suspect that external reasons statements are superfluous.

Having said this, though, I think that Williams is probably right to say that the externalist about reasons should hold that there is some condition implied in statements of the form '*A* has a reason to φ' that is not implied by statements of the form 'There are grounds for *A* to φ,' or the like. The rationale for the inclusion of this additional condition can be more clearly seen if we consider the instructive analogy between reasons for belief and reasons for action to which Elijah Millgram has called our attention. He has noted that while internalism about theoretical reason seems terrifically unconvincing – it does not seem plausible to relativize reasons for belief to an agent's subjective cognitive set – it does seem to be true that we do not ascribe a reason for belief to an agent unless the agent has access to that reason (Millgram 1996, p. 202). Even this availability condition is subject to an important proviso, though: that if the ground for belief is not available to the agent, due to the agent's irrationality, that is no bar to ascribing that reason to the agent

Millgram offers the following cases:

If Joe thinks that Smith will win, but I and my co-conspirators have secretly fixed the computer to make Jones win, we are not entitled to say that Joe has (external) reasons to think Jones will win. But suppose the necessary reasons are available to Joe: they are the common currency of the newspaper he reads, his bar buddies mention them on regular occasions, they are, we would say, staring him in the face; but, because of his faith in the Party, Joe refuses to believe them. In such circumstances, we would say that Joe has reasons, albeit reasons he does not acknowledge. (1996, p. 202)

In the former case, a ground for belief is unavailable, and the agent lacks a reason to have the belief; in the latter case, a ground for belief is unavailable, yet the agent still has a reason to have the belief. The difference is that in the latter case, the agent's theoretical irrationality prevents him from being able to form the evidentiary beliefs that would enable him to believe justifiably that a particular candidate will win the election. Such information would be available if the agent were theoretically rational, and in such a case, the ground for belief constitutes a reason.

We might be tempted to hold that reasons for belief are thus simply grounds for belief that would be available to rational agents, but that isn't quite right, because one of the presuppositions of the ground for belief might be that the agent is irrational: and in such a case, that ground for belief would not be available if the agent were rational. The rough way of putting it is sufficient, though, for our purposes: a reason for belief is a ground for belief that would be available were the agent rational.

A similar condition holds in the case of practical reasons. It seems to me that in addition to the obtaining of Condition X, we should say that the ground for action must be available to the agent if that agent is to have a reason to act. We might offer as an explanation for this condition that if the ground R for ϕ-ing were not available to the agent, that agent could not act under the description 'ϕ-ing on the basis of R.' The qualification noted in the case of theoretical reasons would also need to be applied, though: if the unavailability were the result of the agent's practical irrationality, that would not be sufficient to preclude a ground for action from being a reason for action. A reason for A to ϕ is, roughly, a ground for A's ϕ-ing that is available to A, or would be if A were practically rational.

Now, the fact that the externalist might wish to include this availability condition might leave the internalist wanting to know why we should not take the further step to the internalist view. Suppose that we say that the rationale for the availability condition is just that if the reason to ϕ is not available to the agent, then the agent will not be able to ϕ for the sake of that reason. The internalist might retort, however, that unless we accept the internalist constraint, it will be equally impossible for the agent to ϕ for the sake of that reason: unless A's subjective motivational set is such that A could be motivated to ϕ on the basis of R, then A will not be able to ϕ for the sake of that reason.

It might be held by the internalist to be arbitrary to include an availability condition on reasons without including a motivational condition on them as well. As Williams writes:

It must be a mistake simply to separate explanatory [motivational] and normative [intelligibility-conferring] reasons. If it is true that A has a reason to ϕ, then it must be possible that he should ϕ for that reason; and if he does act for that reason, then that reason will be the explanation of his acting. So the claim that he has a reason to ϕ – that is, the normative statement: "He has a reason to ϕ" – introduces the possibility of that reason being an explanation. . . . This is a basic connection. (1995b, pp. 38–39)

There are two questions to be dealt with here. The first is whether even the internalist view satisfies the connection between intelligibility-conferring and motivational reasons that Williams alleges to hold as a conceptual truth. The second is whether it is plausible to hold that there is such a conceptual connection between intelligibility-conferring and motivational reasons.

There is an obvious response to the internalist's relying on a conceptual connection between the existence of an intelligibility-conferring reason R and R's capacity to motivate the agent: that even on the internalist's view, there are some persons for whom it will not be true that the existence of a reason to act a certain way guarantees the possibility of their being motivated by that reason. The internalist view holds that there is a reason for A to ϕ if A would be motivated to ϕ if procedurally practically rational and informed (and, perhaps, if Condition X obtains as well). But it seems, then, that there will be cases in which the internalist view will ascribe to A a reason for action where A cannot be motivated to perform the requisite act, namely, where A is either misinformed or not procedurally rational. In such cases, A will not be able to be motivated to ϕ even though A has a reason to ϕ.

Since this is an obvious objection to the invocation of this alleged conceptual connection to show the superiority of the internalist view, one would think that there would be a ready response to it. But it is not easy to provide a response that would make the capacity to underwrite this conceptual connection genuinely an independent argument against externalism. The internalist cannot say simply that in determining whether it is possible for A to act on R, we do not keep fixed the agent's practical rationality; for if we do not, then the externalist could also hold that improvements to the agent's practical rationality – understood as the externalist is likely to understand practical rationality, that is, substantively – would make it possible always for agents to act on that reason. It might appear that any argument that the internalist can offer here is doomed either to leave that view on a par with externalism or to rest completely on independent worries about substantive conceptions of practical rationality, worries that could be formulated and defended without invoking internalism.

Let us see, though, whether we can construct an account on the internalist's behalf for the employment of a procedural conception of rationality in the formulation of the internalist constraint. To do so, we can separate the two conditions that appear in the internalist's counterfactual: if there is a reason R for A to ϕ, then A would be motivated by R to ϕ if A were (i) informed and (ii) procedurally rational. We can make the case for allowing the internalist the information condition just by connecting it to a condition that the externalist might allow, that is, the availability condition. The information that is allowed into the formulation of the internalist's account of the connection between reasons and motivation is just that information that is relevant to the constitution of R as a reason to ϕ; if the agent did not have access to this information, then the agent could not ϕ on the basis of R.

The harder case to make is for the procedural rationality condition. The difficulty is to explain why, in connecting reasons and motivation, the internalist can treat the agent's substantive practical rationality as fixed and the agent's procedural practical rationality as open to idealization without losing the reasons/motivation connection as an independent argument for the internalist constraint. But even here there is something to say on the internalist's behalf: we can provide some of what goes by the name 'procedural rationality' by appealing only to the information condition and the circumstances of desire-ascription. This defense rests on the considerations about desires that were raised in our discussion of the Simple desire-fulfillment theory (2.3). There I suggested that a desire for X includes a latent motivation to employ some means believed to transform one's present situation into one in which X obtains, and that a desire for X includes a latent motivation to pursue any state of affairs believed to be an instance of X.

We might say, then, that the procedural rationality in terms of which the reasons/motivation defense of the internalist constraint is formulated is misnamed if it is thought of as some distinctive capacity: rather, all that procedural rationality does is to name those features of desires which, in conjunction with certain kinds of belief, will produce actions that are not simply identical with the objects of the desires. This sort of strategy would enable us to provide an account of the connection between intelligibility-conferring and motivational reasons that does not beg the question against substantive accounts by fixing the state of the agent's substantive rationality, while allowing changes in the state of the agent's procedural rationality in determining whether it is possible for the agent to act on a reason. We might put it this way: in this sense of procedural rationality, agents are guaranteed to be, to some extent, procedurally rational simply by the ascription to them of desires. If an agent believes that y is a means to x and is not motivated in the least to promote y, then we should not ascribe a desire for x to that agent. If an agent believes that y is an instance of x and is not motivated in the least to promote y, then we should not ascribe a desire for x to that agent.

Is this notion of procedural rationality enough for the internalist? It certainly is not enough to cover all of the forms of deliberative rationality that Williams has in mind; for he has in mind the sort of deliberative procedures that concern whole sets of desires and adjudication between rival desires, and the conception of procedural rationality built up here does not seem to allow for this sort of deliberation. Further, it does not allow for the correction of any of the items in the agent's subjective motivational set through deliberation. The formation of additional beliefs about means to ends or specifications allows one to be motivated toward particular states of affairs that will satisfy the interests in one's subjective motivational set, but it will not allow us to hold that it would be irrational to continue to have a certain element in one's subjective motivational set. Perhaps, as the defender of the Simple desire-fulfillment theory did, a hard-line internalist would be willing to accept the severe limitations even on procedural rationality that would result from following this route. But the result is a thinning of practical rationality far greater than the internalist originally conceived.

The internalist might claim, of course, that I have simply constructed an account of procedural rationality for the sake of showing that it is too thin to serve the internalist's purposes. It is not hard, the objection might go, to create an account of procedural rationality that is too thin for the internalist to use. But it seems to me that this is the sort of account of procedural rationality that the internalist would have to offer if he or she is to rely on the intelligibility-conferring reason/motivating-reason connection to defeat the externalist. The notion of procedural rationality suggested here is built entirely out of the concept of availability of reasons and the nature of a subjective motivational set. If the internalist reaches beyond these to an account of rationality that is not rooted in these two items, it will be open to the externalist to ask why the internalist sees fit to alter the conditions of the agent's motivation to include procedural rationality but not to include substantive rationality. I cannot see how the internalist can reply in a way that does not invoke difficulties with theories of substantive rationality that are independent of internalist constraints, difficulties that are independent of the alleged conceptual connections between intelligibility-conferring and motivating reasons.

Besides, it does not seem to me that we have any good reasons to think that the strong connection between intelligibility-conferring and motivating reasons that Williams relies on to support the internalist view is true. What seemed to provide a route to commit the externalist to affirming this connection was the externalist's acceptance of an availability condition on reasons: reasons for action must be available, or else agents won't be able to act on those reasons. The internalist can then point out that it would be arbitrary to accept availability in the sense of 'having an adequate cognitive grasp of' but not in the sense of 'being susceptible to motivation by.' But whatever the merits of this charge of arbitrariness, the externalist can point out that in his or her appeals to the idea of availability, it is availability *to rational agents* that is the relevant test, not availability *simpliciter.* The externalist, to avoid arbitrariness, might be willing to extend the availability condition to a motivational condition so long as the rational agents proviso remains attached: an intelligibility-conferring reason must be such that a practically rational agent – in a substantive sense of practical rationality – can be motivated by it. Once again, for the internalist to take issue with this maneuver requires the internalist to come up with independent arguments against substantive conceptions of practical rationality.

This discussion of internalism is undoubtedly too brief, and likely to appear superficial at points to those who have engaged in greater depth in this debate. But it seems to me that the pattern of the dialectic between the internalist and the externalist yields the following results. When the internalist attempts to forward

an argument against the externalist that is independent of worries about substantive theories of rationality, the argument fails: it turns out that the internalist
view fails the test for adequacy that the externalist view is held to fail, and so we
should conclude either that the test is inappropriate or that there are some difficulties that *any* view of reasons is prone to. It thus seems to me that whatever
merit internalist views have derives not from anything distinctive to internalism
but, rather, from arguments against substantive conceptions of practical rationality that can be formulated without any mention of internalism. Internalism,
therefore, provides no independent grounds to worry about a formally objectivist
theory of well-being like the natural law view defended here; any worries about
the substantive theory of practical reasoning that it embodies can be leveled directly against it without invoking its violation of internalist constraints.

Troubles with Substantive Theories of Rationality

Internalism itself places no obstacle in the way of the acceptance of a formally
objectivist account of well-being; at most, invocation of internalism is but one
way to bring into focus the fact that the defender of this theory of well-being is
likely to affirm a substantive theory of practical rationality, on which an agent's
being practically rational consists at least in part in that agent's being capable
of recognizing certain states of affairs as reasons for action, and being motivated to respond to those states of affairs. Reasons are, on this view, prior to
practical rationality.

Worries about substantive theories of rationality, so far as I can tell, derive
entirely from their presupposition that reasons are prior to practical rationality;
this presupposition raises both ontological questions about the nature of reasons and epistemological worries about how these reasons are known. The central ontological worry is that the existence of these independent reasons for action is (as Mackie puts it; see his 1977, pp. 38ff.) just plain 'queer'; the central
epistemological worry is that the capacity to recognize such reasons for action
is highly mysterious. In both of these respects, substantive theories of practical
rationality are thought to compare unfavorably to wholly procedural or deliberative views, on which reasons for action are posterior to practical rationality:
reasons for action are, on this view, just those states of affairs that an agent
would be motivated to pursue if he or she deliberated well by employing the appropriate procedures. There is nothing ontologically queer about subjective motivational sets and the procedures that agents employ in deliberating; and epis-
temologically, the only real difficulty in explaining how we know what reasons
for action there are is that of answering the counterfactual question of what an
agent would be motivated to do if he or she (perhaps idealized in some way)
employed those procedures in deliberation. I will say something about each of
these worries in turn. But I want first to note that the debate between substantive and procedural conceptions of rationality is not settled, even if it appears

that the substantive conception comes out inferior to the deliberative view in both of these respects. For, after all, given certain plausible assumptions about the possibility of agents' having bizarre subjective motivational sets, the wholly procedural account still has to reckon with the fact that it is sure to generate implausible implications about what an agent has reason to pursue (2.4).

The ontological worry about substantive theories of rationality is that the notion that there are independent reasons waiting to be grasped by agents is just too Platonically lush to endure. In addition to our ordinary world of experience, there is an extra realm of things, reasons, which are quite unlike the usual things that we deal with. But the real identity thesis (1.2–1.4), along with the analogy to first- and third-person judgments on which it is based, suggests that this is but one, not terribly charitable, way to describe the situation presupposed by the defender of a substantive view of rationality. When I say that it is straightforwardly true both that I am in my office and that Murphy is in his office, I am not committing myself to the existence of two worlds, the ordinary world, describable in a third-person way, and a peculiar, shadowy first-person world, in which there is a strange thing called 'I.' Rather, there is but one world, which can be described in one way using indexical concepts and another using nonindexical concepts. When I say that it is straightforwardly true that there are reasons for action, that certain states of affairs are goods, things that make agents better off, this does not – if the real identity thesis is true – require me to say that there is another realm, in addition to the ordinary world with which we are acquainted; rather, I am speaking of a certain aspect of reality using normative rather than nonnormative, practical rather than theoretical, concepts.

The other worry is epistemological. To be practically rational, on the substantive view, has both a cognitive and a motivational element: it is to be capable of grasping and acting on reasons. The critic of the substantive view may wish to know more about the ability that agents allegedly have to grasp these reasons for action. Such a critic will not be satisfied by the inclinationist account offered in 1.1: since that view as articulated presupposes that, characteristically, humans have implicit knowledge of the basic forms of good, knowledge that is made manifest in their tendencies to perform certain types of intentional acts, the critic will want to know more about the source of this knowledge. The very mysteriousness of our knowledge of the good, especially in comparison with the account of practical knowledge offered by the defender of deliberative rationality, may seem to cast grave doubts on the viability of the substantive view.

It is, I agree, not well understood how we know these basic forms of good. But this does not count in any special way against a substantive conception of practical rationality. For, first of all, any conception of procedural rationality that is at all thick will run up against the same sorts of questions. As I have argued, the defender of procedural rationality could content him- or herself with a conception of rationality constructed entirely out of what is present in the concept of a desire: a certain amount of procedural rationality is ascribed to an agent just in virtue of the ascription of a desire to that agent. But this form of procedural rationality is incredibly meager. And if the defender of a procedural view were to move to a more robust and satisfying conception of deliberative rationality, he or she would immediately face embarrassing questions about the fact that it is so ill understood how we know that these deliberative procedures are rational ones.

A final point. It might be suggested that my admission of the mysteriousness of practical knowledge on a substantive conception of rationality, and my attempt to make the procedural rationality view a partner in crime, does not vindicate substantive rationality views so much as to call into question the notion that there is genuine practical knowledge with respect to independent reasons for action *or* with respect to the procedures that are rational to employ in deliberation. But to this I will simply reply that unless we go the route of skepticism, we will acknowledge that much of our theoretical knowledge – that of other minds and of the external world come to mind as the perennial examples – is not well understood, either. (For some comparison of the status of practical knowledge with knowledge of other minds and of the external world, see Chisholm 1977, pp. 119–132.)

The mysteries that arise are of different kinds, and it is hard to judge which ones are deeper and raise more troubling questions about the genuine possibilities of knowledge in those areas. One who thinks that there is knowledge of the external world but worries about practical knowledge might appeal to a thin causal story about knowledge of external objects that is allegedly lacking in the case of knowledge of the good. But it might be plausibly replied that knowledge of the external world is more troubling than knowledge of the good: for while affirmation of the existence of external objects requires a mysterious act of positing the being of such things, affirming that certain things are good requires no such positing, for to say that x is good does not seem on its face to entail the existence of any particular object. While the presence of such deep mysteries is no reason for philosophical quietism, we have no basis to think that any solutions will arrive in the near future that will make these basic kinds of knowing wholly unmysterious; if we are not willing to be skeptics, both with respect to theoretical and practical reason, we shall have to allow that in many cases, the mysteriousness of our knowledge is not in itself sufficient grounds to doubt that we have that knowledge.

A Question Left Open

Even if both strong and weak subjectivism are shown to be inadequate as accounts of the nature of well-being, there still remains the possibility that a hybrid view will be superior to a formally objectivist account. On a hybrid view, for some claims of the form 'x is an aspect of A's well-being,' the truth-conditions will include some mental state of *A*'s with respect to *x;* for some claims of that form, the truth-conditions will not make reference to some mental state of *A*'s. Are there any grounds on which a formally objectivist view can show itself to be superior to a hybrid position?

While I do not doubt that even certain plausible versions of formal objectivism could be inferior to certain hybrid views, formal objectivism has the potential to possess a theoretical virtue as an account of the nature of well-being that any hybrid view necessarily lacks. When one is aiming to provide a theory of the nature of something – whether it be causation, knowledge, number, or whatever – one should, *ceteris paribus,* prefer an account that is not brutely disjunctive to one that is brutely disjunctive. But a hybrid account is inevitably a brutely disjunctive account: *x* is an aspect of *A*'s well-being, on a hybrid account, if and only if (i) *x* fulfills certain objective criteria or (ii) *x* fulfills certain subjective criteria (and perhaps certain objective criteria also). While one might offer a brutely disjunctive objectivist account – Sumner seems to think that this is what defenders of objective list theories of well-being do, though, as I will argue below (2.6), Sumner is almost certainly in error about the theoretical aims of those that offer such lists – there is nothing about formal objectivism that requires such an account, and indeed, a theory of well-being grounded in the real identity thesis would not be brutely disjunctive. Thus, there is a theoretical virtue present in the particular formally objectivist account defended here that is necessarily absent in any hybrid position.

Now, the fact that this formally objectivist account has this advantage over hybrid accounts generally is not dispositive, of course. So far as I know, there are two closely related reasons for holding that a hybrid account is superior to a formally objectivist view. The first is simply that a hybrid view is better able to explain why certain states of affairs that we commonsensically take to be aspects of an agent's well-being are, in fact, aspects of an agent's well-being – especially if the formal objectivist refuses recourse to a brutely disjunctive theory of the nature of welfare. The second is that, more generally, a hybrid view is better able to explain individual differences in what we might call an individual's welfare profile (cf. Griffin 1986, pp. 54–55). It is often supposed that the states of affairs that constitute an agent's welfare differ from agent to agent, and that these differences are the result of differences in agents' preferences, their likes and dislikes, their choices and commitments.

It is impossible, however, at this place to answer these points on behalf of the objectivist view that I want to defend. Whether the first point turns out to constitute an objection to this natural law theory's formal objectivism will depend entirely on the substantive account of well-being offered in Chapter 3: we would simply have to ask if there are any claims of the form '*x* is an aspect of *A*'s well-being' in which we have a great deal of confidence that do not turn out to be implications of the complete substantive theory produced therein. Whether the second point turns out to constitute an objection will also have to wait until the substantive account of welfare is presented. But we can say in advance something about what that theory of the content of well-being will have to look like: it will have to include in it goods that are such that individual differences in preference, attitude, choice, and the like might make a difference to what particular state of affairs would need to be realized for an agent to participate in those goods.

Since the formal objectivist does not appeal to agents' preferences in providing a theory of the nature of well-being, any work in accounting for individual differences will have to take place at the level of the substantive theory. But since formal objectivism does not entail substantive objectivism – it is consistent to hold that the truth-conditions for the claim 'x is an aspect of A's well-being' are wholly objectivist, while holding that some aspects of well-being include the obtaining of certain of A's subjective states – there is nothing to bar the formal objectivist from relying on this sort of strategy in providing a theory of individual differences with respect to the content of agents' well-being. The question of the superiority of this natural law theory's formal objectivism to a hybrid view must, therefore, be left open until near the conclusion of Chapter 3; once the natural law objectivist's theory of the content of well-being is on the table, we will be in a position to assess its merits vis-à-vis the hybrid view.

2.6 'Objective List' Theories

I have argued thus far that a strongly subjectivist account of the nature of well-being is hopeless and that neither an appeal to a distinction between prudential and perfectionist value nor an invocation of internalist constraints on reasons for action gives us any reason to doubt that an objectivist theory of well-being might be correct. As Sumner notes, a theory of well-being must do justice to its formal features; and from our discussion so far, there seem to be at least three such features: goodness, subject-relativity, and reason-giving status. As we have already seen, a teleological theory of well-being, such as that suggested by the account of flourishing developed in Chapter 1 (1.2–1.3), is capable of handling the features of goodness and subject-relativity. The issue, then, is whether such an account can do justice to the reason-giving status of well-being.

It thus unsurprisingly turns out to be the case that the task of evaluating the success of a particular version of formal objectivism about well-being depends in part on the success of the substantive account of well-being suggested by that theory. Just as I argued that strong subjectivism is refuted by its implications about the substance of well-being – it implies that certain states of affairs could be aspects of well-being, even though we would have no reason to promote those states of affairs – I will argue that the particular version of formal objectivism endorsed by this natural law view is supported by its plausible implications about the substance of well-being. (Indeed, I will argue that this objectivist natural law view can explain why desires generate the funny sort of disjunctive reasons that they generate: this version of objectivism is, thus, better able to provide a plausible explanation of the reason-giving status of desires than strong subjectivism is.) The clear superiority in the capacity to do justice to the relationship between well-being and reasons for action is, in my view, what marks objectivism as the superior formal account of well-being.

The argument for the superiority of this particular objectivist theory of the nature of well-being, then, rests in part on the implications that the theory has concerning what states of affairs will appear in a substantive account of aspects of well-being. Sumner has harsh words for those objectivists who put a great deal of emphasis on lists of aspects of well-being, but it is worth pointing out that what Sumner has in mind are those theories of well-being ("objective list theories," to use Parfit's phrase; see his 1984, p. 493) that offer a list of constituents of well-being as an account of the *nature* of well-being (Sumner 1996, pp. 45–46). Sumner is right to complain if those who offer such lists present them as theories of the nature of well-being; they aren't. But it is hard to imagine that those who offer such views present them as accounts of the nature of well-being, rather than simply as an account of its content. The only offender Sumner mentions by name is Finnis, who is, however, innocent: in the same work that Sumner accuses of containing a mere menu of aspects of well-being masquerading as a theory of its nature, Finnis provides a sketch of a teleological theory of well-being in which "the basic forms of good are opportunities of *being;* the more fully a man participates in them the more he is what he can be. And for this state of being fully what one can be, Aristotle appropriated the word *physis,* which was translated into Latin as *natura*" (Finnis 1980, p. 103). Thus, Finnis connects well-being to the fulfillment of human nature.

Even conceding to Sumner that a theory of the nature of welfare must be formal and not just a list of its ingredients, we should still, of course, affirm the view that what one's theory of well-being implies are aspects of well-being is relevant to the assessment of that theory. To think otherwise would be defensible only if we had no access to what constitutes our well-being except by way of a developed theory of well-being, and I don't see any reason to believe this to be true. (This is, I take it, Finnis's rationale for presenting a list of basic goods separately from his sketch of a theory of well-being: on his view, as on my own, one does not need to be a moral philosopher to have a pretty fair idea of what makes him or her well off, even if that pretty fair idea is fallible and subject to reconsideration in light of philosophical analysis.) Thus, we are free to judge the success of a particular formally objectivist theory vis-à-vis formal subjectivism by looking to its claims concerning what are the items the possession of which makes human subjects well off.

3

The Reasons That Make Action Intelligible

3.1 The List of Goods

One of the main goals of a theory of practical rationality is to identify the fundamental reasons for action (0.1). Earlier we considered how a dialectical method, one employing both theoretical and practical reason, might be put to work in defending a catalog of basic goods (1.1, 1.3), and we have seen that the existence of rival subjectivist accounts of welfare does little to call into question the viability of natural law theory's affirming a conception of the good that is both objectivist and welfarist (2.2–2.6). We now turn to an account of those aspects of human well-being that are the basic reasons for action.

There are nine basic goods, nine basic aspects of well-being that are the fundamental reasons for action. These are: life, knowledge, aesthetic experience, excellence in play and work, excellence in agency, inner peace, friendship and community, religion, and happiness.[1] Each of these is a fundamental reason for action, and together they exhaust all of the fundamental reasons for action.

3.2 Pleasure and Pain

In a moment we shall turn to a discussion of each of these goods. At that point I will attempt to describe those goods, to consider some objections to their status as fundamental reasons for action, and to defend that status dialectically. But right now I want to consider the charge that the list of basic goods is clearly not exhaustive because it omits an obvious item: it does not include pleasure, or at the very least the absence of pain, as a basic good. (I do not use 'happiness' as a synonym for 'pleasure' in the list of basic goods in 3.1.) This has the unsavory implication that neither pleasure nor the avoidance of pain is, as such, a reason for action – unsavory because it seems to many to be, in the word of Thomas Nagel, "insane" (1986, p. 159).

Part of the difficulty in handling this question results from the very intransigence of the concepts of pleasure and pain. Recent writers have reaffirmed and persuasively defended an Aristotelian view of pleasure, with the result that it has become questionable whether or not it is a vicious abstraction to attempt to provide an account of pleasure as a reason for action, apart from an account of the activity in which pleasure is taken. There is, on the other hand, pleasure and pain as Bentham characterized them, and such pleasures and pains do not seem to be mere aspects of participation (or lack of participation) in basic goods but characterizable on their own. Consider, then, the sort of brute, physical pain that we are all familiar with, and that I need not attempt to describe. We might ask: why does the natural law theorist not simply include the absence of this kind of terrible pain in the list of basic goods? Why does the natural law theorist not sidestep the charge that his or her view is insane to its foundations by simply adding "the absence of pain" to its catalog of fundamental reasons for action?

One motive for this exclusion is that the absence of pain is so different from the other goods that appear on the list. Recall both the general natural law account of goodness and the specific account of human flourishing discussed in Chapter 1. On the natural law view, goodness is fullness of being, actualized potency; evil (or badness) is emptiness, privation. Badness is not a positive entity but, rather, a lack. Life is the good, death the evil; knowledge the good, ignorance the evil; and so on. But the absence of pain clearly doesn't fit this model. Pain is a positive reality, the absence of pain its lack. (We must try to avoid trivializing this conception of goodness by suggesting that the fullness/privation model is simply an affirmation that good and bad are opposites, so that absence of pain is 'fullness' in some empty and purely formal sense and its presence is a 'privation' in exactly the same sense.) So, absence of pain would differ from the items on the list of basic goods previously offered in that they fit the general natural law model of goodness whereas the absence of pain does not.

Further, the method developed in 1.3 of making explicit one's grasp of human flourishing seems to lend little support to the notion that the absence of pain is a basic good. Recall that on that method, one holds that a certain activity of a human is an aspect of its flourishing only if it is the end of a line in an ordered set of functions, each of which makes intelligible the status of the function before it as a function. But 'not being in pain' doesn't seem to fit the bill. For when we reflect on whether one is functioning properly vis-à-vis one's capacity to experience pain, such proper functioning does not consist in the failure to experience pain but, rather, in the experiencing of pain under certain circumstances and the failure to experience pain under certain other circumstances. And this is, of course, because the human's proper functioning with respect to the experiencing of pain can be made intelligible by pain's role in preventing, or at least limiting, bodily damage. So both the particular account of human flourishing and the general natural law picture of goodness do not sit well with the idea that the absence of pain is a basic good.

Noting the source of the tension does nothing to alleviate it, however: we could say with no small justification that if natural law theory cannot accommodate the avoidance of pain as a fundamental reason for action, so much the worse for the natural law theorist. The natural law theorist might attempt to handle this difficulty by admitting the absence of pain as a fundamental reason for action and modifying both the natural law account of goodness and the specific account of human flourishing previously developed. While the speculative nature of Chapter 1 makes its account of flourishing ripe for modification, that account of flourishing provides me with the best means of which I am aware to defend the view that natural law is grounded in human nature, and so I am not inclined to modify it except under extreme pressure. Another approach would be simply to bite the bullet and to deny the reason-giving force of pain. This approach, as Nagel notes, has an air of insanity about it. A third strategy is to assert the standard natural law line that the absence of pain is not a fundamental reason for action, yet to attempt to find some place for pain within the space of reasons. If this strategy is to be successful, it seems that one will have to provide an explanation for why the avoidance of pain is not a fundamental reason for action (an explanation that is, we might hope, independent of worries about how the existence of such a basic good could coexist with the natural law theorist's favored account of goodness and flourishing), as well as an acceptable explanation for how the avoidance of pain is intelligible even if the absence of pain is not a basic good.

There are three accounts of the nature of pain that have some plausibility, and I will not choose among them here. On one account, pain consists in any sort of experience that one desires to avoid; that one desires to avoid painful experience is a tautology. On another account, 'pain' names a particular sort of experience the 'occurrent phenomenal qualities' of which necessarily generate a desire to avoid it.[2] On a third account, 'pain' names a particular sort of experience the occurrent phenomenal qualities of which characteristically generate a desire to avoid it but which is only contingently an object of aversion. (I mean 'physically contingent' here; on this third account, it is within the actual world with its laws of nature that it is possible that one have a pain yet have no aversion to it.)

Now, it seems to me that no matter which account of pain one accepts, one ought to affirm that it must be the desire to avoid the pain that generates the reason to avoid it. There are, of course, some who hold that one has a reason to avoid pain even if one has no desire to avoid it, and this not on evidential grounds (i.e., that pain is evidence of damage) but on the ground that it is simply the sort of sensation that one has reason to avoid, even if one does not desire to avoid it (see, e.g., Goldstein 1980, p. 357, and Goldstein 1989, p. 261). While there is nothing inconsistent about this view, it seems to me to be wholly unmotivated. To hold that one would have a reason to avoid sensations of pain even if one did not desire to avoid them would be as puzzling to me as to hold that one has a reason to avoid a sensation of blueness even if one does not desire to avoid it. Any difficulty that I have believing that the reason to avoid pain depends on the desire to avoid it is generated by the difficulty I have imagining a case in which I am subject to terrible pain yet lack the desire to avoid it.

If it is true that the avoidance of pain could provide reasons for action only if there is a desire to avoid pain, then we can rely on the argument presented against strong subjectivist theories of well-being (2.4) to show that absence of pain is not an aspect of well-being. For the desire to avoid pain does not give one a reason to avoid pain; rather, it gives one only a reason either to avoid pain or to rid oneself of the desire to avoid pain. Inasmuch as aspects of well-being provide reasons for action, that one does not have a reason to avoid pain as such implies that the absence of pain cannot be an aspect of well-being.

Consider the desire switches again (2.4). Suppose that one of my desire switches is labeled 'that I am not in pain,' and that it is set to ON. I claim that if I were to find myself in a situation in which I am experiencing pain, I would not have a reason to avoid that experience; I have, rather, a reason either to avoid that experience or to flip the switch from ON to OFF. A reason to avoid the sensation of pain or to flip the switch from ON to OFF neither is identical with nor entails a reason to avoid the sensation of pain. Of course, there may be other reasons to choose one of these alternatives. Given the salutary features of the connection between the pain sensation and the desire to avoid that sensation, I might have reason to leave the switch on ON and to try to avoid this particular pain sensation. But, in itself, the desire to avoid pain generates, at most, a reason either to avoid that sensation or to flip the switch.

At this point, it might be objected that the thought experiment with the desire switches makes clear that the argument that the desire to avoid pain does not provide a reason to avoid it is not neutral, as I have claimed it is, among the different theories of pain. If one holds the view that pains are necessarily such that one desires to avoid them, it is not as if one could ever flip that particular switch to OFF; it is as a matter of physical necessity locked into the ON position. And, going one step further, it might be objected that even if pains are only contingently such that humans desire to avoid them, it is a contingency that may as well be necessity for most purposes in life. Even if patients who receive lobotomies of a certain sort or who are placed under anesthesia of a particular kind are reporting accurately when they say that they have sensations of pain just as intense but to which they have no aversion (see Dennett 1981b, pp. 208, 221), these cases are remote from daily life, in which the desire switch controlling the aversion to pain may as well be locked to ON. And it might be asserted that if there is, either as a matter of physical necessity or simply for all practical purposes, an inescapable desire to avoid pain, isn't it thereby true that there is a reason to avoid pain as such, and not just a reason either to avoid pain or to rid oneself of the desire to avoid pain?

The answer is no. The form of the objection is this: if a desire for x generates a reason to secure x or to rid oneself of the desire for x, and ridding oneself of the desire for x is not a practical possibility while securing x is a practical possibility, then there is a reason to secure x. But this implication does not hold. The fact that securing x is a practical possibility while ridding oneself of the desire for x is not does not imply that there is a distinct reason to secure x. Consider the soda machine example (2.4) again. That I had a reason to get a soda generated a reason to put a quarter into the machine, not a reason to put the quarter in my left pocket in the machine. This would be true even if the quarter in my left pocket were the only quarter in the world. The reason to put a quarter into the machine is indifferent between quarters, and that fact is not altered even if there is but one quarter in the world. Similarly, a desire for x generates only a reason either to get x or to rid oneself of the desire for x, and so desires to avoid pain generate only reasons either to avoid pain or to rid oneself of the desire to avoid pain. This fact is not altered even if there is no way that humans will be able to rid themselves of the desire to avoid pain. When humans act intelligibly in avoiding pain, they are not acting on a reason to avoid pain but on a reason either to avoid pain or to rid themselves of the desire to avoid pain.

The absence of the brute sensation of pain is, therefore, not a basic good, not a fundamental reason for action. To generalize: pleasures and pains that can be characterized in abstraction from the activities in which they are generated do not themselves afford reasons for action; they generate reasons for action only by way of desire and, thus, provide reasons for action in the same way that any desired state of affairs provides a reason for action. The task of placing pleasures and pains within the space of reasons in a natural law account, it now becomes clear, is not distinct from the task of explaining why it is that a desire for x produces not a reason to secure x but, rather, a reason either to secure x or to rid oneself of the desire for x. As I mentioned earlier (2.4), this task cannot be carried out until we are well into our discussion of the various basic goods that provide reasons for action, and in particular, of the good of inner peace.

3.3 The Basic Goods

We may now turn to the examination and dialectical defense of each of the nine basic goods that I assert to be aspects of well-being and fundamental reasons for action. Since some other theorists who have recently provided such lists have been satisfied to provide brief descriptions and defenses of the items that they take to be aspects of well-being (see, e.g., Finnis 1980, pp. 86–90; and Griffin 1986, pp. 67–68), some explanation for the length to which I have found it necessary to go in providing accounts of these goods seems appropriate. One reason for the greater length to which I have gone derives from the greater number of sources, both in theoretical and practical reason, to which I think it possible to appeal in providing a defense of the status of a particular item as a basic good. But the main reason for discussing these goods at length is that the natural law view's formal objectivism about well-being is, at least in part, supported by the particular theory of the content of well-being that it offers (see 2.6). Having criticized the strong subjectivist view for getting our reasons for action wrong, the natural law view aims to provide an account of the aspects of well-being that gets our reasons for action right and, thus, to vindicate the natural law view's formal objectivism: there is no satisfactory basis to appeal to subjectivism at the level of the nature of well-being in order to get at a correct account of what we have reason to do. But if the natural law theorist is going to employ an account of the content of well-being in this way, then that account had better be falsifiable: it cannot be an open-ended list to which we can add whenever we might encounter an unusual person whose welfare does not seem explicable in terms of our list of goods; and it cannot be a list of goods described in such abstraction as to place unduly few constraints on its application to particular cases. Surely, some revision of the list in light of further reflection is allowable. But the more falsifiable the manner in which the account of the content of welfare is formulated, the more important the outcome if it turns out that the natural law view can provide a view of well-being that offers a plausible account of our reasons for action.

It is worth noting that almost all of these goods are such that some great moral philosopher, or some important ethical school of thought, has held one or another to be the only genuine good, or the supreme of all goods: life seems to have been treated this way by Hobbes, knowledge by Aristotle, inner peace by the Epicureans (if, as I think, inner peace is close to the Epicurean ideal of *ataraxia*), and so forth. I mention this point not for the sake of appealing to philosophical authority about the status of these goods as such but, rather, to make an observation that has been made by Finnis with respect to the various principles of practical reasonableness that govern conduct, that is, that each of them "has been treated by some philosopher with exaggerated respect, as if it were the exclusive controlling and shaping requirement" (Finnis 1980, p. 102). The substantive natural law account of well-being does not see its main task as correcting radical errors – it is hardly clear how it could aspire to that, given the inclinationist account of practical knowledge on which our knowledge of the good is gained as an effort to make intelligible our directedness toward ends of certain types (1.1). Rather, it aims to remedy the incompleteness caused by arbitrarily focusing on one good at the expense of others.

Life

Life is a fundamental reason for action. When one acts in order to preserve or protect one's life, that action may be immediately intelligible.

The good of life consists in the proper functioning of humans qua animate beings. While I shall not attempt to provide any very precise characterization of this good, we must note at least that participation in it does not consist only in bare survival but also in overall physical integrity and health. Thus, one is motivated by the good of life not only when one acts to avoid death but also when one acts to avoid any sort of disability or disease or to increase one's level of total fitness.

While most everyone would agree that life is, as characterized, a good, many would object to the claim that life should be included on the list of basic goods. Life is, no one denies, a sine qua non condition for participation in other goods and is, thus, in general instrumentally good. What is disputed is whether it is an intrinsic good, apart from its usefulness for enjoying the goods of friendship, practical reasonableness, knowledge, etc. While each of us seems to have a strong directedness toward life that can be made intelligible by positing life as a basic good, the critic of this view wants to claim that this directedness can be explained in terms of life's status as merely instrumental; further, the critic wants to hold that there are some cases in which agents seem to display no inclination toward life, and thus, it would be an error to think that life should be intrinsically good in all cases. I will first try to rebut the arguments that have been put forward to deny that life is in all cases worth having. I will then offer theoretical considerations in favor of asserting that life is an aspect of human flourishing, which, in conjunction with the real identity thesis (1.4), provide a further basis for holding that life is to be counted among the fundamental reasons for action.

The standard type of argument against the view that life is a basic good and not merely a sine qua non condition for participation in other goods is this.[3] Things that are good simply because they are sine qua non conditions for enjoying other goods are not worth having in cases where, for whatever reason, enjoying those other goods is not possible. Thus, the objection goes, one way to test whether life is a genuine basic good and not merely a sine qua non condition for participating in other goods is to construct a scenario in which one is deprived of the possibility of participation in any putative basic good other than life, and then to consider whether one would rather turn out to be the unfortunate agent in this scenario than be deprived of all basic goods *and* life as well. If one does not prefer the former situation to the latter, one must not think that life is, as such, a basic good. Nagel describes one such application of this test when he writes: "[T]he value of life . . . does not attach to mere organic survival: almost everyone would be indifferent (other things being equal) between immediate death and immediate coma followed by death twenty years later without reawakening" (1979b, p. 2). And Jonathan Glover writes that "I have no way of refuting someone who holds that being alive, even though unconscious, is intrinsically valuable. But it is a view that will seem unattractive to those us of who, in our own case, see a life of permanent coma as in no way preferable to death" (1977, p. 45). How can this admittedly weighty objection be rebutted?

Call this argument against the status of life as a basic good, which uses the scenario that Nagel and Glover describe, "the indifference objection." Note, first, that the example used in the indifference objection goes beyond simply depriving one of all the putative basic goods other than life; it, in addition, strips the good of life itself down to its most meager instantiation, that is, mere survival. For, as we noted, the good of life does not consist only in staying alive, but in being properly functioning qua animate, and much more is involved in such functioning besides merely staying alive. Because in a moment I shall criticize the indifference objection's use of a choice scenario like the one Nagel and Glover describe, it might be wondered whether my line of criticism might be easily blocked by imagining one who more fully participates in life, yet is still barred from participation in other putative goods. It seems to me, though, that allowing for a fuller participation in the good of life blunts a great deal of the indifference objection's force. If I imagine the situation of a human substantially barred from participation in other human goods but who enjoys a terrific level of perfection with regard to his or her animate nature – this is hard to imagine, but suppose an agent to be mentally and physically quite healthy though defective in knowledge, friendship, etc. – it does not seem to me in the least obvious that such a person is no worse off not being alive than by participating in the good of life alone.

We must stay, then, with the sort of scenario described by Nagel and Glover: does it call into question the status of life as a basic good? One difficulty with an argument of this sort is that it appears to prove too much. If this argument against the status of life as a basic good is deemed successful, we must likewise grant the success of all sorts of possible arguments against the status of certain objects as basic goods. Against the status of (e.g.) friendship as a basic good, one can imagine not having a preference between a life in which one has a friendship that is extremely tenuous, on the edge of being no friendship at all, and a life in which one lacks such a friendship; if, then, the argument against life as a basic good is held to be telling, this indifference between the most meager of friendships and no friendship at all would show that friendship is not a basic good. Indeed, the indifference objection could be employed to show that for every basic good participation in which admits of degrees (and all of the basic goods are, in my view, of this sort), that putative basic good is no basic good at all.

How, then, ought one to respond to this argument? One could, of course, deny the existence of any basic good participation in which admits of degrees; but this strikes me as a rather far-reaching claim to make on the basis of such a slender argument. One could, however, claim that while life is not a basic good as such, once participation in life reaches a sufficiently robust level, it is a basic good. On this option, it might be the case that while "mere organic survival" is not a basic good, living at a certain level of vitality would be good in itself. Or, on the other hand, one could claim that life is as such a basic good, while perhaps adding that the goodness varies with the robustness of one's participation in it. According to this latter view, mere organic survival is still a basic good, yet a good that is radically diminished due to the meagerness of one's participation in it.

I admit the pull of each of these latter two views. As is obvious, I affirm the claim that life is, at whatever level of vitality, a basic good. I find puzzling how it could be the case that life suddenly becomes intrinsically good upon attaining a certain level of vitality, whereas it lacks any intrinsic goodness prior to that level. It is clear that sometimes *instrumental* goods are valuable as instrumental only when one attains a certain amount of that good: for some agent, perhaps, it might be the case that money has instrumental value only when one has a certain amount of it. Suppose, for example, that one has as an overriding aim the possession of a classic automobile that costs $50,000; one who has this aim needs money in order to achieve it, but any amount of money short of the $50,000 may lack instrumental value. (There is a tight similarity here to what are called "step goods" in problems of collective action.) But the reason that it is easy to understand how this occurs within the realm of instrumental value is that whether something has instrumental value depends, by definition, on its capacity to bring about some other instrumental or intrinsic good. Thus, it is clear why money might only become good once a certain amount of it is acquired.

But this sort of explanation cannot be forwarded in a case involving putative *intrinsic* goods. It, thus, seems to me reasonable to affirm something like the following thesis: if there is some state of affairs the intrinsic goodness of which is constituted by its exhibiting feature(s) F to some degree, then any state of affairs that exhibits feature(s) F to some degree will be to some extent intrinsically good. It would follow that if the intrinsic goodness of any state of affairs is constituted by an agent's participation in the good of life at some level of vitality, any state of affairs in which an agent possesses some level of vitality will be, to some extent, intrinsically good.

Such considerations may be unpersuasive in the absence of an explanation of why the central premise of the indifference objection is correct: that most persons are indifferent between coma for twenty years followed by death and immediate death. Now, according to the theory of reasons for action defended here, reasons are not formally subjective (2.1), and thus, we cannot conclude straightaway from a lack of preference between the living comatose state to the nonliving state that there is no intrinsic goodness to mere life, no reason to prefer the former to the latter. And it is not difficult to believe that if a formally objective account of reasons for action is correct, there may be some slippage between the actual preferences of agents and what there is reason to prefer. If there are such cases, though, the sort of situation described in the indifference objection is precisely the sort of situation in which we would most expect such slippage to be present. After all, it is often the case that participation in some good is accompanied by felt liking for that good, and anticipation of participation in a good often includes anticipation of enjoying that participation.

What is defended here is an objectivist account of goods, and on an objectivist account of goods, it is likely to be the case that there will be some situations in which the structure of preferences of actual agents will not mirror what there is reason to prefer. If there are situations in which the structure of preferences of actual agents does not mirror what there is reason to prefer, then they are likely to include the sort of situation described by Nagel and Glover. It does not seem to be unreasonable to affirm in the face of the indifference objection that life is, at every level of vitality, a basic good – at least no more unreasonable than it is to affirm an objectivist account of goods in the first place.

There is also justification for holding life to be at all levels of vitality a basic good to be found in theoretical considerations regarding human flourishing. Now, given the strategy for determining what are aspects of human flourishing discussed in 1.3, it seems clear that difficulties analogous to those that attend the practical claim that life is a basic good will arise in asserting life to be an aspect of flourishing. For just as one might try to characterize life's choiceworthiness wholly in terms of its being a necessary condition for securing other goods, one might also characterize the human's animate functions as simply supporting other human functions, not as an end of the line in a series of human functions; the function of the human as living might be made intelligible by noting its contribution to other functions, such as knowing, reasoning practically, etc. And it must be admitted that this strategy does not pronounce life to be an aspect of human flourishing. But nevertheless, it seems to me that our judgments do seem to presuppose that life is a part of that set of functions that constitutes human flourishing; while we recognize the function of living can be made intelligible by way of other functions, we also seem to suppose that life's supporting other human functions does not exhaust its capacity to render subsidiary functioning intelligible. When we observe a severely diseased plant, or lower animal, and attempt to assess its state of flourishing, we have no difficulty in judging that while it may not be doing very well, *at least it's alive,* and in this limited way it is flourishing; we thus have with regard to other species a theoretical grasp of the place of life in their flourishing. And it also seems that, if we can manage to put to the side for the moment particular practical concerns, and the distress and horror that we feel upon seeing a human existence terribly diminished, we are likely to make a similar assessment: even humans that are deprived in a number of ways are still flourishing to the extent that they are vital.

It is, of course, true that the real identity thesis, from which we could be justified in concluding from the fact that life is an aspect of human flourishing that life is a basic good and a fundamental reason for action, is not yet proven; and one could accept the view that life is an aspect of human flourishing, yet reject both the real identity thesis and the view that life is a basic good. But, as I noted in Chapter 1, there is some evidence for the real identity thesis (1.4), and given the fact that a number of the basic goods yet to be discussed in this chapter can also plausibly be considered aspects of flourishing, it does seem to be a consideration in favor of the view that life is a basic good that it is an aspect of human flourishing. Thus, I claim that we have both practical and theoretical reasons to affirm that life is, at any level of vitality, intrinsically good.

Knowledge

Knowledge is a fundamental reason for action. When one acts in order to know, to find something out, that action may be immediately intelligible.

To provide a precise characterization of that in which the good of speculative knowledge consists, of course, is a bit beyond me, as it has been a bit beyond the epistemologists working on this problem since Gettier. But there are a few remarks that can be made. The first is that, as those interested in the theory of knowledge seem nearly universally to have been aware, the good of knowledge goes beyond having true beliefs and must include some sort of warrant or justification condition. The second is that the status of knowledge as a good does not depend on whether one pursues that knowledge for itself. It is occasionally suggested that when one affirms that knowledge is a basic good, what is meant is knowledge sought for its own sake, not knowledge sought instrumentally. But in my view, this is not so: knowledge is always, as possessed, intrinsically good, a constituent of well-being. That this is the case in no way precludes the possibility that one may seek knowledge either for its own sake or for its instrumental goodness: if one seeks knowledge for its own sake, this is an intelligible activity, made intelligible by its object; if one seeks knowledge as an instrument, this activity is made intelligible by virtue of the goodness of the object to which the knowledge pursued is a means.

As Martha Nussbaum remarks, Aristotle's view that all humans desire to know stands up "to the most refined anthropological analysis" (1988, p. 48), and it may seem a bit pedantic to dwell on the status of knowledge as a basic good. If one is interested in a careful practical argument for its goodness, one can turn to Finnis, who provides a self-referential argument that one who denies the goodness of knowledge is implicitly committed to affirming its goodness (1977, and 1980, pp. 74–75); and if one is interested in a theoretical argument for its status as an aspect of human flourishing, one may refer back to 1.3, where I illustrated the procedure for making explicit one's knowledge of human flourishing by showing that knowing unhelpful propositions is a human function. (I appealed to unhelpful propositions to cut off the response that knowledge is merely useful for keeping ourselves alive. But I assume that if knowing unhelpful propositions is an aspect of flourishing, knowing propositions that also happen to be helpful is an aspect of flourishing also.) I do want to make a few remarks, though, about a couple of difficulties for the idea that knowledge is, as such, a basic good: one of these difficulties is philosophical, arising from the traditional analysis of knowledge; the other is more intuitive, arising from our differing attitudes toward different sorts of knowledge.

The philosophical puzzle concerning the value of knowledge that I want to address concerns the tension among three claims about knowledge: that knowledge is a basic good; that knowledge is constituted jointly by true belief and warrant for holding that belief; and that warrant is characteristically understood in terms of its aptness for generating true belief. The difficulty is this: it looks as if the reason that we care about having warrant is that warrant tends to produce true belief. Warrant's value is instrumental to the attaining of true belief. And if warrant's value is instrumental in this way, then it is hard to see why we would say that knowledge – which consists in the intrinsic good of true belief and the instrumental good of warrant – is a basic good; why would a basic good be constituted in part by a good that is instrumental? (See Zagzebski 1996, pp. 301 ff., and Sartwell 1992.) Indeed, at least one writer who has called our attention to this difficulty has drawn from it the conclusion that knowledge should be understood as merely true belief (Sartwell, 1992).

But it seems to me that the argument that relies on the instrumental value of warrant has little force against one that makes the following plausible claims regarding the good of knowledge. Part of that good is having true beliefs, and warrant is valuable as a means to acquiring true beliefs. But that warrant is valuable as a means to true belief does not preclude its being valuable in itself, as part of our epistemic good. So, first, there is surely nothing *inconsistent* about holding both that warrant is valuable as truth-conducive and that knowledge consists of true belief and warrant: warrant is an instrumental means to acquiring truth and is a constitutive means to acquiring knowledge.

If there is any worry that arises at this point for the defender of the traditional view who holds that warrant must be truth-conducive, it is that of explaining the relationship between the instrumental goodness of warrant as conducing to truth and the intrinsic goodness of warrant, which grounds its inclusion as a constituent of knowledge. One might argue that unless the defender of the traditional view offers some account of the relationship between the instrumental and intrinsic value of warrant, it seems a mighty coincidence that it should both be an instrumental means to acquiring knowledge and be itself, as epistemically valuable, a constituent of knowledge. Indeed, an even stronger demand might be made. Some might think that an account of the relationship between the intrinsic and instrumental value of warrant must fulfill the desideratum that the relationship between the intrinsic and instrumental value be one of *dependence,* so that warrant would not be intrinsically valuable unless it were instrumentally valuable for acquiring truth.

To carry out this task is for the epistemologists, but there are at least a few remarks that can be made here. The defender of the traditional view of knowledge can point out that it is, in fact, a fairly common occurrence that engaging in some pursuit that is instrumental to a goal also becomes part of a goal, and that it would have never become part of a goal unless it possessed its instrumental status. Consider the aims involved in playing the game of basketball. Presumably, what initially defines a set of dispositions as basketball skills is their contribution to getting the ball into the basket: the capacities to dribble, pass, and shoot well are skills inasmuch as acting from those capacities enables one's team to get the ball through the hoop. But those acquainted with the game also recognize that the goods of playing basketball are not secured merely by getting the ball into the hoop, but by getting the ball into the hoop by performing these activities well. When I, a poor basketball player, through fortuitous antecedent conditions and implacable laws of nature get the ball to go through the hoop, I do not achieve the good of basketball in the way that Michael Jordan does when he deftly dribbles past three defenders and gently lays the ball into the basket. Although it seems right to say that these skills are characterized as such because of their conduciveness to scoring points, the goal of playing basketball well cannot be adequately described unless playing with skill is included as a constituent of that end. (For some explanation of why this is so, see the discussion of the good of excellence in play later in this section.)

It seems to me that the defender of the traditional conception of knowledge might claim that the relationship between warrant and true belief is analogous to that between dribbling, shooting, and passing (well) and scoring baskets. It is plausible that the processes of belief formation that confer warrant are characterized as such because of their truth-conduciveness. But that does not preclude its being the case that our epistemic end with regard to propositions is that we come to hold true beliefs in accordance with those processes that confer warrant. Just as the good of basketball is not merely scoring but scoring skillfully, the good of believing is not simply believing truly but believing truly and warrantedly.

The other difficulty that I want to address is the intuitive worry that the claim that knowledge is as such a basic good is simply overbroad: it counts as valuable kinds of knowledge that really are not. It isn't worth knowing how many blades of grass there are in a square foot of the lawn, or what word appears in the exact middle of the *Oxford English Dictionary*. Such knowledge just isn't like knowledge about God, or of the sciences, or even of moral philosophy. Thus, the objection continues, we should say that it is not knowledge as such that is valuable and worth having, but rather knowledge that contributes to explanation or understanding, or that is about particularly important subject matters.

But it seems to me to be a mistake to restrict the value of knowledge in these ways. It seems to me that so long as one is coming to be aware of some aspect of reality, there is an intelligibility in the pursuit of any knowledge that is not present in, say, the pursuit of not touching brown boxes. Facts about grass density are those in which people can, intelligibly, take an interest – even if devotion of their time to finding out this information may not be the most efficient use of their days. Further, there does seem to be something bad in having *false* views, even in trivial matters, and the badness of having such false views seems best explicable by knowledge being good as such.[4] And, last, I have no idea how one would carry out the task of determining what sorts of knowledge belong in the category of intrinsically valuable and what sorts do not, if one were to admit such a distinction. So it strikes me as the best course to affirm that knowledge is, as such, a basic good.

Aesthetic Experience

Aesthetic experience is a fundamental reason for action. When one acts for the sake of experiencing something aesthetically pleasing, that action may be immediately intelligible.

The concept of aesthetic experience is often taken to include both the experience of contemplating the beautiful and the participation in the artistic process by which the beautiful can be brought into being (as Finnis does; see his 1980, p. 88). But it seems to me that those goods that are involved in the artistic process ought to be distinguished from the goods involved in experiencing the beautiful. Just as it is perfectly clear that the successful physician is not qua physician participating in the good of life but is instead promoting and serving that good, it also seems that the artist is not qua artist participating in the good of aesthetic experience but is instead serving and promoting it. To reject the view that the artistic process is itself a participation in the good of aesthetic experience is not to deny, of course, that there are genuine goods involved in the artistic process (perhaps the good of excellence in play and work, as we shall see), and it is not to deny that in the process of creating, one might be in a special position to experience the beautiful both by knowing it intimately and by witnessing its emergence. But to say that the artist is by virtue of his or her position uniquely capable of appreciating the beautiful in a certain way is not to say that the artist's activity is itself an instantiation of the good of aesthetic experience.

When we consider the good of aesthetic experience, of experiencing the beautiful, the paradigmatic objects of such experience are objects of sight and hearing: paintings, sculptures, mountains, symphonies, concertos, birdsong. Now, there is clearly nothing intrinsically privileged about the objects of these senses; rather, when considering the good of aesthetic experience, we think of these, first of all, because of the human's capacity to make finer discriminations and over a broader range of phenomena with their organs of sight and hearing than with their other senses. (This need not imply that the notion of the 'beautiful' is subjective; it might be, to use David Wiggins's term, an example of an "anthropocentric" predicate [Wiggins 1988, p. 138].) It is, thus, perfectly natural that the concept of the beautiful attaches most obviously to sights and sounds and only clumsily to smells, tastes, and touches.

That the concept of the beautiful most naturally attaches to objects of sight and hearing does not give us any reason, though, to refuse to extend that concept to objects of the other senses for the purposes of a more adequate understanding of the good of aesthetic experience. For if an encounter with certain sorts of beautiful object, those that can be seen or heard, counts as an aspect of well-being, then there is no reason to preclude the possibility that objects of other senses might be appropriate terms of aesthetic relationships. Perhaps the most obvious candidates for this extension are objects of the sense of taste: it is hard to deny that those who appreciate fine wines (or beers, or whiskeys), or who know what good cooking is, are participating in the good of aesthetic experience, even if we would not normally refer to wine tasting and fine dining as instances of experiencing the beautiful. (For further discussion, see Telfer 1993, which argues that "eating and drinking can be an aesthetic experience; simple, undoubtedly, in comparison with some others, but genuine none the less" [p. 109].) And there is, further, no reason to deny that objects of smell or touch can enter into aesthetic experience, even if the present artistic endeavors utilizing objects of these senses, and the present human capacity to make fine distinctions with regard to these senses, are relatively limited.

I hold, then, that the good of aesthetic experience extends to objects of all of the senses. And, like the other goods that we have considered and will consider, participation in aesthetic experience admits of degrees. When we think about aesthetic experience, our thoughts immediately turn to the art lover contemplating a Miró or a Dalí, or to a nature lover looking past a lush valley to the mountains beyond. Fixating on these paradigmatic aesthetic experiences can mask the fact that aesthetic experience is a common feature of our lives, in which we are attuned to and take pleasure in the beautiful to various degrees, even when we are not self-consciously engaged in observing products that were generated for the sake of their beauty.

Consider again the aesthetic experience that can be enjoyed with regard to objects of taste: while paradigmatic participation in that good might be enjoyed only by the gourmet, those who enjoy a simple meal also participate in that good. The aesthetic appreciation of one's surroundings is easy to forget about, given that most of our acts in our ordinary lives are not chosen for the sake of aesthetic experience. But the presence of this experience as a common feature of our lives, a feature that makes our lives better, even if we are not always acting for its sake, might best be brought into focus by imagining it away: the most that we can do is to try to imagine a functional but colorless world to move about in, one stripped of any positive aesthetic features. (It is difficult to imagine this properly, because at least some of what makes a world functional makes it beautiful – that is, orderliness.) Living in such a world would make one worse off, even if one's nonaesthetic aims were just as attainable as in a world like our own. And perhaps there is some testimony to the good of everyday aesthetic experience in the reactions of those who, after a period of deprivation, regain the use of some sense: when the blind regain sight, it is not only the beauty of fine art or majestic natural marvels that they are glad to see, nor is it only for everyday purposes to which their sight is instrumental that they are pleased to be able to use that sense; rather, they seem to regard much of their everyday lives, mundane as they might be, as sources of aesthetic experience.

We do, then, recognize the goodness of aesthetic experience, its contribution to well-being. And there are, in addition, theoretical reasons to affirm its character as a facet of human flourishing. For suppose a human to suffer the following isolated malfunction: a defect in his or her brain prevents him or her from appreciating the aesthetic character of the objects that he or she encounters. From that perspective, it is a beauty-less world. If this malfunction is a serious one (which it seems to be), and if its status as a serious malfunction cannot be put down to its thwarting other human functions (which seems not to be the case), then we must hold that aesthetic experience is an aspect of human flourishing.

Excellence in Play and Work

Excellence in play and work is a fundamental reason for action. When one acts in a certain way just as play, or in order to do a good job, that action may be immediately intelligible.

The fact that 'work' and 'play' are typically used as contrast terms may provoke questions as to why these two are included in the same category within the list of basic goods. And their typical use as contrast terms within ordinary language might be defended by way of an account of the structure of actions of the sorts that are considered work and play: work characteristically aims at the generation of some product external to the activity itself, whereas play is defined by the performance of acts simply for the sake of that performance. We can see, though, why work and play end up classified together if we attend to two questions concerning the status of work and play as goods. With regard to work, one might ask: why is excellence in work a basic good at all? If it aims at a product external to the activity, why is it not instrumentally, rather than intrinsically, good? With regard to play, one might ask: why is the good in question called 'excellence in play,' rather than simply 'play'? Given that play activity is performed for its own sake, for no purpose beyond itself, what is the point of this seeming restriction? Why aren't all cases of play, as defined, instances of a basic good?

Begin with the issue of work. It is true that work characteristically aims at the production of something external to the act of working. But that does not preclude its being the case that this activity of making is in itself something of value, that there are goods enjoyed in productive work that go beyond merely the value of the object produced. In clarifying his views on the aims of practices,[5] MacIntyre writes:

The aim internal to productive crafts, when they are in good order, is never only to catch fish [as in the practice of fishing], or to produce beef or milk [as in the practice of farming], or to build houses [as in the practices of architecture and construction]. It is to do so in a manner consonant with the excellences of the craft, so that not only is there a good product, but the craftsperson is perfected through and in her or his activity. (1994, p. 284)

MacIntyre's characterization of the goods at stake in productive practices illustrates how the good of work need not be construed as merely instrumental.
Rather, if MacIntyre is correct, then to the extent that one succeeds in con-
forming to the highest standards of achievement in a particular productive practice, one enjoys an intrinsic good. In such instances, the good of productive
work consists not merely in ending up with a proper final product but also in
participating in the productive process in accordance with standards of craftsmanship.

And it does appear clear that we do recognize goodness in work other than
that of the merely instrumental variety. Consider an example discussed by Mac-
Intyre: the goods involved in working as part of a fishing crew. When, through
adherence to standards of excellence of skill and teamwork in fishing, a crew
succeeds in catching a large amount of fish, that crew enjoys a good that is lacking in a crew that, in spite of the sheer ineptitude of its members, catches a similar amount through sheer dumb luck. If the good of working on a fishing crew
were merely instrumental, no relevant goodness would be missing in the latter
case that is present in the former. But since we do recognize that there are such
goods missing in the case of the incompetent crew, we must hold that the exercise of craftsmanship and skill involved in productive work is an intrinsic good,
aside from the value of the good that is ultimately produced.

What MacIntyre's remarks suggest is that the status of work as an intrinsic
good depends on that work's being subject to standards of excellence, which
one can achieve to a greater or lesser degree. That is part of what makes certain
types of productive work practices on MacIntyre's view, after all. We should
note one clarification of and one implication of this view. The clarification is
that to say that the intrinsic good of work depends on the presence of standards
of excellence is not to say that one who never achieves excellence in a certain
sort of work completely fails to participate in that good. Rather, it seems that
one enjoys those goods to the extent that one conforms to those standards; participation in that good is a matter of degree. The implication is that there are
forms of work that are not intrinsically good: those that are so lacking in complexity that the notion of 'standards of excellence' fails to apply. To stand at an
assembly line performing simple, tedious, repetitive acts for eight hours is not
to participate in any intrinsic good, at least for normal, unimpaired adults. (I
will say more on this proviso about impairment in a moment.) Thus, some work
is good only instrumentally.

Making clear why work is to be considered not only instrumentally but also
intrinsically good points the way toward an answer to the other question concerning the good of excellence in play: why 'excellence in play,' and not just
'play' *simpliciter?* The reason that I limit the good of play in this way is that it
seems to me that the same points hold true with regard to the good of play that
hold true with regard to the good of work. Unless the play activity is of sufficient complexity that the notion of excellence in that activity can have applica-

tion, the acts of play that are constituted by performance of that activity for its own sake are either unintelligible or intelligible only instrumentally.

Consider two examples of play activity that are lacking in this respect. Imagine, first, the activity of snapping one's fingers at approximately similar intervals. One could perform this activity for its own sake: one could engage in it with intensely focused concentration for minutes at a time. On a definition of play in which playful activity is performed for the sake of the performance itself, surely this particular activity qualifies as play. But it seems to me that, at least for normal, unimpaired adults, one would not claim that this activity is good in itself, intelligible in its own terms. One who engaged in it might be acting unintelligibly. Or, one's engaging in this activity could be made intelligible by noting its status as a means to some other end: one might perform such a ritual for the sake of relaxing, or emptying one's mind, or some other such aim. Or, consider a well-known game that does not meet the standard: tic-tac-toe. MacIntyre disqualifies tic-tac-toe as a practice because its simplicity is such that standards of excellence in it do not seem to apply. Thus, tic-tac-toe as a form of play participated in by normal, unimpaired adults is either unintelligible or instrumental. It is not good in itself.

It might appear from these remarks that I intend to endorse the view that playing and working are not genuine intrinsic goods unless they are performed within the context of a practice as MacIntyre defines it. This, however, is not my intention. Practices of productive work and practices of play are indeed paradigms of the sort of context in which one can enjoy the intrinsic goods of excellence in work and excellence in play. But enjoying these intrinsic goods might not be restricted to practices. All that I am prepared to defend, I think, is that the play or work activity must be of a level of complexity that standards of excellence might attach to it. Put another way, the claim is that to be genuinely intrinsically good, play and work activity must present a *challenge*.

Thus, it becomes clear why in the examples of work and play that fail the complexity/standards of excellence test, one must include the proviso 'at least for normal, unimpaired adults.' For what constitutes a challenge will, of course, depend on one's level of ability vis-à-vis that activity. I therefore leave open that possibility that the good of play might be genuinely instantiated in very small children who have just come across the game of tic-tac-toe, and that the good of work might be instantiated in a severely mentally handicapped person who finds challenging what an adult of normal capacities would find tedious, mindless work. On the opposite extreme, what makes practices as MacIntyre characterizes them paradigms of contexts in which the goods of work and play can be realized is their open-endedness: they always leave room for improvement; they always pose a challenge, even to their most advanced practitioners. While the normal intellectual maturation of a child strips tic-tac-toe of its status as providing an opportunity to participate in the good of play, no such maturation can strip chess of that status.

Thus, I include excellence in work and excellence in play as aspects of a single category of basic good. Their goodness resides in the activities themselves, and this goodness is instantiated to the extent that one realizes excellence in those activities.

It seems that one can also provide an account of the status of excellence in these activities as aspects of human flourishing. Consider a human agent that is such that it is unable to engage in the sorts of performances that we call play activity, or who is unable to carry out any sort of complex productive work. It seems that, even without reference to the effect of these deficiencies on other human functions, we would call these inabilities cases of serious malfunction. Given the strategy for laying bare presuppositions about human flourishing discussed in 1.3, then, there is reason to assert that excellence in play and work is an aspect of flourishing. Theoretical considerations concerning human nature thus confirm the characterizations of the human person both as *Homo ludens* (Huizinga 1955) and as *Homo faber* (Bergson 1911, p. 139).

Excellence in Agency

Excellence in agency is a fundamental reason for action. When one acts a certain way because it is the reasonable way to act, that action may be immediately intelligible.

The notion of excellence in agency has primarily to do with choosing and acting well. This good has two aspects: practical reasonableness, in which one's practical judgments and choices are in accordance with what is reasonable, and integrity of judgment and action, in which one's actions are in accordance with one's all-things-considered practical judgments. While the label that I have given to this category of good may suggest otherwise, I also mean to include, as an aspect of the good of excellence in agency, the state of having appropriate feelings and attitudes. Having appropriate feelings also exhibits this twofold aspect: having feelings in accordance with what is reasonable, and having feelings that are in accordance with one's practical judgments.

While it seems fairly clear what the integrity of judgment and actions consists in, we need to devote some attention to the idea of judging and acting in a practically reasonable way, for this notion admits of both a narrow and a broad interpretation. The narrow interpretation likens practical reasonable judgment and action to responsible practical judgment and action: on this view, excellence in agency is primarily that good of judging, choosing, and acting in a manner that is reasonable, given the resources for practical judgment that are available to the agent. The broader understanding includes the narrow understanding but adds that one does not fully participate in the good of excellence in agency, regardless of the responsibility manifested in one's judging and choosing, if one's acts are not in fact in accordance with the demands of reason.

I think that the broad conception of excellence in agency must be the correct one. Consider, first, the innocent instrument of immorality and the accidental instrument of morality. The innocent instrument of immorality has been deceived through no fault of her own and, thus, responsibly believes that certain acts ought to be performed by her, whereas such acts really constitute grave immorality. Now, we should, of course, say that the innocent instrument of immorality is not culpable for her deeds. But isn't there something bad about being such an instrument, even if what one does is fully practically reasonable in the sense in which practical reasonableness just means responsible judgment and choice? Unless some other good could be implicated here – and the only one that seems remotely relevant is the good of knowledge – we can only explain this person's being worse off if we accept that one's participation in that good is deficient if one acts on the basis of a responsibly reached yet incorrect assessment of the facts. The accidental instrument of morality, on the other hand, judges and acts rightly, but does so on the basis of blameless mistakes of fact. Is this person not worse off than one who acts rightly on the basis of a proper understanding of what the facts of the situation are? Once more, unless we want to ascribe the deficiency to the absence of some other good, we should explain this person's being worse off by holding that participation in the good of excellence in agency can be detrimentally affected by a responsibly reached yet incorrect assessment of the facts.

In assessing the considerations in favor of the broad interpretation, it might also be helpful to note an analogy with the good of speculative knowledge. In characterizing that good, one could go in either of the following ways. One could characterize it as we, in fact, did: as true belief arrived at in a certain way, as a correct grasp of the way that things are that is based on a proper assessment of the facts. One could, on the other hand, characterize it in a way that is independent of the truth of one's beliefs, so that what is at stake is not that one believes the truth and is warranted in believing it but, rather, simply that one does the best that one can with the epistemic resources available.

Why is the former characterization of the good of speculative knowledge the preferable one? It seems simply to be that there is something more to the good of knowledge than merely believing responsibly: it is important not just to do the best that one can, given one's epistemic resources, whatever they happen to be, but also to get things right, and to get things right in the proper way, so that one is warranted with respect to one's true beliefs. There is, then, something to the good of knowledge that is outside the agent's control: sometimes one can responsibly believe falsehoods, and sometimes one can responsibly believe truths but in such a way that one does not possess knowledge; and in these cases, one's participation in the good of knowledge is defective, incomplete. Now, just as speculative knowledge is that good concerned with believing well, excellence in agency is that good concerned with choosing and acting well; and just as there is more to believing well than believing responsibly, it seems that there is more to choosing and acting well than choosing and acting responsibly.

Why do some writers find the narrower conception attractive? I suggest that the best explanation for this attraction invokes the phenomenon of transparency (Finnis 1983, pp. 71–72, and Edgley 1969, p. 90). Transparency holds whenever one state of affairs is indistinguishable from some other state of affairs because of the perspective of the agent: for example, 'I think that p' is transparent for 'p,' because at the point at which one believes that p, that state of affairs is indistinguishable from p's being the case. (Transparency is the source of Moore's paradox, that one cannot consistently affirm that one believes that p but that p is false.)

Now, one's judging and acting in a way that is actually in accordance with the demands of reason and one's acting in a way that is practically reasonable, given one's resources for judgment, are indistinguishable at the point of action: thus, it might appear that the good of excellence in agency is merely responsible judgment and action. But while the states of affairs of acting in accordance with reason and acting responsibly are indistinguishable at the point of action, they are obviously distinguishable in a number of other ways: conceptually, in retrospect, and in other agents. Conceptually, we can see that there is a clear difference between these states of affairs, even at the point of action, so that it is a live issue that is the proper characterization of excellence in agency. And it seems to me that in retrospect, or when observing other agents, the importance of acting well, not just doing the best one can with one's practical resources, becomes apparent. Consider, for example, one who is the victim of lies and responsibly believes and makes decisions on the basis of falsehoods. Such a person is made worse off, even if this person chooses responsibly on the basis of the information that he or she thought correct.[6]

What reasons do we have for thinking excellence in agency an aspect of well-being and a constituent of human flourishing? Why not think that being able to act well is a mere means to some other aspects of well-being? It is difficult to answer this question in the absence of an account of how excellence in agency will manifest itself, an account that we will not begin to sketch until Chapter 5. If the theory of practical reasonableness were to assert that excellence in agency consists in (e.g.) acting in such a way that one's participation in certain aspects of well-being is maximized – a glorified egoism that is not without adherents in the natural law tradition – one might suspect excellence in agency to be a mere means to these aspects of well-being. To project ahead a bit, the account of practical reasonableness sketched in that chapter does not support this suspicion: excellence in agency does not consist in the maximization of one's well-being, or even in maximizing well-being overall. What considerations can be forwarded, though, in favor of the view that excellence in agency is a basic good?

One set of considerations is specifically practical, and some of these practical considerations are obvious, some less obvious. The obvious point is a straightforward appeal to one's interest in acting well, an interest that is not merely for the sake of some other good: it seems to be a good thing to judge and act reasonably, and for one's actions to be integrated with one's practical judgments; and one who is unreasonable or whose actions do not accord with one's own judgments seems to be correspondingly worse off. But there are other ways, less direct, of trying to make manifest the good of excellence in agency.

Here is a pedestrian example of the sort of case that I have in mind. Suppose that I set out to sell my car, and I perform a number of tasks for the sake of that end, believing that these are intelligently crafted means to the attaining of my objective. The car gets sold, but I come to realize that I did an awful job in trying to sell my car: the means I crafted were poor. In such a case, it seems to me that I have reasonable grounds for regret. If my selecting and implementing means to sell my car were themselves mere means to selling the car, I should have no ground for regret: the car got sold, after all. But that such regret is reasonable makes plain that there is an interest in acting well, one that is fundamental.

Or consider the way that being offered more alternatives from which to choose can be cause for reasonable regret. Suppose that one teaches philosophy at Intimate College, which has a small, teaching-oriented department. Now, imagine that one is offered a position at Enormous State U., with a philosophy department of the large research-oriented variety. How could being given such an offer be cause for regret? After all, one could simply disregard this offer, and stay with one's status quo position. It seems that if we construe excellence in agency as a mere means, there could be no reasonable regret in this case. But if we hold the view that excellence in agency is not a mere means but is itself an aspect of well-being, it is clear why being offered a choice can be cause for regret: for an opportunity to choose is often an opportunity to choose wrongly, to make an error. Thus, even if one's job situation is not made worse by receiving an offer from another institution, one can be made worse off by judging and acting poorly in this choice situation: by blindly disregarding the option, by misassessing the goods involved in each position, etc.

Thus, it can be reasonable to regret additional choices, especially those that are difficult to make. (There is further discussion of this point in Dworkin 1982, pp. 50–51.) It is, perhaps, unduly pessimistic to emphasize the fact that having choices makes it possible to choose poorly. It is also true that having alternatives is what makes the good of excellence in agency possible in the first place: one has to be able to choose in order to be able to choose well. (See also Hurka 1987, p. 376.)

There are, then, practical considerations that lead one to affirm the status of excellence in agency as an aspect of well-being. What argument can be given to connect it with human functioning and human flourishing? Suppose that, as most of us believe and as I will try to establish later (5.5), acting well is not simply a matter of acting for the sake of promoting aspects of one's own well-being; it is not just for the sake of living, or knowing, or any other constituent or set of constituents of well-being. Now, typically, when one's brain is functioning well, one is able to act well, in a way that does not always aim at the promotion of one's own flourishing. If one were to become unable to act well, we would, I think, consider this, as such, a serious malfunction. Since this is so, we should affirm the view that excellence in agency is an aspect of human flourishing.

Inner Peace

Inner peace is a fundamental reason for action. When one acts for the sake of inner peace, that action may be immediately intelligible.

Inner peace is a good that is particularly important within this natural law account because it is by means of that good that the formal objectivist natural law view can be brought squarely into contention with subjectivist theories vis-à-vis the reason-giving status of desires. In 2.4 I argued that strong subjectivism as a theory of well-being is mistaken because it implies that a desire for x implies the existence of a reason to secure x; instead, a desire for x implies no more than a reason to secure x or to rid oneself of the desire for x. Now, to this alleged refutation, defenders of a subjectivist theory of the nature of well-being might respond: "There may be difficulties with our theory of well-being, but it at least attempts to explain in what way the fulfillment of desire is related to well-being. Objectivist theories of well-being, on the other hand, tend to be unfortunately silent on this issue." (But see Scanlon 1993, pp. 192–193.)

Now, there is a sense in which formally objectivist theories of well-being *must* be silent about any positive relationship between well-being and desire. A formally objectivist theory, a theory about the nature of well-being, is characterized, in part, by its denial that the agent's desires determine whether a certain state of affairs is included in an agent's well-being. At the level of an account of the nature of well-being, then, the objectivist has nothing positive to say about the role of desire in making an agent well or poorly off. But the formal objectivist can, in addition, affirm a substantive view about the content of well-being: he or she can hold that the formally objectivist view affirmed is consistent with, suggests, or even implies a substantive account of well-being on which the agent's desires are clearly relevant to his or her well-being. Nothing essential to formal objectivism precludes the defender of that view from affirming an account of the content of well-being in which desire has an important part.

One way to establish the relevance of desire to well-being is to show that the satisfaction of desire is somehow instrumentally related to the securing of one or another item in the list of aspects of well-being that the objectivist would accept, so that there is derivative reason to fulfill the desire. This is, in outline, the sort of strategy that Kant uses when he confronts the question of what reason agents have to pursue their own happiness (which Kant identifies with the satisfaction of desire; see *Metaphysics of Morals,* p. 480, and *Critique of Practical Reason,* p. 124): there is reason to pursue happiness "in part because the lack of [happiness] . . . contains temptations to transgress against duty" (*Critique of Practical Reason,* p. 93; see also *Metaphysics of Morals,* p. 388). So, just as Kant holds that there is reason to pursue the satisfaction of desire inasmuch as the satisfaction of desire aids in the performance of one's duties, the objectivist regarding well-being might affirm that one has reason to fulfill one's desires insofar as the fulfillment of those desires is necessary, or useful, for the pursuit of one or another item on the list of aspects of well-being that the objectivist wishes to uphold. While perhaps not entirely inappropriate, such a strategy would not seem wholly to do justice to the intelligibility of the pursuit of objects of desire, and when it is applied to particularly severe cases of the avoidance of pain (see 3.2), it does appear absurd.

There is, however, another strategy available: one can include in one's catalog of aspects of well-being a good the *content* of which implicates desire. Now it would, of course, be troubling if the formal objectivist were to insert such a good into his or her substantive account of well-being without there being some independent plausibility to the notion that this putative good is an aspect of well-being; it will not do to attempt to explain the reason-giving status of desires by positing an aspect of well-being that is unrecognizable as such. In my view, though, there is a good that there is independent reason to regard as such, and the content of which implicates desire in the necessary way. This is the good of inner peace.

What is inner peace? We might say, as a first approximation, that inner peace is the good of having satisfied desires. I don't think that this is quite right, though. If having satisfied desires were an aspect of well-being, then each of us would have a reason to produce desires in ourselves for states of affairs merely because we know that these states of affairs will obtain – such as a desire that water continue to be H_2O, that Christmas be on December 25 this year, and so on. We would also have reason to try to produce trivial desires in ourselves, so that we could easily satisfy them. But this seems wrong; we have no such reasons. To produce desires merely for the sake of having them satisfied is pointless. (See also Parfit 1984, p. 497.) On the other hand, there does seem to be something right about connecting inner peace with the satisfaction of desire. A second, much closer approximation would be to redefine inner peace as the good of not having unsatisfied desires. The effect of this redefinition is to deny that one would have a reason to produce a desire in oneself just for the sake of satisfying it. One has a reason to ensure that one lacks unsatisfied desires, but one has no reason to strive to have satisfied desires.

The inclusion of the good of inner peace in a substantive theory of well-being that is annexed to a formally objectivist account of its nature enables the formal objectivist to explain the relevance of desire to an agent's well-being. But what is particularly noteworthy about the good of inner peace is not merely

that it shows how a good can implicate desire, but also that a formally objectivist theory the substantive view of which incorporates that good provides a
better account of the reason-giving status of desires than a strong subjectivist
theory does.

On a strong subjectivist theory, if one desires x then x's obtaining is an aspect of the agent's well-being; one thus has a reason to secure x. We have seen,
though, that this is false: a desire for x implies not a reason to secure x but a reason either to secure x or to rid oneself of the desire for x. But note that the affirmation of the good of inner peace as an aspect of well-being implies that desires will generate reasons in precisely this way. For suppose that an agent
desires x. Now, the good of inner peace is that of not having unsatisfied desires.
But given any desire for x, there are two ways of achieving the good of inner
peace vis-à-vis that desire: either by securing x, or by ridding oneself of the desire for x. In either case, one will lack an unsatisfied desire for x: the description 'lacks an unsatisfied desire for x' extends indifferently to 'having a satisfied desire for x' and 'not having a desire for x.' An explanation similar in form
can be produced for the way that pleasure and the absence of pain present reasons for action. If one has a strong desire to avoid the sensation of pain, then
the good of inner peace can be secured vis-à-vis that desire either by avoiding
pain or by ridding oneself of the desire to avoid the pain.

These are, I think, important results. For if the negative argument presented
in 3.2 is correct, and if there is some intuitive plausibility to including inner
peace as characterized in a list of objective goods, then it follows that an objectivist theory can present a better account of the reason-giving status of desires than subjectivist theories do, *and* can explain how it is that the pursuit of
pleasure and the avoidance of pain are intelligible actions. This is welcome
news for those sympathetic to objectivist accounts of well-being.

That the list of goods defended here includes the good of inner peace should
not be taken to be more of a concession to the subjectivist than it is. It might er-
roneously be thought that by including the good of inner peace, I am allowing
that there is need for supplementation by subjectivist theories of welfare. Now,
of course, I am allowing that there is need for subjectivist elements in the content of well-being: the theory of the content of well-being offered here is mixed,
rather than fully objective (2.1), but as we have seen, it is consistent with formal objectivism to affirm a mixed conception of the substance of welfare. It is
also important to note that the states of affairs that are held to constitute an
agent's well-being differ on the strongly subjectivist theory of the nature of
well-being and on a mixed substantive view that includes the good of inner
peace. On this mixed substantive view, one aspect of well-being is that of having no unsatisfied desires. This is a state of the person that is valuable for that
person. The claim that inner peace is an aspect of well-being is quite different
from that claim made by the strong subjectivist, which is that states of the world
made the agent well off, and that these states of affairs make the agent well off

because the agent desires them. To put matters another way, on this substantive mixed view, what is valuable is the state of being a person without unsatisfied desires; on the formally subjectivist theory, what is valuable is the obtaining of certain states of affairs that are desired.

The following case brings the difference into focus. Suppose that a depraved person strongly desires to kill a large number of people. On the formally (strong) subjectivist view, it is a constituent of that agent's well-being that this state of affairs obtain. On the substantive mixed view that relies on the good of inner peace, it is a constituent of that agent's well-being that he or she not have this unsatisfied desire. On the subjectivist view, actually killing the people would in itself realize that agent's good. On the mixed substantive view, while killing the people would affect the agent's well-being by producing in him or her a condition of inner peace, the state of affairs in which those people are killed is not itself a constituent of the agent's good. There is a clear difference between these ways of implicating desire in well-being. (And, it seems to me, a difference that in cases like this one favors the appeal to inner peace over the appeal to formal, strong subjectivism.)

Now, it might be argued that this appearance of success in providing a role for desire in well-being without abandoning formal objectivism is an illusion: the formally objectivist theory of well-being is able to provide an account of the role of desire in well-being only by giving up its pure objectivism. Suppose that an agent desires not to touch brown boxes. On this supposition, that agent's well-being will include the obtaining of the state of affairs 'that this agent does not touch brown boxes or that this agent no longer desires not to touch brown boxes.' But that this disjunctive state of affairs is an aspect of this agent's well-being is determined by the agent's having a particular attitude toward the avoidance of brown boxes, and thus on at least some occasions, the truth-maker of 'x is an aspect of A's well-being' is, in some cases, A's subjective states. But if the truth-maker of 'x is an aspect of A's well-being' is some subjective state of A's, then formal objectivism is false.

But the objection fails. First, it misunderstands what is involved in rejecting formal objectivism. To be any kind of subjectivist about well-being, it is necessary not that the truth-maker of 'x is an aspect of A's well-being' is that A is in a certain subjective state, but that A is in that subjective state *toward x*. It is clear, though, that it is not toward the disjunctive state of affairs 'that this agent not touch brown boxes or that this agent not desire not to touch brown boxes' that the agent has the pro-attitude. Secondly, and more importantly, the premise that the states of affairs that constitute an agent's well-being are determined by the agent's desires is just false. The good of inner peace is the good of not having unsatisfied desires. Thus, for any desire d and all agents A, that A does not have d or that A has d and d is satisfied is an aspect of A's well-being. That this is an aspect of A's well-being is independent of any particular desires A has. Of course, what A should do in order to realize this aspect of well-being may differ given A's particular desires and situation, but this will be true of every aspect of well-being on any plausible substantive theory.

There are, however, particular worries about the good of inner peace that need to be addressed; and one of them will call for further modification, hopefully not too terribly ad hoc, to our characterization of that aspect of well-being. It might be objected, for example, that inner peace cannot be characterized as the state of affairs in which one does not have unsatisfied desires, because one can have unsatisfied desires and yet still seem to possess inner peace. At the moment I write these words, I desire to publish a book contributing to the theory of natural law. This is, we might think, an unsatisfied desire. But while I grant that I have not achieved inner peace, I don't think that the fact that this desire is not satisfied contributes to my lack of inner peace. Isn't it false, then, to say that inner peace consists in having unsatisfied desires?

While there are difficulties involved in identifying inner peace with a lack of unsatisfied desires, this is not the sort of case that raises them. The mistake in this objection is the failure to specify the desires at stake completely enough. Desires are time indexed: we do not simply want a certain state of affairs, but we want a certain state of affairs to obtain at, or by, a given time. If I desire that state of affairs S obtain at t, it does not constitute a loss of inner peace for S to fail to obtain at $t - 1$ or $t + 1$. If I desire that S obtain by t, it does not constitute a loss of inner peace for it to fail to obtain at any time before t. Such is the case with the desire I have concerning the publication of a book on natural law. I desire to publish that book at some point in the next, say, ten years or so. That state of affairs does not obtain now, but its not obtaining does not preclude its obtaining in the next ten years. My inner peace is, therefore, not at risk. On the other hand, if 2007 were approaching and I had not yet published a book on natural law, this would constitute a threat to my inner peace.

Or, consider another example: pain. It seems that the desire that accompanies the sensation of intense physical pain has to be characterized in a time-indexed way: "I want to be rid of this sensation *immediately*." Thus, given the nearly universal concomitance of this desire with sensations of pain, the presence of pain is almost a guarantee that the person in pain does not have inner peace. Once one recognizes that desires are time indexed, this sort of concern shows itself to be unwarranted.

A larger worry, which will require the revision of the characterization of inner peace, has to do with Stranger on a Train–type cases (Parfit 1984, p. 494; see also Kagan 1992, p. 171). Parfit imagines a situation in which he meets a stranger who has a disease that is believed to be fatal. Parfit forms a desire that the stranger be cured of the disease. Now, suppose that he never hears of the stranger again, yet the stranger, in fact, recovers from the disease. Does the fulfillment of this desire make Parfit better off? Surely not.[7] But this sort of case also raises difficulties for the notion that the good of inner peace is as characterized. For suppose instead that the stranger does not recover from his ailment.

Parfit's desire thus goes unsatisfied. Isn't it perverse to hold that Parfit's inner peace would be damaged by this turn of events? How could his *inner* peace be damaged by something that is so *outer?*

The obvious way to avoid the implication that Parfit's inner peace is damaged in this case is to include some sort of belief condition. If one really does desire that the stranger recover, and one becomes aware that the stranger has died, then one's inner peace is negatively affected. But one that never becomes aware of this sad turn of events does not suffer any loss of well-being. It is important to note that I am *not* claiming that all that Parfit desired is that he believe that the stranger survive. I am making no such claim. What I am asserting is that while the desire is that the stranger survive, the lack of satisfaction of this desire affects one's inner peace only insofar as one is aware, or believes, that the stranger has died. The good of inner peace, as recharacterized, would be that of having no desires that one believes to be unsatisfied.

This recharacterization of inner peace may appear wrongheaded, but it retains this appearance only if one confuses the different roles that the satisfaction of desire must play in objectivist and subjectivist theories of well-being. Part of the worry about adding an awareness condition proceeds, I think, from concerns that would rightly attend the adding of such a condition within a subjectivist theory of well-being. If one were to hold this sort of view, the consequences of holding that satisfaction of desire need be apparent only would be atrocious: it would imply, for example, that whether one's spouse is unfaithful without arousing suspicion or is completely faithful are equivalent vis-à-vis one's desire that one's spouse be faithful. Having recourse to a Nozick-type experience machine could multiply examples indefinitely (Nozick 1974, pp. 42–45). But we must keep in mind that the implausibility of attaching an awareness condition on desire-satisfaction within a subjectivist theory of well-being does not necessarily translate into implausibility in attaching an awareness condition to desire-satisfaction as the content of inner peace within an objectivist theory of well-being. For there are aspects of well-being other than inner peace; and that one's spouse's infidelity makes one worse off need not be explained in terms of the good of inner peace but, rather, perhaps in terms of the good of friendship (as we shall see in this section), which can be instantiated in faithful marriage.

For the worry about the awareness condition to have bite within an objectivist theory of well-being, one would have to produce examples in which (i) one has a desire for x which is unsatisfied, (ii) one is unaware that one's desire for x is unsatisfied, (iii) one is worse off than one would be if the desire for x were satisfied, and (iv) the condition of being worse off cannot be plausibly accounted for in terms of some item on the list of aspects of well-being other than inner peace. To generate such an example is, in my view, not an easy task.

One might attack the plausibility of the awareness condition more directly, though. On the view that I have proposed, desires generate reasons by way of the good of inner peace. But if an awareness condition is added to the good of inner peace, then my view implies that when one has a strong desire for *x*, one is just as well off when one falsely believes that this desire is satisfied as one would be if the desire were in fact fulfilled. Now, there is clearly a sense in which I am committed to this conclusion: I must claim that *solely with regard to the desire,* the person is equally well off in both cases. But it seems false that this position is counterintuitive.

Consider again the person who has a strong desire not to touch brown boxes. There does not seem to be anything so strange about holding that when we contemplate this person's well-being, solely with regard to the fulfillment of his or her desires, he or she is just as well off falsely believing that he or she is not touching a brown box as he or she would be by actually not touching a brown box. If we consider aspects of well-being other than those in which desire is implicated, we may have a different view: the latter case might be preferable to the former inasmuch as in the latter, the agent has true beliefs, while in the former, the agent has false beliefs; but we are supposed to be considering the agent's well-being only in terms of desire-fulfillment, not in terms of the good of knowledge. It seems, then, that adding the awareness condition to the characterization of inner peace does no violence to our beliefs about the person's well-being in such a case. Or: suppose that we consider someone who strongly desires to act in a way that is reasonable. The recharacterization of the good of inner peace commits me to the view that this person is no worse off vis-à-vis the satisfaction of desire if he or she falsely believes that he or she is acting in a practically reasonable way than if he or she really is acting in a practically reasonable way. But once more, this does not seem counterintuitive: that the agent is worse off in the former case than in the latter is due to his or her not really participating in the good of excellence in agency.

We can generalize from these examples. In cases in which one is worse off falsely believing a desire to be fulfilled than he or she would be if it were actually fulfilled, the damage to well-being results either from (i) the fact that one has a false belief, so that one is worse off with respect to the good of knowledge, or (ii) the fact that what is desired is an item in the catalog of aspects of well-being, so that the desire's not being fulfilled entails that one is deprived of that aspect of well-being. Because this generalization appears plausible, I am willing to accept the conclusion that the fulfillment of desires makes one well off only insofar as it is implicated in the good of inner peace as I have redescribed it.

Having provided an account of the good of inner peace, let us now return to the worry that initially motivated the search for an account of the reason-giving status of pleasures and pains, that is, that pleasure and absence of pain do not fit well into a natural law metaphysics of goodness (3.2). Pain is an evil, but it is not a lack, an absence; it is a positive reality. I dealt with this difficulty not by asserting that the natural law metaphysics trumps the apparent obviousness of pain's reason-giving character but by showing that this character could be accounted for within a substantive account of well-being that affirms the good of inner peace. But the same sort of worry that motivated the search for a better account of the reason-giving status of pain seems to arise with regard to inner peace. How can having no unsatisfied desires be seen as a positive reality, and having unsatisfied desires a negative one, without trivializing the positive reality/negative reality distinction? Can the good of inner peace be accommodated within a natural law metaphysics of goodness?

What I would like to appeal to here is the notion of equilibrium: one who possesses inner peace is in a state of equilibrium, and this equilibrium can without distortion be characterized as a positive reality. One who has no unsatisfied desires, it seems, is in a condition of equilibrium, whereas one who has desires that are unsatisfied is in a state of disequilibrium. This way of viewing the good of inner peace actually fits fairly well with the notion that inner peace is part of human flourishing; recall that on the view defended in 1.2, flourishing is functioning, and on the view proposed there, part of what it is for something to have a function is that it tend toward an equilibrium state. We might say, then, that the human is an entity one of whose characteristic activities is to pursue objects of desire (or modify those desires) until its desires reach an equilibrium state. In addition to being a living, thinking, aesthetic (etc.) being, the human is a desiring being, *Homo appetens*.

Even if we suppose, though, that the notion that a basic good or aspect of well-being must be a positive reality can be preserved by viewing inner peace as a kind of equilibrium, there is a worry that remains. Here is the problem. The account of human flourishing that I have affirmed holds that aspects of flourishing are human functions that are an end of a line of functions, which renders the functions prior to it intelligible as functions. But it seems pretty clear that we are not forced to view the equilibrium state of having satisfied desires in this way. Even if we note that particular human capacities seem to have the function of restoring the equilibrium state of inner peace, we might say that this equilibrium state is solely for the sake of pursuit of the other goods: it is, we might suppose, a mechanism by which knowledge, life, aesthetic experience, etc., are participated in. We might, then, deny that inner peace is an aspect of flourishing; rather, achieving inner peace is typically, though not always, a means to participating in other goods.

I admit that direct appeals to our grasp of human functions do not provide justification for the claim that inner peace is an aspect of flourishing. We can construct interesting thought experiments that partially confirm our views of the other basic goods as aspects of flourishing because we have no suspicion that some are mere means to others. We do not suspect that, if aesthetic experience is a human function, it is mere means to some other function. Thus, if we think that the human who is incapacitated aesthetically is seriously malfunctioning, we might be led to believe that this is because aesthetic experience is an aspect of flourishing. But it is apparent that inner peace differs from aesthetic experience in this respect. I shall not, then, try to construct a theoretical argument for inner peace as an aspect of flourishing: I will, instead, drawing on the accumulated evidence for the real identity thesis, suggest that we should simply affirm that since we have a practical grasp of inner peace as a good, we ought to hold that inner peace is not merely a mechanism for participating in other goods but is itself an aspect of human flourishing.

Friendship and Community

Friendship and community are fundamental reasons for action. When one acts a certain way for the sake of friendship or community, that action may be immediately intelligible.

Human agents can enter into a variety of relationships with one another, but it is only relationships of friendship or community that are intrinsically good. These unifying relationships involved in friendship and community are primarily a matter of action: it is the actions performed by the agents, including the ends that are pursued by them and the descriptions under which those ends are pursued, that mark persons off as being in a relationship of friendship or community with each other. On the view that I will defend here, community is the more inclusive notion: friendship is but one distinctive and particularly intense form of community.

Insofar as community is an intrinsic good, that which makes those who participate in it better off as such, it is instantiated when agents have a common end and aim together to realize that end. (Merely having a common aim is not enough: those who share an end and whose actions further that end are not in a relationship of community unless those actions are cooperative.) Thus, it is crucial to the understanding of community to have a clear idea of what is involved in having a common end; without a clear idea of this notion, it is impossible to distinguish community as an intrinsic good from those forms of community that are good only instrumentally. For on an inadequate account of the ends at which agents aim, some cases of joint action that are merely instrumentally good might appear to count as intrinsically good.

Consider the situation that Hobbes describes as the "natural condition of mankind." In the natural condition of mankind, human agents are predominantly self-interested, roughly equal in mental and physical capacities, in a condition of moderate scarcity, and lacking any coercive political authorities. This condition, says Hobbes, is guaranteed to be a state of war, and the lives of the denizens of the state of nature terrible and short. Hobbes holds, though, that even given the radically disparate aims of those in the state of nature, they must come to realize that peace is good, and will recognize that the only way to achieve peace is to contract together to institute a nearly absolute political authority, the sovereign, which has the right and power to apprehend and punish all those who engage in behavior that threatens the peace. Now, we might ask: Hobbes's own views on community notwithstanding, don't we have a genuine case of the intrinsic good of community instantiated here? After all, the persons involved have a common aim, peace, and they are engaging in coordinated action in order to secure this aim. Is this cooperative activity intrinsically good?

I deny this. The coordinated action of the persons in the state of nature in instituting a sovereign is not, as Hobbes describes it, intrinsically good. There is an intrinsic good involved in what the parties in the state of nature do: it is excellence in agency, participated in to the extent that they recognize that staying alive is a genuine good and carry out the means that they correctly calculate are necessary to the bringing about of this result. But I deny that the intrinsic good of community is present. The reason is that, appearances aside, those in the state of nature do not aim at a common end. What each party in the state of nature wants, given Hobbes's description of those agents, is not peace as such, or peace for all of us in the state of nature, but, rather, that he or she be in a state of peace. The state of affairs aimed at by each party, that is, has an essential self-reference; it is a wholly agent-relative end.

The example of Hobbes's state of nature and the cooperative action that leads out of it is intended to illustrate the point that some cases in which the good of community might initially appear to be present are mere simulacra of community. Community is realized only when the description of the end for the sake of which agents act is itself common. In order to distinguish the sorts of ends that are implicated in the intrinsic good of community from those that are not, we can adopt the terminology used by Gregory Froelich in his persuasive account of the different ways in which Aquinas employs the notion of the common good (1989, p. 38). Some ends are common by way of 'predication.' Suppose that I seek A as an end and you seek B as an end, and A and B are both of kind K. It is consistent, though, with the description of the ends sought that each of these might be realized independently of the other; we might be seeking a good in common only in the sense that they are goods of the same sort. Next, some ends are common by way of 'distribution.' Suppose that there is some state of affairs C which is divisible, either in its concrete realization or in its desired effects, into ends D and E, where you want C for the sake of D and I want C for the sake of E. End C is also common in a sense: prior to its division, or considered apart from its being ordered to D and E, it might be sought by the both of us. (The peace sought by the denizens of Hobbes's state of nature is an end common by way of distribution.)

The pursuit of ends common by way of predication and distribution is not, I claim, the sort of pursuit of common ends that is implicated in the good of community: ends that are common by way of predication are not, as such, the basis of common action at all, for they need not involve the same state of affairs; and ends that are common by way of distribution, while possibly aimed at in common action, might be pursued only for their aspects that are not shared as ends.

The sort of common end involved in the intrinsic good of community is what can be called an end common by way of 'causation.' In defining what it is to be a good that is common by way of causation, Froelich writes that it is "a cause which while remaining numerically one extends to many effects"; it is "common precisely as it is individual" (1989, p. 48). Adapting this characterization to the notion of an end, we can say that an end that is common by way of causation is common precisely as it is individual: it extends to a number of agents as their end without qualification.

Note the sharp contrast between this sort of end and the ends that are common merely by predication and distribution: in the case of ends common merely by way of predication, there is really not a single state of affairs sought; in the case of ends common by way of distribution, there may seem to be a common state of affairs sought, but what is pursued is really distinct aspects of that state of affairs. In ends common by way of causation, on the other hand, it is a single, individual state of affairs that extends to all of the agents involved as a final cause for their actions.

To illustrate this distinction between ends common by way of causation and other sorts of seemingly shared ends, imagine two distinct groups of agents that are involved in the project of founding a small art museum. The structure of the aims of the members of one of these groups is such that each wants the museum to be founded so that he or she will be able to enjoy works of art at will. While the agents in such a group are enjoying and acting for the sake of genuine goods – acting for the sake of aesthetic experience, and enjoying the good of excellence insofar as they deliberate and settle upon suitable means to realize their aim – the end that they have in common is common only by way of distribution. I thus deny that the intrinsic good of community is realized therein. Contrast this group with one the members of which have the common aim of founding an art museum, but who also share the vision that this museum will be a source of benefit for all of those involved in the project, or for the entire wider community. This group is pursuing an end that is common by way of causation: they share as their aim a single state of affairs. In this group, I claim, the intrinsic good of community is realized.

Now, there is no doubt that what I described here are idealized cases. Typically, when there is cooperative action, the structure of the aims of the parties involved will not be so simple: they will share aims to some extent, and to some extent, will not; some of their ends will be common by way of predication, some by way of distribution, some by way of causation. But this does not affect my point: the basic good of community is a matter of genuinely sharing aims, and one can participate in that intrinsic good only to the extent that aims are shared.

This insistence on restricting the good of community to those cases in which ends are shared, in a strong sense, might be thought to cause some difficulty for the idea that friendship is a form of community, let alone its most intense form. For consider the classic analysis of friendship offered by Aristotle, in which paradigmatic friendship obtains when people "wish goods in the same way to each other insofar as they are good"; "those who wish goods to their friend for the friend's own sake are friends most of all" (*Nicomachean Ethics,* 1156b7–10). But this seems to suggest that if *A* and *B* are friends, what makes them friends involves different ends: *A* wills and acts for the sake of *B*'s good, whereas *B* wills and acts for the sake of *A*'s good. Nevertheless, this appearance is illusory. The commonness of the end aimed at by friends, and the extreme intensity of the commonality of friendship, becomes clear when it is noted that for friends, each party's good becomes wrapped up with the other's: "In loving their friend they love what is good for themselves; for when a good person becomes a friend he becomes a good for his friend" (*Nicomachean Ethics,* 1157b34–35).

Thus, in the most intense friendship, there occurs an identification of one's own good with the other's:

> Just as the unknown time of one's prospective death is, in thought, a vantage point from which to distinguish some reasonable alternative plans of life, so friendship establishes an analogous vantage point. In friendship one is not thinking and choosing 'from one's own point of view,' nor from one's friend's point of view. Rather, one is acting from a third point of view, the unique perspective from which one's own good and one's friend's good are equally 'in view' and 'in play.' (Finnis 1980, p. 143)

Friends, then, share common aims in that they act for their own good and for the good of their friends both under the description 'for my own sake' and 'for my friend's sake.' This is, as might be obvious, the most intense form of unifying relationship one can imagine in the practical realm. Relationships of community can be based on long-term ends (promoting the study of philosophy) or short-term ends (helping a philosophy student do well on an exam), on extensive aims (the furthering of justice within a political community) or aims more modest in scope (beautifying one's neighborhood). But no relationship of community more closely unites two persons than friendship: they are devoted to promoting and protecting each other's good, to each other's overall well-being, as to their own.

Now, I have been focusing on paradigm cases of friendship and community, on what it takes for such relationships to be instantiated fully: for it is by understanding such cases that we can see in what ways there can be partial, incomplete instantiations of those relationships, which while defective are at least good as far as they go. One way that friendship and community can be partial has to do with the way that these relationships can be deficient in terms of the action condition; deficiencies of this sort most obviously come to mind with regard to the good of friendship.

The paradigm case of friendship involves, as Aristotle notes, those who live together, who share a life of common action (*Nicomachean Ethics,* 1157b19). Note, though, that in paradigmatic friendship relationships, there is typically more going on than just common action. Given the existence of common action, we can know straightaway that the wills of friends are in concert: they will each other's good, and put that will into action. And, given normal sentiments that are enjoyed in friendship, one will have positive, warm feelings toward one's friend. Deficient cases of friendship often involve those relationships in which a common life is excluded for some reason – other pressing commitments, mere geographical distance, etc. – which are such that the concord of will and sentiment that obtains in paradigmatic friendships is present. Thus, when two persons who were good friends, living and acting together, find themselves separated and unable to carry on that common life, their friendship may remain in an attenuated sense: they may will each other's good, and may persist in their affection for each other. Such persons have, as Aristotle remarks, "goodwill" toward each other, and while he was right to hold that this is not a case of friendship in the paradigmatic sense, we should keep in mind that this is an instance of friendship, incomplete as it might be.

Another way that community can exist partially becomes clear if one notes that relationships of community have both a positive and a negative aspect. The positive aspects of community include primarily that of common action and secondarily common will and common sentiment. But accompanying community in its full-blooded sense is a lack of discord in action, will, and sentiment. This negative aspect of community involves absence of conflict in action and, secondarily, absence of conflict in the wills and sentiments of the agents involved. Now, no relationships of community can be complete if there is only the absence of this sort of conflict: but it is a necessary feature of paradigmatic instances of community, and can be present even without community in a full sense. While on its own a most meager instantiation of community, this absence of discord is, as far as it goes, a good: and it is the good that we call 'peace.' Being at peace with others is thus an aspect of the basic good of community. (See also *Summa Theologiae* IIaIIae 29, 1: there Aquinas treats what I call the negative aspect of community and what I call the basic good of inner peace as parts of one category of good, which he calls "peace.")

While few of us doubt the intrinsic good of friendship, we might sometimes doubt whether community in general is an intrinsic good. Perhaps what drives this doubt is, at least in part, that it is relatively rare that those who engage in the common action which constitutes that good do so for the sake of the good of community. Those who attempt to found art museums rarely do so with the aim of enjoying the good of community among those participating in the project; they do so simply for the sake of realizing that aim. But this fact should not cause us to doubt that community is an intrinsic good. First, just because it is relatively rare to seek community as such, that does not imply that community is not, when participated in, a basic good. When we look upon the activities of those who, with a common understanding of an aim to be achieved, set out to realize that aim, we do seem to recognize that there is a good realized in the cooperative effort itself, aside from the value of the realized aim. Secondly, it is not unknown for people to engage in a shared aim for the sake of the good of community. I have known groups that seek out a choiceworthy goal so that their members can realize it through common action; the aims of such groups go beyond what is chosen as their goal to the fostering of communal relationships among their numbers. Their search for a suitable end that can be shared among them and realized in common action is made intelligible by the status of community as such as a basic good.

And there are, it seems to me, reasons to take friendship and community to be aspects of human flourishing. If a human's brain were to malfunction such that he or she would be unable to participate in friendship, unable to make or to be friends with another, that would count as a serious malfunction, regardless of what other difficulties would be brought about thereby. And, more generally, if one were unable to engage in cooperative action, sharing aims with others, that too would be on its own a quite serious deficiency in human functioning, regardless of what other capacities that person still enjoyed. Thus, in addition to the grounds we have for holding friendship and community to be basic goods and fundamental reasons for action, there is reason to believe that they are both aspects of the human creature's flourishing.

Religion

Religion is a fundamental reason for action. When one acts a certain way for religious reasons, that action may be immediately intelligible.

The good of religion is that good consisting of being in harmony with the more-than-human order (see Grisez, Finnis, and Boyle 1987, p. 108), those aspects of the ways things are that transcend the world of human making, doing, and acting. It seems, though, that the possibility of religion as an aspect of human fulfillment depends, as the name itself might suggest, on the possibility of there being some transcendent intelligent being, not simply an unintelligent cosmos governed by immutable laws of nature. For what could constitute this harmony without some intelligent being? It could not consist in the conformity of human action with those laws of nature: such conformity is guaranteed by the concept of a law of nature (at least in a world without any transcendent intelligent being), for if one performs an act of ϕ-ing, it must not be contrary to a law of nature for one to ϕ. One might claim that even without a transcendent intelligence, one could affirm the existence of a good in the conformity of human willing with those laws of nature, though: for it is possible for one to will to ϕ even while the laws of nature preclude ϕ-ing. But this conformity between human willing and laws of nature seems not to be a distinct good but, rather, just a facet of the good of excellence in agency: after all, it is part of reasonable choosing that one not intend any action that cannot in fact be done. Thus it seems to me that if there is to be such a good as that of harmony between oneself and the more-than-human order, the other term of the harmony relationship must be the sort of being that can be called, whether univocally or analogically, *personal.*

Some might worry about positing as a self-evident basic good something that could not be recognized as such by one who denies the existence of a divine personal being. Finnis worries about this, and notes in reply that it is at least "peculiarly important to have thought reasonably and (where possible) correctly about these questions about the origins of the cosmic order . . . whatever the answer to those questions turns out to be, and even if the answers have to be agnostic or negative" (1980, p. 89). To which Russell Hittinger has responded that this is to transform the good of religion into merely another instance of the good of knowledge (1987, p. 148). But as Finnis goes on to write:

And does not that importance in large part consist in this: that if there is a transcendent origin of the universal order-of-things and of human freedom and reason, then one's life and actions are in fundamental disorder if they are not brought, as best as one can, into some sort of harmony with whatever can be known or surmised about that transcendent other and its lasting order? (1980, pp. 89–90)

Finnis's point is not merely that seeking knowledge of whether there is any divine being is intelligible as an aspect of the good of knowledge (although that is, of course, true on Finnis's view). Rather, his point is that we recognize a *further* intelligibility to seeking information about the existence of a god: that seeking knowledge about the existence of a divine being is also made intelligible by the aim of bringing our wills into harmony with its will, if it turns out that there is such a being. And if seeking knowledge of a god is made intelligible in this way, we must be presupposing that conformity with the will of such a being is a good thing, that religion is itself a basic good.

Indeed, one should not be bothered, in any case, by the fact that one who denies the existence of any divine intelligence will deny the status of religion as a good. Because the human goods are possibilities for human fulfillment, one's recognition of them as goods will depend on one's recognition of them as genuine possibilities. This holds in the case of other basic goods just as surely as it does in the case of the good of religion. If one is a radical epistemic skeptic, claiming that the attainment of knowledge is an impossibility, one may have a difficult time affirming the good of knowledge. If one is an unqualified skeptic with regard to practical reasonableness, one will have a difficult time affirming the good of excellence in agency. Thus, there is nothing special about its being the case that recognition of the basic good of religion requires an openness to the possibility that there is some intelligent more-than-human being.

The status of religion as a basic good might be called into doubt, though, not by questioning the existence of a superior will with which to align our own but, rather, by questioning whether the alignment of our own wills with this superior will is intrinsically rather than instrumentally good. Perhaps, one might object, the tendency to seek out conformity with the will of some divine person or persons can be explained in instrumental terms: we seek the favor of the gods for the benefits to be gained from such conformity, whether in worldly gains (victory in battle, success of the crops) or otherworldly blessings (eternal beatitude). No one denies that people seek the state of affairs that I call the good of religion for further purposes. The question remains, though, whether this conformity can, as such, give point to action. It would strike me as peculiar, though, to hold that it would not be intrinsically good to conform one's will to the will of the divine, given the tight similarity between the good of religion as I have described it and the goods of friendship and community. If being in community with other humans – aiming at and pursuing ends in common with others – is conceded to be intrinsically good, then it seems that being in similar community with a divine being would be intrinsically good as well. If it is good for one to be in a relationship of community with other human beings, how could it fail to be good for one to be in such a relationship with a divine being?

It should go without saying that not all of the religious observances practiced by human agents will constitute participation in the good of religion. Because to participate in the good of religion is to conform one's will to that of some transcendent being or beings, and because the existence and identity of this being or beings (not to mention what is in fact willed by it or them) is not evident to all, it will, of course, be possible for one to think that one is participating in the good of religion when one is in fact not. Once again, this state of affairs is not unusual with regard to the basic goods: agents often think, for example, that they are enjoying the good of knowledge when they are in fact not.

The theoretical argument that religion is an aspect of human flourishing must, of course, have the same conditional form that the account of religion as a basic good has. Suppose that there is some sort of transcendent being, a being that is personal, and that can have intentions about matters regarding which humans might have intentions. Given this supposition, it seems that a person who was incapable of governing his or her intentions sufficiently to bring them into line with the will of this transcendent being would be experiencing a severe malfunction indeed, regardless of how well he or she was otherwise functioning. Thus, we may say that to enter into conformity with the will of the divine, if there be such a thing, is a human function, an aspect of human flourishing.

Happiness

Happiness is a fundamental reason for action. When one acts for the sake of happiness, that action may be immediately intelligible.

By 'happiness' I mean the successful achievement of a reasonable life plan. As I employ the notion of happiness, it has something in common with Aristotle's notion of *eudaimonia* and Aquinas's notion of *beatitudo,* on one hand, and with Rawls's notion of a life plan, on the other. What happiness shares with all three of these concepts is its capacity to structure goods aimed at in one's life and thereby provide a framework for choice in pursuit of those goods. With Aristotle and Aquinas, the goods the structured participation in which are the content of happiness are specifiable independently of one's particular desires; these objective goods are, for reasonable agents, the material of happiness. Thus, on this point, the conception of happiness that I am employing differs from that of a Rawlsian life plan, the content of which is given by one's informed desires. (For the rejection of subjectivism about goods, see Chapter 2.) Against Aristotle and Aquinas, though, happiness as conceived here does not have a definite structure prior to choice: the grasp of goods by practical reason does not itself place those goods into a particular hierarchical framework. (For a discussion of the possibility of a hierarchical ordering among the basic goods, see 5.4.) Thus, this notion of happiness has some kinship with the more subjectivist life-plan idea, where the goods involved in happiness are structured by one's commitments. An agent may commit his or her life primarily to one of the goods, or some combination of them, without violating any natural hierarchy among the basic goods.

Note that this notion of happiness might be considered to be, in effect, another nod to subjectivist theories of well-being: on this view, the structure of happiness is posterior to choice and commitment, not prior to it. While granting that the content of an agent's happiness is subjective in that it is up to that agent to formulate a coherent structure to regulate the pursuit of goods within her or his own life, it is nevertheless important to realize the limited nature of the subjectivism involved in happiness as described here. First, while the structure of happiness is up to the agent, the material that the agent has to work with is not: it is the nine basic goods. Secondly, it would be false to identify happiness as described here with well-being. The reason for this is that there are things that can make one well off other than happiness. Even if a person's commitments are primarily to (e.g.) the good of truth, he or she is still made well off to the extent that he or she participates in the good of life, friendship, play, etc., and is made correspondingly worse off when deprived of these goods.

It is important not to be misled by either a reductionist or a unificationist view of the nature of happiness and its relationship to other goods. On a reductionist view of happiness, the goodness of happiness is reducible to the goodness of the goods that are the material of happiness. On a unificationist view of happiness, the goodness of the goods that are the material of happiness is solely the result of their contributing to the good of happiness. Both of these are, on my view, errors. The reductionist picture fails to see the importance of how the discrete goods in one's life are structured; the importance of this structure is, of course, overlooked if one focuses merely on the goods that are the content of one's conception of happiness. The unificationist picture fails by allowing happiness to swallow the other goods whole, as it were, leaving them with no choiceworthiness or reason-giving force of their own. Thus, it must deny that other goods give one reasons for action, even if they don't contribute to one's happiness; and it must also deny that even a good that contributes to happiness has any force considered apart from its place in one's life plan. (These errors are clearly avoided by Aristotle: as he remarks, there are things that we choose for themselves, even apart from their contribution to eudaimonia [*Nicomachean Ethics*, 1097b2–3]. While eudaimonia structures the goods, the reason-giving character of those goods does not derive wholly from their place in eudaimonia.)

With regard to the grounding of the good of happiness in human nature, it is worthwhile to ask what we would think of the capacity to function of one who, while able to structure commitments to specific goods in a particular way, was incapable of participating in those goods in that way. This does seem like a serious malfunction: even if one is capable of participating in goods, the inability to enjoy them structured in a certain way seems a decided shortcoming in one's functioning. Thus, we must add that, in addition to the various goods that are human functions, the capacity to enjoy them according to a certain worked-out conception of how they are to be ordered in one's own life is a human good.

3.4 Inner Peace, Happiness, and the Hybrid View of the Nature of Well-Being

Having completed our sketch of the nine basic goods, let us return to a question that was left open near the end of Chapter 2 (2.5). After the refutation of both strong and weak subjectivism, I considered whether we had yet discovered any grounds for rejecting a hybrid view on the nature of well-being, that is, a view on which there are some true claims of the form 'x is an aspect of A's well-being' that have as part of their truth conditions some subjective state of A's toward x, but on which not all true claims of that form include A's having some subjective state toward x among their truth conditions. I suggested two grounds that might be put forward for accepting the hybrid view: first, that it is better able to account for our intuitions about states of affairs that are included in an agent's welfare, and secondly, that it is better able to explain individual differences between agents' welfare profiles. Since we now have before us this natural law account's substantive view of well-being, we are in position to say something about the capacity of a formally objectivist theory to meet these desiderata.

With respect to the former desideratum, I can offer no defense other than the sheer breadth of the account of well-being that this natural law theory offers.

Since the hybrid view holds that some claims of the form 'x is an aspect of A's well-being' have A's subjective state toward x among their truth conditions while others do not, the charge of incompleteness is easiest to make if one supposes that there are very few goods that can be established as such without appeal to the agent's subjective states; in such a case, the need for supplementation of a formally objectivist view by adding a disjunctive subjective clause might be felt intensely. But if the natural law view is correct to hold that a large number of aspects of well-being can be affirmed in a non–ad hoc way without appeal to a subjectivist truth-maker, then the motivation to accept a hybrid view is much less pressing.

Even if the natural law view can explain how a variety of human aims could be aspects of well-being, it is not clear how it is to explain how agents' differing preferences, choices, and commitments make a difference in their individual welfare profiles. Indeed, there is a sense in which the natural law view cannot allow for differences in individual welfare profiles: for since human nature determines the content of well-being, and human nature is the same for all humans, then the content of well-being is the same for all humans. But since the substantive account of welfare offered by the natural law theorist is mixed rather than objectivist, it includes some goods the content of which implicates desire, choice, and commitment – namely, the goods of inner peace and happiness. While inner peace is the same for all agents – not having unsatisfied desires – what must happen for agents to enjoy the good of inner peace will differ among agents due to their different desire structures. While happiness is the same for all agents – the successful achievement of a reasonable life plan – the fact that agents can reasonably commit themselves to different life plans will ensure that what must obtain for happiness to be achieved will differ from agent to agent. While the formal objectivist view defended by the natural law theorist commits him or her to the view that there is a clear sense in which well-being is the same for all humans, his or her affirmation of this specific account of the content of welfare allows for individual differences without at all adverting to the hybrid view.

Now, one might hold that this understanding of differences in individual welfare profiles is insufficiently robust. But it seems to me that once we have provided this understanding of individual welfare profiles, it is up to the objector to explain why this understanding is too weak. Consider the following analogy. It does seem to be an important criterion for the adequacy of a conception of moral norms that it allow that there be differences in individuals' 'moral requirement profiles,' that is, in what individual agents are morally required to do. This seems true: I am bound to render certain services to Georgetown University; you (likely) are not. One might explain this situation by claiming that it is an objective truth, not dependent on any agent's desires, choices, preferences, etc., that those who freely enter into a fair agreement to ϕ are morally bound to ϕ; and thus, since I have freely entered into such an agreement with George-

town University that you have not, I am under moral requirements to Georgetown that you are not.

It seems to me that if it were complained that this isn't a satisfactory explanation of individual differences in moral requirements because it rests on the
supposition that, deeply, it is the same moral norms that apply to all of us, this
complaint would be wholly without merit. Now, one might say: morality is not
welfare, and welfare might have to respond more deeply to individual differences than morality does. This is the argument that I am looking for; until I see
it worked out, I cannot see how the hybrid view has any clear advantage over
the natural law theory's substantive mixed view in dealing with individual differences in well-being.

3.5 The Real Identity Thesis Revisited

The natural law theorist claims that the basic goods are grounded in human nature. The interpretation of this claim that I have offered is the real identity thesis, according to which, states of affairs of the form 'x is a good worth having'
are identical to states of affairs of the form 'x is an aspect of human flourishing' (1.1). In 1.4 I indicated what sorts of evidence would count in favor of this
thesis. I noted that it has the theoretical benefit of unifying power: it enables the
natural law theorist to affirm a tight connection between the normative and nonnormative orders; and as we saw in 2.5, it allows the natural law theorist to cir-
cumvent Mackie's queerness objection. Moreover, the identification of aspects
of flourishing with goods worth having avoids a great deal of the implausibility that often attends cross-category reductions: I have made no claim that the
practical is in any way *conceptually* reducible to the nonpractical, and the identification of goods worth having and aspects of flourishing is entirely within the
category of states of affairs that are irreducibly evaluative (1.4). Further, aspects
of flourishing and goods worth having display similar structural features.

What remained to be argued at the end of 1.4 was an identity in content –
that those states of affairs that we take, on reflection, to be goods worth having
are just those states of affairs that we take, on reflection, to be aspects of human flourishing. How much have we added to the argument for the real identity thesis by the consideration of the human goods in this chapter?

For each of the nine basic goods I have tried to explain, if only sketchily,
what states of affairs are participations in these goods. I have argued that we do
recognize these states of affairs as making us better off, and that there are theoretical considerations in favor of affirming their status as aspects of human
flourishing. For most of them – knowledge, aesthetic experience, excellence in
play and work, excellence in agency, friendship and community, religion, and
happiness – I have held that the method of knowing aspects of flourishing described in 1.3, which appeals to our grasp of what counts as serious malfunctions, suggests that they are aspects of flourishing. For two of the goods – in-

ner peace and life – I have conceded that I cannot show that they are aspects of flourishing using the method in 1.3, but have maintained that it is not inconsistent to hold them to be aspects of flourishing. Given the generally tight correspondence in content between the basic goods and aspects of flourishing, and the other reasons in support of the real identity thesis laid out in 1.4, I thus conclude that the real identity thesis is correct. Natural law is grounded in human nature.

4

Welfarism and Its Discontents

4.1 Welfarism in the Theory of Practical Rationality

The natural law theory of practical rationality holds that the fundamental reasons for action are the basic goods; it also holds that these basic goods are aspects of agents' well-being. The natural law view is therefore a welfarist conception of practical rationality: it holds that all reasonable action is ultimately grounded in well-being, that rational action is action that constitutes an appropriate response to agents' welfare. Or, as Andrew Moore and Roger Crisp have more precisely put it (*mutatis mutandis,* for they are concerned with welfarism in moral theory and not in the theory of practical rationality generally), the welfarist view is the conjunction of three theses: the existence thesis, that "there is such a good or value as individual well-being"; the significance thesis, that "some individual well-being has [practical] significance, qua individual well-being"; and the exclusiveness thesis, that "individual well-being is the only good or value which has basic [practical] significance" (Moore and Crisp 1996, p. 598). Whatever one thinks about the particular account of the existence and significance of well-being defended in the first three chapters, it should be conceded that the main worries about welfarism in the theory of practical rationality are not about the existence or significance of well-being but about the exclusiveness of that theory's focus on welfare: the worry is that a welfarist theory will inevitably be incomplete, and thus, any adequate theory of practical rationality will have to hold that items aside from aspects of well-being are of fundamental practical significance.

This charge of incompleteness is serious but answerable. In the main, the appearance that welfarist theories of practical rationality are inevitably incomplete arises from a single source: the failure to appreciate the breadth allowed by welfarism's claim that rational action is action that responds *appropriately* to agents' welfare. That welfarism must be an incomplete theory of practical rationality is an appearance that is generated by associating the welfarist thesis with some distinct thesis about how, in particular, it is appropriate to respond to agents' well-being. Having thus narrowed the welfarist thesis, constricting *ab initio* its capacity to account for the intelligibility of certain types of clearly intelligible conduct, the objector can plausibly claim that welfarism is as such an untenable type of theory of practical reasonableness. But once we sever welfarism's entangling alliances with other theses about practical rationality, the charge of inevitable incompleteness becomes far more difficult to sustain. Whether welfarism turns out to be incomplete will, thus, turn out to depend on whether the best welfarist system of practical reasonableness, once worked out, will be sufficiently robust.

4.2 Welfarism Does Not Imply Egoism

In casting about for a way to defend welfarism in moral theory, Sumner dismisses the possibility that it can be defended as an implication of welfarism in the theory of practical rationality. He writes:

If welfarism [in moral theory] cannot be supported by psychology, it is tempting to turn to practical reason. The argument might run as follows: while welfare is not the only thing that people are capable of seeking for its own sake, it is the only thing which it is rational for them to seek, and therefore it is the only rational basis for ethics. The problem is that the premiss of this argument is blatantly false. (1996, p. 188)

The premise of the argument – that welfare is the only thing that it is rational for agents to promote – is blatantly false because, says Sumner, to affirm that premise is to affirm a self-interest theory of practical rationality, a theory that "requires individuals to maximize their own welfare" (1996, p. 188). Since welfarism in the theory of practical reasoning entails the self-interest theory of rationality, and the self-interest theory of rationality is blatantly false, then welfarism in the theory of practical rationality must also be false. But it is hard to see why Sumner thinks that the thesis that welfarism is the correct type of account of practical rationality implies the truth of the self-interest theory of rationality. For, after all, the welfarist view as such says only that well-being is the ultimate source of reasons for action; it does not as such put forward the additional thesis that the only subject whose well-being is relevant is the agent that is trying to decide what to do. It is compatible with the welfarist thesis – which is not to say that all welfarists need affirm it – to hold that practical reason requires the maximization of the overall well-being of all welfare subjects, not merely that of the agent. Indeed, it is hard to know why Sumner would think that welfarism in practical rationality would bring in its wake an egoistic conception of practical rationality, given his own view that all welfare reasons are agent-neutral: a subject's well-being is a reason for all agents to act, not merely a reason for the subject whose well-being it is (Sumner 1996, p. 185; see 2.2 for a discussion of agent-relativity).

Now, one might retort: just because Sumner thinks that welfare reasons are agent-neutral, that does not mean that they are; it could be the case that the best welfarist conception of practical rationality would hold that welfare reasons are agent-relative. If welfare reasons are without exception agent-relative, then the claim that the only basic reasons for action are aspects of well-being would seem to commit one to a self-interest conception of rationality. And, one might add, there is at least some reason to think that affirmation of a welfarist conception of the basic goods exerts pressure toward the affirmation of an agent-relativist stance on the nature of the reasons for action: since the goods that are the fundamental reasons for action are such in virtue of an agent-relative description – these states of affairs are of fundamental practical relevance because they are good *for some agent* – it seems reasonable to hold that the fundamental reasons for action are such in virtue of an agent-relative description as well. (See, for a view that suggests an argument akin to this one, Rasmussen 1999, pp. 3–10.)

This argument is, however, far from decisive in favor of the claim that aspects of well-being generate only agent-relative reasons for action. I will consider it in more detail in Chapter 5 (5.3): I will argue there that the natural law theorist should affirm that while aspects of well-being do generate agent-relative reasons for action, they also generate agent-neutral reasons, and so there does not exist the quick route from the claim that the basic goods are agent-relative to the claim that egoism is mandated by a welfarist conception of practical rationality. The welfarist natural law view I defend rejects the self-interest theory of rationality: egoism is not one of the discontents of welfarism.

Before we turn to another of welfarism's alleged discontents, it is worth considering an argument that Sumner employs against the self-interest theory that is capable of being transformed into a genuinely independent argument against welfarism:

That the self-interest theory is in any case false is easy to see from our response to someone who knowingly makes himself worse off in pursuit of some rival category of value: the ethical, perhaps, or aesthetic, or perfectionist. We do not normally regard such persons as irrational, or even unreasonable. (1996, p. 188)

We can transform this into an argument against welfarism that is independent of the implausible essential connection between welfarism and the self-interest theory by eliminating self-interest as the middle term: we might say, that is, that there may be other types of value besides the prudential to which an agent might reasonably respond – the ethical, perfectionist, or aesthetic. If so, then the welfarist view would be incomplete, not by restricting the scope of practical rationality to what benefits the agent but by restricting the scope of practical rationality to but one of a number of types of value.

To rebut the charge of incompleteness supported by this modified argument, we would need to make a case that, insofar as these other types of value give reasons for action, it is in virtue of their relationship to well-being. If morality is a matter of practical reason, which I will argue in Chapter 6 (6.1–6.2), and correct practical reasoning is welfarist, then we will have eliminated any tension between the fact that we regard pursuit of ethical value as reasonable and the claim that considerations of well-being are the only fundamental reasons for action. If prudential value and perfectionist value are one, as the real identity thesis claims (1.2, 2.5, 3.4), then the reasonableness of the pursuit of perfectionist value will be secure. Aesthetic value is not so easy to deal with, inasmuch as Sumner understands aesthetic value here not in terms of the value of experiencing the beautiful but, rather, in terms of the value of one's life itself being an aesthetic object (1996, pp. 21–23). If Sumner had the former in mind, then we could account for the reasonableness of pursuit of aesthetic value in terms of the good of aesthetic experience as it appears in the natural law theorist's substantive account of well-being (3.3). Even though the latter is less easy to deal with in terms of the account of well-being offered in the first three chapters, it does not strike me as implausible to hold that insofar as having a life that is high in aesthetic value in this sense is genuinely something that it is reasonable to strive for, its value derives from welfare considerations, perhaps from the good of excellence in agency realized in creatively ordering one's pursuits in a free and reasonable way.

To answer the charge that a welfarist theory of practical reasonableness must be too narrow because it is unable to accommodate the reasonableness of responding to ethical, perfectionist, or aesthetic value is not, of course, to show that a welfarist theory will be able to handle all of the types of value that our intuitions might urge us to accommodate. But it is worth keeping in mind that the very breadth of this natural law theory's substantive account of well-being seems likely to insulate it to some extent against this objection; a welfarist theory of practical rationality grounded in a thinner theory of well-being, like those of the classical utilitarians or even of Sumner himself (1996, pp. 171–183), would be easier to call into question by the invocation of this sort of incompleteness.

4.3 Welfarism Does Not Imply a Maximizing Theory of Rationality

Another type of incompleteness to which a welfarist theory of practical reasonableness is alleged to be susceptible has been emphasized by Sen (1982b, p. 363) and again recently discussed by Moore and Crisp (1996, pp. 611–612). The worry is that welfarist theories of practical rationality do not recognize the goodness of states like justice, fairness, and equality, and thus cannot provide an adequate account of the reasonableness of promoting these states of affairs. Moore and Crisp have us imagine two worlds that are identical in terms of the levels of well-being displayed, but in one (and only one) of those worlds, those who are worse off have a lower level of well-being through no fault of their own, perhaps even as a result of coercion (1996, p. 611). If, as one might be tempted to say, one of these worlds is worse than the other, then it must be on account of something besides the well-being of the inhabitants of those worlds. And if something besides the well-being of the inhabitants of those worlds makes one of the worlds worse than the other, then we must conclude that there is something apart from well-being that is of fundamental practical significance.

Moore and Crisp offer a response on behalf of the welfarist with which I am in agreement, as is clear from the general strategy articulated in 4.1: they argue that the welfarist can explain the reasonableness of promoting (e.g.) fairness without introducing nonwelfare goods by distinguishing between basic goods (what Moore and Crisp call "values") and what constitutes a reasonable response to those basic goods (what Moore and Crisp call – a bit misleadingly, in my view – "reasons"). Thus, they argue, the point of promoting fairness can be made simply by reference to well-being itself, as promotion of fairness is an appropriate response to well-being. And even if there are some lingering worries that the welfarist view is incomplete because unable to provide an account of the independent value of these states of affairs, the welfarist can take solace in the fact that one who harbors such worries is, in any case, not the typical defender of the ideals of fairness, justice, or equality.

Egalitarians, for example, do not typically assert that equality is a good, in the sense that the objector wants to say that it is a good but, rather, that a state of affairs in which persons are equal is the result of a proper response to the nature of what is basically of value – perhaps persons. Thus, to summarize briefly an egalitarian position: because persons are what is basically valuable, and they are equal with respect to their personhood (or sentience, or status as images of God . . .), the only rational response to persons is to act in such a way that their condition is equalized. This seems to me to capture the characteristic egalitarian stand on the value of equality: its importance resides in the way that it constitutes a peculiarly appropriate rational response to what is basically of value; its importance does not reside in the state of affairs itself as a basic value. And, further, the welfarist has a ready account of why there might be these lingering worries about the essential incapacity of welfarism to assert that (e.g.) justice has, as such, fundamental practical significance, that is, that its pursuit is a reasonable response to the nature of the basic goods, which are aspects of well-being. It is the appropriateness of this response that leads people to think, naturally yet nonetheless mistakenly, that justice is of independent value.

Now, the ease with which the welfarist wields this response might lead one to wonder whether something of the force of the objector's criticism has been missed: even conceding the legitimacy and importance of the distinction between goods and reasonable response to goods, perhaps there is some thesis essential to a welfarist conception of practical rationality that, in fact, rules out the possibility of a satisfactory welfarist account of justice (etc.) as an appropriate response to the nature of the basic goods. Why might one be tempted to hold that the welfarist is unable to account for the import of justice, fairness, and equality?

What generates this appearance is, in my view, the conjunction of welfarism with a maximizing theory of rationality – the idea, that is, that it is not only true that the only item of basic practical significance is well-being, but also that the only possible reasonable response to well-being is that of maximization, of producing as much of it as possible. The conjunction of welfarism with a maximizing conception of rationality – along with the assumption that welfare reasons are, as Sumner thinks, agent-neutral – yields a utilitarian theory of practical reasonableness, as I will argue in greater detail in Chapter 5 (5.2). The reason that it has been thought that *welfarism* cannot provide an account of the reasonableness of promoting justice, fairness, and equality is, I think, that it is thought that *utilitarianism* cannot provide an adequate account of the reasonableness of the promotion of these states: as every introductory ethics text notes, there is at least an apparent tension between the utilitarian notion of maximization and the ideals of justice, fairness, and equality, which ideals do not seem readily explicable in maximizing terms. Once the thesis that practical rationality is maximization is conjoined with the welfarist thesis, then the discontents of utilitarianism become the discontents of welfarism. And if one remains committed to this maximizing picture and to the view that a utilitarian conception of practical reasonableness cannot adequately account for the reasonableness of justice, fairness, etc., the only other option is to give up unqualified welfarism.

Consider, as an example of this sort of maneuver, the strategy offered by Scanlon on consequentialism's behalf against Rawls's criticisms of utilitarianism (Scanlon 1973). In *A Theory of Justice,* Rawls complains against utilitarian theories that they imply that the life prospects of the worst-off are to be sacrificed if such a sacrifice would produce greater overall good according to utilitarian calculations; in place of utilitarianism as a theory of how the basic structure of society ought to be organized, Rawls offers two principles of justice, which have among their conditions that the life prospects of the worst-off members of society be maximized. Now, Scanlon showed that a consequentialist who accepts a maximizing conception of practical reasonableness could formulate a theory of the good that, in conjunction with the maximizing conception, would mimic the requirements of Rawls's two principles. Suppose that one were to offer an account of the good that is, to use Scheffler's phrase, "distribution-sensitive": "its rankings of states of affairs . . . are directly affected by the ways in which benefits and burdens are distributed within those states of affairs" (Scheffler 1994, pp. 29–30). According to Scanlon's particular distribution-sensitive account of the good, the better state of affairs is the one in which the position of the worst-off group is maximized; if two states of affairs are equal with respect to the position of the worst off, the better of the two will be a state of affairs in which there are fewer in this position (given the constancy of the population in these two states of affairs); if two states of affairs are equal with regard to the position and number of the worst-off, the better of the two is the one in which the position of the second-worst-off group is maximized; and so forth.

A consequentialist account with this theory of the good would mimic the distribution resulting from Rawls's theory. It is thus clear, a consequentialist might say, that modifying utilitarianism's account of the good while adhering to the consequentialist conception of practical rationality as maximization can enable the consequentialist to avoid charges that his or her view must inevitably sanction injustice. There is, of course, nothing about this strategy that is restricted to justice; it could be used to explain the reasonableness of promoting fairness, equality, or any other state of affairs that seems to be insusceptible to full explanation in utilitarian terms. And there is nothing that requires the consequentialist to give such an absolutely central place to these goods: rather, he or she could make them simply goods among others (see also Kagan 1989, pp. 6–7).

Now, as I will argue in Chapter 5 (5.3), the variety of goodness to which this nonwelfarist consequentialist appeals here is obscure, and so I doubt that this way of providing an account of the reasonableness of promoting justice (etc.) is a satisfactory one for a chastened utilitarian to affirm.[1] But my main point is not to criticize the nonutilitarian consequentialist for taking this route, but to note that the motivation behind this maneuver derives not from a difficulty that is shown to arise from welfarism as such but from a difficulty that is thought to arise from welfarism conjoined with a maximizing theory of rationality. Suppose that one is a utilitarian and considers to be failures utilitarian attempts to deal with justice and equality, such as the attempts that appear in Mill's *Utilitarianism* (pp. 41–63), or in Sidgwick's *Methods of Ethics* (pp. 439–448), or in Hare's *Moral Thinking* (1981, pp. 147–168). One can at this point give up either utilitarianism's welfarism or its maximizing conception of rationality. The movement of utilitarianism from a theory of morality with a distinctive account of the good into a consequentialist conception that refrains from affirming any such account makes clear that the overwhelming preference has been to cling to the notion of rationality as maximization. But one could, of course, reaffirm welfarism and reject the notion that the appropriate response to well-being is that of maximization. If one rejects maximization as the peculiarly appropriate response to well-being, then one preserves some room for the welfarist to provide an account on which aspects of well-being are such that they call for justice-, fairness-, or equality-promoting responses.

One might be suspicious of this response, finding it hard to see how there could be a welfarist conception of practical rationality that really is able to provide an account of the reasonableness of these types of responses. These suspicions could be grounded in one or another of the following thoughts: that even if welfarism does not logically imply maximization, it is obvious that a welfarist theory will be a maximizing view; or that if a welfarist theory is not a maximizing theory, it will be terrifically unhelpful, unable to give important practical guidance; or that even if a nonmaximizing welfare theory is able to give important practical guidance, it is not likely to be able to provide accounts of justice and equality. The latter two of these worries cannot be answered except by providing positive accounts both of the nature of the welfare reasons upon which the natural law theorist relies and of how the most promising account of the justification of practical principles yields, together with an account of the nature of those reasons, a set of principles that is both nonmaximizing yet still helpful; I provide these accounts in Chapter 5 (5.1, 5.3, 5.5). But I want to say a few words here about the notion that welfarism is deeply connected to a maximizing theory of rationality. This just seems false.

Welfarism says nothing about maximizing; so it can hardly be a logical implication of welfarism that the best account of practical rationality is a maximizing view. Perhaps welfarism is so tightly connected with maximization just in virtue of the self-evidence of maximization as a practical strategy: any theory of practical rationality, including welfarism, must affirm maximization or else will be doomed to obvious falsehood. But this obviousness claim again seems false. Maximization is not at all an obviously correct strategy. First, it only fits with a theory of fundamental reasons for action in which the fundamental reasons for action are producible ends, ends that can be brought about by action; but since there are comprehensible theories of the fundamental reasons for action – namely, Kantian views (5.2) – that reject the notion that the fundamental reasons for action are producible ends, it cannot be that the maximizing strategy is a part of every live option in the theory of practical reasonableness. Secondly, if maximization is the way to go in the theory of practical reasonableness – assuming for the moment that we are restricting our consideration to those theories that take the fundamental reasons for action to be producible ends – it will be in virtue of those reasons themselves; there will be something about them that makes maximization the appropriate strategy to follow with respect to them.

As I will argue in more detail, it is surely true that one of the features of reasons that would make them candidates for a maximizing strategy would be their commensurability as reasons. But, again, commensurability is not uncontroversial; and, indeed, the natural law theory of practical reasonableness that I will defend rejects in a wholesale way the commensurability of distinct goods (5.3). There is nothing, then, that should lead us to believe that a welfarist conception of practical reasonableness is inevitably a maximizing view. The discontents of utilitarianism are not ipso facto the discontents of welfarism.

None of this shows, of course, that the other suspicions about a welfarist view that is not a maximizing theory – that is, that it will be unhelpful or will still fall short of dealing satisfactorily with justice, equality, etc. – will not turn out to be correct. Whether they will turn out to be correct will depend on the merits of welfarist but anti-utilitarian theories of practical rationality, such as that articulated in Chapters 5 and 6, and not from any illicit linkage between a welfarist theory of the good and a maximizing theory of the right.

4.4 Welfarism Does Not Imply Promotionism

There is yet a third way that the welfarist thesis that the only items of basic practical significance are aspects of agents' well-being might be thought inevitably to result in incompleteness. The difficulty concerns the incapacity of welfarist views to deal with 'backward-looking' actions, such as actions performed as a result of commitment, or on the basis of considerations of gratitude or retribution. (While gratitude is itself, strictly speaking, a retributive notion, I reserve the term 'act of retribution' only for acts of harming.) It appears that welfarism lacks the resources to explain the intelligibility of acts of this sort, for there is a fundamental tension between the essentially forward-looking character of reasons for action recognized by the welfarist and the essentially backward-looking character of the rationales for actions performed as a result of commitment, gratitude, or retribution. Adherence to the claim that the only reasons for action are aspects of well-being to be promoted renders impossible the task of adequately accounting for the intelligibility of actions of this sort.

Consider, first, the difficulty that the welfarist will have in accounting for the intelligibility of acting out of commitment. By 'commitment' here I do not understand anything like a promise, or contract: I do not mean the performance of some act that, by virtue of the constitutive rules of some institution or social practice, results in an obligation by the agent that performs the act (cf. Rawls 1971, pp. 344–348). Rather, by 'commitment' I mean a decision made by the agent to perform some act at some future time. On occasion, agents have sufficient grounds to form commitments; there may be goods that they wish to promote that cannot be promoted, or cannot be promoted as well, unless they were to undertake that commitment. Now, there are occasions on which agents act out of commitment: they perform actions the rationale of which is that they had previously committed themselves to perform them. On at least some of these occasions, agents acting out of commitment would not have performed the actions in question except for that commitment. But it is not clear how the welfarist is to provide an adequate account of the intelligibility of acting out of commitment. For, one might say, on the welfarist view, reasons for action are always certain goods that can be promoted by action; but the rationale offered for performing the acts in question in these cases is something past, the decision itself.

It seems that in attempting to account for the intelligibility of keeping commitments, the welfarist can treat the commitment only as causally, not normatively, relevant to the status of the act as eligible: perhaps making the decision foreclosed other options by making it psychologically impossible for the agent to choose otherwise, or certain courses of action that would have been available for the agent had the agent not made the commitment are now not open to the agent, thus leaving this particular action as the only eligible choice; or perhaps the agent is so psychologically constructed that acting contrary to the prior decision would generate deep regret, or other sorts of psychological instability, with resultant deprivation of other goods. But this kind of response is deeply flawed: for not only are these explanations not universally true, and thus not a satisfactorily complete account of the intelligibility of acting out of commitment; the explanation still seems to be of the wrong sort, placing the rationale for keeping commitments wholly in the future and stripping the past act of commitment of any deeper normative effect.

Consider, next, gratitude and retribution. By 'gratitude' and 'retribution' here I mean certain types of acts, both of which have as part of their rationale some act or event that occurred in the past. An act of gratitude occurs only if one performs an act of benefiting another because of what that other did on some previous occasion; an act of retribution occurs only if one performs an act of harming another because of what that other did on some previous occasion. Acts of gratitude are performed only if one, acting out of gratitude, sees the other's past act in a favorable light; acts of retribution are performed only if one, acting out of retribution, sees the other's past act in an unfavorable light. Again, the difficulty concerns explaining how, if all reasons for action are aspects of well-being to be promoted, acts of retribution and gratitude – which take as their rationales some past act – could possibly be intelligible actions. It looks as though acts of gratitude and retribution could be made intelligible only by noting the tendency of those acts to promote future positive (welfare-promoting) acts or to deter future negative (welfare-diminishing) acts. But again, it seems that the intention to promote or deter seems unnecessary for the intelligibility of such actions; indeed, many would deny the title of 'gratitude' or 'retribution' to acts performed out of motives such as these.

Now, against these prima facie cases for the impossibility of reconciling a welfarist conception of practical rationality with the intelligibility of these backward-looking types of actions, it might be held that the difficulties can be resolved merely by offering a more sophisticated welfarist theory. One might appeal to the now common utilitarian distinction, suggested by Rawls (1955) and elaborated by Hare (1981), between two levels of moral thinking: the critical and the intuitive (Hare 1981, p. 25). At the intuitive level, we appeal to ordinary prima facie principles that are quite proximate to action; they are easily available, require for their application little practical thought, and so forth. Characteristically, agents will have dispositions to adhere to these prima facie principles, along with the associated moral sentiments. At the critical level, we appeal to all of the resources provided by the best theory of morality, which is, on Hare's view, preference-utilitarianism: there is no guarantee, then, that this sort of thinking will be commonly available in the course of our moral lives.

The main tasks carried out in critical thinking are two: to settle on the best set of intuitive principles to accept and affirm, and to deal with conflicts between intuitive principles.

Now, one might claim that the welfarist in the theory of practical rationality can appeal to this two-level view: practical judgment can take place at the critical level, at which all of the resources of the best welfarist theory of practical rationality are available to one, or at the intuitive level, at which we appeal to prima facie principles that would be selected in critical practical thinking. And this appeal to two levels of practical thought might be claimed to make available to the welfarist an account of the intelligibility of backward-looking acts within an essentially forward-looking scheme of practical rationality. While at the critical level of practical thought, all practical reasoning is forward looking, it does not follow from that fact alone that the set of practical principles that would be selected for use at the intuitive level would be all forward looking as well.

Critical practical thought might select, for forward-looking reasons, a set of prima facie principles that dictate the performance of certain types of action as responses to certain past acts: as responses to one's own decisions, or to others' welfare-promoting or welfare-diminishing action. In order to put oneself in a position to reap the rewards of long-term commitment, it might be reasonable to adopt a disposition to keep one's commitments; in order both to encourage others to promote well-being and to discourage them from diminishing it, it might be reasonable to adopt a disposition that would cause those that benefit others to be rewarded and those that harm others to be penalized. And if it is complained, as I complained earlier, that this account does an injustice to the motivations of those who perform these actions, it may be responded that once one has adopted these principles, the content of one's motivation does not include that one is acting for the sake of promoting well-being: for not only would this supposition be false on many occasions, it would also fail to describe accurately the intentions of those acting on considerations of commitment, gratitude, or retribution. Rather, one who adopts these principles does not think that 'one thought too many' when acting; at the intuitive level, backward-looking actions are performed simply on their backward-looking rationales.

If the welfarist theory of practical rationality aims at preserving the intelligibility of acts of this sort, though, it seems to me that the two-level approach does not succeed. I put to the side here whether intuitive and critical thinking is sufficiently separable in action to prevent the one-thought-too-many criticism from applying. Rather, the concern I have with this sort of approach is that it does not seem plausible to hold that the procedure by which principles are chosen at the critical level is sufficient to confer intelligibility on the acts performed on those principles: the fact that, at the critical level, practical reason would endorse adoption of a principle according to which (e.g.) keeping commitments is something worth doing does not suffice to make intelligible one's keeping one's commitments.

There are at least two reasons for this worry. First, I cannot see how the intelligibility of actions of this sort is to be explained by the fact that they *would be* selected at the critical level of practical thinking. Surely, if action according to intuitive principles is somehow to inherit the intelligibility present in the choosing of such principles, there has to be some real causal link present: the agent must act on those principles *because* those principles would be chosen in critical practical thinking. Since almost no one adopts principles on the basis of this sort of thinking, the most straightforward way of establishing the causal link is not available. The story would instead have to be very much like the complex – and in my view implausible – story that Sidgwick tells about the "unconsciously utilitarian" character of the morality of common sense (*Methods*, p. 453), in which an inchoate awareness of the utilitarian principle and improving knowledge of means for promoting happiness result in a movement of common morality toward the set of principles that the utilitarian would acknowledge in critical thinking.

Secondly, even if the requisite causal link were established, it seems to me that the two-level approach would still fail to make intelligible acts of this sort. As Parfit has convincingly argued, the claim that "If it is rational or right for me either to cause myself to be disposed to act in some way, or to make myself believe that this act is rational or right, this act is rational or right" is not true; "Rationality and rightness cannot be inherited in this way" (1984, p. 40). For, as Parfit notes, it could be to one's advantage to be a threat-fulfiller, one who always carries through on one's threats, even when this makes one worse off. But that does not show that, once the threatened party refuses to yield to the demand backed by the threat, it is rational for the threat-fulfiller to carry through. What makes it rational to adopt a threat-fulfilling disposition is that it is reasonable to expect others to respond in a certain way to one's being a threat-fulfiller, so that there will rarely be occasions on which one has to carry out the threat; it is not that it is always reasonable to perform the action that flows from a threat-fulfilling disposition (Parfit 1984, pp. 19–23; for a contrary view, see Gauthier 1986, pp. 184–187).

The same seems to hold true of intelligibility, as well as of rationality and morality: the fact that a disposition to act a certain way is a disposition worth having, a disposition that it makes sense to pursue or not to rid oneself of, does not show that action out of that disposition is in the least intelligible. When one acts out of such dispositions, what one is doing might in no way at all be worth doing. Even if there is, then, in welfarist terms some point to the adoption of backward-looking principles of conduct, that would not in itself make action from those principles intelligible. If (e.g.) one adopts a retributive disposition in order to discourage others from acting in a certain way, that does not mean that once others act in that way, it follows that one acts intelligibly in acting retributively. It could be that in acting retributively, one is acting unintelligibly, for no reason at all.

There are, of course, certain extra premises that can be added that would make acting on such principles intelligible. If it is assumed that adopting these principles involves having a certain fundamental desire to act on them, and that it is sufficient for the existence of a reason to act in a certain way that one has a basic desire to act that way, then the adoption of a principle would guarantee the intelligibility of acting on it – not from any inheritance of intelligibility from the critical level, but just from what it is to adopt a principle and what is sufficient for having a reason. But we have rejected the view that having a desire is sufficient for having a reason (2.4, 2.5), and so we still lack an account in welfarist terms of the intelligibility of backward-looking action. I would offer a similar response to those like Mackie (1982), who would account for retribution and gratitude as acts arising from emotional responses selected in evolution. This would not on its own be enough to make these acts a whit more practically intelligible.

It seems to me, then, that the welfarist's appeal to a two-level view does not show that acting out of commitment, retribution, or gratitude is even minimally rational. Now, one might reply: surely it is no objection to a theory of practical rationality that it implies that sometimes it is rational to place oneself in a position such that one will act irrationally, or that one might have a reason to place oneself in a position such that one will act for no reason at all. This seems to be true. What is more worrisome, though, is to hold that this is the strategy that must be employed to find some place for an entire class of extraordinarily familiar actions, that is, backward-looking actions. From the discussion thus far, it appears that there is not a single instance of a backward-looking action the intelligibility of which can be accounted for on a forward-looking welfarist conception of practical rationality, even when the more sophisticated two-level approach is employed. The best that can be gotten from the welfarist view with respect to such actions is intelligible unintelligibility; we have not yet produced any account by which the welfarist can hold that backward-looking action is itself intelligible.

What, then, is the welfarist to do? Should the welfarist concede that the inability to handle backward-looking reasons is one of the discontents of welfarism, but that this shortcoming is acceptable in the context of welfarism's many strengths? No: there is nothing that forces welfarism to this concession, for there is nothing in welfarism's thesis that only well-being is of fundamental practical significance that precludes the welfarist from providing a more satisfactory account of the intelligibility of backward-looking action.

Consider, first, action performed out of commitment, the intelligibility of which seems to be explicable in welfarist terms, even without challenging the notion that welfarism is an essentially forward-looking conception of practical rationality. (Keep in mind that I am not here arguing that commitments generate rational requirements, in the sense that it is never reasonable to act contrary to an earlier commitment, or that it is never reasonable to act contrary to a reasonably made commitment, or even that there is a strong prima facie requirement in favor of acting in accordance with reasonably made commitments. All that I am arguing here is that keeping commitments is intelligible as such, and that its intelligibility is explicable in welfarist terms.) What the welfarist – or at least the defender of the natural law version of welfarism that I have defended thus far – can say is that there is a reason to keep commitments because to keep commitments is to promote a good, an aspect of well-being. The connection between the keeping of the commitment and the promotion of the good is not merely instrumental, though; the keeping of the commitment is itself a basic good, an aspect of the good of excellence in agency. Recall that the good of excellence in agency is just that of judging and choosing in a reasonable way, and of acting in accordance with one's judgments and decisions (3.3). If excellence in agency thus characterized is a basic good, then acting in accordance with one's commitments – one's past decisions about what is to be done at some future time – will itself be an instance of that good. Indeed, the past decision constricts the range of present actions that can constitute completely reasonable actions.

Consider the following analogy. The aspect of the good of community that I called 'peace' involves agents' wills not being in conflict with each other (3.3). Suppose that you have a neighbor who is a bit finicky aesthetically, and has the following very strong views about the color scheme of the outside of your house: if the main color that you use is tan, then you should paint the shutters brown (but not, for goodness's sake, red); if the main color that you use is white, then you should paint the shutters red (but not, for goodness's sake, brown). One day you paint the sides of the house tan, and you now must decide what to paint the shutters. Clearly, you can choose intelligibly to paint the shutters brown, based on the following consideration: you have already painted the sides of the house tan. This reason refers to a past act of yours, but can be explained wholly by welfarist considerations: the good of peace between you and your neighbor is (partially) realized by your going on to paint the shutters brown. With respect to the good of peace in this case, it is indifferent whether you employ the tan/brown or white/red color scheme; but once you have painted the sides of the house tan, then this past act constrains what actions you might perform in order to promote the good of peace. Likewise, the aspect of the good of excellence of agency involves a choice: either decide to ϕ and then ϕ, or do not decide to ϕ. Once one has decided to ϕ, what one can do to participate in the good of excellence in agency with respect to decisions to ϕ is narrowed to the act of ϕ-ing.

So far as I can see, then, there is nothing that is inconsistent with the welfarist thesis to hold that acting in accordance with one's commitments necessarily involves the realization of an aspect of the agent's well-being, and as such provides the agent with a reason to act in accordance with those commitments. Any objection to the view that welfarism can account for the intelligibility of such action will have to be framed, then, in terms of the justification for including excellence in agency thus characterized on the list. But excellence in agency thus characterized does seem to be something good, something that makes the agent well off. Put to the side issues about whether agents should ever form commitments or under what conditions they should, for such issues are not relevant here. The issues are: after the agent has settled on a certain course of action, has deemed it worth carrying out and has set him- or herself to performing the requisite acts, is that agent, as such, a more practically reasonable agent by performing rather than not? And isn't one better off, as such, being practically reasonable rather than not? (For further discussion of the good of excellence in agency, see 3.3; for a discussion of the strength of the requirement to keep one's commitments, see 5.6.)

Even if there is a coherent welfarist account of the intelligibility of action performed out of commitment, however, it does not seem that this account can be extended to cover acts of retribution and gratitude. Action out of commitment is made intelligible by appeal to an independently defensible basic good that is realized in such action. But it seems that no item on the list of goods (3.3) affirmed by this welfarist view is such that it would enable us to find a place for the intelligibility of retribution and gratitude within a forward-looking account of practical rationality. How, then, should the welfarist deal with this very different type of backward-looking action?

As might be guessed from this chapter's prior treatments of alleged gaps in the welfarist account of practical rationality, the welfarist can attempt to disentangle what is central to his or her theory from other theses about practical rationality commonly associated with, but not essential to, that theory. What seems to generate the trouble for welfarism vis-à-vis backward-looking actions is that welfarism's view of practical rationality is essentially forward looking, whereas the rationales for acts of gratitude or retribution are backward looking. But the welfarist might point out that there is nothing in welfarism as formulated that implies that it is an essentially forward-looking theory of practical rationality.

The claim that welfarism is as such incapable of dealing with backward-looking action results from conjoining the thesis of *promotionism* with the welfarist theses. Promotionism is the thesis that the basic reasons for action are essentially and exclusively ends *to be promoted.* Conjoined with welfarism, promotionism yields the conclusion that the basic reasons for action are aspects of well-being to be promoted. But if some state of affairs is wholly in the past, its obtaining cannot be promoted; and so if some state of affairs is entirely in the past, it cannot be a reason for action. Since reasons are what make action intelligible, welfarism and promotionism together rule out the possibility of intelligible action with a backward-looking rationale. But the welfarist might note that promotionism is a thesis distinct from anything that the welfarist qua welfarist asserts: if promotionism can be plausibly denied by the welfarist, the argument that there is an essential tension between welfarism and the existence of intelligible actions with backward-looking rationales fails.

The welfarist *can* plausibly deny promotionism. The welfarist can admit that the most obvious response due to the basic goods is that of promotion. But there may be other ways of responding appropriately to the basic goods. Consider, for example, the way that Raz employs the notion of an expressive action. Raz has us note the way that friendship can be the rationale for at least two different kinds of action: even if friendship is most characteristically cited as a reason for acting in welfare-promoting ways, that is, to promote the good of one's friend, one has reasons, on the basis of this friendship, to perform other actions that do not benefit the friend at all; such actions are, rather, symbolic of the relationship that exists between them. These acts are expressive, for they "express the relationship . . . involved" (1979, p. 255). To employ Raz's example, even if one's friend will not be harmed by confirming innuendos that are made about him or her, one's confirming them would be inappropriate given the relationship that exists between friends. Such an action appears to be an intelligible one, yet the nature of its response to what is valuable cannot be understood in terms of the response of promoting that value.

The welfarist can claim, then, that in addition to the response of promoting well-being, well-being can make expressive action intelligible as well. It does seem pretty clear that we do recognize that welfare reasons can be reasons for responses other than those of promotion. The very fact that emotional responses can be intelligible or unintelligible, and that the intelligibility of some of these responses can be provided by reference to an aspect of well-being, manifests this recognition. One can be pleased by the presence of a certain good, or distressed by its absence; and these conditions of being pleased or distressed are rendered intelligible by the agent's relationship with – namely, participation in, or lack of participation in – those goods. (It would be unintelligible to be pleased by the absence of a good and distressed by its presence in the absence of some further reason.) And the intelligibility of these types of responses cannot be captured by attempts to reduce these to promotion-responses, for they are of such different sorts: note that when we are told that it does no good to be distressed over the absence of a good ("don't cry over spilled milk"), this piece of information just misses the point, for one does not feel distressed over the absence of a good in order to promote the good, and the fact that being distressed does not help one to achieve some other good is not relevant to its status as a fitting response to that good. It seems possible, then, that the welfarist can, without detriment to the welfarist theses, hold that there is a type of response to aspects of well-being that is distinct from the response of promotion, that is, the response of expression.

The importance of the category of expressive action as being distinct from promotion yet intelligible by appeal to welfare reasons is that it could provide a route for the welfarist to acknowledge and account for the existence of intelligible action with backward-looking rationales. For, unlike the act of promoting the good, there does not seem to be anything intrinsically forward looking about expressive action and emotion. One can intelligibly regret the absence of a good in the past, as well as fear its future absence; one can intelligibly be glad that some good was enjoyed in the past, as well as hope for its realization in the future. One can intelligibly build a monument to express the goodness of something past; or intelligibly beat one's breast to express the badness of something past. But this account of the intelligibility of such emotions and actions remains welfarist: for it asserts that in all cases, what renders intelligible these expressive actions is some aspect of well-being, some good realized (or not) in the past, enjoyed (or not) in the present, or anticipated (or not) in the future.

The welfarist can provide some account of backward-looking action, then, if he or she rejects promotionism. What should we say, then, about the cases of retribution and gratitude that motivated this discussion in the first place? First, the welfarist should hold that what makes acts of retribution or gratitude intelligible is an aspect of well-being: either the aspect of well-being promoted by the benefactor to whom gratitude is to be shown, or the aspect of well-being that is attacked by the malefactor upon whom retribution is inflicted. This is highly plausible, just from the definitions of gratitude and retribution: such acts are performed on the basis of some benefit or harm. Secondly, the welfarist should hold that gratitude and retribution are instances of expressive action. This, too, is at least initially promising, as evidenced by the number of recent discussions of punishment that make central its expressive function (see, e.g., Feinberg 1965; Nozick 1981, pp. 370–374). Thirdly, it seems to me that while the simple cases of expressive action with respect to well-being concerned the expression of the agent's relationship to some instance of a basic good, the welfarist account of gratitude and retribution should appeal to the expression of a relationship that possesses three terms: that between the benefactor/malefactor, the beneficiary/victim, and the good promoted or attacked. Fourthly, the welfarist should hold that the positive character of the response in cases of gratitude – the promotion of a good – is fitting, due to the positive character of the relationship between benefactor, beneficiary, and the good; the negative character of the response in cases of retribution – the deprivation of a good – is fitting due to the negative character of the relationship between malefactor, victim, and the good. Indeed, unlike most expressive actions, which have their particular expressive content as a matter of convention, the positive and negative character of the respective expressive actions of gratitude and retribution can be understood as naturally fitting responses, as they involve the promotion or deprivation of what is good by nature.

Needless to say, I have not shown here that the welfarist can easily provide an account of retribution and gratitude. Working out precisely the nature of the three-term relationship for which gratitude or retribution is a fitting response

and why precisely gratitude or retribution is a fitting expression of this relationship – and doing so without moving beyond the resources allowed by welfarism – remains a serious task for the welfarist account of practical rationality.
But perhaps the weightiness of this burden is relieved a bit by keeping in mind
that what initially generated worries about welfarism's status with respect to
gratitude and retribution – the allegedly essentially forward-looking character
of welfarism – is not what makes retribution and gratitude hard to deal with.
The claim that welfarism cannot, in principle, deal with backward-looking action has been disposed of. And further, while few of us doubt that reasons can
render expressive action intelligible, explaining precisely how certain actions
are fitting responses to express relationships to value is bound to be difficult.[2]
I think that this will probably hold true of any view, and is no particular objection to a welfarist account of practical rationality.

5

The Principles That Make Choice Reasonable

5.1 A Justificatory Framework for Principles of Practical Reasonableness

The choiceworthy alternatives for action embarrassingly outstrip our capacity to act on them. We will therefore be unable to act on all such opportunities. How will we select which opportunities will be acted upon and which must be forgone?

As it will turn out, particular choices made by the practically reasonable agent will be, to a great extent, governed by his or her life plan, which agents are required by reason to formulate (5.6) but the content of which is largely left open to the exercise of creative free choice (6.5). Nonetheless, there are some guidelines for choice that are available apart from the commitments to particular goods that constitute a plan of life. These guidelines for choice are requirements of practical reason itself. What I want to do is to set up a framework within which we can see how a set of principles of practical reasonableness can be justified, and which can then be used to assess the merits of the natural law theory I am defending vis-à-vis rival normative views, such as egoism, consequentialism, and Kantianism. (Thus, the framework that I present will have to be neutral among these various theories of practical reasonableness, so that adherents of these rival views can recognize that framework as doing justice to their accounts of the principles of practical reason.) What we need to determine, first of all, is what it is that principles of practical reasonableness are supposed to assess.

Plans of Action and Principles of Practical Reasonableness

In judging the merits of the different principles of practical reasonableness proffered by natural law theory and its rivals, I shall hold that what these principles of practical reasonableness are supposed to evaluate are primarily *plans of action,* where a plan of action is an ordered set of performances that has as its end some fundamental reason for action.[1]

Why is the plan of action the appropriate object of assessment? Keep in mind the two separate (but related) tasks that a complete theory of practical rationality has to accomplish: it must both characterize what makes action intelligible and explain how action is made reasonable (0.1). Now, part of the reason for distinguishing these tasks is that it is only intelligible action that is a candidate for the status of reasonable or unreasonable; the brutely unintelligible is not a species of the unreasonable but, rather, is a separate genus altogether. Once it is agreed that the candidates for assessment as reasonable or unreasonable are instances of intelligible action, it is clear why the plan of action has to be the fundamental unit of assessment by principles of practical reasonableness. For it is only as part of a plan of action that any action is intelligible or unintelligible. (This is not to preclude the possibility that a plan of action might include only one basic action within it; 'part' here does not mean '*proper* part.')

Consider the act of taking a copy of Descartes's *Meditations* from a bookshelf. In itself this action is not intelligible: it is only intelligible as part of a larger plan of action (perhaps a plan in which one carries the book back to one's easy chair, opens it, reads it, and thereby gains from it a bit of philosophical understanding; or perhaps a plan in which one throws that book into the fire on a cold night to keep oneself alive; or . . .). Considered in itself, the action lacks the intelligibility that is a prerequisite for the assessment of acts as reasonable or unreasonable.

This account of what principles of practical reasonableness assess calls for some immediate clarifications. First, one might object that not all intelligible plans of action terminate in some fundamental reason for action. One might, for example, contemplate entering into an investment scheme with the intention of securing greater wealth; yet one does not have a fundamental reason to secure wealth. And surely it would be perverse to claim that investment schemes are not the sort of thing that are the proper object of assessment as practically reasonable or unreasonable. Now, I of course agree that investment schemes can be intelligible, and that they are an appropriate object of assessment by principles of practical reasonableness. But I deny that the definition of 'plan of action' that I offered must be interpreted so as to preclude the investment scheme. For when one says that it is of the nature of a plan of action that it terminate in some fundamental reason for action, one need not be committed thereby to the view that every plan of action has some particular fundamental reason in mind. One might, that is, have an intelligible plan of action in which it is indeterminate for which fundamental reasons one is acting: one can pursue a set of instrumental goods as such without knowing to which basic goods one will employ those instrumental goods as instruments. Thus, it is clear that the investment scheme can count as a plan of action, and therefore as an object of assessment by principles of practical reasonableness: even if one is not investing in order to secure some particular basic good, one's investing might be for the sake of having wealth that will aid one in the pursuit of yet-to-be-specified basic goods. (Of course, if one is not aiming either at specified or unspecified basic goods by investing, that course of action will be unintelligible, and thus will not be the sort of act that principles of practical reasonableness are needed to assess.)

Secondly, one might argue that in affirming that plans of action thus conceived are the appropriate objects for assessment by principles of practical reasonableness, I have gone back on the claim, made in 4.4, that promotionism is not necessarily an exhaustive account of intelligible response to the basic goods. It might be thought that a plan of action by its very definition involves a set of actions the aim of which is the realization of a particular good; it is this particular good that makes the set of actions ordered toward its realization intelligible. Now, I do not doubt that the paradigm case of the plan of action is a set of actions that culminates in the obtaining of a good. But I deny that promotionism is built into the definition of a plan of action. A plan of action could have as its end a good that is not *to be realized* by those actions, but which is in some way *to be respected,* or otherwise appropriately responded to, by those actions. (For those skeptical of this use of the notion of an 'end,' see the discussion of the contrast between producible and subsistent ends in the discussion of Kant's view in 5.2.) While my attention will be focused mainly on plans of action concerned to promote the good – the nature of reasonable expressive action is, in my view, even less well understood than the nature of reasonable action that aims to promote some good – the concept of a plan of action does not entail that these are the only kinds of actions that constitute a plan of action in the defined sense.

Another worry about making plans of action the object of assessment of principles of practical reasonableness is that this would imply that those principles would be unable to pronounce on the reasonableness or unreasonableness of basic actions as such. Now, this is, strictly speaking, correct: for since actions are not intelligible except as part of a plan of action, it is not appropriate to classify them as reasonable or unreasonable. But that is not such a great loss: for in place of practical conclusions such as "killing the innocent is practically unreasonable" or "lying is practically unreasonable" that the objector wants to be able to affirm, principles of practical reasonableness might imply conclusions such as "any plan of action that includes the killing of the innocent is unreasonable" or "any plan of action involving lying is unreasonable." If the objector wishes to say, for shorthand, that murder and lying are unreasonable, the danger of misunderstanding need not be great.

Here is a fourth worry. On the proposed view, principles of practical reasonableness assess plans of action. In order for there to be anything to assess, agents must already be acting for the sake of some good, forming plans of action the intelligibility of which derives from some worthwhile end. What this precludes, then, is the possibility that failing to act for the sake of a good or that failing to form a plan of action be shown practically unreasonable. For if to be practically unreasonable is to be ruled out by a correct principle of practical reasonableness, and those principles apply only to proposed plans of action, it could not be the case that failing to act for the sake of a good could ever, as such, be contrary to practical reason. Again, I concede the claims of the objection while denying that it counts against my view. Whether one acts for the sake of a good or not is not something with which the theory of practical reasonableness deals; that is a matter for the theory of intelligible action. The theory of practical reasonableness assumes that agents are acting on reasons, and aims to specify what ways of acting on reasons are reasonable and which are unreasonable. The theory of practical reasonableness, thus, does not prescribe the pursuit of any good by any agent. If there is an objection to agents' not acting for goods at all, it is an objection that should be framed not in terms of the agent's unreasonableness but in terms of the agent's unintelligibility.

The Formulation and Defense of Principles of Practical Reasonableness

Principles of practical reasonableness cannot, in my view, be derived from prior principles. But neither are they intuitions, in the sense that Sidgwick thought that the first principles both of egoism and of utilitarianism were intuitions. (For Sidgwick's account of the characteristics of intuitions, see *Methods,* pp. 338–343.)

The method of formulating and defending principles of practical reasonableness that I will employ is grounded in the following considerations. First, since the principles of practical reasonableness have as their function the selection of plans of action that have their eligibility from their ends – the fundamental reasons for action that render those plans intelligible – the content of those practical principles should flow from those reasons. Secondly, once we allow that the content of the practical principles should flow from those reasons, we should keep in mind Rawls's dictum, later appropriated by Samuel Scheffler, that "the correct regulative principle for anything depends on the nature of that thing" (Rawls 1971, p. 29; see also Scheffler 1994, p. 57). Principles of practical reasonableness, that is, should adequately respond to the nature of the fundamental reasons that make action intelligible. Thirdly, given the variety of ways that one can act on reasons, and the indefinite number of plans that one could formulate, principles of practical reasonableness best function negatively, as ruling out certain plans of action (or, better, classes of plans of action) as unreasonable. Assessment of plans of action as practically reasonable follows the *via negativa:* any plan of action that principles of practical reasonableness do not deem unreasonable counts as a reasonable plan of action.[2]

These considerations together suggest the following method for defending a principle of practical reasonableness. A principle of practical reasonableness is correct if and only if it rules out some plans of action, and all of those plans that it rules out do injustice to the specific characteristics of the fundamental reasons for action. Now, to say that a principle must rule out only those plans that do injustice to the nature of reasons for action is, of course, to be altogether too metaphorical, but it can be made more precise. The objects assessed by principles of practical reasonableness are plans of action. Plans of action need assessment because agents must choose among alternative plans of action. But these plans of action always contain presuppositions about the nature of the reasons for action that are implicated in those plans. Since these presuppositions are truth-valuable, we can deem unreasonable those plans of action that contain false presuppositions about the characteristics of the fundamental reasons for action.

It is obvious that it is essential to this framework for assessing principles of practical reasonableness that we be able to give at least a tolerably clear idea of the notion of 'presupposition.' My claim is that plans of action all have presuppositions; and since presuppositions are propositions, presuppositions are the sorts of thing that could be true or false. Under what conditions, though, can we say that a plan of action presupposes the truth of a certain proposition? The basic idea is that a plan of action presupposes the truth of a certain proposition if the truth of that proposition – or the belief in that proposition's truth by the agent – is necessary to render that plan of action intelligible, that is, worth choosing under the description under which the action is performed (0.1). It is important to note that when one holds that an agent's plan of action presupposes the truth of a certain proposition, one is not thereby claiming that the agent does, in fact, believe that proposition to be true. The reason that we are entitled to call that proposition a presupposition of the plan of action, even if it is not actually believed or relied on by the agent who formulated that plan of action, is that we are entitled to assume that the plan of action is an intelligible one, since principles of practical reasonableness have as their aim the ruling out of plans of action that are otherwise intelligible and therefore eligible.[3]

Now, given that the presuppositions I have in mind here have to do with the nature of the fundamental reasons for action, it seems that any given presupposition of a plan of action might err in one of two ways: it might hold that one or more of the reasons implicated in that plan has some characteristic that it actually lacks, or it might hold that one or more of those reasons lacks some characteristic that it actually has. A principle of practical reasonableness rules out plans of action that err in at least one of these ways. If, however, that principle excludes plans of action that have only true presuppositions about the nature of the reasons for action, then that principle does not do justice to the characteristics of the fundamental reasons for action and is therefore false.

Accounts of principles of practical reasonableness can therefore be criticized in at least two ways. On one hand, they can be criticized with regard to their theories of what the relevant characteristics of the fundamental reasons for action are. On the other, they can be criticized for how the principles proposed by that theory attempt to embody an appropriate response to those characteristics. In the next section, 5.2, I argue that, given their accounts of the relevant features of the fundamental reasons for action, egoism, consequentialism, and Kantianism all possess plausible accounts of the principles of practical reasonableness. Later, in my own account of the relevant characteristics of reasons for action (5.3), I shall explain in what ways egoism, consequentialism, and Kantianism embody inadequate accounts of the relevant characteristics of the fundamental reasons for action.

There are, of course, other ways to try to defend principles of practical reasonableness. But the framework presented here has two desirable features that are worth emphasizing.[4] The first is that it provides a way to bring a variety of normative views into contention with one another. If, as I shall show, a number of competing normative theories can be accurately portrayed in terms of this framework, it brings into relief the exact points of dispute among these theories. The second is that if one or another normative theory shows itself superior to the others in terms of this framework, then we would have grounds to believe that that theory provides a particularly deep understanding of the normative order. For, according to this framework, all of these competing theories are engaged in the ambitious task of connecting the domain of the intelligible tightly to the domain of the reasonable. If a set of principles emerges victorious from this framework, its victory is not merely that it (e.g.) was able to fit more neatly with our pretheoretical intuitions about how it is reasonable to act but, rather, that it has established a unified theory of the normative domain.

5.2 Egoism, Consequentialism, Kantianism

Egoism, consequentialism, and Kantianism each present a single principle of practical reasonableness that is superordinate to all other principles of action. Each of these theories defends its principle of practical reason as the only principle that adequately responds to the nature of the fundamental reasons for action.

Egoism

The fundamental principle of egoistic systems of practical reasonableness asserts that each agent ought to maximize his or her own good. Or, to put this principle in terms more amenable to the framework discussed in 5.1: any plan of action that does not maximize the agent's good is to be ruled out as unreasonable.

Now, whether this principle of practical reasonableness is the correct one depends on the characteristics of the fundamental reasons for action. Given the content of the egoist's principle, the egoist would have to show that any plan of action that does not maximize the agent's well-being is dependent on a false presupposition about the nature of the reasons for action that there are. Egoistic systems of practical reasonableness hold that the following are the relevant characteristics of the fundamental reasons for action: first, that those reasons for action are grounded in agent-relative goods; secondly, that those reasons for action are themselves agent-relative; and thirdly, that those reasons for action are commensurable. On the egoist's view, these are the only relevant characteristics of the fundamental reasons for action; every line of defense of the egoist principle of practical reasonableness must make reference to one or another of these features. We can treat each of these characteristics in turn, considering for each how it contributes to the final form of the egoist's first principle.

For the egoist, the fundamental reasons for action are grounded in agent-relative goods: what there is fundamental reason to promote are states of affairs that are intrinsically good for agents. Thus, the egoist system of practical reasonableness is, like the natural law account sketched thus far, welfarist: all of the basic reasons for action are welfare reasons. As is perhaps obvious, this view of the nature of the reasons for action immediately rules out any candidate set of principles of practical reasonableness that does not preclude from the status of reasonable any plan of action that has among its ultimate aims the obtaining of a state of affairs that is not an aspect of someone's well-being. For if one has the obtaining of a state of affairs of this sort as part of the ultimate aim of one's plan of action, one presupposes that this state of affairs provides a reason for action; but according to egoism, this presupposition is false, for the only fundamental reasons for action are reasons of well-being. This is why the egoist's principle of practical reasonableness rules out all plans except those that propose to advance an agent's well-being.

Egoism does not claim only that the fundamental reasons for action are grounded in states of affairs that possess agent-relative goodness, though: it also claims that the reasons for action that flow from these agent-relative goods inherit those goods' agent-relative character. (This is not an uncontroversial claim, even for those who affirm the existence of agent-relative goods: some writers hold that while the fundamental reasons for action are grounded in agent-relative goods, the reasons generated by those goods are agent-neutral. The utilitarian variant of consequentialism is such a view, as I argue in this section; so is Finnis's natural law theory [5.3].) The idea, that is, is that the essential reference to the agent necessarily present in the characterization of agent-relative goods is transmitted to the reasons that are generated by those goods. Suppose that G is a goodness-predicate of the agent-relative variety: for all agents x and all states of affairs y, then if G is true of y then with regard to x, y is good, where the predicate G contains a free occurrence of x. According to the egoist view of the connection between goods and reasons, the reason-statement corresponding to this good-statement will contain a reason-predicate R that is also agent-relative. If the obtaining of a certain state of affairs is good for an agent, then that agent has a reason to promote that state of affairs; but that does not mean that any other agent has a fundamental reason to promote that state of affairs.

If this account of reasons for action is correct, then no set of principles of practical reasonableness can be correct that does not rule out as unreasonable any plan of action that has as (at least part of) its end a state of affairs that is good for someone other than its agent. For any agent who has such a plan presupposes that some other person's well-being provides a reason for the agent to act. But this is a false presupposition, if all of the reasons for action produced by aspects of well-being are agent-relative.

Finally, the egoist theory of reasons holds that reasons for action are commensurable. The commensurability of reasons for action affirmed by the egoist is the result of the commensurability of the goods that generate those reasons. While for the egoist the list of aspects of well-being might be just as variegated as that presented in 3.3, each state of affairs that is an aspect of an agent's well-being can be assessed and compared with other such states of affairs to the extent to which those states of affairs contribute to an agent's overall good. With regard to any two aspects of an agent's well-being, then, we can say it either must be the case that one of those aspects possesses less goodness than the other or that it possesses at least as much goodness as the other.

Now, the way that the feature of commensurability enables the egoist to rule out certain classes of plans of action as unreasonable differs from the way in which the welfarist and agent-relativist conception of reasons enabled the egoist to rule out certain classes of plans of action as unreasonable. With regard to the welfarism and agent-relativity of the reasons for action, any adequate set of principles of practical reasonableness can rule out certain classes of plans of action as deficient in themselves, without reference to other eligible plans of action. But the commensurability feature does not support this sort of principle: it cannot rule out plans as such, but only as compared to other eligible plans.

Suppose that agent A has before him or her eligible plans P_1 and P_2, where P_1 and P_2 terminate in the securing of aspects of A's well-being S_1 and S_2 respectively. Since S_1 and S_2 are aspects of A's well-being, their goodness is commensurable, and the reasons for action that they generate are likewise commensurable. Because they are commensurable, it is either the case that S_1 contains at least as much goodness as S_2 (that is, S_1's goodness is greater than or equal to S_2's), or S_1 contains less goodness than S_2. The egoist wants to make two claims here: first, that if S_1's goodness is less than S_2's, then any set of principles of practical reasonableness that fails to rule out P_1 is incorrect; and, secondly, that if S_1's goodness is at least as great as S_2's, then any set of principles of practical reasonableness that rules out P_1 is incorrect.

Suppose, first, that the goodness of S1 is less than the goodness of S_2. Now, according to the egoist, any set of principles of practical reasonableness must be incorrect if that set of principles does not imply that, given this supposition,

P_1 is to be ruled out. For S_2 contains all of the goodness that S_1 has and additional goodness as well; the agent A thus has every reason to act on P_2 that he or she has to act on P_1, plus additional reasons as well. There is thus reason for A to prefer P_2 to P_1, but no reason for A to prefer P_1 to P_2. It would thus be unreasonable for A not to prefer P_2 to P_1 when S_2's goodness is greater than S_1's; any set of principles that did not rule out P_1 in comparison to P_2 would be incorrect.

Suppose, next, that the goodness of S_1 is at least as great as the goodness of S_2. According to the egoist, any set of principles is incorrect if it holds that P_1 is to be ruled out. For P_1 could be ruled out only if there is some reason to prefer P_2 to P_1. But since there is no such reason, there is no basis for ruling out P_1. When choosing between any two plans, if one plan promises at least as much good as the other, the former cannot be ruled out as unreasonable.

A complication surfaces at this point. I have been arguing that the maximizing character of egoism's principle of practical reasonableness arises from the commensurability feature of the fundamental reasons for action. But, one might point out, what I have been discussing is the comparison of two plans by way of comparison of their *aims,* while egoistic theories of practical reasonableness characteristically compare plans of action by way of a comparison of *all* of the effects on an agent's good that would result from the implementation of that plan, whether part of the agent's aim or not.

Consider, for example, the following scenario. Agent A is deliberating between plans of action P_1 and P_2, where P_1 and P_2 have as their aims S_1 and S_2 respectively. In addition to these aims, though, it is foreseeable that P_1 will have among its consequences state of affairs T_1 and P_2 will have among its consequences state of affairs T_2. Now, suppose further that S_1 possesses greater goodness than S_2 does, but S_1 and T_1 together have less goodness for A than S_2 and T_2 together have. It would seem that, as developed so far, the egoist's principle of practical reasonableness counsels the ruling out of P_2; after all, the goodness of the aim of P_1 is greater than the goodness of the aim of P_2. But classic egoism denies this: it holds that one ought to select the plan that promises greater good for the agent, and that plan is P_2: for it promises the greater goodness of S_2 and T_2. How can we bring our attempt to defend egoism in terms of this framework closer into line with the standard egoist position?

What seems clear is that modification of our results to mesh with the standard egoistic line involves rejecting the normative importance of the distinction between the intentions involved in a plan and the foreseeable effects of the implementation of a plan. What we want to show, that is, is that the agent who chooses P_1 over P_2 holds a false presupposition, that is, that whether a good is intended as the aim of a plan or is merely foreseen is a relevant consideration in comparing plans. Now, I shall take as given that there is an important conceptual difference between the intended and the foreseen, which it is the task of the philosophy of action to characterize. At issue is how it can be determined whether this conceptual difference makes a normative difference. Some consequentialists attack the alleged relevance of this distinction by example, showing that in many cases, our intuitions seem to undercut this position; some anti-consequentialists seem to think that it is sufficient to note the clear conceptual distinctiveness of these notions in order to show that there must be some normative difference lurking somewhere. But if the framework for defending principles of practical reasonableness that I have put forward is correct, whether the intended/foreseen distinction carries normative weight will have to depend in some way on the characteristics of the reasons for action themselves.

It seems to me that the irrelevance of the intended/foreseen distinction within egoism (and also consequentialism) results from the commensurability of the reasons for action. If a state of affairs that is a foreseeable effect of the implementation of a plan is good in the same way as the fundamental reason that is the aim of that plan, and this type of goodness is held to be the only thing that can make a state of affairs a reason for action, then it would seem to be irrational to hold that the intended aim of the plan of action is relevant to the assessment of that plan, while the foreseeable effects of the plan are not. Thus, those who hold that the aim of the plan counts in comparison with other plans, while the foreseeable effects of that plan do not, presuppose something that is false.

This sort of argument would, if successful, secure the result that we need to complete the defense of the egoist's principle of practical reasonableness in terms of the egoist's account of the nature of the fundamental reasons for action. Another way to secure it would be to show that plans in which goods are intended are to be preferred to plans in which goods are foreseen only. Suppose that an agent is considering adopting a plan that is for the sake of good state of affairs S_1, and which is such that it is foreseeable that good state of affairs S_2 will result if that plan is implemented. Why would an agent prefer this plan to a similar plan in which both S_1 and S_2 are parts of the plan's aim? Once again, both S_1 and S_2 are good in the same way, and possess the sort of goodness that generates reasons for action: is it not arbitrary to act for the sake of S_1, merely accepting S_2 as a side effect, when one could act for the sake of both?

To conclude, then: if the egoist's account of the relevant features of reasons for action is accurate and complete, the egoist has grounds for holding that his or her principle of practical reasonableness is accurate and complete also. For we have dismissed any proposed principles of practical reasonableness that (1) allow plans that have, as any part of their aims, states of affairs that are no part of anyone's well-being; (2) allow plans that have, as any part of their aims, states of affairs that are no part of the agent's well-being; (3) allow plans that do not promote the agent's well-being at least as well as any alternative plan; and (4) rule out any plans that promote the agent's well-being at least as well as any alternative plan. Thus, the necessity and sufficiency of the egoist principle that all plans that are suboptimal vis-à-vis the agent's good are to be ruled out as unreasonable.[5]

A comment about the commensurability feature is in order here. It might be wondered whether the egoistic theory of practical reasoning is committed to the view that all reasons for action are commensurable. While it seems to me that commensurability is a common assumption of egoism, this strong claim about commensurability could be denied by an egoist. There is some cost to this maneuver, though: it would mean that egoism in its classic formulation has nothing to say about choices between plans that involve incommensurable reasons for action. It is important to note the difference between egoism's counsels regarding plans involving equal goods and those involving incommensurable goods. With regard to equal goods, egoism has clear and unequivocal counsel: it counsels indifference; from the point of view of practical reason, it is irrelevant whether one selects one such plan rather than another. With regard to incommensurable goods, though, it is not as if egoism counsels indifference; rather, it has no counsel to offer at all. With regard to incommensurables, classical egoism is silent.

Consequentialism

The fundamental principle of consequentialist systems of practical reasonableness asserts that each agent ought to maximize the overall good. Or, to put this principle in terms of the framework for defending practical principles: any plan of action that does not maximize the overall good is to be ruled out as unreasonable.

If consequentialism is a correct account of the principles of practical reasonableness, it is due to the nature of the reasons for action. Consequentialism, unlike egoism, is not committed to the view that reasons for action are all welfare reasons (though, as we shall note, its most prominent version does affirm this view). It does, however, affirm that all reasons for action are goods. Further, no matter what sort of goods generate the fundamental reasons for action from the consequentialist standpoint, consequentialism asserts that the fundamental reasons for action are agent-neutral. And, further, consequentialism asserts that these reasons for action are commensurable, in virtue of the commensurability of the goods that generate those reasons.

Consequentialism affirms that the reasons for action are goods. This is, in itself, not a very illuminating claim – far less illuminating than (e.g.) the claim that reasons for action are all welfare reasons. But consequentialists might hold that this is a benefit rather than a difficulty for their view: it is not trapped into any confining or overly restrictive account of what generates reasons to act. It does seem, though, that if the consequentialist is going to give an account of practical reasonableness based on the nature of the good, the consequentialist should give some idea as to how the good is to be specified.[6] At any rate, given a specification of the good, this feature of the reasons for action implies that any plan of action that does not aim at producing what is (according to that specification) a good is to be ruled out as unreasonable. For one who aims to secure what is not (according to that specification) a good presupposes what is false: that one's aim provides a reason to act.

Next, the reasons for action that are generated by goods are agent-neutral. Recall that, given the generic form of reason-statement $(x)(y)(Ry \rightarrow$ there is a reason for x to promote $y)$, reason-predicate R is agent-neutral if it contains no free occurrences of x. The agent-neutrality of reasons for action imposes constraints on plans of action that are to count as reasonable: for the universally agent-neutral character of reasons for action implies that any plan of action the aim of which contains an ineliminable self-reference is to be ruled out, for all such aims are agent-relative rather than agent-neutral. (The notion of self-reference here involves the use of indexical terms. A plan that aims at the state of affairs *Murphy's acquiring knowledge* differs from a plan that aims at the state of affairs *my acquiring knowledge*. The former can enter into an agent-neutral reason for action, but the latter cannot; thus, consequentialism implies that only the latter is ruled out as an unreasonable plan of action.)

Finally, consequentialism, like egoism, affirms the commensurability of these agent-neutral reasons for action; the commensurability of these reasons derives from the commensurability of the goods that generate those reasons. I need not repeat here the reasoning from the commensurability of reasons for action to the maximizing character of the principle of practical reasonableness: the same rationale that gives egoism its maximizing character gives consequentialism that same character. Similarly, the commensurability feature denies the intended/foreseen distinction any practical significance within consequentialism, just as surely as it does within egoism. Thus, we see the basis for the consequentialist principle of practical reasonableness: the features of the reasons for action that consequentialism emphasizes would rule out any proposed set of practical principles that (1) allow plans that have, as any part of their aims, states of affairs that are not intrinsically good, (2) allow plans that have, as any part of their aims, a state of affairs with an ineliminable self-reference, (3) allow plans the aims of which do not promote the overall good at least as well as any alternative plan, and (4) rule out plans that promote the overall good at least as well as any alternative plan. Thus, given the features of the reasons for action emphasized by generic consequentialism, the rational basis for affirming the consequentialist first principle seems clear.[7]

It is worth briefly noting what the most well-known version of consequentialism, utilitarianism, adds to the generic consequentialist principle: it specifies the good to be promoted as well-being. Utilitarianism is welfarist, just as the version of egoism described here and the natural law account of the good described in Chapters 2 and 3 are welfarist. Thus, it affirms the constraint on principles of practical reasonableness that the correct set of principles will rule out any plan of action that does not aim at promoting someone's well-being. Unlike egoism, though, it holds that while the goods that generate the fundamental reasons for action are agent-relative, the reasons that they generate are agent-neutral.[8] Thus, the utilitarian holds that reason requires agents to maximize overall well-being, that all plans that fail to maximize well-being are contrary to reason.

Kantianism

The fundamental principle of Kantian systems of practical reasoning is that humans ought to be treated as ends-in-themselves, that is, that every plan of action that fails to treat humans as ends-in-themselves is to be ruled out as unreasonable.

The fundamental principle of the Kantian theory stands in stark contrast to the principles of both egoism and consequentialism. As is to be expected, given the framework for defending principles of practical reasonableness, the differences between Kantianism and these other views are due to their divergent accounts of the nature of reasons for action.

Perhaps the most striking difference between the egoist and consequentialist account of reasons for action and the Kantian account is that the fundamental reasons for action are, on these views, very different kinds of thing. For the egoist and the consequentialist, reasons are states of affairs that can be made to obtain through action; thus, the generic form of a reason-statement employs variables that range over states of affairs to which reason-predicates might apply and variables that range over agents whose acts might promote those states of affairs. On this view, the fundamental reasons for action are, to use Donagan's helpful phrase, "producible ends" (Donagan 1977, p. 227). The Kantian holds, by contrast, that while it is true that there are some nonfundamental reasons for action that are producible ends, the fundamental reasons for action are not states of affairs at all but are, rather, *persons*. To hold that humans are ends-in-themselves is just to hold, I think, that humans themselves, and not just states of affairs involving them, are the fundamental reasons for action.

While the Kantian notion of the end-in-itself has been found by some writers to be incomprehensibly muddled, the Kantian can bring to bear both intuitive considerations and arguments of considerable philosophical appeal in favor of this view. The intuitive considerations that support this idea of human as end-in-itself have to do with common sense's affirming that reasons for action can be persons. Consider, for example, the facts that we explain the rational motivation of our actions in terms of 'for the sake of' relationships and that we sometimes speak of acting for the sake of persons just as we speak of acting for the sake of some state of affairs; this suggests that we sometimes do take reasons for action to be persons. (One could take part in an electoral campaign for the sake of getting Candidate X elected, or one could take part in that campaign for Candidate X's sake. In the former case, the reason for one's action is some state of affairs, a producible end; in the latter case, the reason is a person, an end-in-itself.)

If one should dispute this evidence from common sense, the Kantian can bring forward an argument that holds that no producible ends are intelligible as the aims of action except when referred to some person. For, the Kantian claims, it is simply untrue that pursuit of any producible end – and we can include here those states of affairs that are instantiations of the basic goods defended in Chapter 3 – is intelligible in itself. To act for the sake of John's happiness – to take just one example of a producible end – is not something that makes sense unless one is doing this for John's (or someone else's) sake. Indeed, the Kantian might go on to say, anyone who affirms an account of basic goods while failing to note that action in pursuit of them is pointless unless it is for the sake of the persons that those goods fulfill is confused about where the value of those states of affairs resides. Since the basic reasons for action are, on this Kantian view, persons and not states of affairs, the principles of practical reasonableness affirmed by the Kantian must likewise refer not to states of affairs but to persons. (For fuller discussion of these points see Donagan 1977, pp. 224–239, and Anderson 1993, pp. 17–30.)

If human persons are ends-in-themselves, then any plan of action that fails to treat persons as ends-in-themselves is as such unreasonable, for such plans of action falsely presuppose that human persons are not ends-in-themselves. We might put it this way. To act for the sake of some producible end by failing to treat a human as an end-in-itself is to undercut the rationale of one's own action: for producible ends confer intelligibility on action only when sought for the sake of persons. Thus, the agent, in acting for an end in this way, undercuts the only thing that could give the pursuit of that end intelligibility in the first place. To act for the sake of some end-in-itself by failing to treat some person as an end-in-itself is to be self-contradictory or arbitrary: either self-contradictory, both affirming and denying that humans are ends-in-themselves, or arbitrary, in affirming that one human is an end-in-itself while another is not (*Grounding*, pp. 428–429). Thus, given the Kantian characterization of the fundamental reasons for action, this principle of practical reasonableness seems inevitable.

It is worth noting, though, the relative lack of content that the Kantian principle possesses. Part of its abstractness derives from the fact that to hold that persons are ends-in-themselves and to offer some account of what confers the status of end-in-itself on a being are two different things. Since we might think that what constitutes treating a being as an end-in-itself will depend on what exactly makes a being an end-in-itself, the fundamental Kantian precept must be meager without a spelling out of what gives a being this status. (For Kant, being an end-in-itself is tied to being a free, end-setting being; thus, to fail to treat persons as ends-in-themselves will, on this specification, involve treating them as if they were mere objects, unfree, incapable of passing judgments on potential pursuits.) Another source of the abstractness of the Kantian precept derives from the abstractness of the action concept employed in the principle, that is, 'to treat as'; or, in some other formulations, 'to respect.' This abstractness is not so easily remedied: indeed, it has been argued with some persuasiveness that to specify what counts as treating a being as an end-in-itself, or what counts as respecting humans' rational nature, depends on some background normative view, so that the Kantian principle is actually incomplete without supplementation from some other normative position (e.g., consequentialism) (see, e.g., Kagan 1987, esp. p. 652).

Now, it might be held that since the defense of the Kantian principle offered in terms of the framework allows these sorts of difficulties to beset the Kantian principle, Kantians should not take the framework to present accurately their position on the source of the authoritativeness of that formulation of the categorical imperative. But this seems to me to be the wrong response. Regardless of whether one thinks that Kantians can overcome the abstractness of this formulation of the Kantian principle, and can do so in a way that is nonarbitrary, does not require appeal to some other background normative theory, and solves the paradox of deontology,[9] it cannot be denied that these are the very difficulties that set the agenda for contemporary Kantians. That the account of the Kantian principle put forward in terms of a Kantian view of the nature of reasons for action explains why this should be the problematic for present-day Kantians is a virtue, rather than a vice, of this account.

I have tried to show that the principles of practical reasonableness put forward by egoists, consequentialists, and Kantians can be defended by them by reference to their views on the nature of the fundamental reasons for action; given their diverse account of those reasons, the principles of practical reasonableness they offer seem plausible ways to assess plans of action as reasonable or unreasonable. Further, each of these normative views can be plausibly interpreted as trying to offer a deep account of the connection between the reasons that make action intelligible and the principles that make choice reasonable.

I shall now turn to the task of trying to show the superiority of a set of natural law principles that bears some similarity to those held, either explicitly or implicitly, by adherents of the natural law tradition. This defense will consist in two stages. In the first stage (5.3), I try to show that a particular account of the nature of the fundamental reasons for action is superior to the accounts offered by egoists, consequentialists, and Kantians. In the second stage (5.5), I try to explain how this particular account of the nature of reasons for action determines the shape of a distinctively natural law set of principles of practical reasonableness.

5.3 The Nature of Reasons for Action

Our discussion of the egoist, consequentialist, and Kantian theories of practical reasonableness suggests that the account of practical reasonableness offered by the natural law theorist must take a stand on at least the following issues: (1) whether the correct account of reasons for action is welfarist; (2) whether the fundamental reasons for action are agent-neutral or agent-relative; (3) to what extent commensurability holds among the basic reasons for action; and (4) whether the fundamental reasons for action are producible ends (states of affairs) or ends-in-themselves (persons). Addressing these issues will both determine the distinct shape of the natural law theory of principles of practical reasonableness and make clear the source of the differences between the principles of that theory and the principles affirmed by egoism, consequentialism, and Kantianism.

Welfarism about the Good

Consider the distinction between agent-relative and agent-neutral goodness-predicates mentioned in 2.2. If A ranges over agents and x over states of affairs, G is a goodness-predicate when $(A)(x)(Gx \rightarrow$ with regard to A, x is good). Agent-relative goodness-predicates contain a free occurrence of A in G; agent-neutral goodness-predicates do not. Thus, if some state of affairs is good in virtue of an agent-relative goodness-predicate's applying to it, it is good for some agent; if some state of affairs is good in virtue of an agent-neutral goodness-predicate's applying to it, it is good *simpliciter.* Now, aspects of well-being are good in virtue of agent-relative goodness-predicates' applying to them; this is part of the concept of well-being, and so nothing could be considered an aspect of well-being unless it were good by virtue of an agent-relative goodness-predicate's applying to it. To be a welfarist in the theory of practical rationality is, in part, to hold that the basic items of practical significance are all aspects of well-being, things that are good in an agent-relative sense (4.1). At the most basic practical level, agent-neutral goods have no role to play.

As we have seen, egoism and the utilitarian variety of consequentialism both adhere to this welfarist thesis; consequentialism considered generically, though, has no commitment to welfarism. The natural law view defended here rejects the agnosticism about the nature of the good present in generic consequentialism, siding with the egoists and utilitarians in holding that any states of affairs that are intrinsically good are, in virtue of their being instances of welfare, good by virtue of satisfying an agent-relative goodness-predicate. From within this natural law view, there is a straightforward rationale for affirming welfarism: it is a thesis about the good that fits well with the real identity thesis and the particular account of flourishing developed in Chapter 1. According to the real identity thesis, goods grasped by practical reason are identical with aspects of human flourishing grasped by theoretical reason (1.2–1.4). But the notion of flourishing is essentially relational: a state of affairs is an aspect of flourishing in relation to some being and the kind of thing that it is. Since the items of basic practical significance are held by the real identity thesis to be identical to states of affairs that are essentially relational, it coheres well with the natural law view to affirm a welfarist, agent-relative conception of the good.

Now, one might respond that there are strong reasons to be suspicious of any account of practical rationality that rejects the existence of agent-neutral goods. "There are," one might say, "some states of affairs such that, necessarily, all agents have a reason to promote them. The absence of suffering, the presence of well-being, the existence of beauty – all of these are instances of such states of affairs. Since all agents have reason to promote these states of affairs – and, I might add, since all agents have reason to promote these states of affairs just because these states of affairs are good in some way – it follows that there are agent-neutral goods: the absence of suffering, the presence of well-being, the existence of beauty, among others." But this argument does not go through, at least not in a straightforward way that does not involve the affirmation of additional controversial premises. For even if it is true that *x* is a state of affairs that all agents have a reason to promote, that is, that *x* is an agent-neutral *reason for action,* it does not follow that *x* is a state of affairs that is good with respect to all agents, that is, that *x* is an agent-neutral *good.* It does not even follow from the fact that there is an agent-neutral reason to promote some end and that the reason to promote that end is that it is good in some way that the end in question is an agent-neutral good. For it could be, after all, that the good at stake is agent-relative, and not agent-neutral – it is good only with respect to some particular person, not good simpliciter – but that there is an agent-neutral reason to promote that which is good in an agent-relative way.

We still have not seen, though, any grounds independent of the particulars of this natural law view in favor of affirming a welfarist view. Are there any such independent grounds, or is the case for welfarism simply the case for the natural law conception of goods presented in the previous chapters? It seems to me that there are reasons available for being favorably disposed toward welfarism: that at present agent-neutral goods are highly mysterious, and that at present the affirmation of the existence of these mysterious goods is accompanied by no compensating theoretical benefit. Since we should not multiply mysteries beyond necessity, we should reject the claim that there exist agent-neutral goods.

The mysteriousness of agent-neutral goods does not reside in the obscurity of the very idea of an agent-neutral good: we can, as we have seen, spell out what it is for a good to be agent-neutral. What makes agent-neutral goods mysterious is that it seems that we can at present say so little about the nature of such goods, apart from their answering to that concept. In this respect, agent-neutral goodness compares rather unfavorably with agent-relative goodness.

Consider, by way of contrast, the extent to which welfare is subject to plausible explication, that is, the extent to which we can provide plausible formal accounts of the nature of well-being. A state of affairs is good *for an agent* insofar as it is pleasing *to that agent,* or insofar as it satisfies the desires *of that agent,* or insofar as it is perfective *of that agent.* Accounts of the nature of agent-relative goodness are numerous and rich, rich enough that they can be falsified – at least if the argument of Chapters 2 and 3 is correct. But when we look for explications of agent-neutral goodness to compare to the numerous plausible candidate theories of the nature of agent-relative goodness, we find nothing that comes close to the rich array of theories of well-being. At most, we find a list of states of affairs that are allegedly instances of agent-neutral goods. But – to adopt an objection that Sumner levels against objective list theories of well-being (Sumner 1996, pp. 45–46; see 2.6 for a discussion) as an objection against objective list theories of agent-neutral goodness – it would be wrong to think of a list of agent-neutral goods as anything like a theory of agent-neutral goodness; such a theory would have to tell us something informative about the formal features of the concept, rather than simply to catalog states of affairs that happen to fall under the concept. To be told that agent-neutral goods include justice, fairness, beauty, well-being, rich personal relations, freedom, the advancement of knowledge, etc., is not to learn anything new about the nature of agent-neutral goodness.[10]

Now, one might say that even if agent-neutral goods are mysterious, because we have not seen any plausible account of the nature of agent-neutral goodness, we should posit such value anyway, because either it is obvious that there are such goods or it is clear that we need to posit such goods to explain what there is reason to do. This claim was considered with respect to justice, fairness, and equality in 4.3, and there I argued that there is no reason to suppose either that we do intuitively think of these things as agent-neutral goods or that we need to suppose that these things are agent-neutral goods in order to explain our reasons to promote these states of affairs. I shall not multiply examples here. I will leave it to the reader to determine whether it appears that we are inclined on reflection to acknowledge the agent-neutral goodness of certain states of affairs, rather than merely to acknowledge that there are agent-neutral reasons to promote certain states of affairs. I will also leave it to the reader to determine whether the reasons to promote these states of affairs can be adequately explained in wholly welfarist terms. If this welfarist view can adequately account for the reasons to promote these allegedly agent-neutrally good states of affairs, it seems to me that the present obscurity of agent-neutral goodness is an adequate basis to affirm the welfarist thesis.

Agent-Relativity and Agent-Neutrality

According to egoism, the fundamental reasons for action are agent-relative. According to consequentialism, the fundamental reasons for action are agent-neutral. It is obvious that the resolution of this issue will have tremendous bearing on the content of the principles of practical reasonableness, especially when one's stand on this matter is coupled with the view that the goods that generate the fundamental reasons for action are all grounded in the good as the welfarist conceives it.

Natural law theorists have not spoken with one voice on this issue. (Nor have they spoken with one voice on issues of welfarism and commensurability.) Both Aquinas and Hobbes, in my view, conceived reasons for action in a completely agent-relativist way. With Hobbes, this is clear from the account of goodness in terms of which he frames the notion of rational action. With Aquinas, the agent-relativity is not always so clear, but it seems to me that the tenor of his view is agent-relativist, and that any apparently neutralist conception of goodness employed turns out to be, as such, not fundamentally relevant to practical reasoning. On the other hand, contemporary natural law theory tends to rely on an agent-neutral conception of reasons for action. From his earliest writings on natural law to his most recent discussions, Finnis has advocated agent-neutralism:

[O]ne is confronted not only with the pull of one's experienced desire for self-preservation [for example], but also with the concept that human life [for example] is a value to be realized and respected, and an awareness that the value is realized as much in your life as mine. Intelligence thus faces the problem, which realization of the value to pursue, and cannot solve the problem by declaring that my life is more valuable, as such, than yours. (Finnis 1970, p. 368)

[T]he basic goods are human goods, and can in principle be pursued, realized, and participated in by any human being. Another person's survival, his coming to know, his creativity, his all-round flourishing, may not interest me, may not concern me, may in any event be beyond my power to affect. But have I any reason to deny that they are really good, or that they are fit matters of interest, concern, and favour by that man and by all those who have to do with him? (Finnis 1980, pp. 106–107)

One can consider as desirable the participation of other people in goods of the same sort, i.e. one can think it good that other people, even people who do not engage one's affections at all, should be able to act (or to share in the results of action) under the same description: what at the level of mere feeling is radically different (his securing a good and my securing a good) becomes, at the level of understanding, significantly 'the same.' (Finnis 1983, p. 46)

On Finnis' view, everyone has a reason to promote the good of each person. I may be moved to promote my own good with indifference toward yours, but this sort of selfish action is the result of emotion, not of the recognition of intelligible reasons for action (Finnis 1992, p. 149).

Natural law theorists are thus divided over the issue of whether to affirm an agent-relativist or an agent-neutralist conception of the fundamental reasons for action. Which of these conceptions should be affirmed? As I suggested in 4.1, there is at least a prima facie reason for preferring an agent-relativist account of the reasons for action: that the goods that generate those fundamental reasons for action are such in virtue of an agent-relative description. (That those goods are agent-relative is an implication of the affirmation of welfarism: if all basic goods are aspects of well-being, and well-being is insusceptible of anything other than an agent-relativist interpretation, one must of course hold that the basic goods are agent-relative.) Now, if we say that every state of affairs that is an instance of a basic good is such in virtue of an agent-relative goodness-predicate's applying to it, and instances of basic good are the fundamental reasons for action, it seems reasonable to hold that the fundamental reasons for action are such in virtue of an agent-relative reason-predicate's applying to them.

A defender of an agent-neutralist natural law theory would, of course, resist this sort of argument. Finnis, for example, might deny that the basic goods are to be understood in an agent-relative way; and, indeed, his remarks occasionally strongly suggest an agent-neutralist account of the good at work. But if he means to assert this, he must give up his firm view that the basic goods are aspects of well-being, since it is impossible to characterize something as well-being in a way that is agent-neutralist. I therefore suggest that we read Finnis not as making a claim about the agent-neutrality of the good that is incompatible with his welfarism but, rather, as affirming the view that agent-relative goods generate agent-neutral reasons for action.

I have suggested that there is a good reason to hold that the fundamental reasons for action are agent-relative: that instances of basic goods are the fundamental reasons for action, and instances of the basic goods are such in virtue of agent-relative goodness-predicates. Now, this is not an entailment, of course: one can hold that while the states of affairs that are instances of basic goods have this status in virtue of their fitting an agent-relative description, they have their status as reasons in virtue of their fitting an agent-neutral description (e.g., while a state of affairs is good with regard to me in virtue of its fitting the description 'being an instance of my knowing,' that state of affairs is a reason in virtue of its fitting the description 'being an instance of someone's knowing'). But it does seem a ground, albeit defeasible, for affirming agent-relativity with regard to reasons for action. Why would someone like Finnis affirm an agent-neutralist conception of reasons for action?

Henry Veatch and Joseph Rautenberg have argued that Finnis's agent-neutralism stems from his severing the concept of a good from that of human needs and interests; but, as should be abundantly clear, this charge is completely groundless: on Finnis's view, the goodness of any basic value is constituted by its contributing to human fulfillment, and the reason to promote the basic values is their contribution to human fulfillment. To judge that something is a basic good is to judge that it is "a general form of human well-being" and a "fulfillment of a human potentiality" (Finnis 1980, p. 72); "The basic goods are basic reasons for acting because they are aspects of the fulfillment of persons" (Grisez, Finnis, and Boyle 1987, p. 114). It is, thus, obvious that this is not the reason that Finnis endorses agent-neutralism. (For a fuller discussion of Veatch and Rautenberg's arguments and a refutation of them, see Murphy 1996a, esp. pp. 53–63.)

Occasionally, Finnis argues that the absence of proper names in the descriptions of the states of affairs that are instances of basic goods shows that the reasons for action that arise from them are agent-neutral: "As intelligible, the basic goods have no proper names attached to them. So that they can be understood as goods and provide reasons for acting whether, in a particular case, the agent or another may benefit" (Grisez, Finnis, and Boyle 1987, p. 114). But this won't do. The agent-relativist does not assume that any proper names are attached to the goods; the agent-relativist simply denies that the lack of proper names in a reason-predicate implies that the reason-predicate is agent-neutral and, in addition, suggests that there is some basis for holding that the fact that goods are aspects of well-being indicates that the reasons arising from them are agent-relative. Indeed, the proper names issue is beside the point: a goodness-predicate or reason-predicate's containing a proper name is neither necessary nor sufficient for making that predicate agent-relative.

Recall the definition of an agent-relative reason offered by Nagel: given that R is a reason-predicate – that is, $(x)(y)(Ry \rightarrow$ there is a reason for x to promote $y)$, where x is an agent and y a state of affairs – R is an agent-relative reason-predicate if and only if there is a free occurrence of x in R. If there are no free occurrences of x in R, then, no matter how many proper names are included in R, R will be an agent-neutral reason; all agents will thereby have reason to promote y. It thus seems that Finnis errs here in thinking that the supposition that reason-predicates employ only general terms is either necessary or sufficient to guarantee the agent-neutrality of those reasons. (The same would hold true, *mutatis mutandis,* of goodness-predicates; so if the 'no proper names' point is offered in support of an agent-neutral conception of goodness, that conception would be similarly lacking in support.)

What basis is there, then, for the natural law theorist to affirm agent-neutralism? It seems to me that the strongest grounds that can be put forward for holding that the agent-relative basic goods generate agent-neutral reasons for action would rely on the same type of considerations that were employed in formulating a list of the basic goods (1.1). Consider the following plan of action: that of giving food to a complete stranger in order that this stranger might stay alive. Is this an intelligible action or not? It seems to be; and it is the sort of action toward which many of us display a tendency, an inclination. How is the agent-relativist to account for the intelligibility of actions that seem to be for the sake of promoting others' good?

Veatch and Rautenberg hold that the agent-relativist has an easy answer to this question. In defending eudaimonism, a thesis the content of which is closely approximated as the conjunction of welfarism and agent-relativism, they write:

If one should try to make a rejoinder [to eudaimonism] . . . by asking whether in an Aristotelian or Thomistic [i.e. a eudaimonist] context there can be no such thing as a love of neighbor, or no sacrificing of oneself for the good and well-being of others, the reply is that not only is provision made for such a thing as an individual's love of his friends, but also and more generally a love of neighbor is actually something morally requisite for each and every human being. Yet this certainly does not mean that such a love of neighbor for Aquinas is ever to be construed as an exercise in utilitarian impartiality. . . . No, for Aquinas, as for Aristotle, a love of neighbor is to be construed as a love for one's friend in which one's friend's good is identified with one's own good, and where to pursue the good of one's friend is to show even a definite partiality for one's own happiness and well-being, of which the good of one's friend becomes an integral part. (Veatch and Rautenberg 1991, pp. 820–821)

We might read Veatch and Rautenberg's treatment of the problem of others' good as an effort to turn the tables on a view like Finnis's, since it is part of Finnis's view both that friendship is one of the basic goods and that it is constitutive of friendship that the good of one's friend becomes an aspect of one's own good. In participating in friendship, one necessarily finds oneself in a situation in which one's good is bound up with the good of others: as Finnis writes, "self-love (the desire to participate fully, oneself, in the basic aspects of human flourishing [including friendship]) requires that one go beyond self-love (self-interest, self-preference, the imperfect rationality of egoism)" (1980, p. 143).

The Veatch-Rautenberg position may be fairly summarized as this: the way to handle the problem of others' good is, on an agent-relativist account, to make the others somehow *less other* – that is, to emphasize the existence of special relationships, such as those of friendship and community.[11] Now, there is no doubt that on both agent-relativist and agent-neutralist natural law theories, the reasons for action arising from these special relationships have an important place. But to rely wholly upon them as a way of handling the problems surrounding others' good is ill-advised, for two related reasons. First, to rely wholly on contingent unifying relationships to explain one's reasons to foster others' good is to allow that in the limiting case of the person who does not participate in the good of friendship, for whatever reason (commitment to other basic goods, emotional distaste for friendships, serious chemical imbalance in the brain), such a person has absolutely no reason to promote others' good. Secondly, even for those who participate to a great extent in the goods of friendship, there are still many who remain completely other – perhaps the stranger on the roadside who has been set upon by thieves, or perhaps the stranger on the other side of the earth whose environment we might contaminate for our own convenience. With regard to such people, we have no reason to promote their good, if all reasons to respect others' good derive from special relationships in which another's good becomes assimilated to one's own.

So the Veatch-Rautenberg account is unsuccessful. But neither do I find wholly satisfactory the two solutions that I proposed in earlier work on behalf of agent-relativism (Murphy 1996a, pp. 71–80). On one solution, the agent-relativist can hold that it is a principle of practical reasonableness that each person respect what is a source of value for him or her, and thus, one has reason to respect others' participation in the basic goods by promoting it or refraining from impeding it. On the other, the agent-relativist can hold that since religion is a basic good, and all human participations in the basic goods are imitations of the divine goodness, it is partly constitutive of being in a proper relationship to the divine that one respect others' participation in the basic goods. I now find the former solution problematic because I am unsure whether such a principle of practical reasonableness could be defended within the framework I have offered for assessing principles of practical reasonableness; and I now find the latter solution problematic both because it depends so heavily on a conception of the relationship between the divine goodness and human goodness and because it rests on a very loosely articulated conception of the good of religion. But I confess that my main concern with these proposals has to do not with the details of how these agent-relativist responses can be worked out but with the simple worry that these responses offer too derivative an account of the intelligibility of promoting others' good.

By contrast, an agent-neutralist view like Finnis's is easily able to handle the issue of others' good. On his view, the basic goods that are good in virtue of fulfilling persons are such that for each instance of a basic good, all agents have a reason to promote it. For every goodness-predicate G that contains a free occurrence of a variable ranging over agents, there is a reason-predicate R that contains in its place a variable bound by an existential quantifier: if G is 'is an instance of A's knowing', G gives rise to R, 'is an instance of someone's knowing.' Thus, the reason is had by all agents; and the reason is a reason to promote any state of affairs that is an instance of some person's knowing. On this view, if y is good for agent A, then all agents have a reason to promote y. It is, therefore, easy to explain the intelligibility of giving food to the stranger, or indeed of any action that aims at promoting an instance of a basic good in oneself or another.

The view that agent-neutral reasons for action arise from the basic goods thus has as an argument in its favor its capacity to provide a much more natural and plausible explanation for the intelligibility of other-regarding actions than the agent-relativist view is able to offer. It might be thought that since the agent-neutralist view is clearly superior in accounting for the intelligibility of actions of this type, there are sufficient grounds to reject the simple view of the relationship between goods and reasons that the agent-relativist offers. But matters are not so clear-cut.

The central worry about agent-relativism is that even where it can provide some account of the intelligibility of the pursuit of others' good, it seems to make concern for others a far too derivative matter. It seems to me, though, that agent-neutralism falls prey to an analogous worry: it makes special concern for one's own good a far too derivative matter. On the agent-neutralist view, special concern for one's own good is sensible only insofar as one is in a better position to promote one's own good (either for the straightforward reason that we are better able to promote the good of those close to us, and no one is closer to us than ourselves, or for the less straightforward reason that there are some goods constituted by choice such that it is necessarily up to each person to promote that good for him- or herself). But, just as the agent-relativist solutions to the problem of others' good seem to me to be too derivative, the agent-neutralist solutions to the problem of one's own good seem to me too derivative also. One could, of course, deny that any such nonderivative concern for one's own good is intelligible; but this is a claim that one could with equal plausibility make with regard to others' good. The fact that the dualism of practical reason discussed by Sidgwick (*Methods,* pp. 497–509) is such a central issue in practical philosophy is a theoretical manifestation of the common conviction that concern for oneself possesses a peculiar, unique intelligibility. And if there is such intelligibility to pursuit of one's own good, then there is a feature of practical life of which agent-relativism provides a better account: for if the reasons for action grounded in the basic goods are agent-relative, then the intelligibility of the special concern that agents have for their own good is easily explicable.

To hold that the fundamental reasons for action are agent-relative commits one to a tortured account of how pursuit of others' good is intelligible; to hold that the fundamental reasons for action are agent-neutral commits one to a tortured account of how self-preference in pursuit of the good is intelligible. There is a third option, though, and it is one that does justice not only to the immediate intelligibility of pursuit of others' good and to the nonderivative concern for one's own good, but also to the theoretical consideration that I first mentioned as a point in favor of an agent-relativist conception of reasons. The basic idea is due to Thomas Nagel. In *The Possibility of Altruism,* Nagel claimed that in order to be legitimate, a putatively agent-relative reason for action has to be reformulated as an agent-neutral reason. But in reconsidering his view, he realized that his argument entailed a different conclusion, that is, "That there are [agent-neutral] reasons corresponding to all [agent-relative] ones. This by itself does not imply that all reasons are [agent-neutral]. It remains possible that the original [agent-relative] reasons from which the others are generated retain some independent force and are not completely subsumed under them" (Nagel 1970, p. vii).[12]

What these remarks of Nagel's suggest vis-à-vis the various considerations that have been raised in favor of natural law theory's affirming an agent-neutralist or agent-relativist conception of reasons is that it is possible to incorporate all of these positive features within a single theory of fundamental reasons for action. One might affirm the simple view, that agent-relative reasons result from agent-relative basic goods. But, in addition, one might claim that from these agent-relative reasons for action there arise fundamental agent-neutral reasons for action. Within this system of reasons there will be, as Nagel suggests, an agent-neutral reason corresponding to every agent-relative one. Such a system of reasons is capable of explaining both how pursuit of others' good is intelligible, in that such action is sanctioned by agent-neutral reasons for action, and how special concern for one's own good is intelligible, in that such action is sanctioned by independent agent-relative reasons for action.

Now, it might be thought that there is incoherence here in the idea that a fundamental agent-neutral reason for action arises from an agent-relative reason. How can a fundamental reason arise from another reason? Isn't what makes a reason fundamental just that it does not arise from another reason? We need to make a distinction between two ways that a reason for action can be fundamental. It can be fundamental in that in explaining how that reason is generated, one need not appeal to the existence of any other reason in one's explanation. Or, it can be fundamental in that in offering a practical account of the normative force that the reason possesses on a given occasion, one need not refer to the normative force of another reason.

Now, it may be the case that a reason that is not fundamental in one of these senses will fail to be fundamental in the other sense also. Consider, for example, instrumental reasons and specificatory reasons. (If, indeed, there really are any reasons of these sorts. The principle of individuation for reasons offered in 2.4 would, I think, imply that there really are no such reasons.) An instrumental reason arises from another instrumental or noninstrumental reason, and as instrumental, it derives all of its normative force from that other reason. A specificatory reason (that is, a reason to promote some state of affairs that is an instance of some state of affairs that one has reason to promote, as when one has a reason to play basketball inasmuch as one has a reason to take exercise) arises from another reason, and as specificatory, it derives all of its normative force from that other reason. But while there are grounds for supposing that all reasons nonfundamental in the latter sense are also nonfundamental in the former sense, the converse need not hold. It is thus possible that reasons that arise from other reasons have independent normative force. This seems sufficient, however, to answer the worry. For my claim is that while agent-neutral reasons are not fundamental in the former sense, in that they arise from agent-relative reasons, they are fundamental in the latter sense, in that they are distinct reasons, of independent normative force. In making one's action of promoting another's good intelligible, one need appeal only to the agent-neutral reason, though in a metapractical account of why one has that agent-neutral reason, one would need to make reference to the corresponding agent-relative reason for action.

I offer no account here, though, of how agent-neutral reasons arise from agent-relative reasons, for I possess no such account. The best-worked-out view is Nagel's (1970, pp. 99–124). Let it suffice to say that while I think that his emphasis on the practical need to avoid dissociation between the subjective and the objective points of view is not the kind of account that fits with natural law theory of the sort that I am developing, his argument that the generation of agent-neutral reasons results from some sort of objectifying function of reason seems surely right. If I were to try to work out such an account, I would focus not, as Nagel does, on the conception of the self as one being among others, but on the states of affairs that practical reason grasps as worth pursuing. The states of affairs that are grasped as reasons for action under agent-relative descriptions are all, when realized, susceptible of both an agent-relative and an agent-neutral description.

What needs to be understood is how practical reason comes to view this state of affairs as something worth pursuing, not only under the original agent-relative description that still applies to it but also under the agent-neutral description that applies to it. For, of course, if an instance of the agent's good is worth pursuing under that agent-neutral description, so too are all of those states of affairs that are instances of others' well-being to which that agent-neutral description also applies. If, for example, my reason to promote my own knowledge generates a reason to promote someone's knowledge, I would have a reason to promote the knowing of any person capable of participating in that good.

I admit that I have left mysterious how this process occurs. But we do have good reasons to think that it does occur; and as Hume writes, "it is no just reason for rejecting any principle, confirmed by experience, that we cannot give a satisfactory account of its origin, nor are able to resolve it into other more general principles" (*Enquiry,* p. 213). It is worth reminding those who are skeptical about this objectifying function of practical reason that this sort of activity is mysterious also in the theoretical domain. How do we move from affirming descriptions of the world that are subject-centered to affirming descriptions of the world that are not subject-centered? In the absence of an impossibility proof, the lack of a detailed picture of how this movement toward agent-neutrality occurs gives us no reason to doubt that it does.

Incommensurability

It is difficult to underestimate the extent to which the structure of egoism and consequentialism is dictated by their affirmation of the commensurability of the goods that generate the fundamental reasons for action. The two features that are defining of consequentialist thought – a maximizing account of practical reasonableness,[13] and a rejection of the relevance of the intended/foreseen distinction – both flow from the commensurability thesis (5.2). To a great extent, the form of the natural law theory of practical reasoning put forward here results from a strong denial of this claim about commensurability.

The basics of the argument for a strong incommensurability thesis are due to Germain Grisez (1978). The argument for this claim takes the form of a practical proof, in the sense that Kant's argument that human beings are 'negatively free' is supposed to be a practical proof (*Grounding,* pp. 447–448). Recall that on Kant's view, the practical proof for the freedom of the human agent is that the positing of such freedom is a necessary condition for making sense of the activity of deliberation. This proof is practical in that the positing of freedom is done for the sake of accounting for a feature of action. As Thomas Hill has pointed out, though (Hill 1992, pp. 117–118), it is also important that theoretical considerations not stand in the way of the conclusion of this practical proof. If determinism could be shown to be true by theoretical reason, we would have reason to dismiss the result of the practical proof: but since, as Kant argues in the first *Critique,* the sort of causal relationships on which determinist claims are made can be known to hold only in the phenomenal realm, it leaves open the possibility that the noumenal self is a free agent. Thus, in this practical proof, we have both the affirmation of a claim as needed to make sense of a feature of action and at least an openness to the possibility of the truth of that claim from the perspective of theoretical reason.

The incommensurability thesis is proved practically. Recall the situation of practically significant choice described in the Introduction (0.1): it is the situation in which it is possible for an agent to act intelligibly in either of two (or more) incompatible ways; that is, he or she may ϕ intelligibly or may ψ intelligibly, but it is impossible for the agent both to ϕ and to ψ. More precisely, an agent A confronts a practically significant choice if (a) A has a reason to ϕ which is not identical with any reason that A has to ψ; (b) A has a reason to ψ which is not identical with any reason that A has to ϕ; (c) it is possible for A to ϕ; (d) it is possible for A to ψ; and (e) ϕ-ing is incompatible with ψ-ing. It might be thought that since reasons are what makes actions intelligible, it is strange that conditions (a) and (b) are not simply 'A has a reason to ϕ' and 'A has a reason to ψ' respectively. Why add the proviso that these reasons are not identical with any reasons to perform the other action? The answer is that the conditions for the intelligibility of the performance of an action are not identical to conditions for the intelligibility of the performance of one action *rather* than another. The adducing of a reason to ϕ is sufficient for the answering of the question 'Why did he or she ϕ?' But when the question is, 'Why did he or she ϕ rather than ψ?' the adducing of a reason to ϕ is not sufficient for the answering of that question; rather, one will have to provide a reason that one has to ϕ which is not a reason that one had to ψ. If one were to adduce reason R as the reason that one ϕ-ed rather than ψ-ed, yet R is a reason for ψ-ing as well as for ϕ-ing, one will not have made one's performance of the act of ϕ-ing rather than ψ-ing a whit more intelligible.[14]

From this description of practically significant choice follows what I will call the *general* incommensurability thesis. Consider a situation in which an agent A faces a practically significant choice between two plans of action, one of which, the plan of action of ϕ-ing, has reason (or set of reasons) R as its rationale, and the other of which, the plan of action of ψ-ing, has reason (or set of reasons) S as its rationale. According to the general incommensurability thesis, in all such cases R and S are incommensurable. If they were commensurable, then A would not face a practically significant choice between them: for either it would be the case that every reason that A had to ψ would be a reason that A had to ϕ, and A would have additional reasons to ϕ as well, or it would be the case that every reason that A had to ϕ would be a reason that A had to ψ, and A would have additional reasons to ψ as well. If the former of these options hold, then A cannot ψ intelligibly; if the latter, then A cannot ϕ intelligibly. In either case, A does not face a practically significant choice. Thus, in every practically significant choice, the reasons for action involved are incommensurable.

The general incommensurability thesis makes a claim about the connection between practically significant choice and the incommensurability of reasons for action, just as the conclusion of Kant's argument asserts a connection between deliberation and freedom. What neither the deliberation-freedom connection nor the choice-incommensurability connection gives is the *scope* of deliberation or choice, so that we can explain the extent of freedom or commensurability. If there is an instance of deliberation, or practically significant choice, then there is freedom, or incommensurability. But in an account of the principles of practical reasonableness that is built on the nature of reasons for action, we need to know how far incommensurability extends. Three sorts of incommensurability will be important for our treatment of the principles of practical reasonableness: incommensurability that arises (i) between the categories of basic good that generate the fundamental reasons for action, (ii) between distinct instantiations of basic goods, and (iii) between agent-relative and agent-neutral reasons for action.

(i) I claim that incommensurability holds between the categories of the basic goods in the following strong way: each of the categories of basic good is incommensurable with every other. Now, by making this claim, I do not (yet) make the assertion that for every instance i of good G and every instance j of distinct good H, i and j are incommensurable. The thesis that the categories of good are incommensurable is not meant to have this implication. Rather, it is only to say that none of the goods is better in kind than any other, considered generically.

The basis for this claim regarding the incommensurability of the categories of basic good is that (a) we can, in fact, encounter choices of a fairly abstract sort between these different categories and (b) when we do encounter these choices, they are invariably practically significant. One can face choices regarding the devotion of one's life to one type of good rather than another: to become a physician (life) or a philosopher (knowledge), to get married (friendship) or to take holy orders (religion). And it does seem clear that when one encounters these choices, one can intelligibly choose one or the other. If this is so, then, by the general incommensurability thesis, the categories of basic good are incommensurable.

(ii) Presumably, if the categories of basic good are incommensurable, then at least some of the different instances of basic good are incommensurable. But how far does the incommensurability of instances of basic goods extend?

I claim that the incommensurability among the instances of the basic goods is pervasive: every two instantiations of basic goods that are wholly distinct are incommensurable with each other. Now, it seems clear from the universality of this claim that any plausibility that it possesses will depend on some presupposed, at least partial, account of how the notion of 'wholly distinct' is to be understood. The general idea is that two states of affairs are wholly distinct when those states of affairs are not identical and neither state of affairs includes the other. More specifically, but not exhaustively, here are some sufficient conditions for two instances of basic goods to be wholly distinct: instantiations i and j are wholly distinct if there is some person in which i is instantiated and j is not, or vice versa; instantiations i and j are wholly distinct if i and j are instantiations of distinct categories of basic good; instantiations i and j are wholly distinct if i and j contribute to distinct dimensions of the same category of basic good. Here is a sufficient, but not very informative, condition for two instances of basic goods not to be wholly distinct: instantiations i and j are not wholly distinct if i and j differ in no relevant respect other than the degree to which i and j instantiate a particular dimension of a basic good.[15]

Now, this incommensurability thesis is quite strong. The basis for it is just that all of the cases in which one is choosing between wholly distinct instantiations of basic goods are cases in which the choice is practically significant: either option can be intelligibly chosen; for each action, there is a reason to perform that action that is not a reason to perform the other.

One way to see the support for this claim is simply to imagine cases involving undoubtedly wholly distinct instances of basic good, and see whether it is not obvious that in these cases, one faces a practically significant choice. While this sort of appeal does, I think, work in many cases, there are some cases of wholly distinct goods in which we are strongly disposed to reject incommensurability. I thus offer the following alternative route to seeing that all such choices are practically significant. Consider the concept of 'not unreasonable regret.' It seems clear that in many cases, one can choose a plan of action, confident that one has made the best, or at least a reasonable, decision, while still not unreasonably regretting not taking the other option. For this sort of regret not to be unreasonable, there would have to be something worthwhile in the unchosen plan that is not present in the chosen plan: for if the chosen plan had everything that the unchosen plan had, and some more as well, regret would be completely out of place, and totally unreasonable.[16] It is clear, then, that the notion of not unreasonable regret is quite closely tied to situations of practically significant choice: what makes choice practically significant is that for each option, there is something to be gained in that option that is not to be gained in the other. So, for any choice, if it is one such that both options could be the source of not unreasonable regret, that choice is practically significant.

Now, it seems to me that whenever there is a choice between two wholly distinct instances of basic goods, either option could be the source of not unreasonable regret. When we opt for one instance of a basic good, rather than a wholly distinct other, we do not gain all that is of interest and more besides; we miss out on something genuinely good, worth realizing, whose goodness is not captured in the instance of a basic good that we do settle on. If, as I suggest, the possibility of not unreasonable regret invariably goes along with choices between wholly distinct instances of basic goods, then all such choices are practically significant. If all such choices are practically significant, then every two instances of basic goods that are wholly distinct are incommensurable.

(iii) Grisez and Finnis emphasize the sorts of incommensurability discussed in (i) and (ii), though my argument departs from theirs at points. But since they seem to affirm that all of the fundamental reasons for action are agent-neutral, neither of them considers a third kind of incommensurability: that between the agent-relative and the agent-neutral reasons for action. Just as we can consider choices between acting on one category of basic good or another in the abstract, we can consider choices between acting on agent-relative and agent-neutral reasons in this way. Consider as a stark version of such a choice the decision whether to live an egoistic life or an impartial one. This kind of choice does seem to be a practically significant one: the person who opts for egoism may be unreasonable, but that person is not acting unintelligibly. Neither is the person who chooses to live a life of impartiality, acting only on agent-neutral reasons, acting unintelligibly. Thus, I claim that there is incommensurability between the agent-relative and agent-neutral reasons for action. (See also Nagel 1979c.)

Now, these arguments for deep and pervasive incommensurability among the fundamental reasons for action take the form of a practical proof, and, as I mentioned, practical proofs can be called into doubt by the conclusions of theoretical reason. While I know of no such arguments, it will be worthwhile to present a model of how incommensurability might arise, in order to carve out some conceptual space for it.

We can see why this incommensurability might be present by reconsidering some of the claims made in Chapter 1 in the discussion of the real identity thesis. The real identity thesis connects aspects of human flourishing to aspects of well-being: for a particular state of affairs to contribute constitutively to one's well-being is for it to contribute constitutively to one's flourishing. If, then, we can see how these states of affairs might be incommensurable with regard to the extent that they contribute to human flourishing, we can see that there is conceptual space for incommensurability of goods.

First, it seems clear how states of affairs that contribute to different persons' flourishing could be incommensurable. Even if state of affairs S were to contribute to *x* degree to *A*'s flourishing, and *T* were to contribute to *y* degree to *B*'s flourishing, we lack a common measure to commensurate the two: there is no third object to whose flourishing both *S* and *T* contribute that could serve as a common measure for S and T. Secondly, it seems clear how states of affairs that contribute to one person's flourishing could be incommensurable, if they are instances of different categories of basic good. For it seems possible that the function that constitutes human flourishing is an inclusive function – living and knowing and experiencing aesthetically and . . . But this sort of function, in itself, provides no standard with which to commensurate the various functions that are conjoined in it. Thirdly, it seems clear how states of affairs that are instances of a single basic good might nonetheless be incommensurable with each other, that is, that it not make sense to say of any two instances of good *G* that one of them instantiates *G* more fully than the other. For any of the items included as part of the human's inclusive function that is its flourishing might have a number of dimensions to it (think of the different kinds of knowledge that there are, and how it might seem senseless to say that one is a greater participation in knowledge than the other), or might have instances that are related only analogically, so that there is no univocal notion that could be used in providing a common measure for greater or lesser instantiation (think of the different ways one might participate in play). Thus, it seems to me that we can provide an account of human flourishing that would make sense of there being tremendous incommensurability among the fundamental reasons for action.

Given the arguments for the incommensurability of goods and the consistency of incommensurability with what we know of human flourishing from theoretical reason, I will proceed to treat incommensurability as a feature of the fundamental reasons for action to which any adequate set of principles of practical reasonableness will do justice. Since incommensurability is so powerful, it is clear that the consequentialist principle of practical reason must be severely limited in scope. And indeed it is: see 5.5 to see the limits on the application of that principle in the face of almost complete incommensurability.

Producible Ends and Ends-in-Themselves

Throughout our previous discussions of the natural law view's welfarism about practical rationality, I have spoken of welfare reasons as states of affairs that as such make some subject better off. It seems clear, then, that I am in some way committed to rejecting the Kantian view that the fundamental reasons for action are subsistent ends, or ends-in-themselves, in favor of the view that the fundamental reasons for action are producible ends.[17] But I think it would be misleading to characterize the natural law view as simply rejecting the Kantian picture in favor of the standard welfarist position. Rather, its conception of the relationship between the basic goods and the humans who can participate in them enables it to move beyond the subsistent-end/producible-end dichotomy.

The main reason that I take the Kantian view to be unsatisfactory is that it requires a dualism between the person and the goods in which that person can participate, which strikes me as both implausible in itself and without foundation. Its inherent implausibility can be seen by way of its implications about what occurs when one is deprived of an instance of a basic good. Suppose, for example, that a thug were to aim at injuring you. On the Kantian view, this attack on you is one step removed: it is not an attack on you directly, but only on one of the goods that you happen to be enjoying. Now, this sort of description might be accurate if the thug were, say, to burn your house down – this sort of attack on you is clearly at a remove from your person. But to hold that an attack on your health, a good that is intrinsic to you, is not an attack on you directly but only through a good you happen to be participating in seems to me to render implausible the dualism of person and goods that implies it.

It seems to me that the Kantian could defend this distinction only by rejecting the intrinsicness to the person of the goods in which one can participate or by holding that their status as goods is dependent on some exercise of one's personhood. But both of these strategies strike me as unpromising. Perhaps within Kant's own view, the intrinsicness to the person of goods could be denied: on his view, the person who is capable of agency exists in the noumenal realm, while any goods that might be pursued belong to the phenomenal realm. Any deprivation of goods would be, on this view, at a remove from the person; for the person is, on this account, pure agency. But contemporary Kantians have, for the most part, rejected this view of the person, along with other functionally equivalent dualisms that would render comprehensible a strong distinction between persons and the goods that they can enjoy.

The other way to generate the needed distinction between person and goods is to make the status of goods as such dependent on some free exercise of agency by the person; on this view, the self would be prior to the ends that it pursues, inasmuch as the status of these ends as goods would depend on the agent's choice. In depriving a person of a good, then, one would be depriving him or her of something that is good only by way of the victim's agency, of something worthy of protection only because it is the end of an agent. But this is, in my view, just another version of subjectivism about goods; it relies on the claim that prior to choice there is no intrinsic intelligibility to the pursuit of certain objects. Since this subjectivism about goods is false (2.2–2.5), it is false to say that the self is prior to its ends in any sense that would sustain the strong distinction between the basic goods and the person who participates in them.

What renders the Kantian account of fundamental reasons for action as subsistent ends hard to believe, on this view, is the status of the basic goods as intrinsic to persons. But one sympathetic to the Kantian view might offer the following retort. Surely, this sympathizer might say, even on the natural law view there is an important difference between the person and the goods that the person can enjoy. After all, no instance of a basic good – apart from, of course, the minimal participation in the good of life that is the sine qua non for the continuing existence of the person – is essential to a person; a person can exist without enjoying any particular instance of a basic good. There is, then, a metaphysical priority of person to goods that surely will be reflected in the view that the ultimate reasons for action, the most basic items of practical significance, are persons, rather than the goods that fulfill those persons. And, further, the defender of the subsistent ends view can appeal again to the considerations in favor of that view mentioned in 5.2, that is, that it can be plausibly argued that no action for the sake of some producible end is intelligible unless directed for the sake of some person.

The natural law theorist cannot entirely deny the force of these considerations: for, on the natural law view, the status of the basic goods as such depends on their fulfilling, perfecting, the humans who can enjoy them. But this is, I think, where the natural law theorist can hold that his or her view does not involve simply a rejection of the Kantian conception of the end-in-itself as the fundamental kind of reason for action but, rather, a movement beyond the end-in-itself/producible-end dichotomy.

To hold that the fundamental reasons for action are subsistent ends is to hold that what makes action intelligible is its relation to what is, to what exists. To hold that the fundamental reasons for action are producible ends is to hold that what makes action intelligible is its relation to what is to be, to what can be brought about. On the Kantian picture, then, it is agents – subsistent ends – that are the fundamental reasons for action. But the natural law theorist, drawing on the particular account of human functioning and flourishing defended in Chapter 1 (1.2–1.4), can say that it is misleading to think of action for the sake of persons as being action simply for the sake of some existing thing. On this alternative conception, the existence of humans as we know them is always partial, incomplete; to act for their sake is to help complete them, actualize them, make them exist more fully. On this alternative conception, the clear distinction between subsistent and producible ends breaks down. There is not: the person; and, in addition, the goods in which that person participates. Rather, the participation of the agent in these goods is the very being of that person; he or she exists to the extent that he or she participates in these goods.

Now, this way of calling into question the subsistent-end/producible-end distinction is likely to draw protests from those who hold that this way of talking about existence, as a matter of more-or-less rather than as a matter of all-or-nothing, is both contrary to all ordinary understandings of existence and sure to bring nothing but obfuscation. I have no wish to deny that there is clearly and unquestionably a sense – perhaps the most common sense – in which all beings who exist exist to the same extent. Like the backward-E of existential quantification, 'there exists' is in this sense an all-or-nothing matter. But while I cannot hope to provide anything like a complete defense of the claim that to speak of existence as a more-or-less matter is clearly appropriate and not at all ob-

fuscating, I can at least say something about what the defender of this natural
law position might offer as a way of clarifying this idea.

When a thing is such that it has a proper end in virtue of the kind of thing
that it is, when a thing is such that it belongs to the thing's nature to perform a
certain kind of activity, yet such that its performance of that activity is not guaranteed, that thing can meaningfully be said to exist to the extent that its condition exhibits the activity that is its flourishing or proper functioning. A mere
pile of rubble, the configuration of which is not a matter of design, upon which
no purposes have been imposed – if such a thing can exist at all, it presumably
either does or doesn't, and there would be little sense to the idea that it exists
partially. A vacuum cleaner, not yet completely assembled, is by contrast the
sort of thing to which partial existence can be meaningfully ascribed. The difference is just that the vacuum cleaner, unlike the pile, does have an end that
constitutes its functioning well, and to the extent to which it has realized its capacity to exercise that function, it exists.

Once we affirm, then, the notion that the human has a function, and flour-
ishes to the extent that it exercises its function (1.2), then we can make comprehensible the idea that the human being can exist to a greater or lesser degree.
On this view, to promote the human's functioning is to promote a human's becoming more complete, more actual. This understanding of the relationship between the person and the goods in which the person can participate breaks down
the clear distinction between producible and subsistent ends. To respond to a
basic good as such is just to act, in some specific way, for the sake of a person.
(For further discussion of the way that natural law theory tries to get beyond the
producible-end/subsistent-end dichotomy, see Boyle 1984, pp. 401–407; Grisez,
Finnis, and Boyle 1987, p. 115; and George 1988, pp. 1417–1419.)

5.4 A Note on Hierarchy among the Basic Goods

In providing an account of the principles of practical reasonableness that govern plans of action, then, I will rely upon the fact that reasons for action are welfare reasons; that for each agent-relative welfare reason, there is a corresponding agent-neutral welfare reason; and that all of these distinct reasons are
incommensurable. I will not refer to any other feature of the reasons for action
in providing an account of practical principles. This stance sets this natural law
account in opposition, though, to an eminent natural law tradition that holds that
the basic goods exhibit a hierarchical ordering, and that this hierarchical ordering is relevant in determining how it is appropriate to respond to the basic goods.
In contrast to this tradition within natural law theory, Finnis, George, and others have recently argued against the notion that the basic goods exhibit any such
practically relevant hierarchy. It might be thought, then, that my failure to appeal to theses about hierarchical ordering among the basic goods is an implicit
endorsement of Finnis's and George's position. But it seems to me that nothing

that I have argued thus far commits me to the endorsement of their view, and indeed, the arguments that they offer for this position are far from decisive. While I think that we can spell out, in a way that avoids Finnis's and George's criticisms, what it would be for there to be a practically relevant hierarchy among the basic goods, I do not think that these conditions are, in fact, met.

It seems that Finnis holds that the absence of a hierarchy among the categories of basic goods is a result of their incommensurability: there is no hierarchy among them because "none of the basic goods can be said meaningfully to be better than another" (Grisez, Finnis, and Boyle 1987, p. 137; Finnis 1980, p. 92). Since a hierarchy among the basic goods could exist only if some of these goods were, as such, better than others, the incommensurability of the basic goods forecloses the possibility that there might be a natural hierarchy among them. In addition to this worry about the compatibility of incommensurability and hierarchy among the basic goods, George raises questions about what precisely such a hierarchy would come to if an agent were faced with decisions between goods that occupy different levels in the hierarchy.

George considers the frequently offered suggestion that religion is superordinate to the other basic goods, and wonders just how this would, if true, play out in the agent's decisions concerning the promotion of that good. Suppose that an agent, in keeping with the view that religion is the highest in the hierarchy of goods, devotes Sunday to church. How far does the good of religion control the rest of that agent's life?

We are likely to have trouble figuring out what he ought to do on Monday morning when he faces the option of going to a morning church service or getting to work on time. Does the supposed hierarchical priority of religion release him from the moral obligation (to be at work promptly) entailed by his prior commitment to his employer? Perhaps the principle of hierarchy does not control this particular choice; perhaps we can conclude that, despite the priority of religion, our subject ought to go to work in this case rather than to church. But what if he can manage to attend the service and still make it to work on time, thus avoiding any violation of moral norms? Does the priority of religion entail that he behaves immorally if he opts instead to spend his time before work reading the paper, or listening to some jazz recordings, or playing with his children? Suppose he does forgo all these possibilities in favor of a morning church service. Is he also morally required to forgo a pleasant walk in the park after lunch in order to attend a noontime religious observance? Does the priority of religion over the other human goods mean that in every situation of choice in which one is under no moral obligation to do something else, one must, if possible, act specifically for the good of religion? (George 1988, p. 1427)

George admits that this picture may be a caricature of what the defenders of the hierarchy thesis have in mind, while "welcom[ing] correction": on his view, none of the opponents of his and Finnis's position have offered anything like a sufficiently detailed account of what would be involved in choosing reasonably with respect to a hierarchy of goods.

Finnis and George offer, then, challenges of two sorts to the defender of the hierarchy thesis: first, to show either that the incommensurability thesis applied at the level of basic goods is false or that incommensurability is consistent with hierarchy; and secondly, to show what requirements of practical reasonableness would follow from the affirmation of the relevant hierarchy among the basic goods. In a moment we will turn to the task of offering responses to these challenges on behalf of the defender of the hierarchy thesis. But it should be noted that there is available to the defender of that thesis an obvious *tu quoque* rebuff to Finnis's and George's challenges. Both Finnis and George hold that each person is under a practical requirement to form a life plan that includes a subjective prioritization of the basic goods in his or her life (Finnis 1980, pp. 100–105). While the incommensurability of the basic goods implies, on their view, that there is no such hierarchy prior to choice, one can reasonably place these goods in a hierarchy in one's own life plan and can reasonably adhere to that life plan in making more particular choices. But to affirm that one can reasonably impose such an order of priority upon the basic goods is to give up the idea that there is any sort of inconsistency between holding that the basic goods are incommensurable and that they by nature exhibit a hierarchical ordering. For if one can reasonably place the goods in a hierarchy and adhere to that hierarchy in making choices, then in so doing, one is doing nothing that is at odds with the incommensurability of those goods. But if one is doing nothing at odds with the incommensurability of the goods by treating them as hierarchically ordered, then there is no reason to believe that there is anything inconsistent in affirming both that those goods are incommensurable and that they are *by nature* hierarchically ordered. And if George asks what particular requirements on choice are generated by the goods' naturally forming a hierarchy, the defender of that view can respond that it is the requirements on choice that would be generated by the goods' forming a structurally identical hierarchy through the agent's commitment.[18]

The recognition of Finnis and George of the reasonableness of prioritizing the basic goods in one's life and of responding to that hierarchy in particular ways undermines their claims that there is something inconsistent or obscure about holding that the basic goods form some sort of hierarchy that constrains the range of practically reasonable responses to those goods. The mistake in thinking that the incommensurability thesis rules out the existence of a hierarchy among the basic goods seems to be that of supposing that the only relationship among the basic goods that could be relevant to the formation of a practically relevant hierarchy among them is that of 'better than' or 'worse than'; if so, the truth of the incommensurability thesis would decisively rule out the possibility of a hierarchy among the basic goods. (Since this natural law view affirms the incommensurability thesis, I will not recommend its rejection to the friend of the hierarchy thesis as a way of upholding that latter thesis.) But it seems to me that the defender of the hierarchy thesis could appeal to a distinct relationship that might hold by nature among some of the basic goods, the 'for the sake of' relationship, and this relationship seems consistent with the presence of incommensurability among the basic goods, while capable of underwriting a practically relevant hierarchy among those goods.

The idea is this. The defender of the hierarchy thesis could claim that while all of the basic goods are intrinsically good, worth pursuing for their own sakes, some of them are naturally – that is, prior to all individual choice and commitment – also for the sake of others. If some basic good G is for the sake of some basic good H, while H is not for the sake of G, then there does seem to be a kind of hierarchy among the basic goods. And this relationship does not seem to depend on the goods in question being commensurable: there is no obvious logical relationship between H's having (or failing to have) all of G's intrinsic goodness, and more as well, and G's being (or not being) for the sake of H.

How, though, would the hierarchical structure of the basic goods manifest itself in constraints of practical reason? Perhaps the defender of the hierarchy thesis could offer the following: if a certain good is by nature for the sake of another, then it is by nature a means to the achievement of that other; and so what practical reasonableness would require would be that in one's plan of action, one should never fail to treat the former as a means to the latter. To do otherwise is to presuppose falsely that the former is not for the sake of the latter.

It is obvious, though, that this preliminary formulation of this principle of practical reasonableness would require interpretation: we would need to determine, that is, the most reasonable way to understand the idea that certain basic goods must be treated 'as means.' One natural, but far too strong, reading would go as follows. Suppose that G is for the sake of H, and H is not for the sake of G. To fail to treat G as a means to H is to pursue G other than as a means to H (or as a means to some other good for whose sake G is). On this reading, if a basic good is for the sake of another, then the proposed principle of practical reasonableness rules out any promotion of that good except as a means to a good for whose sake it is. To continue employing the example that was the focus of George's attention: if religion were thought of as a superordinate good, a good for the sake of no other but such that all others are for the sake of it, then knowledge (e.g.) should never be pursued except as a means to the religious good. But this understanding of the principle of practical reasonableness that would result from the truth of the hierarchy thesis is too strong. After all, knowledge is an intrinsic good (3.3), even if it is also for the sake of the good of religion; it would seem not to do justice to the nature of knowledge as intrinsically good if, by its very nature, it can never be reasonably pursued except as an instrument.

There is, however, an alternative reading of this principle that seems better in doing justice to goods that are both intrinsically good and hierarchically ordered by the 'for the sake of' relationship. We might say that pursuit of each of the basic goods is as such reasonable, but only if one's pursuit of those lower in the hierarchy is regulated by the pursuit of those higher in the hierarchy. (I take the idea that the for-the-sake-of relationship involves the way that pursuit of one good is regulated in light of another from Richardson 1994, pp. 53–57.) One might (e.g.) hold that one can reasonably pursue knowledge for its own sake, even apart from its being a means to the religious good, if the pursuit of knowledge is regulated by what is necessary to promote the religious good.

Call this the 'regulation' interpretation of what follows from the hierarchy thesis. Again, there is a stronger and a weaker way of reading the regulation interpretation. On the strong reading – one that resembles the 'caricature' assumed by George – a for-the-sake-of relationship between knowledge and religion would imply that while one may pursue knowledge for its own sake, to do so in a way that in any way lessens one's capacity to participate in the religious good is inadequately to respond to the fact that knowledge is naturally for the sake of harmony with the divine. (Consider, by way of comparison, Aristotle's own treatment of the good of pleasure: while he holds that pleasure is an intrinsic good, it is to be subordinated to the goods of the proper functioning of the rational animal; pleasures are to be pursued only insofar as they "make for health and good condition" or "are not hindrances to these ends, or contrary to what is noble, or beyond [one's] means" [*Nicomachean Ethics,* 1119a15–18].)

George thinks that this is silly, I suppose, because he seems to think that it will result in the domination of one's life by a particular good. But it is far from clear either that this is true or that, if true, it would be an objection to the view. First: it is far from clear that domination of one's life by a particular good would result from this understanding of the regulation principle. Least importantly, but perhaps most obviously, goods can often be means to other goods, either directly (knowing things can help one to participate in the good of religion) or indirectly (pursuing a good other than knowledge can help recoup one's energy for pursuit of the good of knowledge). Further, it is sometimes true – and is almost certainly true in the religious case, which is part of why George's caricature misses the mark – that what is needed to participate in one good requires participation in another good, or that participation in that good has an upper limit, beyond which one could pursue other goods without damaging it in the least. Secondly, even if it were to follow that one's life would be dominated by pursuit of this good, it is hard to know whether that would count as an objection to the view. For those who take the religious good to be superordinate, either naturally or through choice, I imagine that George's caricature is of very little force indeed. If it were true that participation in the religious good were really threatened or undermined in any way by these other pursuits, rather than unaffected by or actually furthered by them, I imagine that without batting an eyelash those committed to the good of religion would agree that it would be unreasonable to pursue these other aims.

The stronger of the two readings of the regulation interpretation, then, seems to me not obviously mistaken. But there is a weaker reading of it that also strikes me as plausible: one might claim that the principle should be understood as conditional, rather than unconditional: it does not demand that we regulate one good in light of the other; rather, it demands that *if* one deliberates concerning how to handle conflicts between these goods, then one must regulate one good in light of the other. I might, when facing a choice between pursuing the good of knowledge or the good of religion, just go for knowledge without deliberation. This would not be unreasonable, according to the weaker, conditionalized interpretation. But if I attempt to deliberate on the place to give each of these goods in my aims, then it would be unreasonable not to regulate the pursuit of knowledge in light of the good of religion.

None of this, of course, shows that there is, in fact, a hierarchy among the basic goods such that a practical requirement along these lines embodies the only appropriate response to it; thus far, all I have argued is that Finnis's and George's worries are not decisive with respect to the issue of hierarchy among the basic goods. Suppose that, in order to illustrate the way that this natural law view could try to defend the hierarchy thesis, we were to take up the task of showing that religion stands superior to all of the other goods in a for-the-sake-of hierarchy. Call a basic good that is not for the sake of any other basic good a 'final basic good,' and call a basic good that is for the sake of another basic good a 'nonfinal basic good.' Our task, then, is to show that religion is a final good with respect to which all other basic goods are nonfinal. Now, in order to defend this claim, it is clearly not sufficient to note that the other basic goods can be pursued as means to the achievement of the good of religion; it is true of *all* of the basic goods that the other goods can be employed as means to them. The argument that all of the other basic goods are naturally nonfinal with respect to the good of religion would likely depend instead on one or both of the methods employed in providing an account of the basic goods in Chapter 3: the inclinationist method of making explicit our implicit grasp of fundamental practical truths (1.1) or the employment of our theoretical understanding of human functions, together with the affirmation of the real identity thesis (1.3).

Recall that the version of inclinationism endorsed in Chapter 1 derives from Aquinas's view that fundamental goods are known through our *inclinationes,* our tendencies to act purposively to secure certain ends. These 'directednesses' are made intelligible through practical reason's affirming the theses that the objects of these inclinationes are good. Interestingly, though, in the passage where Aquinas discusses the relationship between inclinationes and goods, he affirms not only that the objects of the inclinationes – he mentions life, procreation, social relationships, and knowledge of God – are good; he affirms that an order among the inclinationes makes clear that there is an order among the fundamental goods: "the order of the natural inclinationes corresponds to the order of the precepts of the natural law" (*Summa Theologiae,* IaIIae 94, 2).

MacIntyre offers the following gloss on Aquinas's remark:

It is important that these *inclinationes* are ordered: we educate our children for the sake of their being able to participate in the good of knowledge; we subordinate our need for self-preservation if the lives of our children or the security of our community are gravely endangered. It is not of course that everyone always orders their inclinations this way, but that the general patterns of distinctively human behavior evince those directednesses in such a way that it is the ends toward which they are directed that provide our primary experiences of the pursuit of particularized goods. (MacIntyre 1988, p. 174)

It is not just the fact that some goods can be used as means to achieve other goods that makes clear that there is a natural for-the-sake-of relationship between them. Rather, the positing of such a natural relationship is needed to make intelligible a tendency to order the goods in this way.

It is clear, then, what sorts of tendencies toward purposive action would have to be present in order for one employing the inclinationist method to posit the thesis that all of the other basic goods are for the sake of the good of religion: the distinctive human tendency would have to be toward subordinating all of the other goods to the good of religion, to regulating their pursuit of other goods in terms of what is needed to achieve the religious good. Does this method of defending a hierarchy of goods support the claim that religion sits atop such a hierarchy? It is, I think, far from clear whether there is, in fact, a tendency to subordinate other goods to the religious good that needs to be made intelligible at all, or whether this tendency is best made intelligible by the positing of a natural for-the-sake-of relationship between the goods.

Even correcting for differences in theoretical judgment – judgments about whether there is a God and whether His will can be known in any way are especially important – it is not obvious that the religious good is one toward which agents characteristically subordinate the pursuit of other ends. And even if it were, it is far from clear that positing the thesis that all other basic goods are naturally for the sake of the good of religion is the best way to explain this tendency: it might be best explained simply by the fact that the other basic goods are more apt to be used as instrumental means than the religious good is. The fact that the other goods are (at least apparently) more efficient instruments for bringing about the religious good than the religious good is for bringing about other goods should not be confused with the claim that religion is a final basic good with respect to which the other basic goods are nonfinal. The fact that the other goods are more apt to be instruments implies only that if one decides to pursue the good of religion, securing these goods can be an excellent way to go about doing so; the fact that all other basic goods are for the sake of the good of religion is supposed to show that pursuit of the religious good is to be made one's supreme aim, if one pursues any aims at all. It is unclear, then, whether the mere fact that agents tend to pursue other goods for the sake of religion far more than they pursue the good of religion for the sake of other goods should lead us to affirm that the other goods are for the sake of religion or just to recognize that the religious good is not as efficient an instrumental means to promoting other goods.

Theoretical reason, together with the real identity thesis, may be able to provide grounds for affirming that religion is the final basic good, even if unaided, practical reflection cannot do so. Recall that on the view defended in Chapter 1, the functions that are constituents of human flourishing – and thus, according to the real identity thesis, fundamental reasons for action – make intelligible the subsidiary functions of the human. It seems that the way to show that religion is a superordinate good, according to this method, would be to show that even if all of the aspects of human flourishing are ultimate in the sense that each is capable of being viewed as an 'end of the line' of human functions, not in need of any further function to be intelligible, all of these aspects, other than the religious good, gain some intelligibility as functions in terms of their contribution to the human's capacity to gain harmony with the divine will.

This is the argument that one employing this method would have to make, but it is a difficult argument to make, for the following reason. This method for making explicit aspects of human flourishing is most successful when its task is to separate those human functions that are merely instrumental to the securing of aspects of human flourishing from the aspects of human flourishing themselves. It has more difficulty when there are both grounds for thinking the function an instrument and for thinking the function an aspect of human flourishing: think of the good of inner peace, which could be viewed both as a mere means to securing other aspects of well-being and as a good in itself (3.3). The way that this difficulty is resolved is to resort to the verdict of practical reason: practical reason's suggestion that inner peace is an aspect of well-being provides a basis for resolving the difficulty in favor of the view that inner peace is an aspect of human flourishing. Now, in this case, the difficulty is to figure out whether the other basic goods need to be viewed also as being for the sake of the good of religion in order to be fully intelligible as functions, or whether their intelligibility as functions is sufficiently explained by their being aspects of human flourishing. It seems to me that in this case, as in the case of inner peace, there is no way to resolve this issue apart from an appeal to the judgment of practical reason. But, as we have just seen, there are reasons to doubt that practical reason affirms that all other basic goods are for the sake of the religious good. Thus, it appears that theoretical reason does not provide an independent reason to think religion to be a superordinate good.

To claim that we lack adequate grounds to say with any confidence that religion holds a higher place in the hierarchy of goods than does knowledge, life, or the other basic goods is not to offer a general argument against any of the goods having hierarchical priority over some others. The most plausible candidate for such a good would be – unsurprisingly – happiness. Perhaps it is true that agents display a tendency to regulate the pursuit of other goods for the sake of happiness, and thus, we can assert the priority of happiness to the other goods in the hierarchy of natural human ends. But note that, unless we are able to provide some further hierarchical ordering among the goods, the status of happiness as superordinate end will not provide us with much in the way of constraints on reasonable conduct prior to the agent's choice and commitment. For since happiness consists in the realization of the agent's reasonably chosen system of ends, the way that happiness will regulate the pursuit of other ends will depend just on what place the agent gives to these other ends within the content of happiness. At most, the assertion that happiness is a superordinate end will be a reminder to us that once we have reasonably settled on a system of ends, we should not be distracted from its pursuit by occasional, more particular ends that are themselves choiceworthy, but the pursuit of which would detract from our reasonably settled-upon life plan. But since we have independent reasons, grounded in the principles of practical reasonableness, to hold firm to our commitments (5.6), this reminder is not needed for doing any work in this theory of practical rationality. To sum up: even if happiness can plausibly be held to be a superordinate good, its status seems to add little to what we can independently say about what practical reasonableness requires.

5.5 Principles of Practical Reasonableness Governing Plans of Action

We now turn to a defense of the principles of practical reasonableness that govern plans of action. I will defend four such principles: against dismissing or devaluing any aspect of well-being; against dismissing or devaluing any person within the context of agent-neutral ends; against intentionally destroying an instance of good for the sake of promoting another; and against acting inefficiently in pursuit of the good. Following my defense of these principles in terms of the account of the nature of reasons for action offered in 5.3 and the framework for assessing principles of practical reasonableness offered in 5.1, I will turn to the issue of whether this set of principles of reasonableness is complete. The answer will be no: there is a gap in the theory of practical reasonableness that must be filled by an account of principles that apply directly to agents. The elaboration of these principles is carried out in 5.6.

Against Dismissing or Devaluing Aspects of Well-Being

The first principle of practical reasonableness governing plans of action rules out all plans that involve the dismissal or devaluing of any aspect of well-being. Any plan of action that dismisses an aspect of well-being presupposes the falsity of the view that all aspects of well-being provide reasons for action. Any plan of action that devalues an aspect of well-being by treating it as of less value than some other aspect of well-being presupposes the falsity of the incommensurability thesis as applied to categories of basic good. To dismiss or to devalue an aspect of well-being in one's plan of action is, therefore, inevitably to pre-suppose something that is false about the nature of the fundamental reasons for action; all such plans of action are ruled out as unreasonable.

It is difficult to employ this principle of practical reasonableness (and, we shall see, the second principle of practical reasonableness also) in order to show that any particular plan of action is unreasonable, for plans of action typically do not, on their face, show a devaluation or dismissal of an aspect of well-being. Consider, for example, the plan to spend seven dollars for admission to an art museum, thereby enabling oneself to participate in the good of aesthetic experience. Does this plan of action involve a dismissal or devaluation of other goods – life, knowledge, friendship, etc. – toward the realization of which one's money might have been spent? Obviously, from the characterization so far of this plan of action, there is no way to tell. Does this mean that this principle of practical reasonableness is contentless, incapable of ruling out any plan of action as unreasonable?

No. That with regard to many, or most, plans of action it is extremely difficult to determine whether they are in compliance with the principle does not show that with regard to all plans of action, it is impossible to have a fair idea whether they are in compliance. Further, once we see that some plans of action give indications of being out of compliance with the principle, we can see how this principle can guide choice, not only with regard to that type of plan but also with regard to all plans of action.

The principle that rules out the dismissal or devaluation of any aspect of well-being is most difficult to apply in cases where the plan of action is a limited one with a narrowly defined objective. Particular plans of action, after all, will often need no reference to any more than one good; such is the case with regard to the plan to go to the art museum. But from the absence of reference to other types of good in one's limited plans of action, it of course does not follow, or even suggest, that other goods have been dismissed or devalued. The absence of reference to other goods in this type of plan of action is precisely what we would expect. What we would have less reason to expect, though, is that with regard to the most inclusive plans of action – what I have called life plans – certain goods would be omitted entirely. Given that all nine of the basic goods are equally aspects of well-being, an inclusive plan of action that had no place for one or another of these basic goods would be a suspicious one.

To say that a life plan that omits reference to any aspect of well-being is a suspicious one is to give an epistemic standard for the violation of the principle, not a normative one; and it is not to propose a logically sufficient condition for violation of that principle. With regard to this first remark: when I say that the omission of any aspect of well-being from a life plan is an epistemic standard for the violation of the principle, I mean that a life plan's displaying this feature gives us some reason for believing that the principle has been violated; I do not mean to say that this sort of omission constitutes a violation of the principle. With regard to the second remark: the omission of any aspect of well-being from a life plan does not give us sufficient reason to assert that a violation of the principle has occurred; it seems to me that one's life plan might, in some cases, omit reference to an aspect of well-being without violating the principle. Practical reason does not require pursuit of at least some of all of the basic goods, so that life plans that omitted one or another would thereby be unreasonable: the natural law does not require dilettantism.

Why is the absence of mention of a good in a life plan not itself a violation of the first principle of practical reasonableness? If this is not a violation, what is? The important point is that this principle rules out plans of action that are formulated on the basis of false presuppositions that the agent relied upon in formulating that plan of action. Thus, the reasonableness or unreasonableness of a plan of action vis-à-vis this first principle is tied to the deliberation and judgment, prejudices and presuppositions, of the agent that formed that plan of action. Two plans of action that seem alike in all intrinsic features – the aim of the plan, the means to be used in order to promote it – may nonetheless differ with regard to their reasonableness, if one of the plans was formed on the basis of false presuppositions about the good and the other on true presuppositions.

That two plans of action alike in intrinsic features might differ in their reasonableness does not seem an implausible claim, given that we often take a choice to be reasonable or unreasonable because of the quality of the deliberation that gave rise to that choice, and we sometimes think that two persons' choices for the same option might differ in their rationality due to differences in the way that the persons set about making their choices. What we have in the case of this principle of practical reasonableness is just the conjunction of this idea with the claim that one way deliberation can go awry is through false views about the nature of the good.

Consider, for example, the difference between the following two people, both of whom are dedicated to the pursuit of the aesthetic good to the exclusion of the pursuit of other goods. One of these persons settled on her life plan with full recognition that this sort of pursuit of aesthetic enjoyment brings with it a real loss, a missing out on a number of the other worthwhile ends that one can enjoy. The other settled on his life plan without recognition of the genuineness of the other goods, holding that life is a mere instrument, that knowledge is worthless except where it might help promote the pursuit of the aesthetic good, etc. Or, perhaps the error was not so great: perhaps, while recognizing the other goods as such, he held that they were of a lower kind, less important than the good of aesthetic experience. Given the conclusions reached earlier concerning welfarism and the account of aspects of well-being, we should affirm that while these two life plans may be alike in their intrinsic features, the life plan of the latter is unreasonable, whereas the life plan of the former is not.

On the view that I have proposed, that one does not give each of the forms of basic good a place in one's life does not itself constitute unreasonableness in choice, for the requirement not to dismiss or devalue any good is a requirement on how a particular plan of action is formed, not on the content of the resultant plan of action. But there is a way that one might nevertheless defend the claim that omission of a good from one's life plan is an infallible mark of violation of the principle. The argument would have to be formulated in terms of an account of what deliberation in forming a life plan is like, and it would rest on the premise that anyone who neither dismisses nor devalues any category of basic good will, as a matter of fact, include every category of good in his or her life plan. Perhaps evidence of a less direct sort could be offered by way of the claim that for all persons who do not have all the goods represented in their life plans, each of those persons in fact dismissed or devalued one of the goods. But I don't see any reason why this need be so, why someone could not, with awareness of what he or she would be missing out on, settle on pursuit of some forms of human good to the exclusion of others.

Having framed this discussion primarily in terms of the reasonableness or unreasonableness of life plans, I should perhaps emphasize that this principle of practical reasonableness does not apply only to life plans but also to all plans of action. Any plan of action, regardless of its level of generality, that is formed on the basis of the denial of the goodness of any aspect of well-being is unreasonable.

Against Dismissing or Devaluing Persons
within the Context of Agent-Neutral Ends

The second principle of practical reasonableness governing plans of action rules out all plans that involve the dismissal or devaluation of any person's good within the context of agent-neutral reasons for action. Suppose that an agent is acting on a set of agent-neutral reasons for action. Any plan of action that involves dismissing the good of a person described by an agent-neutral reason-predicate is to presuppose falsely that the identity of a person is relevant in the context of agent-neutral reasons for action; any plan of action that involves devaluing the good of a person described by an agent-neutral reason-predicate by treating that person's good as of lesser value is to presuppose falsely the commensurability of distinct instantiations of basic good among persons. Thus, to dismiss or to devalue a person's good within the context of agent-neutral reasons for action is to presuppose something that is false about the nature of the fundamental reasons for action.

This principle is similar to the first principle of practical reasonableness in that the requirement it imposes applies primarily to the formation of a plan of action and only derivatively to the plan of action thereby formed. On its face, a plan of action the end of which is an agent-neutral reason but which does not make reference at all to some person's good that falls within the reason-predicate's description cannot be seen to violate the principle. For just as a plan of action might innocently focus on one aspect of well-being to the exclusion of others, a plan of action might innocently focus on some persons' well-being to the exclusion of others'. What this principle does rule out, though, are all those plans of action within the context of agent-neutral reasons for action that were formed by taking identity of persons into account.

The particular formulation of this principle of context-limited impartiality is indebted to several different features of reasons for action discussed in 5.3: the agent-neutral character of some of the fundamental reasons for action; the agent-relative character of others; and the incommensurability between these categories of reason for action. It is clear that if the principle as stated is to be nonvacuous, there must be agent-neutral reasons for action; and if the principle as stated is to be correct, these agent-neutral reasons must be characterized in a particular way. As I argued, the intelligibility of the pursuit of others' good gives us reason to affirm the existence of agent-neutral reasons to promote aspects of basic good in any person, reasons that correspond to the agent-relative reasons to promote aspects of one's own well-being (5.3). The existence of such reasons ensures that this principle is not empty: there is a wide variety of contexts in which the principle might apply. I also suggested that the agent-neutral reason-predicates contain an existentially quantified bound variable in place of the free variable of the agent-relative reason-predicate: so, for example, in addition to the agent-relative reason-predicate 'is an instance of x's living,' which arises directly from the status of life as a basic good, there is an agent-neutral reason-predicate 'is an instance of some person z's living.' Given the existence of agent-neutral reason-predicates of this sort, it is clear that one who acts on such reasons, yet excludes a particular person from consideration to whom that predicate might apply, is acting arbitrarily, acting in a way that could make sense only if the false claim that this sort of agent-neutral predicate can distinguish between persons on the basis of identity were presupposed.[19]

This principle of practical reason requires impartiality in the realm of agent-neutral reasons for action. But the form that this principle takes is also due to the existence of independent agent-relative reasons for action. The existence of agent-relative reasons for action makes the principle's scope-restriction ('within the context of agent-neutral reasons') a genuine restriction. It is the particular characterization of agent-relative reasons for action that precludes a less qualified version of the principle, one that requires impartiality *tout court* and not just with regard to agent-neutral reasons. For, given the existence of agent-relative reasons as characterized in 5.3, we have no basis for condemning as unreasonable those agents who consider the identity of the person in which an instance of good is located – whether it is in oneself, or in another – when one is acting on agent-relative reasons for action.

Nor can we retrieve an unlimited impartiality by asserting the preeminence of agent-neutral over agent-relative reasons for action. Even if we affirm the existence of independent agent-neutral and agent-relative reasons, we might think that we could rescue a fuller impartiality by holding that agent-neutral reasons hold sway over agent-relative ones: so, in any case where there is tension between agent-neutral reasons and agent-relative reasons, the former emerge as relevant to determining rational action in that situation; and given the relevance of only agent-neutral reasons in those cases, the requirement of impartiality will be, in effect, unqualified. But the preeminence of agent-neutral over agent-relative reasons is not a premise upon which one can rely in defending a principle of unqualified impartiality, due to the incommensurability of agent-neutral and agent-relative reasons for action.

It is worth noting the differences between the sort of impartiality principle that Finnis affirms within his natural law theory and the impartiality principle affirmed here. On Finnis's view, all of the fundamental reasons for action are agent-neutral, and he employs this conception of reasons in support of an unqualified principle of impartiality:

The basic goods are human goods, and can in principle be pursued, realized, and participated in by any human being. Another person's survival, his coming to know, his creativity, his all-around flourishing, may not interest me, may not concern me, may in any event be beyond my power to affect. But have I any reason to deny that they are really good, or that they are fit matters of interest, concern, and favour by that man and by all those who have to do with him? . . . [W]e can add . . . a third requirement [of practical reasonableness]: of fundamental impartiality among the human subjects who are or may be partakers of those goods. (Finnis 1980, pp. 106–107)

It is because of this requirement that Finnis thinks self-preference in pursuit of the basic goods can be condemned: Finnis's impartiality requirement is "a pungent critique of selfishness, special pleading, double standards, hypocrisy, indifference to the good of others we could easily help ('passing by on the other side'), and all the other manifold forms of egoistic and group bias" (Finnis 1980, p. 107).

Frankly, I wish I could defend a more stringent principle of impartiality as a requirement of practical reasonableness. But, in my view, there is no such requirement. Quasi-egoistic life plans, the ends of which are all agent-relative goods, can be practically reasonable. (I call such plans 'quasi-egoistic,' rather than 'egoistic,' for two reasons. First, egoism is usually a maximizing idea, and the maximizing idea is ruled out by the pervasiveness of incommensurability. Secondly, the egoist does not recognize agent-neutral reasons as at all relevant to the reasonableness of his or her action; but, as I show with regard to the next principle of practical reasonableness, the reasonable quasi-egoist will have to restrain him- or herself in pursuit of his or her good by a principle that is both self- and other-regarding, even if the ultimate aim of the quasi-egoist's life plan is completely self-regarding.) A plan of life that is devoted to a decidedly partial pursuit of one's own good – a pursuit that is not justified by appeal to agent-neutral reasons – need not run afoul of the constraints of practical reasonableness. But that does not make this principle of practical reasonableness any less real: when one is acting on agent-neutral reasons, impartiality is rationally required.

To show why this requirement, though restricted, is an important one, let us consider an important context in which agent-neutral reasons are inevitably at stake: communities. The principle of limited impartiality rules out all plans of action that involve respect of persons within communities. ('Respect of persons' is a summary term for devaluation or dismissal of goods because of the identity of the person or persons partaking of those goods.) As I argued in Chapter 3 (3.3), community is marked by cooperative action in pursuit of shared ends. But, as I noted, the sense in which the end had to be shared is a rather special one: it has to be an end common by way of causation, so that agents are acting for the sake of the same state of affairs under the same description. Ends that are common in this way, though, have to be specified in an agent-neutral way. Thus, the qualified principle of impartiality places rational restrictions on any plan of action that is formed within the context of community. It is within communities that the requirement of impartiality has its full force.

Against Intentional, Instrumental Destruction of Instances of Basic Good

The third principle of practical reasonableness governing plans of action rules out all plans of action that involve the intentional destruction or impeding of an instance of a basic good for the sake of bringing about some other instance of a basic good. Any plan of action that involves the intention to destroy or impede an instance of a basic good for the sake of bringing another into existence presupposes that the good to be promoted is at least as good as the good that is intentionally destroyed. But according to the incommensurability thesis as applied to all distinct instantiations of basic goods, the distinctness of the good to be destroyed and the good to be promoted entails that those goods are incommensurable. Thus, any plan of action that includes an intentional, instrumental destruction of an instance of a basic good is to be ruled out as unreasonable.

This principle has been called the 'Pauline principle,' in light of Paul's rejection of the notion that evil may be done that good will come of it (Romans 3:8; cf. Donagan 1977, pp. 149–164, and Finnis 1983, p. 109). The Pauline principle is a strong claim about practical reasonableness, and a great deal of its strength derives from the strength of the incommensurability thesis upon which it relies. I have no more to say in defense of the thesis that incommensurability among distinct instances of basic good is pervasive. The question to be taken up is whether one who accepts this extreme incommensurability thesis could, nevertheless, reasonably reject the Pauline principle. The elaboration of the defense of this principle will consist in two stages. In the first stage, I try to show that acting in accordance with the Pauline principle is at least a reasonable response to the nature of distinct instances of basic good as incommensurable.[20] In the second stage, I try to show why it is not only a reasonable response but the only appropriate response.

Adherence to the Pauline principle is at least a reasonable response to the incommensurability of distinct instances of basic goods. Consider, by way of contrast, the way that consequentialism argues for a conception of practical reasonableness that requires maximization and renders irrelevant the distinction between what is intended and what is foreseen but unintended: these views rest on claims about commensurability. By consequentialist lights, the reason that it would be unreasonable in some cases not to intend the destruction of an instance of a basic good is that in those cases, that destruction could bring about a greater good. Since by that sort of act one would bring about all of the good that would exist had one not performed such intentional destruction, and some more good as well, it would make no sense at all not to intend the destruction of that good; refraining from such destruction would be rationally unmotivated. But this is manifestly not the sort of argument that one can offer in the face of massive incommensurability, for one can show that there is something lost by intending destruction: the incommensurable good that is destroyed, irreplaceable because incommensurable with all others. It cannot be shown that it would be unreasonable not to destroy one good for the sake of a greater one if all distinct instances of good are incommensurable.

Unless there is an argument against refraining from destroying instances of basic good for the sake of other goods that does not rest on commensurability – and I know of no argument extant – we have no grounds for believing that adhering to the Pauline principle is not a reasonable response to the nature of the fundamental reasons for action. But the Pauline principle is not merely a permissive principle: it states a requirement. It does not just say that refraining from destroying an instance of a basic good, in order to bring about another, need not be based on a false presupposition; it says that intending such destruction is always based on a false presupposition. One way to get at the rationale for this requirement is to see why one might dispute the Pauline principle even while affirming incommensurability. I claimed that the false presupposition of intentional attacks on instances of basic goods is that the good to be promoted is at least as valuable as the one to be destroyed or impeded. But this might be disputed: one might grant that while this presupposition is false, given the nature of instances of basic good as incommensurable, this presupposition is not essential to acts of intentional damage to instances of basic goods. Rather, the necessary presupposition is only that the good to be promoted is *no worse than* the good to be destroyed. And clearly, this presupposition is compatible with the massive incommensurability defended in 3.3, and indeed, entailed by it. For g to be worse than h is for h to be better than g; but if g and h are incommensurable, then h is not better than g; so, if g and h are incommensurable, then g is no worse than h, and h is no worse than g.

The distinction between the intended and the foreseen but unintended becomes practically relevant with regard to the distinction between a state of affairs' being at least as good as another and a state of affairs' being no worse than another. When one intends instance of good i and foresees (but does not intend) that instance of good j will thereby be damaged, thwarted, or prevented, it seems to me to be sufficient for making sense of that sort of action to ascribe the presupposition that j is no worse than i. But it also seems to me that the situation is altered in a case where one intends the damaging, thwarting, preventing of j in order to bring about i; to make sense of this type of action, it is necessary that good i be at least as good as j is. Why? Goods like i and j are reasons for action; they give point to what we do, and they give point to our actions in virtue of our intending them. However, the world is such that we invariably forgo a number of goods when we act for the sake of others. But to forgo such goods is not to treat them as nonreasons: when we attempt to provide a practical explanation for why we have forgone these goods, the explanation can be framed wholly in terms of the nature of the world and the limits of our time, energy, and ability in pursuing the good (see Finnis 1992, pp. 147–148). When asked why we pursued some goods and allowed others to go unpromoted, the answer will do that the goods that we pursued are no worse than the ones we left to languish. But this sort of explanation cannot be given in the case of intentions to damage goods: for the nature of the world, and our limited capacities for agency, does not guarantee that we will ever have to intend the destruction of any of the goods that are reasons for action.

Thus, the explanation offered in the case of unintended but foreseen impeding of instances of basic good is insufficient: if one is to intend damage to an instance of the good for the sake of another, one will have to claim not only that the good to be destroyed is no worse than the one to be promoted, but also that the former is at least as good as the latter is. It is clear, then, why consequentialists reject the intended/foreseen distinction: for consequentialists, insofar as they take their principle of practical reasonableness to guide action, affirm commensurability, and in cases of commensurability, *no worse than* and *at least as good as* are coextensive. Thus, any situation in which one can justify acting with the foreseeable result that a good will be damaged will be one in which one can justify acting with the intention of damaging a good. But the consequentialists are wrong about commensurability. While we know what kind of justification is necessary for performing an act of intentionally damaging an instance of a basic good in order to promote instrumentally a distinct good, we also know that a necessary condition for providing such a justification is not to be had. That is why acting in accordance with the Pauline principle is not only a reasonable response to the incommensurability of instances of basic good; acting in accordance with the Pauline principle is rationally required.

Against Inefficiency

The fourth principle of practical reasonableness governing plans of action rules out all plans that involve inefficiency in pursuit of instances of basic goods. This fourth principle is essentially comparative: just as to label any action, process, or method 'inefficient' is always to compare it to some other action, process, or method, so too the requirement of efficiency does not pronounce on plans of action as such but only on the reasonableness of a plan in comparison to other eligible plans of action.

Consider a certain stock of instrumental goods M, which is instrumentally good in that it is useful for realizing instances of basic goods. If plan of action P_1 consumes M, and only M, in order to bring about only instance of basic good i, plan of action P_2 consumes M, and only M, in order to bring about distinct instances of basic good i and j, and neither P_1 nor P_2 is otherwise ruled out as unreasonable, then P_1 is to be ruled out as unreasonable. For the state of affairs at which P_2 aims contains all of the good that the state of affairs at which P_1 aims contains (since both P_1 and P_2 aim at realizing i), and some more as well (since P_2 aims at realizing j, and P_1 does not); thus, there is a reason to prefer P_2 to P_1, but no reason to prefer P_1 to P_2. To fail to prefer P_1 to P_2 is to falsely presuppose that j is not a reason for action, that it is not a distinct reason for action, or that the state of affairs consisting of i and j is not more worth promoting than the state of affairs consisting of i alone.

The inefficiency most clearly ruled out by the nature of the fundamental reasons for action is that in which a single stock of instrumental means is employed for a lesser rather than a greater good. But seeing the unreasonableness of this inefficiency allows us to make clear the unreasonableness of the other type of inefficiency, where one employs a larger stock of instrumental means to promote an instance of good, rather than using a smaller stock to promote that good.

Consider two (otherwise eligible) plans of action P_1 and P_2, where P_1 and P_2 both aim to realize instance of basic good i. P_1 employs a larger stock of instrumental means to realize i, whereas P_2 employs a smaller stock to realize i. In this case, P_1 is to be ruled out as unreasonable: for if one were to act in accordance with P_2, there would be some stock of instrumental means left over to be used to promote some distinct, as-yet-unspecified instance of basic good j. But since no matter what good j is, i and j together are better than i alone is – i and j contain all of the good that i has, plus some more as well – it is unreasonable to act in a way that can realize only i, and not j also. To fail to prefer P_2 to P_1 is to presuppose falsely either that P_2 employs a larger stock of instrumental means than P_1 (for the size of a stock of instrumental means is ultimately defined in terms of its capacity to bring about intrinsic goods), that j is not a reason for action, that j is not a distinct reason for action, or that the state of affairs consisting of i and j is not better than the state of affairs consisting of i alone.

This principle forbidding inefficiency thus rules out using a larger stock of instrumental means than is necessary to promote a given good and using a given stock of instrumental means to secure less good than is possible. What constricts the range of application of this principle is not just the clause that the plans between which the choice is made must be 'otherwise eligible,' that is, not ruled out by some other principle of practical reasonableness. It is obvious that the massive incommensurability holding between the instances of basic good narrows the scope of this principle. By contrast, consequentialism can be formulated as simply the conjunction of the affirmation of commensurability and this principle of efficiency: consequentialism tells us to use the instrumental means at our disposal to secure as much good as is possible; and given the commensurability of all goods, there are no restrictions on this principle that prevent it from being a self-sufficient master dictate directing us simply to maximize the good.

5.6 Principles of Practical Reasonableness Governing Agents

In 5.1 I argued that the principles of practical reasonableness primarily assess plans of action, and in 5.5 I provided an elaboration and defense of these principles in terms of the nature of the fundamental reasons for action. But in 5.1 I said that plans of action are the primary object of assessment by principles of practical reasonableness, not the only object of assessment. The reason for this qualification is that to offer an account of practical reasonableness only for plans of action would be to leave a lacuna in the theory of practical reasonableness, in that we now lack any account of the reasonableness of agents in forming, revising, and acting on their plans. We know what constraints such plans must meet. But we have no idea, yet, whether agents are under any such constraints with regard to the way that they form, revise, and follow plans of action. I shall argue in this section that there are such principles of practical reasonableness, and that they apply to agents directly and not by way of application to particular plans of action.

There may be an objection to the formulation of principles of this type. Recall that in 5.1 I suggested that there are no principles of practical reasonableness requiring one to act for any good. Does my affirmation of a need for principles dictating how agents are to form, revise, and follow plans of action involve a recantation of that view? After all, since plans of action are for the sake of some good, doesn't a requirement to form and act on such a plan amount to a requirement to pursue a good? The answer is no. What these principles of practical reasonableness applying directly to agents describe are ways that an agent can be unreasonable, given that the agent is attempting to form plans of action at all. They do not require an agent to make any plan of action: they only state that if an agent sets about forming plans of action, certain ways of dealing with those plans of action are unreasonable.

The framework in terms of which these principles for agents is to be defended is similar to that in which the principles for plans of action were defended. Just as plans of action based on false presuppositions concerning the nature of the reasons for action were ruled out, ways of forming, revising, and following plans of action are to be ruled out if they presuppose false views either of the nature of those reasons or of the nature of plans of action. The general idea will be that certain ways of dealing with plans of action involve a kind of inconsistency: treating a plan of action in a certain way undercuts what gives point to plans of action in the first place.

Against Over- and Under-Specificity in Planning

The first principle of practical reasonableness for agents is that in forming plans of action, the agent must not refrain from forming such plans at various levels of specificity. To wit: the agent must not form such plans always at a highly specific level, and the agent must not form such plans always at a highly general level.

Against over-specificity, we may say that the agent who sets him- or herself to form a plan of action presupposes that the goods for the sake of which the agent forms that plan are worth pursuing. But these goods are not just valuable on a specific occasion; participation in them is a lifetime possibility, and the particular goods in which one can participate and the extent to which one can participate in these various goods will depend on how one orders them in one's life. This gives an agent reason to form plans of action that are broad enough in scope that they can be referred to in order to determine which goods one shall pursue in more specific plans of action. This requirement against over-specificity also implies a constraint on rational planning analogous to the moral 'agglomeration principle': that if an agent forms plan P_1 and plan P_2, that agent should also plan on performing P_1 and P_2. The point of this requirement is not obvious if one conceives the agent following this requirement as forming one plan, forming another, and then merely conjoining them: rather, the idea is that the agent should not form two plans of action that are incapable of being put together into a single plan of action. If the point of planning is to promote certain goods, then one undercuts that point by forming distinct plans that cannot be joined together into a unified plan of action. (For a discussion of this principle of rational intending, and its moral analog as the principle of agglomeration, see Gowans 1994, pp. 70–72, 75–77, 81–83. Williams discusses, and names, the agglomeration principle in his 1973b, pp. 180–182.)

Against under-specificity, we may say that the agent who forms only highly general plans of action seems inconsistent: the point of forming such plans is to find out how one can enjoy the goods ordered in those plans, but one will not be able to realize these goods by planning unless one descends to specific plans that dictate how one can achieve a good on a particular occasion. An agent who forms plans of action over-specifically leaves his or her life as a whole unplanned, leaving pursuit of the good prey to conflict, temptations to dilettantism, and missed opportunities; an agent who forms plans of action under-specifically fails to descend to the level of the particular, where the basic goods are in fact realized, leaving his or her planning vain and empty. Thus, to form plans of action under- or over-specifically is contrary to practical reasonableness.

This requirement against over-specificity, when followed, yields what I briefly described in Chapter 3 as a life plan. While the formation of a life plan is, for those who form plans of action at all, a rational requirement, the fulfillment of that life plan is itself a basic good, the good of happiness (3.3).

Against Flightiness and Stubbornness

The first of the principles of practical reasonableness applying directly to agents places requirements on the way that agents form plans of action. The second places requirements on the way that agents treat the plans of action that they have formed. The need for such a principle arises from the fact that plans of action are not typically formed and then immediately and instantaneously completed; rather, they involve ordering one's actions over a stretch of time. The fact that plans of action order an agent's actions over time, along with the fact that agents form plans of action in order to pursue well certain goods, together support a requirement against flightiness and stubbornness with regard to one's plans of action.

With respect to flightiness: once formed, plans of action should not be altered or abandoned at will; they should be altered or abandoned only in cases where there is a sufficiently good reason for doing so. Now, it seems clear that it cannot be reasonable to alter or abandon a plan of action without having *some* reason for doing so. After all, to transform one's plan of action intentionally would not even be an intelligible act if there were not some reason or other for so doing. Further, there is an instructive analogy that can be exploited here with theoretical rationality. It seems that at all times, a theoretically rational believer must affirm of the beliefs that he or she holds that those beliefs should not be altered or abandoned without there being a reason for so doing. For if he or she did not affirm this claim, then the holding of the belief does not appear reasonable to begin with; it is hard to see how holding a belief could be reasonable if one could, within reason, abandon it on no basis at all. The same holds true, I think, in the realm of practical rationality: the practically reasonable agent must affirm at all times, with respect to his or her formed plans of action, that it would not be reasonable to abandon them at will; it is hard to see how having that plan of action could be reasonable if one could, within reason, alter or abandon it for no reason at all.

If one is not to violate the principle forbidding flightiness with respect to one's plans of action, one will not alter or abandon one's plans of action without a sufficiently good reason for doing so. What, though, constitutes a sufficiently good reason? While I can offer nothing like exhaustive criteria, the following points may provide some guidance. First, what would *not* count as a sufficiently good reason would be any reason that one has already adequately considered in the deliberation leading up to the formation of the plan of action, so long as that deliberation could not be faulted in a way that is relevant to the consideration of that reason. (Suppose that I commit myself to finishing a philosophy paper, rather than to spending the afternoon drinking with friends. In the midst of my work my friends stop by, and I feel like abandoning my plan to finish the paper. While there is, no doubt, a reason to abandon the philosophy work that I am doing – after all, to go with my friends is not sheerly unintelligible, for I can cite a reason that makes choiceworthy the afternoon trip to the pub – it would be unreasonable to do so, if I indeed were adequately cognizant in my deliberation of the goods that would be set aside by working on the paper.)[21]

Secondly, what would count as a sufficiently good reason draws some content from the other principles of practical reasonableness, as well as from one's more embracing plans of action. One good reason for altering or abandoning a plan of action is that the plan of action either involves the violation of a principle of practical reasonableness or was formed in a way that involved the violation of a principle of practical reasonableness. If executing one's plan of action turned out, in the specific and unfortunate circumstances at hand, to require the intentional destruction of an instance of a basic good (5.5) – if, for example, one needed to lie in order to achieve some personal goal – then there is sufficient reason to abandon or alter the plan of action. If the deliberation the outcome of which was the plan of action involved devaluing some basic goods (5.5) – if, for example, one formed a life plan without adequate appreciation for the status of aesthetic experience as worth having – then there may be sufficient reason to alter or abandon that plan of action. Aside from reasons to alter or abandon plans of action deriving from the principles of practical reasonableness themselves, what counts as a sufficiently good reason will be determined by the content of one's more embracing plans of action, especially one's life plan, which will determine the relative priority of the various goods that one might pursue.

On the other hand, since the point of forming plans of action is to pursue well various goods, one should not display stubbornness in sticking to one's plans, refusing to alter or abandon them when one becomes aware of important changes in circumstance, errors in deliberation, or alterations in one's more general and embracing plans of action. To exhibit this sort of stubbornness with regard to one's plans of action is to undercut the rationale of forming plans of action, that is, to select among the various goods to which one might respond and to select among the various plans of action by which one can respond to the goods thus selected.

Against Idleness

Plans of action on their own don't respond to any goods; goods are responded to by agents acting in accordance with those plans. The third principle of practical reasonableness applying directly to agents rules out, as unreasonable, idleness, that is, the failure to act on the plans of action that one has settled on. Again, while this may look as if I am taking back the claim that a principle of practical reasonableness does not require the pursuit of any good, this principle does not state such a requirement: what it states is that it is unreasonable to form a plan of action and then to refrain from acting on that plan; it does not state that the formation of any plan of action or the pursuit of any good is rationally required.

The rationale for this principle is that the formation of a plan of action, yet refusing to act on it, involves a performative inconsistency. The point of forming a plan of action is to guide one's conduct. If one refrains from acting on a plan of action, then there is no point to the forming of that plan of action. Thus, when one settles on a plan of action, it is unreasonable for that agent to refrain from acting on that plan of action.

5.7 Virtue Theory

The greatest of all natural law theorists was Aquinas, yet natural law theory is only one strand of Aquinas's moral thought: he organizes his moral theory in terms of the virtues, and indeed, the prominence of the virtues in that theory has led some recent commentators to downplay the natural law elements of Aquinas's account (see Goerner 1983 and Nelson 1992). Aquinas seems to have thought that there is a place within moral theory for both natural law and virtue. But the revival of virtue theory in the past few decades as an account of the moral life to rival Kantian and consequentialist conceptions has led to interpretations of virtue theory that seem to be incompatible with the natural law theory that has been developed here. While I can no more attempt a full-fledged response to virtue ethics as such than I could to egoism, consequentialism, and Kantianism, it is worth spending some time trying to discern the extent to which this natural law view can incorporate the theses that are characteristic of virtue theories and the extent to which it must simply reject them.

There seems to be no particular thesis that is common to all of the moral views that have been put forward recently as varieties of virtue ethics – save, of course, the claim that understanding the virtues is an indispensable task within moral theory. But two theses appear quite frequently and thus have as good a claim as any to define virtue ethics. One of these theses has to do with the way that the virtues enter into the specification of the standard of correctness for practical judgment. The other has to do with the way that virtuous motivation affects the evaluation of action. While only the former of these two theses poses a direct challenge to the natural law theory of practical reasonableness presented thus far, the latter has also been taken to show that there is something inadequate about theories that rely heavily on practical principles, as my own view does; we shall therefore consider both.

Virtue and the Correctness of Practical Judgment

The thesis of virtue ethics that most directly challenges the natural law theory of practical principles defended in this chapter is that the standard of correctness for practical judgment makes essential reference to the virtues. We may take Aristotle's statement of this position as the paradigm: on Aristotle's view, to act well is to hit the mean, avoiding both excess and defect; the mean is, however, determined by the way that the person of practical wisdom (*phronesis*) would decide; and on Aristotle's view, the possession of practical wisdom presupposes the possession of all of the virtues (*Nicomachean Ethics,* 1105b36ff., 1144b20ff.). Thus, on Aristotle's view, the standard for the correctness of practical judgment is what the virtuous person would decide. To what extent is this account of the correctness of practical judgment compatible with the natural law view I have defended?

There are several different ways to understand this sort of theory of practical correctness. One dimension along which interpretations of this thesis vary concerns what type of standard the virtuous person's decision is supposed to be. One interpretation of this claim is metaphysical: the virtuous person's decision is the truth-maker for practical judgments; it is the fact that the virtuous person would decide in a certain way that makes a practical judgment correct or incorrect. (Michael Slote refers to this sort of virtue theory as "agent-based," as opposed to merely "agent-focused": see his 1996, pp. 83–84.) Another interpretation is epistemological: the virtuous person's decision is a standard by which we can know what practical judgments are correct; it is a perfectly reliable indicator of which practical judgments are correct and which are incorrect.

As is clear, the natural law theory presented here must reject the metaphysical understanding of this virtue thesis. Correctness of practical judgment – or absence of incorrectness, to keep in mind the negative function of the principles of practical reasonableness (5.1) – is the result of the nature of the fundamental reasons for action; the nature of the reasons dictates the nature of the appropriate response by agents. At any rate, I doubt that many virtue theorists are attracted by this sort of interpretation. (For a rival view, see Zagzebski 1996.) Aristotle almost certainly did not accept it: he treats the virtues as states that dispose us to respond appropriately, that is, reasonably, to various goods and evils. So courage is the state that disposes us to respond appropriately with respect to dangers (especially the loss of life) and the goods that can be preserved and promoted by facing those dangers (especially the common good of one's political community) (*Nicomachean Ethics,* 1115a7–1117b24); temperance is the state that disposes us to respond appropriately with respect to bodily pleasures and the goods that can be impeded by partaking in those pleasures (*Nicomachean Ethics,* 1117b24–1119b19); and so forth. Besides, it is hard to see how the virtue theorist is to interpret the notion that virtues are excellences on this conception.

On the Aristotelian conception, a virtue is an excellence because it enables one to choose well, which, given the human function, involves responding to goods in a reasonable way. But on the view that the virtuous agent's decisions determine the standard of correctness for practical judgment, it is hard to see by what measure these qualities are to be accounted excellences. I also have trouble seeing what sort of formal characterization we are to offer with respect to the nature of the virtues given the metaphysical interpretation: while on the Aristotelian view, the notion of a state that enables one to respond appropriately to goods and evils provides an account of what fixes the status of a state as a virtue – the nature of human good and human evil – it is unclear what the metaphysical theory is to offer in its place. While perhaps these worries could be removed by the formulation of a well-developed virtue theory that takes this metaphysical stance – one that would be, I suppose, more Nietzschean in cast than Aristotelian – I think that the initial implausibility of this view and the near consensus of virtue theorists against it suggest that it is no problem for this natural law view that it would have to reject this interpretation of virtuous-agent-as-standard thesis.

How, though, are we to understand the epistemological reading of that thesis? As it is stated, it seems unfortunately susceptible to a reading that would render that thesis undistinctive. One who defends a natural law conception of practical reasonableness could agree with that thesis by affirming that the virtuous person is one who adheres to the principles of the natural law: since the principles of the natural law are the standard for practical correctness, the judgment of the virtuous person could equally well serve as such a standard. But we are entitled to assume that the virtue theorist means to make a substantive and distinctive claim in affirming the virtuous-agent-as-standard thesis. What would make the epistemological reading of this thesis substantive, distinctive, and congruent with the views of many virtue ethicists would be the inclusion of the notion that the virtuous agent's decision is the *ultimate* epistemological standard of practical correctness.

We might put it this way. Suppose that the virtue theorist holds, as I and my imagined egoist, consequentialist, and Kantian interlocutors held (5.1–5.2), that the correctness of practical judgment depends on the appropriateness of the response to the reasons for action at stake in one's judgment. Aristotle, I say, held such a view, and it is a plausible construction to place on the views of Nussbaum and other neo-Aristotelians (see, e.g., Nussbaum 1988 and Nussbaum 1990b). The point on which they differ is how best to characterize the ultimate standard for the appropriateness of the response to the goods at stake in one's decision. The virtue theorist's claim is that the ultimate standard for the appropriateness of the response is just the virtuous person's decision.

There are, again, two ways of understanding this substantive version of the epistemological reading. The stronger interpretation is that the virtuous person's decision is the ultimate standard for the correctness of any particular practical judgment. On this view, there is no standard for any practical judgment that can be stated in a way that does not logically depend for its warrant on the decision of the virtuous agent. The weaker interpretation holds that the virtuous person's decision is the ultimate *complete* standard for practical judgment. This view allows for the possibility that there may be some standards for correctness of practical judgment that can be stated in a way that does not logically depend on the decision of the virtuous agent. Any such standard would be, however, incomplete: the virtuous person's decision is able to serve as a standard for all of the practical judgments on which any set of these independent standards can pronounce, plus some more as well.

Now, the natural law theory defended here must reject the stronger interpretation of the virtuous-agent-as-standard thesis. The reason it rejects this view is its theory of practical principles contained in 5.1, 5.3, and 5.5: that theory asserts that there are principles of practical reason that rule out any plan of action that presupposes something false about the nature of reasons for action, and thus are always unreasonable responses to instances of the basic goods; these principles are not defended by way of the assertion that these principles state what types of plan of action virtuous agents would favor.

We should, however, leave open the possibility that the weaker interpretation of the virtuous-agent-as-standard thesis is correct, even given the present account of the principles of practical reasonableness. In stating and defending that set of principles, I relied only on features of the fundamental reasons for action that lend themselves to articulation and that attach to those reasons universally; I used those features to defend the view that plans of action of certain types inevitably contain certain false presuppositions and are, therefore, invariably unreasonable. But even if we were to stipulate that no other principles of practical reasonableness could be defended under these constraints, it would be unjustified to conclude that there must, therefore, be no other constraints of reason on how we respond to instances of basic goods other than those constraints formulated in practical principles. To conclude thus would be to confuse an artifact of the process of principle construction with a substantive thesis of the theory of practical reasonableness, that is, that principles govern the entirety of the reasonable.

To put the possibility I want to leave open a bit more precisely: it may be the case that there are certain responses to the instances of basic goods at stake in a practical judgment that are inappropriate; the inappropriateness is due, as always, to the nature of the goods at stake; no agent could formulate a correct universal practical principle based on articulable features of the goods at stake to explain why those responses would be inappropriate; and that the most that we can say about our justification for holding that these responses are inappropriate is that the virtuous person would hold them to be so. To recognize the possibility of the correctness of this view is not to devalue the place of practical principles in explaining the normative status of plans of actions; rather, it is just to allow that the reasons for action may have certain features that defy being transformed into comprehensive principles. This limited affirmation of the sort of moral particularist view forcefully urged by Dancy (1993), McNaughton (1988), Little (2000), and others was, after all, quite clearly affirmed by Aquinas;[22] it can hardly be entirely outside the spirit of natural law theory.

Having noted the compatibility of this interpretation of the virtuous-agent-as-standard thesis with the natural law view, and having admitted its attractiveness, I will nevertheless decline to rely on its truth in reaching any normative conclusion in this book. To use it to reach normative conclusions requires, of course, more than evidence for the truth of that thesis; it would require me to be, or to be able clearly to recognize, the virtuous agent that can serve as the standard for practical correctness. Sufficient self-knowledge bars me from affirming that the first option is satisfied; a lack of confidence in my capacity to pick out or even accurately to envision the fully virtuous agent precludes me from holding that the second option is satisfied. I will, therefore, rely only on those principles of the natural law defended in 5.5 and 5.6, even if that restricted reliance will produce thinner conclusions than those reached by a number of writers in the natural law tradition (see 6.3–6.5).

Before we turn to the second thesis that is characteristic of virtue ethics, I want to note that making room for virtue within a natural law conception of practical reasonableness does not imply that on such a view, virtues would be merely dispositions to choose on the basis of practical principles, or even (given the possibility of correct practical judgment that is not principle guided) that within the domain of the reasonable governed by practical principles, they are merely dispositions to choose on the basis of those principles. It seems to me that the virtuous agent *could* simply possess such dispositions: there seems to be no reason that an agent who has a disposition to choose in accordance with the principles of the natural law, and who knows that these principles characterize how it is reasonable to respond to goods, should be denied the status of 'virtuous.' On the other hand, it is consistent with the natural law doctrine to hold that there could be agents whose dispositions are not best characterized as tendencies to decide on the basis of principles but who are nonetheless to be considered virtuous. A virtuous agent could be disposed to respond to instances of goods in a more particular way, not by way of rules that express general truths about the nature of instances of the basic goods. Even in this latter case, the principles of practical reasonableness would have much to say about the agent's conduct, but they would speak of such conduct *descriptively:* even if the agent does not act on those rules, the agent acts in ways that conform to those rules.

I claim that natural law theory admits the possibility of at least two patterns of moral virtue: one that is best understood as deciding on the basis of rules, another that is best understood as responding to the character of particular goods. While not apparent at the level of brute performance, these differences would perhaps manifest themselves in the way that we describe their patterns of deliberation. Suppose, for example, that two virtuous agents aim to get extensions on a deadline. Both know that a lie to the editor would easily bring about the extension. Yet for both, the lie is ruled out because it violates the goods of knowledge and excellence in agency (see 6.3). But their patterns of deliberation differ. One virtuous agent acts on the rule 'one ought not lie,' which is derived from the Pauline principle; the other does not act on that rule but, rather, decides that the particular good to be brought about by the lie cannot justify the telling of the lie with its harm to the editor. Both agents might resist the lie on the basis of the incommensurability of goods and the nature of the lie as an attack on a good for the sake of some distinct good. But the former agent treats the rule against lying as a premise of practical reasoning, subsuming the editor's good and his or her own good under that premise, in order to reach the conclusion that the lie would be unreasonable; the latter agent makes no such appeal to a rule, but simply sees the editor's good as not being the sort of thing that can be justifiably attacked to promote his or her own good.

If these patterns of deliberation were entrenched in these respective agents' dispositions, the differences in their deliberations would be, I claim, no grounds for calling one agent virtuous and the other not. In both cases, their patterns of deliberation are responsive to the nature of the goods involved in their decisions. Their practical reasoning displays what we might think of as different sensibilities: the former displays a tendency toward the general, to think in abstract terms; the latter displays a tendency toward the particular, to think in concrete terms. But neither view must involve any deficiency at all with respect to reasonableness in responding to instances of basic goods. And if that is so, then a universalistic, rule-governed conception of the virtues and a particularistic, situation-governed conception of the virtues need not be competitors within a natural law account.

Virtues, Principles, and Motivation

With respect to the first virtue ethics thesis we considered, the virtues have a cognitive role: possession of the virtues enables one to form appropriate judgments with respect to the pursuit of the goods and evils at stake in the context of decision. With respect to the second, the virtues have a motivational role: possession of the virtues motivates the agent to act in appropriate ways in response to those goods and evils. (One need not hold that these are totally distinct roles: see, e.g., McDowell 1978.) We might put the second virtue ethics thesis in this way: possession of the virtues is indispensable for the excellence of one's action (see, e.g., Stocker 1976).

Now, there is clearly an important sense in which the natural law theory defended here agrees with this view. The good of excellence in agency is that good consisting in choosing and acting well and in having one's judgment and feeling in harmony with one's choices and actions. We might say, then, that the possession of the virtues is important in two ways with respect to the good of excellence in agency. First, possession of the virtues is a means to performing excellent actions, those in line with the requirements of practical reasonableness. Secondly, possession of the virtues is a constituent of the good of excellence in agency: having one's dispositions and feelings aligned with the good is not only a means to proper action but is itself intrinsically good for an agent.

There is, however, a way of understanding this virtue-as-motivator thesis that does not fit so easily with the natural law view. One might claim that in affirming the notion that virtue is indispensable to the good of excellence in agency, I miss the strength of the claim made by the defender of the virtue-as-motivator thesis: this thesis does not merely claim that virtue is necessary to being an excellent agent, but that possession of virtue is necessary for a particular action to be excellent, that is, not lacking anything relevant to that act's goodness. One's act of courage, it might be claimed, is not as good as it could be if it does not proceed from the virtue of courage; and so on with respect to the acts of the other virtues.

I reject this view, and so should, I think, virtue theorists. First, it seems to be possible that an agent perform an act with full awareness of the nature of the goods at stake in his or her choice and of the response that would be appropriate given the nature of those goods; that the agent perform that action on the basis of that practical judgment; yet that agent lacks the relevant virtue. (If this is not possible, it is due to some cognitive thesis about the virtues, that only the virtuous person could form such a justified judgment. This is a very strong claim, much stronger than the claim that only the virtuous person can serve as a reliable standard of the correctness of practical judgment.) Given the correct intention and employment of means suitable to circumstances, formed on the basis of well-grounded assessments of the goods at stake, why would the absence of a virtue be sufficient to detract from the goodness of the action? To have a virtue, one might say, is just to have the requisite motivational and intellectual dispositions toward such action; it is hard to see why an action could not be excellent in the absence of a tendency to perform such actions.

Secondly, it is unclear whether the view that possession of a virtue is necessary for the excellence of an act of that virtue makes sense of the virtue theorist's characteristic view that the virtues are acquired by habituation. It seems that if habituation to a virtue is the correct account of how the virtues, at least the moral virtues, are acquired, then at least at some time prior to the acquisition of a virtue one is performing the same action without possessing the relevant virtue that one would later perform when one does possess that virtue. If not, it seems strange to call what is supposed to be going on 'habituation.' But if the action that is performed prior to the possession of the virtue is the same as the action that is performed after the acquisition of the virtue, then it does not seem to me to be possible that the former is lacking in some excellence as an action that the latter enjoys.

We can offer an explanation for why one would suppose that the action of the virtuous agent must be better than the action of the nonvirtuous agent: it is that the nonvirtuous agent is worse off with respect to the good of excellence in agency than the virtuous agent is. Even if the nonvirtuous agent were able to perform the act of a virtue without using the virtue as a means, he or she would still lack that harmony between decision, judgment, and feelings/dispositions that is characteristic of the agent that is fully participating in the good of excellence in agency. But that does not mean that there is anything that need be deficient about any particular act of the agent that lacks the virtues.

I do not pretend to have surveyed here the various theses that virtue theorists have put forward that provide some challenge to natural law theories; I have examined interpretations of only two prominent virtue theory theses. With respect to some of these claims – such as the weaker epistemological interpretation of the virtuous-agent-as-standard thesis and the weaker interpretation of the virtue-as-motivator thesis – natural law theory can incorporate the virtue theory insights without loss. With respect to some of these claims – such as the metaphysical interpretation of the virtuous-agent-as-standard thesis and the stronger interpretation of the virtue-as-motivator thesis – we have strong reasons to doubt them, even independently of their inconsistency with the natural law view presented here. And with respect to one of the claims we considered – the stronger interpretation of the epistemological virtuous-agent-as-standard thesis – the only thing that I have said against it is that it is inconsistent with this natural law account. But that is all I aim to say here on that matter: that thesis presupposes the negative claim that no correct practical principle can be formulated without reference to the virtuous agent. The best response to such a claim is to produce an example of such a practical principle; and so my response is just the defense of the principles of practical reasonableness laid out in 5.5 and 5.6.

6

What Ought to Be Done

6.1 'Ought'

In this chapter I will bring to completion my treatment of natural law as a theory of practical rationality. In order to conclude this treatment, I need to consider what resources natural law theory has for answering that most basic of practical questions, 'What ought I to do?' While it is obvious from the previous chapters that natural law theory holds that what one ought to do has a great deal to do with the goods worth pursuing and the principles of practical reasonableness governing choice, we need to see precisely how these goods and those principles bear on the truth of ought-judgments. In order to bring this question into focus, let us turn to the notion of 'ought' itself to see how the natural law theorist should characterize that idea.

The first thing that the natural law theorist should say about ought-judgments was presupposed in the previous paragraph: it is that ought-judgments are genuine propositions – they are objects of belief, they are the sort of thing that can be true or false, they can enter into logical relationships with other propositions. The second thing is that within a natural law view, the notion of 'ought' is connected closely to the possibility of acting well, that is, to instantiating in the good of excellence in agency as that good was characterized in Chapter 3 (3.3). One ought to perform a certain action, that is, if by the performance of that action one will thereby be acting well, participating in the good of excellence in agency.

While there might be a number of senses of 'ought' – we shall consider another sense of it in a moment – the sense of 'ought' that is immediately tied to the good of excellence in agency is, according to natural law theory, the most fundamental practical sense of 'ought.' But we would do well to see whether this sense of 'ought' admits of further explication.

Consider Alan Donagan's account of what makes moral judgments true, which can be adapted into an account of the truth of ought-judgments:

The elementary deliverances of common morality are . . . true or false according to the realist, or correspondence, theory of truth. They are true if and only if practical reason, functioning without error, would make certain prescriptions. Thus elementary moral prohibitions of the form "Actions of kind *K* are unconditionally contrary to reason" are true just in case practical reason, functioning without error, would prescribe that actions of kind *K* unconditionally may not be done: or, in a more recent idiom, just in case anybody in any possible world, who thinks about the matter to a practical conclusion and makes no error, prescribes that actions of kind *K* unconditionally may not be done. (1977, p. 53)

To be fussy about this: Donagan should have dropped the word "may" from the statement of what reason prescribes, for by including the "may," a moral concept reappears in Donagan's explanation of the truth conditions for moral 'ought' judgments. Given this alteration, Donagan's view can be transformed easily into a theory of 'ought' judgments that satisfies the desiderata that such judgments be propositional and that they be appropriately related to practical reasonableness: '*A* ought to φ' is true if and only if any practical reasoner would, if his or her or its practical reason were functioning without error, prescribe that *A* φ.

I would like to adopt the main thrust of Donagan's strategy, but there are several reasons that I am unwilling to adopt it as it stands. First, the counterfactual, abstract cast of the notion of 'ought' does not sit well with the idea that acting as one ought involves a participation in the good of excellence in agency; for excellence in agency consists first and foremost in acting in accordance with one's correct judgment. Thus, the fundamental practical sense of 'ought' must refer not to just *anybody's* practical reason but to the agent's; and it must refer not to what an agent would reach as a deliberative conclusion but what the agent in fact does reach. Secondly, I find the notion of 'prescription,' while not completely improper, a bit strange once the previous modification is adopted: if the correctness of the fundamental 'ought' depends on the practical reasoning of the agent whose act it is to be, then one is always prescribing to oneself. While this carries some Kantian tones of legislating for oneself, this sort of locution is too high for me. Better to say, in keeping with the idea that what is assessed by principles of practical reasonableness are plans of action among which agents are trying to decide (5.1), that ought-judgments have to do with agents' decisions, rather than agents' prescriptions. I thus propose the following standard for the truth of ought-judgments in the most fundamental practical sense of 'ought': *A* ought to φ if and only if *A,* whose practical reason is functioning without error, decides to φ.

Even if one agrees that there is a rationale within natural law theory for characterizing the fundamental practical 'ought' in this manner, one might raise an obvious objection to it. In contrast to Donagan's account of the truth of moral judgments, my characterization of the correctness of ought-judgments depends too much on subjective factors, in particular, the agent's decision. Consider the following case to bring the objection into focus. Many of us would want to make claims of the following sort: 'John ought not to lie to Mary.' In many cases in which we make such claims, we think that what John in fact decides to do is irrelevant to the truth of this claim. But if '*A* ought not to φ' means '*A* ought to refrain from φ-ing,' though, then on the characterization of 'ought' offered by natural law theory, this common view must be false: for whether John ought to refrain from lying to Mary depends on whether John has decided to refrain from performing that act.

This is only a worry if we cannot capture the sense of our claim about John's lying within some other meaning of 'ought' that is definable in terms of natural law theory's fundamental practical 'ought.' This sense of 'ought,' like Donagan's account of the precepts of the common morality, will not be dependent on subjective factors. Call this the moral 'ought.'

6.2 The Moral 'Ought'

The natural law theorist can provide a characterization of a certain type of 'ought' statement in which the 'ought' is independent of the agent's decision; I want to say that this concept is sufficiently close to that presupposed in moral theory to be called the moral 'ought.' *A* morally ought to φ if and only if it is not possible that *A*, whose practical reasoning is functioning without error, decide to ψ, where ψ-ing and φ-ing are incompatible. This moral 'ought' is untainted by subjective factors: whether *A* reaches any particular decision is a contingent matter; whether it is possible for *A* to reach a certain decision errorlessly is not a contingent matter. On this explication of the moral 'ought,' we can provide an interpretation of the claim that John ought not lie to Mary on which John's actual decision is irrelevant to the correctness of that ought-judgment: in saying that John ought not lie to Mary, our judgment is true only if it is not possible for John to make a decision about how to act that is incompatible with refraining from lying without some error of practical reason. We are denying, that is, that John could, without practical error, decide to lie to Mary. This sort of claim could be true even if John decides to lie to Mary, or makes no decision at all on the matter.

Before considering an important objection to the idea that this is an adequate characterization of the moral 'ought,' we should first clear up some misunderstandings that this analysis might be prone to generate. One might object that by making every true moral ought-judgment, by definition, necessarily true, I have by fiat transformed every moral truth into a moral absolute. To make such a charge, though, is to misunderstand what is at stake between those who affirm and those who deny the existence of moral absolutes. While the necessity of certain moral judgments may be a necessary condition for the existence of moral absolutes, it is not a sufficient condition. What is required, in addition, for the existence of moral absolutes in the philosophically and practically interesting sense is that there be acts, describable in a certain way, that are exceptionlessly prohibited. Without committing myself to a detailed view of the way that such acts must be describable in order for their prohibition to count as a moral absolute, I may offer examples of what I have in mind: the affirmation of the claim that it is necessarily true that one morally ought not to perform immoral acts of deception is compatible with the rejection of moral absolutes in a philosophically interesting sense, while the affirmation of the claim that one morally ought not to assert falsehoods with the intention to deceive is incompatible with the rejection of moral absolutes in a philosophically interesting sense. Since I have placed no restrictions on what sorts of circumstances can be included in the act of φ-ing in the explications of the fundamental practical 'ought' and of the moral 'ought,' there is no reason to think that my account of the moral 'ought' implies that all true moral ought-judgments will turn out to be moral absolutes.

There is still a reason to be unsatisfied: one might wonder whether any moral ought-judgments turn out to be true if subjected to this necessity condition, apart from those that are analytically true. Part of the response to this will be the discussion carried out in 6.3, which will indicate how moral ought-judgments are established as true and give some examples of the derivation of such judgments. But, even apart from that presentation, there is no reason to think that the only correct moral ought-judgments would be analytically true.

Suppose that there is a merely prima facie duty not to lie, where 'lying' is specifiable in nonmoral terms as the assertion of falsehoods with the intention to deceive. Now, on the explication of the moral 'ought' that I have offered, the universal judgment 'for all agents A, A morally ought not to lie' does turn out to be false – for if this duty can be overridden, there may be some cases in which one can, without error, decide to lie. But one can state the prima facie duty more exactly, in a way that could be true: 'for all agents A, A morally ought not to lie in the absence of sufficiently strong reasons for doing so.' While this statement is not very informative about how strong the reasons have to be in order to be able to make an errorless decision to tell a lie, that is not the fault of the account of the moral 'ought,' but, rather, of the imprecision of the formulation of the prima facie duty not to lie. It does not seem to me, then, that this account of the moral 'ought' reckons all moral judgments false save ones that are trivial on account of their analytic truth.

A further problematic issue to be dealt with concerns the explication of the moral 'ought' and its relationship to the fundamental practical 'ought.' It might be held that the introduction of the moral 'ought' as a way to understand how an ought-judgment can be independent of an agent's decision does not wholly solve the problem raised by the case of John's lying to Mary. For we might want our accounts of the fundamental practical 'ought' and the moral 'ought' to exhibit the following logical relationships: if A morally ought to φ, then A ought to φ; and if A morally ought not φ, then A ought not φ. But these relationships clearly do not hold between the moral and the fundamental practical 'oughts,' given the inclusion of the agent's actual decision in the statement of the truth conditions for ought-judgments in the fundamental practical sense. That A morally ought to φ does not imply that A ought to φ, but that it is not the case that A ought to perform any action incompatible with φ-ing; that A morally ought not φ does not imply that A ought not φ, but that it is not the case that A ought to perform any action incompatible with refraining from φ-ing. So, to return to our example: even if we are glad to know that John morally ought not lie to Mary, we might be nonplussed that this does not imply that John ought not lie to Mary. Rather, it implies only that it is not the case that he ought to do anything that includes lying to Mary.

I admit that these implications stray from common usage, and may be counterintuitive. But it seems to me both that these implications are very much in keeping with natural law theory's account of excellence in agency and that the distinction between 'A ought' and 'it is not the case that A ought,' in conjunction with other senses of 'ought' definable in terms of the fundamental practical 'ought,' does all of the work that we need the term 'ought' to do.

First, what is troubling about the implications of the fundamental practical 'ought' is that in cases where John does not decide not to lie to Mary, there is no condemnation of John's lying to her that we could offer at the fundamental practical level other than 'it is not the case that John is doing what he ought'; we could not, that is, put forward the stronger 'John is doing what he ought not to do.' Now, if it were moral 'oughts' that we are concerned with, there is clearly a difference between the condemnatory force of the two: 'it is not the case that A morally ought to φ' means that it is possible for A to decide, without error, not to φ; 'A morally ought not φ' means that A's deciding to φ guarantees that A is in error. But it is true that, in the circumstances described, we cannot say that John ought not lie to Mary in the fundamental practical sense. It seems to me, though, that this is precisely what we should expect from the natural law theory of practical reasonableness. For, after all, all badness is, on this natural law view, a lack, a deficiency, a falling short in some way (1.4). Given the tight connection between 'ought' and excellence in agency, to say that one is acting in a way that it is not the case that one ought to act is to indicate that one's action is deprived in some way, that it is lacking something needed to be a full participation in the good of excellence in agency on this occasion. This is condemnation enough, on the natural law view. If we say that in lying, John is doing something that is not something he ought to do, we are not expressing that his act is merely indifferent; we are expressing that John's actions lack some goodness that they are capable of having. For a type of action to be morally wrong is to guarantee that any action of such a type will be deficient in this way.

Secondly, if this account of the fundamental practical 'ought' has an implication that is contrary to our ordinary way of thinking about ought-judgments, that fact is a philosophical consideration against that account only if our ordinary notion of 'ought' fulfills some function in practical thought that the fundamental practical 'ought' (or notions definable in its terms) cannot. I doubt this claim, though: for the fundamental practical 'ought,' along with the moral 'ought' defined in terms of it, clearly captures that there are some ways of acting that are excellent, some that fall short of excellence, and some that are incompatible with excellence. Until I am persuaded that there are other important practical functions of 'ought,' I see no reason to think that the explication of the fundamental practical 'ought' is inadequate to our ordinary usage in a way that constitutes an objection to that explication.

Even if one does not balk at the logical relationships that I hold to obtain between the moral 'ought' and the fundamental practical 'ought,' one might still claim that it is badly misleading to call this former type of ought-judgment the moral 'ought': it might be objected that the moral 'ought,' thus conceived, does not give the privileged place to the impartial point of view that the moral 'ought' should embody. Nowhere in the statement of the satisfaction conditions for the moral 'ought' is reference made to impartial reasons. This omission is perhaps even more damaging when this conception of the moral 'ought' is deployed within the natural law view, for the details of that view suggest that partial reasons will have an undue influence on what we morally ought to do. For an agent to be morally required to ϕ, it must be impossible for the agent reasonably to decide to perform any act incompatible with ϕ-ing. But the way that agent-relative welfare reasons function in this account of practical rationality – they are the most basic reasons for action, and are incommensurable as a class with agent-neutral welfare reasons (5.3) – implies that the presence of these agent-relative reasons will place tremendous limits on what we are by nature morally required to do. Think again of the principles of practical reasonableness governing plans of action formulated in 5.5. There is an important limitation on the principle of impartiality: the requirement to be impartial holds sway only when one is acting on agent-neutral ends, and one is not rationally constrained to act on agent-neutral, rather than agent-relative, ends. It thus turns out that the grossest partiality is not morally wrong, for it is possible for one reasonably to act in grossly partial ways, and since it is possible for one reasonably to act in grossly partial ways, gross partiality cannot be one of those ways that we morally ought not to act.

I do not think that it will be possible to put this worry entirely to rest. As I mentioned in 5.5, I wish that I could defend a less qualified principle of impartiality; but I find it impossible to deny the existence of basic agent-relative welfare reasons, and I find it implausible to hold that agent-neutral reasons are somehow superior in kind to agent-relative reasons, so that we could affirm the dominance of neutral over relative reasons in deliberation. The worry that the moral 'ought' on my view does not embody an entirely impartial perspective is not to be handled, then, by adjusting the account of reasons for action. Perhaps, then, we should handle it by adjusting the account of the moral 'ought.' In order to make certain that the moral 'ought' reflects an impartial perspective, we could qualify the characterization of the moral 'ought' so that it is concerned only with the practically reasonable agent's response to agent-neutral reasons. An agent A morally ought to ϕ, then, if and only if the following is true: if A were acting on only agent-neutral reasons for action, then it would not be possible for A, whose practical reason is functioning without error, to decide to ψ, where ψ-ing and ϕ-ing are incompatible. Given the impartial character of the moral point of view, why shouldn't we incorporate this qualification into the statement of the satisfaction conditions for the moral 'ought'?

One reason not to take the impartiality consideration as a decisive reason to modify the characterization of the moral 'ought' is that it is not clear that the moral 'ought' embodies so strictly the impartial point of view. It is often thought that there are, as Shelly Kagan puts it, "limits" on morality (1989, pp. xi): the range of moral demands to which we are susceptible is limited by partial concerns. (Of course, Kagan's interest is in rejecting, rather than defending, this view.) If we take this common view seriously, it does not seem as such an objection to my view that what we are morally required to do is shaped by the presence of agent-relative welfare reasons.

Now, one might respond in a couple of ways here to this anti-impartialist point. One might say, first of all, that the way that morality is shaped by agent-relative reasons is far greater on the natural law view that I have defended than the ordinary believer in the limits of morality is likely to have imagined. If this is the reply that is offered, though, then the argument is no longer being carried by a certain essential connection between impartiality and the moral point of view; rather, the argument is being carried by a particular account of how impartiality and partiality come together to determine the precise shape of the best theory of morality. I have nothing further to say to this point than to reaffirm the account of reasons for action and principles of practical reasonableness defended in the first five chapters.

One might say, though, that I have misunderstood the way that partiality can shape moral requirements. Even if partial considerations do have an effect on what one morally ought to do, they have effect only through the approval of impartial considerations: whether reasons to promote one's own good that one has can affect the particular moral requirements by which one is bound is determined by the agent-neutral reasons for action that there are. On this view, agent-relative reasons can affect what one morally ought to do only derivatively: if the correct assessment of the agent-neutral reasons for action implies that agents may act on certain agent-relative reasons, then agent-relative reasons may help to determine the shape of their moral obligations.

Suppose that this view were worked out in tolerable detail, and were sufficiently plausible to underwrite the thesis that the limits of morality were themselves the result of morality's essential impartiality. Would this provide an adequate basis to adopt the modified account of the moral 'ought,' which is defined not in terms of what is a possible reasonable response to the set of all reasons but in terms of what is a possible reasonable response to a proper subset of reasons? I would still be suspicious of such a proposal, for the following reasons. The rationale for the modified account of the moral 'ought' is that impartiality is commonly held to be a formal feature of moral requirements. But *overridingness* is also commonly held to be a formal feature of moral requirements. An effect of reinterpreting the moral 'ought' in terms of agent-neutral reasons only is to give up the present interpretation's capacity to capture overridingness: as the moral 'ought' is presently formulated, correct judgments that *A* morally ought to φ are practically overriding – practical reason demands that one never act in a way that one morally ought not act. Once we move to the modified understanding of the moral 'ought,' though, the focus on the proper subset of reasons strips such judgments of their overriding character.

It seems to me, then, that our ordinary understanding of the moral 'ought' exhibits a tension between impartiality and overridingness, and given the most defensible account of reasons for action, no theory of the moral 'ought' could capture both.[1] The tendency of recent writers has been, I think, to emphasize the impartiality of moral judgment and to give up on its overridingness. My decision to go the other way – to give up the impartiality of the moral 'ought' in favor of its overridingness – reflects the fact that my main concern is to exhibit the contours of natural practical reasonableness, of what can be said about reasonable action apart from agents' choices and decisions. (This concern with the contours of natural practical reasonableness, regardless of the extent to which its prescriptions depart from what is ordinarily included under the rubric of 'morality,' is the reason that Sidgwick allowed egoism, somewhat paradoxically, to count as a "method of ethics"; see *Methods,* p. 119.) To accept the restricted notion of the moral 'ought' is to lose this idea: for whether this kind of moral ought-judgment will govern the deliberation of the practically reasonable agent will depend on the agent's decision, to wit, whether and to what extent to act on agent-neutral reasons. Thus, I understand the moral 'ought' as dealing with what we can say about constraints on conduct that hold independently of the agent's decisions, even if the extent of these constraints is drastically limited by the various kinds of reasons on which the agent might choose to act.

Let us now turn, then, to drawing out some implications of this notion of 'ought' in conjunction with the claims of the natural law theory developed in Chapters 4 and 5. We shall begin by considering the constraint mentioned in the characterization of both the fundamental practical 'ought' and the moral 'ought': that practical reason not err in reaching its decision. In what ways is practical reason susceptible to error in reaching its decisions, and to what extent does this constrain what one ought to do?

6.3 How Practical Reason Can Err

In the fundamental practical sense of 'ought,' one ought to φ if and only if one whose practical reason is functioning without error decides to φ. The proviso that the agent's practical reason must be functioning without error is in need of some clarification, both with regard to its precise meaning and with regard to what would actually constitute errors in the functioning of practical reason.

The main clarification that needs to be made with regard to the no-error proviso is that the condition that practical reason function without error applies only to that particular decision: that is, A ought to φ if and only if A decides to φ, and A's practical reason functions without error with respect to the decision to φ. The fact that I might have erred in coming to a particular decision does not in itself call into question its being the case that I ought to perform an action in accordance with a distinct decision. Its being the case that one ought to perform a particular action does not have as a precondition perfection of practical reason in all of one's decisions.

So, its being the case that one ought to φ requires only that practical reason function without error with respect to the decision to φ. There are two ways that this condition could fail to be met with regard to any particular decision, and these two ways correspond to the traditional distinction between fact and right: practical reason can err with regard to claims about nonnormative truths, and it can err with regard to claims about normative truths.

Strictly speaking, practical reason does not itself err concerning claims about nonnormative reality. The claims about nonnormative reality that it employs in the deliberative decision-making process are taken from theoretical reason. But since theoretical reason can err in its affirmation of nonnormative propositions, which propositions are then used by practical reason in deliberation, practical reason can inherit the errors of theoretical reason. Since practical reason is incompetent to judge on these matters, and the part of natural law theory being developed here is part of practical reason, I will say nothing about the sorts of errors that theoretical reason makes that might be used by practical reason in reaching its decision. But one issue does call for a bit more elaboration, and that is whether all factual errors that appear in deliberation call into question the decision that results from that deliberation.

Consider the following case. Suppose that Mary wants to make a contribution to charity. She believes that contributing x dollars to a particular charity will promote the good of Y persons. She thus decides to contribute x dollars to that charity. But it turns out that Mary was wrong: x dollars contributed to that charity will promote the good only of $Y-1$ persons. Does Mary's being mistaken on this point show that Mary's practical reasoning was not proceeding without error when she reached the decision to make the contribution, and thus, that it is not the case that she ought to make that contribution?

The answer is, unsurprisingly, that it depends on further facts about the history of Mary's deliberation. While it seems obviously true that errors inherited from theoretical reason can call into question whether an agent ought to act in the way that he or she decides to act, it also seems that we need a bit more precision on the issue of how errors of theoretical reason have to be implicated in one's decision-making process in order to count as an error in the functioning of practical reason. It does not seem to me that every error of theoretical reason that appears in the flow of deliberation is sufficient to invalidate the decision resulting from that deliberation. We might offer as first approximation of how errors in theoretical reason must be implicated in deliberation in order to count as an error of practical reason that the false proposition appearing in the flow of deliberation must be one upon which the agent relies in reaching that decision. (Hence, the qualification that the error must be *with respect to that decision.* If the error of fact is not relied upon by the agent, the agent does not, to that extent, err with respect to that decision.) The difficulty is in explaining what precisely it means for an agent to rely on a certain proposition in coming to a decision.

My view is that while it is inappropriate to give a counterfactual analysis of what it is for an agent to rely on a certain fact in making a decision, counterfactual considerations give the clearest guidance in specifying, as precisely as we can, which facts an agent is relying on. To return to the example: was Mary relying on the fact that the x dollars would benefit Y people? Or was she relying on the fact that the x dollars would benefit more people if contributed to that charity than to any other? Or was she relying on the fact that the x dollars would benefit at least a certain number of people? By asking about what Mary would have decided had she held different beliefs, we can get a clearer idea as to which facts Mary was relying on. But I think that counterfactual analyses will invariably fall short of giving necessary and sufficient conditions for whether an agent was relying on a particular fact, since the notion of reliance is a causal notion, and I doubt that causal notions can be adequately captured by counterfactual analyses, however helpful they are at guiding us in making more precise what our causal beliefs are. (For the contrary view, see Lewis 1973.) Regardless of how we are ultimately to test whether a decision is flawed by an error of theoretical reason, the general claim that I make is that the falsity of nonnormative propositions constitutes an error in the functioning of practical reasoning in reaching a decision only if the truth of those propositions was relied upon in reaching the decision.

With respect to the normative domain, we have already provided an account of how practical reason can fall into error. So long as the agent is choosing and deciding intelligibly, what he or she will decide upon is a plan of action, as that notion is characterized in 5.1. But, as I noted there, plans of action have presuppositions that are truth-valuable. Practical reason can err in that it presupposes falsehoods about the nature of the reasons for action implicated in a plan of action. Thus, practical reason errs whenever it runs afoul of one or another of the principles of practical reasonableness described and defended in 5.5, for those principles were shown to be correct by reference to the nature of the fundamental reasons for action.[2]

Given the characterization of the moral 'ought' presented in 6.2, and the account of the principles of practical reasonableness defended in Chapter 5, it is clear that natural law theory conceives these principles of practical reasonableness as the basis of most fundamental moral ought-judgments. For A morally ought to ϕ if and only if it is not possible that A, whose practical reasoning is functioning without error, decide to ψ, where ψ-ing and ϕ-ing are incompatible. But all of the principles of practical reasonableness for plans of action are based on the fact that a certain type of plan of action invariably involves an error with respect to the nature of the fundamental reasons for action. Thus, if a principle of practical reasonableness rules out ϕ-ing as unreasonable, then A morally ought not to ϕ. It can therefore never be the case that an agent A ought (in the fundamental practical sense) to ϕ if a principle of practical reasonableness rules out A's ϕ-ing.

The principles of practical reasonableness upon which moral requirements are based are highly abstract, however. To provide derivations of all of the interesting moral requirements that can be generated from these fundamental principles would be extremely tedious, though; and, besides, this study is not primarily for the sake of dealing with the more casuistical questions that arise within natural law theory. But it is worthwhile at least to illustrate how some of these principles imply clearly action-guiding moral requirements by producing a few derivations from these principles, which derivations can serve as models for further expansion of the stock of moral requirements that are part of the natural law. I will also use the formulation and defense of these moral requirements to indicate some of the limitations to which this natural law theory is subject.

Against Discrimination

Most of us think that discrimination of various sorts – of race, sex, and religion, to take a few examples – is morally wrong. Natural law theory explains the wrongness of discrimination in terms of the principle of practical reasonableness that rules out dismissing or devaluing persons within the context of agent-neutral reasons.

Recall that this principle of practical reasonableness is incapable of ruling out any plan of action on the basis of that plan's intrinsic features: what is relevant is how the agent formed that plan of action, and whether the decision in favor of that plan was reached by way of a devaluation or dismissal of some person. The fact that a plan of action would impose some burdens on one person and not others, or provide benefits to some and not to others, is insufficient to show that there is anything morally suspect about that plan of action, just as the fact that a plan of action ignores goods of one kind and promotes goods of another kind is insufficient to show that there is anything morally suspect about that plan of action. At most, the character of these plans is a *sign* that the agent has chosen in a way that is practically unreasonable.

If discrimination is to be declared morally prohibited, then, by appeal to this principle, what is prohibited is primarily a certain way of deciding how to act and only secondarily a certain way of acting. Take racial discrimination: to discriminate with regard to race is primarily to come to decisions with regard to how one will act in a way that inappropriately takes the race of those affected into account. This way of characterizing racial discrimination might seem to turn the claim 'racial discrimination is unreasonable' into a tautology: for it might seem analytic that *inappropriate* consideration of race is unreasonable. But the notion of appropriateness at work in this characterization of racial discrimination is not the generic 'inappropriate to practical reason' that would render the prohibition on racial discrimination tautologous; rather, whether consideration of race is appropriate is determined by the nature of the agent-neutral reason (or reasons) for action that provides the aim of the plan of action, and which therefore governs the application of this principle of practical reasonableness. When one is acting on an agent-neutral reason – and only those acting on such reasons are constrained by this principle of practical reasonableness – the nature of that reason will determine, together with facts about the world, what sort of characteristics are relevant in the forming of a plan of action.

Consider, in this regard, the recently debated issue of whether the exclusion from the United States military of those living a homosexual lifestyle constitutes immoral discrimination. On the view proposed here, whether such exclusion amounts to immoral discrimination depends on whether the agent-neutral end being pursued is such that it picks out as relevant the distinction between those leading such a lifestyle and those not. Given that at least one of the purposes of the common project of the military is to provide an effective fighting force, the contributions to the debate of those who presented evidence for or against the claim that allowing gays in the military would undermine the effectiveness of that force were clearly to the point in the assessment of that policy's moral status.

Now, to the formulation and defense of this rather formal rule against discrimination, one might retort that the rule possesses too little force against those intent on racial discrimination. For one aiming at the promotion of an agent-neutral end could simply modify the end pursued until that end supported the imposing of burdens or the denial of benefits to an individual or class of persons. But this reply would be in error. First, the assumption behind the principles governing plans of action is that those plans of action have ends that are supported by reasons for action. Thus, even if one comes up with some end formulable in an agent-neutral way that will support de facto discrimination, that end must be backed by reasons. (One could not, in attempting to justify a university admissions policy discriminating against blacks, affirm that the aim of the university is to promote knowledge for white people, and hold that this end does support a difference of treatment between whites and blacks. While there is an agent-neutral reason to promote knowledge, there is none to promote knowledge for white people.) Secondly, it must be recalled that not every trans-formation of plans of action is allowed by principles of practical reason. Since the principles of practical reason governing agents precludes flightiness, one cannot reasonably alter one's aims without a sufficient reason for doing so. It will, however, be difficult to come up with a reason for transforming one's plan that is a reason to deny benefits or impose burdens on a particular individual or group.

What this criticism does bring out, though, is an important truth about the way that this formulation of the principle forbidding discrimination functions in deliberation. The verdict that a particular policy is a discriminatory one may lead those engaged in a common project to reconsider their conception of the aims of that project, to take part in a debate that may transform – for good rea-son – their view of the ends that are being pursued. Consider, for example, an affirmative action policy in the hiring of faculty. Given a particular conception of the aims of an educational institution, such a policy might seem to amount to immoral discrimination. The recognition of this fact might lead those inside and outside of that institution to pause to reconsider the aims of such institu-tions, whether (e.g.) some end might be ascribed to those institutions in light of which an affirmative action policy might be completely justified. As the abstract cast of this example suggests, I offer no brief on behalf of a conception of ed-ucational institutions that would either support or preclude the permissibility of affirmative action practices. But it does seem to me that this is the direction in which the debate over affirmative action has turned, in that those involved in that debate seem now to be most concerned with what the role of institutions of higher learning is within the larger society, what sort of aims should be pursued by those institutions, and whether affirmative action policies are justified by those aims.

Now, the rule against discrimination that I have been defending derives from a principle of practical reasonableness concerned with the way that agents act on agent-neutral reasons. One might wonder, though, whether an agent that acts only on agent-relative reasons would be able to evade the rule and perform acts of discrimination. Consider, in this regard, the way that James Rachels argues against egoism (Rachels 1999, pp. 93–95). Rachels argues that the egoist is ir-rationally arbitrary because the egoist treats his or her own good as being of fundamental importance to action and others' good as being of no fundamental importance to action, though there is no relevant difference between them. The egoist, therefore, arbitrarily treats him- or herself as special. In this, the egoist's irrationality is akin to that of the racist, who treats members of certain races as superior or inferior without reason for doing so. Now, Rachels's argument against egoism is unsuccessful. If all reasons were agent-neutral, it would be forceful: if there is a reason to promote (e.g.) knowledge as such, then it would be arbitrarily irrational for me to promote my own knowing and to fail to promote yours, simply because mine is instantiated in me and yours in you. But if some reasons for action are agent-relative, then the fact that some good is instantiated in me might be a perfectly good reason to promote it, rather than some good to be instantiated in you. In doing so, I am not treating myself as special for no reason: I do have a reason to promote my good over yours. (And, of course, you have a reason to promote your good over mine.)

But if Rachels's argument fails, one might say, then surely the similar argument purporting to rule out all racial discrimination as unreasonable must fail also. One who claims that whites' good should be promoted while blacks' good should not can be convicted of irrational arbitrariness. But one might be an agent-relative racist, holding that everyone has a reason to give preferential treatment to members of his or her own race. Since I am white, I have reason to give preferential treatment to whites under the description 'members of my race'; if I were black, I would have reason to give preferential treatment to blacks under the description 'members of my race.' If there were agent-relative reasons of this sort, then discrimination could be justified by one who is acting not on agent-neutral but on agent-relative reasons for action. But the simple response is that there are no such reasons. While there are agent-relative reasons to promote one's own good, there are no agent-relative reasons to promote the good of members of one's own race, just as there are no agent-relative reasons to promote the good of members of one's own zip code, of one's own hair color, or of one's own height. Given the fact that the fundamental reasons for action are goods that fulfill individual persons, it is perfectly clear why there would be no such reasons.

This principle of practical reasonableness forbidding the dismissing or devaluing of persons, and the rule precluding discrimination that follows from it, is the foundation for claims of justice. Whether a plan of action – either an individual's plan of action, or that instituted within a cooperative scheme – is just depends on how that plan was formed, whether it was formed in a way that did not dismiss or devalue the good of anyone within the context of the agent-neutral end for the sake of which the one or the many are acting.

Consider, in this regard, Rawls's original position procedure for deciding issues of basic justice. The original position embodies a decision procedure in which knowledge of certain features of the parties in that position is denied to them. Two important aspects of the application of this principle of practical reasonableness are embodied in Rawls's procedure: that what is primarily relevant is the way that the decision is reached, and that the decision procedure must not give weight to any irrelevant characteristics of those that are to be affected by the decision. Given the inevitable brevity of any such treatment, it would be hopelessly silly to try to engage Rawlsian justice theory in any meaningful way here. But we may note at least the following. First, there is nothing incompatible in affirming both the natural law theory presented here and Rawls's original position device as the best way to specify what this principle of practical reasonableness rules out as unjust within a political community. Secondly, to say that Rawls's procedure can be employed within a natural law theory to specify what sorts of policies would be unjust within a political community is not to say that this principle is the only or ultimate regulative principle within political communities: certain policies might be ruled out not as unjust, but as violating some other principle of practical reasonableness. Thirdly, one might, within a natural law theory, stop short of calling Rawls's original position procedure the best for political communities while still endorsing it; one might call it an appropriate procedure for settling questions of justice, though not one required by natural reason.

There is an important limitation on this principle of practical reasonableness. While it implies that within communities – where communities exist only where there is common pursuit of an end – justice is a requirement of reason, it does not bring everyone into a domain where rules of justice limit their conduct. The reason for this is just that there is no requirement of reason to enter into communities, or indeed to pursue an agent-neutral end of any sort. Natural law thus permits one to be a quasi-egoist, one whose ultimate aims are all agent-relative. (I discuss in what ways the egoism allowed by reason is 'quasi' briefly in 5.5 and in more detail in this section.) While the principle of practical reasonableness discussed in this section is as true for the quasi-egoist as for anyone else, the quasi-egoist's failure to pursue agent-neutral ends precludes that principle from guiding that agent's conduct.

Against Lying

I shall illustrate an application of the principle of practical reasonableness that rules out intentional, instrumental destruction of an instance of a basic good by showing how it generates a moral requirement against lying. Let us stipulate, in keeping with tradition, that for A to lie to B is for A to assert a proposition to B believed by A to be false with the intention to deceive B. (But note that Aquinas [*Summa Theologiae* IIaIIae, 110, 1]) denies that the intention to deceive is part of the essence of the lie.) This definition of lying employs no moral terms: the concepts of assertion, falsehood, and deception are not themselves moral terms, and so the absolute prohibition on lying that I will defend cannot be construed as mere tautology, as it would be if lying were defined as 'wrongful deception,' or the like.

Now, there is a straightforward argument that lying is wrong that appeals to the Pauline principle, an argument endorsed by Finnis, among others. Lying is an act the intention of which is to deceive. To intend to deceive is to intend to cause someone to believe that which is false. But to intend to cause someone to believe a falsehood is, however, to act against the good of knowledge, which is a basic good. As we have seen, though, acting against any basic good is contrary to the Pauline principle. Therefore, one morally ought not to tell lies.[3]

This argument is successful, I think, but in my view, it does not provide the best natural law explanation for the wrongfulness of lying. In my view, the best explanation for the wrongfulness of lying invokes the good of excellence in agency, not the good of knowledge. While knowledge is, as possessed, always intrinsically good, it can be pursued either qua instrumental or qua intrinsic good. And it seems that when the liar intends to cause the deceived to believe that which is false, he or she attempts to damage the good of knowledge precisely insofar as it is an instrument to the good of excellence in agency, at least in paradigm cases of lying: for the liar typically aims at getting the deceived to act or feel in a certain way by manipulating the process of practical reasoning, by attempting to insert a false premise upon which the deceived will rely in making his or her assessment regarding how to act or how to feel. Since, as we have seen, reliance on mistaken normative or nonnormative propositions undermines one's participation in the good of excellence in agency, the liar's act characteristically constitutes an intentional attack on a basic good.

So, in paradigm cases of lying, the good of excellence in agency is at stake, along with the good of knowledge.[4] Are there any reasons for taking one of these goods to hold explanatory priority over the other in a natural law account of the wrongness of lying? Consider Aristotle's remark in Book V of the *Ethics* that the person who commits adultery in order to steal is more unjust than intemperate, because such a person acts in order to satisfy his or her *pleonexia,* rather than his or her sexual appetites (*Nicomachean Ethics,* 1130a25–29). The context of this passage makes clear that what Aristotle is remarking on is that we make judgments regarding the presence of habits by noting the actions that proceed from them: one who commits adultery in order to steal is acting from the habit of pleonexia, rather than intemperance, for it is only (we may suppose) to enrich oneself that one engages in the illicit sexual act. Even though the subject of Aristotle's remarks is the relationship between habit and action, I think that his comments are important for our consideration of how the wrongfulness of lying is to be explained. One who commits adultery in order to steal is unjust, rather than intemperate, yet one who commits adultery while stealing (yet not in order to steal) would, in Aristotle's terms, be considered both unjust and intemperate – *not* unjust, rather than intemperate, *not* more unjust than intemperate. And the reason for this difference is that in the former case, the acts of adultery and theft are ordered to one another in a certain way, whereas in the latter case, these acts display no such order. The ordered relationship, we might say, is that of specification of means: in Aristotle's imagined case, the act of adultery is a means to the act of theft, and indeed constitutes part of the complex that is the act of theft.

The general principle suggested by these considerations is that if an act against good *G* is a means to and is part of an act against good *H,* then the explanation of the wrongfulness of that complex act should give priority to the fact that the complex act is against good *H*. If this principle is correct, then we should hold that although the lie is an act against the intrinsic good of knowledge and an act against the intrinsic good of excellence in agency, explanatory priority for the wrongfulness of lying ought to be afforded to the good of excellence in agency. For the act against the good of knowledge carried out in the lie is both for the sake of the act against the good of excellence in agency, and indeed is a component of the complex act against the good of excellence in agency. Thus, we ought to give the good of excellence in agency explanatory priority in accounting for the moral rule against lying. (For a more detailed discussion of this issue, see Murphy 1996b.)

The Pauline principle rules out any action where one of the intentional objects of the agent's plan of action is the destruction or impeding of a state of affairs that constitutes a participation in a basic good in order to bring about another state of affairs that constitutes a participation in a basic good. In the natural law argument against lying, Finnis's argument and my argument focus on, respectively, the state of affairs of an agent's knowing some proposition and the state of affairs of an agent's acting in accordance with an accurate assessment of what is to be done. What this discussion illustrates, apart from the bare fact that the Pauline principle can be used to rule out certain sorts of act as unreasonable, is that in employing the Pauline principle, great care needs to be given to characterizing properly the nature of the act that is being morally assessed. Often our everyday names for acts do not clearly enough distinguish between relevantly different plans of action that are referred to by those names. We call acts of intentional deception 'lying,' whether they are typical acts against excellence in agency or less typical acts against the good of knowledge alone. We should not, however, be blinded by traditional or commonsense categories of actions in providing accounts of moral rules: since moral requirements are ultimately such in virtue of the character of the basic goods, it should be those goods themselves, and how particular actions are structured in relation to them, that govern our explanations.

The example of lying illustrates the point that we need to pay careful attention to what goods are at stake in using the Pauline principle in defense of a moral requirement. But we also need to pay careful attention to the nature of the plan of action that bears on those goods. One obvious point is that the Pauline principle applies to what is intended, not to what is unintended but merely foreseen: while unintended damage to goods is clearly a matter of practical relevance, it is not governed by the Pauline principle. This is why the various formulations of the principle of double effect include, as conditions of its application, both that the proposed act not violate the Pauline principle (that is, that the harm involved is not intended) and that the proposed act not violate any other principle of practical reasonableness. Another, less obvious point is that in my formulation of the Pauline principle, I have restricted its application in a controversial way: to be forbidden by the Pauline principle, the intentional destruction must be instrumental, that is, for the sake of bringing about a distinct good. This restriction limits the capacity of the Pauline principle to rule out acts of intentional harm in two ways.

First, it might be possible that an intentional act of destruction be performed that is not for the sake of a distinct good, but which is, in itself, an instance of a good. This possibility was once endorsed by Finnis. On that view, the order of justice is an aspect of the common good, and is itself a basic good. In some cases, the performance of a judicially sanctioned execution might further the common good of justice, not as an instrument to it, but as a constituent of it. While the deprivation essential to such punishment is "in one sense, an intentional attack or suppression of basic human goods," that deprivation "is intended neither for its own sake nor as a means to any further good state of affairs. Rather, it is intended as itself a good, namely the good of restoring the order of justice" (Finnis 1983, p. 129).

This argument succeeds only if the defense of the Pauline principle that I have offered fails to go through in the case of intentional attacks on basic goods that themselves constitute instances of basic goods. I am uncertain, though, what to say on this matter. On the one hand: an intentional attack on a basic good is no less an attack by its constituting a good, and it is an attack that is made intelligible only by reference to the good that it is held to instantiate. On the other, one might say, as Finnis once did, that the sort of weighing of goods that is presupposed in instrumental destruction of a good is not necessary in destruction of a good that itself constitutes a good. I simply do not know what to think here. Until I am able to construct, or see constructed, better arguments for one of these positions, I will keep to a restricted formulation of the Pauline principle so that it applies only to the instrumental destruction of instances of basic goods. (Finnis has recently indicated that he no longer accepts the defense of capital punishment suggested in Finnis 1983, but offers no explanation of what he took to be deficient in that account: see Finnis 1998, p. 293.)

Even if it were shown, though, that all destruction of basic goods performed for the sake of promoting basic goods – whether instrumental or not – should be ruled out by the Pauline principle, that still would not provide adequate warrant for holding that every plan of action involving the intentional destruction of a basic good is as such unreasonable. Recall that, as was argued in 4.4, it is open to the welfarist in the theory of practical rationality to reject promotionism, the thesis that any reason that makes an act intelligible is always a good to be promoted by that action. An act might be made intelligible by way of some relationship to the good other than that of promoting it; I mentioned that expressive action is a common, if not well understood, kind of action that cannot be easily subsumed under the category of promoting the good. Suppose that expressive action can be made intelligible by reference to well-being. If so, and among these intelligible instances of expressive action are those that involve the destruction of an instance of a basic good, nothing in the argument offered for the Pauline principle would militate against the reasonableness of such expressive action. For, after all, the argument for the Pauline principle was framed in terms of a comparison of the goods to be destroyed by the proposed action and the good to be promoted by means of that destruction; since such plans of action involve the false presupposition that the good to be gained is at least as good as the good to be destroyed, all such acts are unreasonable (5.5). But expressive action does not contain this presupposition of commensurability, for an expressive act that involves destruction of an instance of a basic good – think of retributive action – is not, qua expressive, for the sake of promoting a distinct good. (This is, of course, not to say that retributive acts, if intelligible, are automatically reasonable: they might be criticized by appeal to principles of practical reasonableness, other than the Pauline principle.)

Now, I have not shown that promotionism is false, only that commitment to welfarism does not obviously involve commitment to promotionism (4.4), and so I cannot say with confidence that some intentional acts of destruction of instances of basic good are not ruled out by the Pauline principle. My aim here has been only to make clear why I have limited the application of that principle as I have: that at present, we lack sufficiently good arguments to say how broadly the Pauline principle applies.

Against Callousness

I shall illustrate an application of the principle of practical reasonableness that rules out inefficiency by showing how it generates a moral requirement against callousness, that is, a refusal to promote the good of those that one could easily help.

As I mentioned earlier, one of the features of the natural law theory that I have defended that many readers are likely to find distasteful is its inability to rule out a certain kind of egoism as an unreasonable way to live. The recognition of agent-relative reasons irreducible to agent-neutral ones, and a refusal to affirm natural commensuration between these types of reasons, precludes the condemnation of the promotion of agent-relative over agent-neutral ends as a way of life. But it is clear that this 'quasi-egoism' is not standard egoism. On the typical egoist view considered in 5.2, what is practically reasonable is to maximize one's own good. But the quasi-egoism permitted by the natural law theory defended here involves significant departures from this principle. First, quasi-egoism is obviously not, according to natural law theory, a *requirement* of reason. Secondly, since all distinct instances of basic goods are incommensurable (5.3), the notion that one ought to maximize one's own good makes no sense as a master requirement of practical reasonableness. Thirdly, even if the ultimate aim of one's plan of action is the promotion of one's own good, the quasi-egoist must, in order to be reasonable, admit the existence of agent-neutral reasons for action and allow one's own plans of action to be dictated, to some extent, by those reasons. For example: while typical egoism would allow, and sometimes even require, the intentional destruction of others' good in order to promote one's own, the quasi-egoism that is within reason would include no intentional, instrumental destruction of goods, whether in oneself or in others. Thus, one's pursuit of one's own good is significantly constrained by the nonegoistic rule against certain intentional attacks on basic goods.

Another rule that all agents, including the quasi-egoist, are bound by reason to adhere to rules out callousness toward others' good. Consider the following case, described by Hume for a different purpose.

> Let us suppose . . . a person ever so selfish, let private interest have ingrossed ever so much his attention, yet in instances where that is not concerned, he must unavoidably feel some propensity to the good of mankind, and make it an object of choice all other things be equal. Would any man who is walking along tread as willingly on another's gouty toes, whom he has no quarrel with, as on the hard flint and pavement? (*Enquiry*, pp. 217–218)[5]

All are bound to avoid others' gouty toes, if it is indeed all the same to them whether they walk on the left side of the path or the right. (For it to be 'all the same' to an agent which side of the path to walk on is for that agent to miss out on no basic good by walking on one side, rather than the other.) This follows from the moral requirement against callousness: that one morally ought not to refrain from promoting another's good when one can costlessly do so.

This requirement is, of course, much weaker than many would like, but it would be an error to think of it as toothless. One might think it toothless due to a mistaken reading of 'costlessly,' supposing that every act of promoting another's good must have some cost to it. This universal claim seems false – walking on one side of the path, rather than another, seems to be costless, and that is why Hume's example has force both against psychological and ethical egoism. Even if we concede, though, that most promotion of others' good has a cost, that does not render the proposed rule nonaction guiding: for what is relevant is not that most acts of promoting others' good require some expenditure of instrumental means but that many such acts lack an *opportunity* cost. It is often the case, that is, that the instrumental means that are the cost of promoting another's good will not be available later for the promotion of one's own good, regardless of whether one uses it in carrying out other-regarding plans of action or not. Not to employ these means in such cases would be a waste, and thus a violation of the principle of practical reasonableness ruling out inefficiency.

These moral rules against discrimination, lying, and callousness are but a few of the rules that can be derived from the principles of practical reasonableness defended in Chapter 5. While it is clear that many other rules besides these can be drawn from those principles, it is also clear that the account of moral rules derivable within this natural law theory is much thinner than those brought forward in other typical natural law theories, such as Aquinas's or Finnis's. While there are, in my view, moral requirements grounded in reason itself, natural law theorists too often overstate what reason demands. This is a theme to which I will return in 6.5 and 6.6.

6.4 Moral Dilemmas

Before we turn from the discussion of the constraints placed on choice and action by practical reason to a consideration of the positive side of decision making, I want to devote some attention to an issue in moral philosophy that has been much discussed over the past thirty-five years: moral dilemmas. The main issues concerning moral dilemmas are (i) how such dilemmas should be characterized and (ii) whether they are, as characterized, genuine possibilities. Despite attempts to show the impossibility or possibility of moral dilemmas, either by appealing to formal deontic principles or by drawing attention to the phenomenological character of situations of moral conflict, there seems to be little evidence that progress can be made on the subject outside of the context of a more embracing normative theory. (As Alasdair MacIntyre has recently remarked, "it has become continually more evident that answers to questions about moral dilemmas stand or fall in systematic conjunction with answers to questions about moral theory in general" (1990b, p. 382).) Given the systematic (if necessarily incomplete) character of the moral theory presented in this work, it is worth considering the implications of this theory of practical reasonableness for the problem of moral dilemmas. I will first present what I take to be a fairly standard understanding of dilemmatic situations and then consider the extent to which the existence of moral dilemmas is consistent with both the understanding of moral ought-judgments proposed in 6.2 and the account of principles of practical reasonableness defended in Chapter 5.

What is essential to the dilemmatic situation is not, of course, the fact that two moral requirements come into conflict. What is essential to the dilemmatic situation is the inescapability of wrongdoing, the impossibility of performing an action that does not violate the requirements of morality. If it is possible that there be cases in which no matter what one does, one will be acting in a way that one ought not to act, then moral dilemmas are possible. The dispute over the possibility of moral dilemmas, then, is a dispute over the truth of the following proposition. Given that S is a variable ranging over states of affairs, A is a variable ranging over agents, and ϕ is a variable ranging over actions, moral dilemmas are possible if and only if it is possible that there is a state of affairs S and an agent A such that necessarily, if S obtains, then for any action ϕ that A might choose in S, A morally ought not to ϕ. According to the natural law theory defended here, are moral dilemmas in this sense a genuine possibility?

According to the account of ought-judgments sketched in 6.1 and 6.2, an agent morally ought not to perform a given action just in case it is not possible for that agent errorlessly to decide to perform that action. Now, it seems clear that if we restrict our attention to those principles of practical reasonableness governing plans of action – at least, with regard to the applications of those principles that make no reference to the agent's decisions or judgments – then no dilemmas can arise. (The importance of the qualification to this claim will be discussed shortly.) For recall how these principles were generated: they specify, and rule out as unreasonable, any plan of action that does injustice to the nature of the fundamental reasons for action. To do injustice to the nature of those reasons is to make a false presupposition about the nature of those reasons. But since reasons for action – like everything else in the world – cannot possess inconsistent features, it must always be possible that there be some plan of action that would presuppose nothing false about the nature of those reasons.

The thrust of this argument seems to show that the conception of the moral 'ought' employed within this natural law theory, together with its account of how principles of practical reasonableness are formulated, implies that there could be no dilemmatic situations. But the argument just presented was explicitly restricted in scope: it claimed that within a certain subset of the principles of practical reasonableness, no dilemmas could arise. I want to exhibit the possibility of moral dilemmas arising within the other subset of practical principles, that is, those that make reference to the agent's judgment and decision.

Consider a putative moral requirement that we may call 'the conscience principle': that one ought never to act against the dictates of one's conscience. (The introduction of the notion of 'conscience' perhaps calls for some explication. I do not take conscience to be either a distinct faculty or an infallible source of moral knowledge. Conscience is, rather, ordinary fallible human reason functioning in a certain capacity, that of providing answers to particular practical questions, questions of the form 'what am I to do here?') Those who defend the conscience principle often do so by appealing to some good that is compromised when one acts contrary to conscience. Thus, John Granrose offers what he calls a "prudential" argument for the conscience principle, on which acting according to conscience is a necessary condition for mental health: one who violates conscience will have guilt feelings that preclude the sort of integrity of mind essential to one's well-being (1970, pp. 208–209). Larry May also seems to endorse a version of the prudential argument. On his view, during the process of forming a dictate of conscience, one comes to see that if one were to perform a certain act, one would later look back on that action with regret, and this would "violate the inner harmony or integrity of the self" (1983, p. 59). Because "performing [an act against conscience] will produce disharmony within oneself when one comes to examine one's conduct later" (1983, p. 61), one should not act against conscience.

Now, while the advocates of the prudential argument seem to me to be correct to hold that (at least part of) the explanation for the conscience principle should rely on the concept of the agent's integrity, I think that there is something fundamentally wrong with the notion that the conscience principle is founded on an assessment of how one's later self will react to one's action. One problem with this view is that feelings of regret and guilt typically follow from one's judgment that one has done something wrong, and that leaves the question unanswered why it is wrong to act contrary to conscience. But even putting this difficulty to the side, the prudential view is burdened by the assumption that those who act against conscience inevitably experience guilt feelings, and this would seem to be a false empirical generalization. Some people who seem to form judgments regarding how they ought to act do not experience pangs of guilt when they fail to act in accordance with these judgments. But even for agents who typically experience guilt when they act against conscience, it is sometimes the case that the choices that they are tempted to make that are contrary to conscience are such that if they carry them out, they will not later look back upon them with regret.

The least interesting of such cases are those in which one will not be in a position to look back with regret at all, because one will not be in a position to look back: consider a choice contrary to conscience to commit suicide. More interesting are those cases in which the self is transformed by one's choice so that one will no longer regret acting against conscience; indeed, one might be pleased that one did so. Suppose, for example, that Jane is a sincerely religious person who is offered a job in which either the sort of work that she will have to do or the sort of people she will deal with will put her religious belief to a severe test. Jane might be tempted by the rewards that attend this position, but might judge that she ought not accept it because of the danger to her faith. If she were to imagine the consequences of acting against conscience by accepting the job, she might realize that by acting against conscience, she would later not regret her choice against conscience at all – if she were to lose her faith, she might be *glad* that she lost it. There would be no internal disharmony resulting from that choice against conscience.

The prudential argument, as stated, seems to go astray in two important ways. First, it goes astray by placing the disharmony that results from acting against conscience somewhere down the line, a merely foreseeable consequence of such actions: as we have seen, these consequences need not follow. Secondly, it goes astray by characterizing the disharmony as a sort of interior psychological discord: as we have seen, this leaves unanswered the question of why agents would experience this sort of discord, and, further, not all agents experience this mental distress when they act against conscience. How can one save the important idea of the prudential argument – that the agent's integrity is part of the explanation for why one ought to act in accordance with conscience – while avoiding its difficulties?

It looks as if the problem with the prudential argument is the fact that violating conscience is only tenuously and contingently connected with the good to which that argument appeals, the good of inner peace (see 3.3). The pruden-tial argument would have a more solid basis were it to appeal to a good that pos-sesses a tighter connection to acting in accordance with conscience: excellence in agency. For recall that it is constitutive of the good of excellence in agency that the agent's actions display integrity with the agent's practical judgments. Given the conception of dictates of conscience as judgments of practical rea-son specifying what an agent ought to do on a particular occasion, it is clear that any act that flouts conscience will constitute a disintegrity between judgment and action and will, therefore, be a diminished participation in excellence in agency.

Thus far, we seem to have an explanation for why one would have a reason to act in accordance with conscience: to do so is to participate to some extent in the good of excellence in agency. What grounds do we have, though, to af-firm a moral *requirement* not to act against conscience? The basis for affirming the conscience principle is the Pauline principle, which rules out intentional de-struction of instances of basic goods (5.5). Since by acting contrary to con-science one acts against an instance of the good of excellence in agency, thus violating the Pauline principle, one morally ought never to act against con-science.

Conscience is, however, fallible. It is a commonplace, brandished by Anscombe against Butler's moral views, that "a man's conscience may tell him to do the vilest things" (Anscombe 1958, p. 2); an agent's conscience obviously can dictate that one perform acts that one ought not to perform. It follows from the truth of the conscience principle and the fallibility of conscience that there are cases of moral dilemmas. For suppose that one's conscience mistakenly dic-tates that one ϕ, where ϕ-ing is ruled out by one or another principle of practi-cal reasonableness. In such a case, one morally ought not to refrain from ϕ-ing (for, if one does, one violates the conscience principle), and one morally ought not to ϕ (for, if one does, one violates some other requirement of practical rea-sonableness). Suppose, for example, that the axe murderer is at Ben's door, in-quiring as to the whereabouts of his potential victim. Ben judges that he ought to tell a lie; but the Pauline principle forbids the telling of lies. Ben is in a moral dilemma: if he lies, he violates the moral requirement against lying defended in 6.3; if he refrains from lying, he violates the conscience principle.

In my view, moral dilemmas can arise *only* through errors of this sort. Re-stricting the domain of moral dilemmas in this way enables natural law theory to avoid the difficulties that could be pressed against views that allow a more expansive place for dilemmatic situations. Consider how limiting the place of moral dilemmas to those arising from agents' errors exempts those dilemmas from the argument against moral dilemmas presented earlier in this section. There I argued that since plans of action are unreasonable only if they presup-pose something false about the nature of the reasons for action, and those rea-sons do not exhibit inconsistent features, there must always be a plan of action that presupposes nothing false about the fundamental reasons for action. But the sort of situation in which moral dilemmas arise, on my view, is not susceptible to this argument. For it is part of the description of the dilemmatic situation S that the agent A has erred: it thus is no surprise that it is impossible for A errorlessly to decide on a plan of action in S, given that it is stipulated to be a *condition* of S's obtaining that A has made just such an error.

Dilemmas generated by mistaken conscience also escape the argument against moral dilemmas recently formulated by Christopher Gowans. While Gowans allows the possibility of moral dilemmas in an attenuated sense, he rejects the possibility of moral dilemmas in the robust sense that I have described here. Gowans relies on a standard argument against moral dilemmas: since it is the case that if A ought to ϕ, then it is possible for A to ϕ ('ought implies can'), and it is the case that if A ought to ϕ and A ought to ψ, then A ought to ϕ and to ψ ('agglomeration'), moral dilemmas are impossible. For suppose that A ought to ϕ and A ought not to ϕ. It follows by agglomeration that A ought to ϕ and to refrain from ϕ-ing. But it is impossible for A to ϕ and to refrain from ϕ-ing, and so it follows from 'ought implies can' that there can be no such moral requirement. Thus, the affirmation of dilemmatic situations implies a contradiction. It is Gowans's contribution to this argument to provide support for the invoked deontic principles by connecting them to tenets of rational intending (1994, pp. 66–87).

Gowans argues that if A is a rational agent, then A cannot believe that A ought to ϕ, that A ought to ψ, and that A's ϕ-ing and A's ψ-ing are incompatible. The main premise of his argument is that of intention-prescriptivism: if A sincerely believes that A ought to ϕ, then A intends to ϕ (Gowans 1994, p. 79). Consider, next, two principles of rational intending, which are intentional analogs of the deontic ought-implies-can and agglomeration principles: that if A intends to ϕ, then A believes that ϕ-ing is possible, and that if A intends to ϕ and intends to ψ, then A intends to ϕ and to ψ (1994, pp. 70–71, 75). Now, suppose for *reductio* that a rational agent believes him- or herself to be in a moral dilemma: the agent believes that he or she ought to ϕ, that he or she ought to ψ, and that he or she cannot both ϕ and ψ. By intention-prescriptivism, the agent intends to ϕ and intends to ψ. But by the intentional counterpart of the agglomeration principle, he or she intends both to ϕ and to ψ; and so, by the intentional counterpart of the ought-implies-can principle, he or she believes that ϕ-ing and ψ-ing are jointly possible. But, by hypothesis, the agent does not believe this. Therefore, no rational agent could believe him- or herself to be in a moral dilemma; and since it does seem plausible to think there is some connection between what can be rationally believed vis-à-vis morality and what is actually the case, this fact gives us reason to think that there could not be moral dilemmas.

Does Gowans's argument call my defense of moral dilemmas into question? It does not. For any two true propositions 'A ought to ϕ' and 'A ought to ψ,' Gowans's intention-prescriptivist argument shows that ϕ-ing and ψ-ing must be compatible only in cases in which A can believe at the same time both 'A ought to ϕ' and 'A ought to ψ.' Gowans's argument establishes at most that, for any two ought-judgments that are simultaneously accepted by a rational agent, these judgments cannot conflict; he does not argue that all pairs of true ought-judgments can be accepted by a rational agent. If there is a pair of true ought-judgments that cannot be simultaneously accepted by a rational agent, Gowans's argument does nothing to show that these ought-judgments cannot form a moral dilemma.

The presence of this lacuna allows for moral dilemmas that result from affirmation of the conscience principle and the possibility of mistaken conscience. Consider Ben's situation again. If the conscience principle is true, then Ben ought to lie; but Ben also ought not lie, because the Pauline principle forbids it. Does Gowans's intention-prescriptivist argument cast any suspicion on the possibility of a moral dilemma like Ben's? No. Even if it is granted that Gowans's argument shows that there cannot be moral dilemmas in which an agent can accept both of the allegedly conflicting ought-judgments, Ben's situation does not fit this description. For if Ben were to form the belief that he ought to tell a lie because the conscience principle, conjoined with his mistaken dictate of conscience, demands it, then it is not possible for him also to believe that he ought not lie, for his conscience is (ex hypothesi) mistaken, unaware of the moral absolute against lying. This example is, of course, generalizable. If A believes that A ought to ϕ because one ought always to act in accordance with conscience, then of necessity, A is unaware of the true ought-judgment of objective morality that A ought not ϕ. That A cannot accept both judgments is given by A's conscience's being mistaken. And because both judgments cannot be simultaneously accepted by A, the possibility of moral dilemmas resulting from mistaken conscience cannot be rejected by relying on Gowans's intention-prescriptivist argument against moral dilemmas.

It is worth noting that Gowans's argument is built on a deeper supposition about the role of moral principles. The motivation behind intention-prescriptivism, says Gowans, is that ought-judgments are supposed to be action guiding (1994, p. 68). And it is, I think, part of the concern that motivates the denial of moral dilemmas that it is hard to see how action can be guided by moral requirements in cases in which they produce conflicting ought-judgments. Since the principles of practical reasonableness are formulated for the purpose of guiding choice, one might worry whether allowing the possibility of moral dilemmas undercuts the success of those principles in fulfilling this purpose. But note once again how moral dilemmas arising from applications of the conscience principle are special, invulnerable to this general worry about the capacity of ought-judgments to guide action. For one can be guided by a correct moral principle only if one is aware of it; but in the case of mistaken conscience, one is, ex hypothesi, not aware of the truth of that moral principle (or the proper application of that moral principle) regarding which one's conscience is mistaken. So, no moral principle loses its capacity to guide action by coming into conflict with the conscience principle; its capacity to guide action is already blocked by the agent's ignorance. If one's worry about moral dilemmas has to do with their depriving moral requirements of their capacity to guide action, one has no reason to worry about the moral dilemmas generated by the conscience principle.

One might argue, on the other hand, not that my admitting dilemmas of this sort has unacceptable implications but, rather, that I have failed to present a case of a genuine moral dilemma. As I characterized them, moral dilemmas are cases of inescapable moral wrongdoing. And one might deny that dilemmas of the sort allowed by the conscience principle are in fact inescapable: one can, after all, change one's mind about what one ought to do, so that the conscience principle no longer generates moral conflict. To this I respond that the objection only succeeds if 'changing one's mind' can be a plan of action that the agent can decide to act upon without violating any moral requirement. Even granting that this can be part of a plan of action – which I find dubious – it seems to me that it could not be acted upon without wrongdoing by one who is in a moral dilemma due to mistaken conscience. For it is characteristic of such dilemmas that those involved do not recognize themselves as being in a dilemma (see Potts 1980, p. 59, and MacIntyre 1988, p. 186). Ben surely does not: if we accept the conscience principle, what should we say if Ben, judging that he is bound to tell a lie, sets himself to the task of changing his mind about the wrongness of lying? It seems that we should say that he is violating the conscience principle: so long as he judges that lying is the thing to do, any plan of action that he decides upon that does not include his lying to the axe murderer would be contrary to the conscience principle.[6] Thus, the fact that an agent would no longer be in the dilemma were that agent to change his or her mind does not cast doubt on the dilemmatic character of that situation.

6.5 Positive Norms, Life Plans, and the Partial Constitution Thesis

To this point in our discussion of ought-judgments, we have been occupied with the negative side of such judgments: how some decisions err with respect to practical reasonableness, how some decisions inevitably err with respect to practical reasonableness, and whether there are cases in which no matter what one decides, one's decision will err with respect to practical reasonableness. We have not yet spoken of the positive side of such decisions. Given that one is willing to adhere to the constraints imposed on choice by the nature of the fundamental reasons for action, what additional guidance can be had by an agent who is trying to decide, positively, what to do?

To this question the natural law theory defended here responds: apart from the constraints imposed by the principles of practical reasonableness previously discussed, the decisions that an agent makes are ultimately a matter of the agent's free choice. (Again: I am putting to the side the possibility, granted in 5.7, that there are constraints on practically reasonable conduct that are recognizable by the virtuous agent but not formulable as principles of practical reasonableness.) Deciding how to act in a manner that is excellent is, thus, a matter of constrained creativity: each agent is, within the bounds set by the nature of the reasons for action themselves, free to choose.

Some moral philosophers have derided ethical views that make claims like this, on the basis that these views have too little to say on the issue of what to decide. Theories of moral rules provide, they say, no guidance on the issue of how one should live, however much they say on how one should not live. I am unpersuaded, though, by criticisms of this sort. It is perfectly clear, first of all, that every plausible moral theory allows that at some point, agents must simply make decisions that are unguided by that moral theory. Even classical Benthamite utilitarianism must allow that when alternative courses of action promise equal balances of pleasure over pain, one must simply choose one of those alternatives.

But perhaps we are missing the real point of the criticism. Perhaps the criticism appeals to the size of the range of choices that practical reason is unable to dictate, together with an assumption about the nature of choice undictated by practical reasonableness. On Bentham's view, those choices that are not dictated by practical reason are arbitrary because the alternatives are a matter of complete indifference. This may not seem objectionable within Bentham's theory, for the class of such choices is relatively quite small. But on the natural law view, the domain of choice unfettered by practical reasonableness is relatively quite large; and if this natural law theory holds that all choices within that range are as arbitrary and indifferent as they are within Bentham's scheme when there are equal pleasures at stake, surely that is a point against the natural law view. For it is obvious that many of the choices that we make that are not dictated by practical reason are not arbitrary; yet natural law theory treats them as if they are by offering no guidance in the making of these choices. If one is trying to decide whether to become a philosopher or a lawyer, surely that is not a matter of mere indifference; but natural law theory treats it as if it were, as if flipping a coin were a perfectly appropriate way of making the decision (just as the choice between courses of action offering equal pleasure would be appropriately solved by a coin flip within the Benthamite view).

There is an important difference, though, in the way that the natural law view and classical Benthamite utilitarianism allows a place for choice undictated by practical reason. In the Benthamite scheme, all such choices are arbitrary, because the options are indifferent: since the only reasons for action are pleasures – for simplicity's sake, I'll ignore pains – if two courses of action promise equal pleasure, there is every reason to choose one course of action as there is to choose the other. This is sheer, arbitrary choice between indifferent alternatives. But the natural law theory defended here denies that cases of choice unfettered by practical reason are (typically) of this sort. Since the choices that are to be made within the constraints set by practical reason are between distinct goods, and the distinct goods involved are invariably incommensurable (5.3), it would be misleading to label such choices as between indifferent alternatives: for it is not the case that there is every reason to choose one alternative as to choose the other.

These choices are, unlike the choices in Bentham's scheme, practically significant. If one is deciding whether to become a lawyer or a philosopher, for example, there are reasons to choose one of these ways of life, and distinct reasons to choose the other. There is something genuinely at stake in which of these alternatives one opts for, and that is why flipping a coin is not a fully reasonable way to choose among incommensurables. What makes a coin flip an appropriate way to deal with choices between indifferents is that practical reason has no way at all to distinguish between the options: the decision to take whatever option is picked out by the coin flip is a way to make the options distinguishable. But with options that are incommensurable in value, practical reason *can* distinguish between them, even if (assuming no other principles of practical reasonableness are relevant) practical reason does not determine that only one of them is ultimately eligible. In such cases, the use of a coin flip to decide between the options strikes me as a failure of reasonableness: there is reason to take either one of the options, and one must simply go for what is appealing in one of the options; to use a coin flip, or any other proxy for choice, is to close one's eyes to the distinctive appeal of each option. (I do not deny that a coin flip might be second best: one who finds him- or herself unable to make choices in the face of incommensurables may have reason to use coin flips, but only as a remedy for this infirmity of choice.)

So, the natural law theory denies that the absence of complete guidance in making such choice implies that all such choices are matters of indifference: in making these choices, one invariably opts to realize some goods and to forgo others. If one objects to natural law theory's inability to guide choice in these cases, the reply must simply be that what makes practically significant choices like this possible – the massive incommensurability of goods worth pursuing – is the very same thing that precludes the possibility of more highly detailed guidelines for choice.

Now, the fact that practical reason itself is unable to formulate guidelines drawn from the nature of the reasons for action themselves to govern fully such decisions does not imply that the agent's decisions will be patternless, random. After all, the principles of practical reasonableness applying to agents require the agent to form broad plans of action, that is, life plans, and to adopt less comprehensive plans of action congruent with that life plan (5.6). This life plan will set priorities among the goods to be pursued and will settle, at least in outline, the issue of how such goods will be pursued. This life plan is, of course, open to modification. But since practical reason also requires that one not be flighty with regard to the plans of action upon which one has settled (5.6), this broad life plan will be less malleable than the smaller scale plans that are formulated closer to the occasion of action. Thus, the freedom of the agent in deciding positively what to do is not an invitation to random, chaotic pursuit of goods.

A very important conclusion follows from this conception of creative decision making, together with the notion of the fundamental practical 'ought' defended in 6.1. There is a popular view of natural law theory, one bolstered by a plausible but mistaken reading of Aquinas's remarks on the eternal law, that an agent's reflective decision making is nothing more than an effort to generate decisions that mirror objective truths about what that agent ought to do in those circumstances. But given the previous remarks in this section, it is clear that this is not the picture endorsed by this version of natural law theory. If what an agent ought to do depends on what the agent errorlessly decides to do, and an agent can errorlessly decide to φ even where φ-ing is not dictated by the principles of practical reasonableness, it follows that an agent's decisions go beyond the principles of practical reasonableness in determining what an agent ought to do. If in a given set of circumstances an agent errorlessly decides to φ, then that agent ought to φ; nevertheless, had that agent errorlessly decided otherwise, it would have been the case that the agent ought to act otherwise.[7] To take the example of a choice between becoming a philosopher or a lawyer: since practical reason rules out neither choice, whether I ought to become a philosopher or a lawyer depends on my free decision to pursue one sort of life, rather than the other.

This view involves two sorts of concession to subjectivism about 'ought.' First, whether it is the case that one ought to φ or it is not the case that one ought to φ depends on whether one makes the decision to φ: even if φ-ing is required by practical reason, so that one morally ought to φ, it will not be the case that one ought to φ in the fundamental practical sense of 'ought' without a decision to φ. Secondly, if φ-ing and ψ-ing are both plans of action eligible for an agent, neither of which is ruled out by practical reason (that is, it is neither the case that one morally ought not φ or morally ought not ψ), whether one ought to φ or ought to ψ will depend on whether one decides to φ or to ψ. Thus, an agent's decision is implicated in whether or not one ought to perform a certain action (even one required by practical reason), and it is implicated in which of a number of morally permissible actions one ought to perform. But this subjectivism is tightly bound by objective considerations. One objectively has reasons to decide properly, for only by deciding properly will one act well, thereby participating in the good of excellence in agency. And how it is proper to decide is, if not completely determinate, constrained by objective principles of practical reasonableness formulated on the basis of the nature of the reasons for action, reasons that make objectively intelligible the different plans of actions among which one might choose.

Since my view contains elements both of subjectivism and of objectivism regarding ought-judgments, it is open to criticism from both sides. My response to subjectivism about reasons for action is contained in Chapter 2, and I have no additional remarks on the issue of why subjectivism about reasons is an untenable thesis. But there still may be worries from more objectivist views. Some might persist in worries about how many decisions natural law theory leaves underdetermined by practical reason: but, as I said, every view allows some decisions to be underdetermined by reason, and natural law theory does not imply that such decisions are indifferent. Some might worry, on the other hand, about holding that an agent ought to act in accordance with those decisions that go beyond what practical reason dictates. This is an objection not so much to natural law theory's leaving a large number of decisions unspecified by principles of practical reasonableness, but to the characterization of the fundamental practical 'ought.' The objector, that is, would have us hold that one ought to φ only if one decides to φ, and φ-ing is required by principles of practical reasonableness. But this characterization of the fundamental practical 'ought' is not in accordance with the good of excellence in agency, which is participated in (I claim) every time one acts in accordance with one's error-free decisions, not just when one acts in accordance with those decisions required by principles of practical reasonableness. Given the close connection between excellence in agency and the truth of ought-judgments, this is the set of truth-conditions of ought-judgments that I must affirm.

One might pose an objection to this view from the more objectivist camp that rests partly on a sort of phenomenological consideration concerning deliberation and partly on the view that the activity of deliberation contains certain presuppositions. When one is engaged in deliberating over a decision, one asks questions of the form, 'what ought I to do here – ought I to φ or ought I to ψ?' But this way of posing questions presupposes, one might think, that there is an answer to these questions apart from and prior to decisions about how to act. If someone asks 'ought I to φ?' and the answer comes back 'it depends on whether you decide to φ,' the respondent would simply have missed the point of the question. And this can only be explained by supposing that there is an answer out there prior to decision about what the agent ought to do, an answer that the agent is attempting to uncover in deliberation. Phenomenologically, we might say that deliberation ends with a decision that has the feel of getting the answer, not like simply making a choice. The feel of deliberative conclusions gives evidence against the idea that it is our decisions that determine, even in part, what we ought to do.

Deliberation involves both judgment and decision. Insofar as it involves judgment, these considerations are very much to the point. The agent who asks the deliberative question 'what ought I to do?' could be seeking information about the requirements of practical reasonableness, which constrain all deliberation by constraining the range of ought-judgments that could become true through decision. In this sense, one is asking 'what ought I, morally speaking, to do?' as part of one's decision-making process. Given a more-or-less well-defined life plan, the answers to be found might be fairly determinate: given a life plan that an agent has settled on and lacks sufficient reason to modify, the principles of practical reasonableness ruling out respect of persons and inefficiency might have a lot to say for or against various plans of action. But, on the other hand, the agent who persists in asking the question 'what ought I to do?' in deliberation, after gathering all morally relevant information about what practical reasonableness requires, does not give evidence against my partly subjectively defined notion of 'ought': in my view, that agent merely displays a lack of awareness that, or a refusal squarely to face the fact that, judgment must end and free decision must begin; in other words, the relevant question is not at that point 'what ought I to do?' but, rather, 'what *shall* I do?' So, my response to the argument from presupposition is that while objectivism is presupposed by the judgment portion of deliberation, it is not presupposed by the decision portion of deliberation; and if one makes the additional claim that all deliberation is judgment, my response is that this is simply an error against which the natural law theory defended thus far is my argument.

With regard to the phenomenological argument, I agree that the decision reached at the end of deliberation often has the feel of hitting the brick wall, of coming up with the answer. With regard to much of what goes on in deliberation, there is room to concede that objectivism explains the phenomenology best: part of deliberation is, of course, coming to understand what it is reasonable to do. Even with regard to that part of deliberation that consists in decision, there is an alternative interpretation of the phenomenology that fits with the more subjective conception of the fundamental practical 'ought' and the underdetermination of decisions by practical reason: it is that the decision settles the issue, creating the wall, so to speak, rather than running up against it. (Similarly, one can interpret the openness of the feeling of deliberation not as being simply an epistemic openness – the agent doesn't know the answer yet – but to normative openness – there may be no fact of the matter yet as to what the agent ought to do.) It therefore seems that phenomenological considerations against the claims about ought-judgments that I have made are not very weighty.

Call the thesis that I have been defending – that there are acts of ϕ-ing that agents ought to perform, even though ϕ-ing is not required by practical reason, and that its being the case that agents ought to perform these acts of ϕ-ing is due to agents' decisions – the 'partial constitution thesis.' Contrast this thesis with two other views. On some views, practical truths are wholly constituted: humans invent right and wrong. On other views, practical truths are not at all constituted by human decisions: while human action can provide a circumstance for the application of a practical principle, practical truths are not up to human making at all. The truth of the partial constitution thesis would allow us to cut between these views, allowing a place both to the constraints placed on us by the nature of the normative and nonnormative orders and to human creativity in how we respond to the good.

6.6 Normative Openness and Natural Law Theories of Authority

We have seen that human nature determines the forms of good available for intelligible pursuit (1.2–1.4, 3.1–3.5), and that the nature of the instances of these goods determines what constraints there are on fully reasonable choice and action (5.1, 5.3, 5.5–5.6, 6.1–6.3). But, as we have also seen, these constraints leave a great deal of openness in how fully reasonable agents may act (6.5). I want to conclude this book by noting a special problem that the normative openness of the natural law creates within social groups, even social groups containing none but fully reasonable agents. Seeing how the normative openness of the natural law generates this problem, and how the resources internal to the natural law are powerless to remedy it, will help to make clear why it is not just happenstance that the title 'natural law theory' names both a theory of practical reasonableness and a theory of authority: rather, the natural law theory of authority is an attempt to remedy the difficulties that arise within the natural law account of practical reasonableness.

In every group situation in which agents are actively pursuing their ends, there is potential for practical conflict. There are a variety of species of practical conflict, but generically we can say that there is practical conflict between agents A and B when A wills the obtaining of state of affairs S and B wills the obtaining of state of affairs T, where states of affairs S and T cannot both obtain. Now, every moral theory allows that there might be practical conflict that arises when one or both agents have committed some sort of moral error: A may will the death of B, while B wills no such thing. Presumably, the solution to this sort of conflict involves either moral education or physical restraint. What is more interesting is the extent to which practical conflict can occur without the existence of practical error, and how the difficulties involved in such conflict can be overcome.

As I mentioned in 6.5, while all plausible normative theories imply some degree of normative openness, such theories differ on how far that normative openness extends. Within natural law theory as I have presented it, normative openness obviously extends very far indeed. And the particular account of 'ought' defended in 6.1 adds a wrinkle to the problem of error-free practical conflict. For if two agents errorlessly decide on conflicting courses of action, it is not as if they can innocently fail to pursue them: rather, their errorless decisions to pursue those courses of action bind them by the nature of the fundamental practical 'ought' to prosecution of those plans.

There are a number of ways that practical conflict can arise. Consider a type of conflict that is paradigmatically Hobbesian, and that is at the front of our minds when we imagine cases of practical conflict. This sort of conflict occurs when agents in no sense share the ends that generate the conflict, and those ends involve incompatible states of affairs. Thus, if you are pursuing this apple in order to preserve your life, and I am pursuing this apple in order to preserve my life, we have a case of Hobbesian practical conflict. Practical conflict can occur in other ways, though. Consider two Benthamite utilitarians who share the end of maximal happiness, where this end can be specified independently of anyone's plans of action. If these agents aim to realize this end by cooperative action, yet there is more than one possible set of coordinated plans of action that would equally well achieve this end, there is potential for practical conflict: there may be disagreement over which set of plans of action should be acted upon to realize that end. Further, there is a mode of practical conflict that figures prominently in Aquinas's political theory. Even if two agents share at some level of abstraction a common end, they may not be in agreement as to how that end is to be concretely realized; they may have different specifications or determinations of that common end in mind. While they abstractly share a common will toward realization of that end, they may be in practical conflict with regard to its mode of realization. This may sound as if it is a case of conflict resulting from practical error. But it need not be. It could be that such ends can display normative openness, so that prior to an agent's determination, there is no definite answer as to how that end should be specified. This is, I believe, Aquinas's view (Murphy 1997b, pp. 335–343).

Why is practical conflict of these types a bad thing, something that normative theories should worry about? There is a straightforward answer to this question, one to which all normative theories that treat this problem appeal, and a less straightforward answer, one that depends on a special characteristic of this theory of practical reasonableness. The straightforward answer, of course, is that practical conflict tends to result in the frustration of the agent's ends, that for which he or she is acting in the first place. If agents are acting for completely distinct ends, whether agent-relative ends or different agent-neutral ends, the implementation of conflicting plans of action makes it more difficult for one or both of them to be achieved. If agents are attempting to pursue an end in common, they will be frustrated if unable to settle on instrumental means for bringing about that common end. And if agents aim to realize an abstract common end, one that lacks determinate content prior to specification by some agent, they will be unable to act in concert if they lack a common specification of that end. In each case, practical conflicts result in the frustration of at least some of the ends that the agents involved are pursuing.

There is, however, a distinct reason to worry about cases of practical conflict. Recall that according to the account of the fundamental reasons for action sketched in 3.3, community is a basic good. Community has both full-blooded and diminished forms: full-blooded, where agents have a common end and pursue that end by common action, and diminished, where agents are not in a state of discord with one another. Given that community is a fundamental reason for action, it is clear that there is reason to avoid practical conflict, apart from the fact that it frustrates the implementation of those plans involved in the conflict. For that very conflict is itself a deprivation of even the negative aspect of the good of community.

It is clear, then, that while the normative openness of the natural law brings with it a great good – the opportunity to order the basic goods creatively in one's life and to determine appropriately the means to respond to those goods – it also brings with it a threat, even among practically reasonable agents: that of practical conflict. The characteristic solution to this problem is – to put it in a backhanded way – to alter the circumstances of action so that the existence of practical conflict implies that at least one of the parties to the conflict is acting in a way that is practically unreasonable. And the characteristic alteration in circumstances favored in order to bring about sufficient closure in the normative openness of the natural law is that of the institution of *practical authority* – some person, persons, or set of rules such that practically reasonable persons will adhere to their dictates as a way of overcoming the problem of practical conflict.

We can, therefore, see that there is more than a contingent, merely historical connection between natural law theories of practical rationality and natural law theories of authority: the latter emerge logically as an attempt to overcome some of the practical problems that the former cannot handle alone. Authority, within these natural law conceptions, is justified in large part by its capacity to promote, in a reasonable way, the good of agents by solving problems of practical conflict that arise from the normative openness of the natural law. (See, for two otherwise disparate natural law theories of political authority that agree on this point, Aquinas's *De Regno* and Hobbes's *Leviathan*.) But while acknowledging that the natural law account of practical reasonableness will require supplementation by an account of practical authority, we should equally emphasize the inevitably central presence of a natural law theory of practical rationality within the account of authority: for while it is the incompleteness of the natural law that makes necessary the institution of practical authority to resolve conflict between reasonable agents, nothing can be said of normative importance about the nature, content, and binding power of such authority that does not ultimately rest on the natural law. The normative openness of the natural law makes it a limited sovereign, but it is sovereign nonetheless.

Notes

Introduction

1. Rawls 1993 distinguishes between the rational and the reasonable, where rationality concerns the capacity to advance one's own ends, and reasonableness concerns the willingness to adhere to fair terms of cooperation. This work makes nothing of this distinction: 'rational' and 'reasonable' are used interchangeably to refer to appropriate cognitive, affective, and volitional responses to what there is reason to do.

Chapter 1. The Real Identity Thesis

1. Derivationism and inclinationism are not, of course, exhaustive of the possibilities. Derivationism holds that the principles that are first in the practical realm are derived from propositions in the theoretical realm. Inclinationism holds that the principles that are first in the practical realm are underived, either from principles in the speculative realm (for, if they were derived, the account would be derivationist, rather than inclinationist) or in the practical realm (for, if they were derived, they wouldn't be first principles). The reason that the derivationism/inclinationism divide is not exhaustive is that inclinationism adds a claim about how one comes to be aware of the first principles in the practical realm. So, there are other nonderivationist possibilities, e.g., straight and unadorned intuitionism.
2. I don't think Aristotle was a natural law theorist because I am not convinced that his view meets the third criterion for natural law theory discussed in 0.1: that there are principles of practical reason that can specify how it is reasonable to respond to those goods. The only candidate offered by Aristotle for such a principle, the doctrine of the mean, relies on a reference to the determination of the person of practical wisdom to have content. For more on the disagreement between virtue theories of practical reasonableness and natural law conceptions, see 5.7.
3. Consider, for example, his Aristotelian arguments against the intrinsic goodness of wealth, fame, honor, and power (*Summa Theologiae* IaIIae 2, 1–4): these arguments function by showing that the intelligibility of their pursuit comes not from the objects themselves but from some goods realized through them (such as in the case of money and power) or from some goods of which they are concomitants (such as in the case of honor).

4 This is, in effect, the problem with strong subjectivist conceptions of the good. While, if correct, they would classify as intelligible many of our intelligible actions, they allow too much, classifying as intelligible acts that are pointless. See 2.4.

5 Hume allows that reason also has a role in discovering causal connections, so that one can effectively pursue the objects of one's desires, but this is not implicated in the most basic forms of evaluation.

6 This is clearly a problem for Aquinas as interpreted by Lisska: on his interpretation of Aquinas, natural law principles are known by investigation of essences, which are on both Lisska's and Aquinas's views extremely difficult to know (Lisska 1996, p. 112). This seems to imply that very few persons can know even the most basic principles of the natural law. This implication makes Lisska's view dubious, both in itself and as an interpretation of Aquinas (since Aquinas clearly held that the most fundamental natural law principles are evident to all; see *Summa Theologiae* IaIIae 94, 4).

7 There is a great deal of evidence in Finnis's works that he would support the weak grounding thesis. He writes that anthropological and psychological accounts of human nature are relevant to ethics because they present "an assemblage of reminders of the range of possibly worthwhile activities and orientations open to one" (Finnis 1980, p. 81); one needs "theoretical knowledge about one's own powers . . . to know what one might choose to do" (Grisez, Finnis, and Boyle 1987, p. 111). He emphasizes that "[t]he possibility of human fulfillment . . . presupposes both the given reality of human nature – with its capacities and natural inclinations – and people's actual abilities, skills, and resources. . . . In general, what still can be presupposes what already is; in particular, what one naturally is grounds all that one is to be" (Grisez, Finnis, and Boyle 1987, p. 116). Finnis thus supports at least the weak grounding reading of the grounding thesis: human nature determines what sorts of goods are available for humans to participate in.

8 On Moore's view, we are intuitively aware of what things are objectively good, regardless of whether it is possible that these states of affairs ever be produced by human action. Thus, the goodness of a state of affairs and the possibility of its achievement by humans pulls apart on Moore's account. See *Principia,* §§50, 55.

9 There is some evidence that Finnis would accept not only the weak grounding thesis but the strong grounding thesis as well. He writes that human nature determines "why [the self-evident practical] principles are principles of natural law" (Grisez and Finnis 1981, p. 22). And Finnis presents a list of the basic goods in which he introduces each good by providing what seems to be an explanation for its character as a good: "As *animate,* human persons are organic substances. Life itself, . . . health, and safety are one category of basic good. As *rational,* human persons can know reality and appreciate beauty and whatever intensely engages their capacities to know and to feel. Knowledge and esthetic experience are another category of basic good" (Grisez, Finnis, and Boyle 1987, p. 107). The "as X" locution employed seems to be a mark of explanation; the character of life as a good is explained by the animate aspect of human nature, the character of knowledge as a good is explained by the rational aspect of human nature, and so on. This suggests that Finnis goes beyond the weak grounding view by holding that the various aspects of human nature explain why each of the basic goods is a good.

10 Recently, Robert George (1992a) has taken Finnis's critics to task both for misinterpreting Finnis's claim that practical principles are not derived from theoretical

principles to *mean* that the principles of natural law have no basis in human nature, and for holding that the absence of a derivability relationship *entails* the absence of any grounding in human nature. Nothing I have said here takes issue with either of George's contentions. Certainly there is ample testimony in Finnis's writings that he does think that practical judgments regarding goods to be sought are grounded in human nature; and it may be possible for practical judgments regarding goods to be sought to be grounded in human nature in the absence of a derivability relationship. What this argument calls into question is whether Finnis (or George) is *entitled* to the claim that human nature strongly grounds the principles of the natural law in the absence of some known implication from the former to the latter. Without an account of the grounding relationship that does not depend on derivability, it appears that a strong relationship between human nature and natural law must become a matter of faith, rather than the object of a philosophical explanation.

11 It is sometimes suggested that the object of my belief that I am in my office and my belief that Murphy is in his office are the same proposition. See, for an example of this view, Perry 1993c, pp. 123–129. I find this view hard to believe, since I lean toward the view (that Perry labors mightily to rid us of) that belief states are individuated by propositions, and it seems possible for me to believe that I am in my office while not believing that Murphy is in his office. But suppose that there is only a single proposition believed here. This could be good news for both the inclinationist and the derivationist: for one could analogously claim that certain beliefs about human nature and about certain natural law principles have as their objects the same propositions, even if they are expressed differently. And, if that is the case, the propositions of the natural law could be derivable from propositions about human nature, using the rule that *p* entails *p!* This is, in essentials, the view suggested in Murphy 1995a, which I now hesitate to affirm simply because I hesitate to commit myself to the view of propositions that it seems to presuppose.

12 On Aquinas's view, *synderesis* consists in habitual knowledge of the natural law, which knowledge is possessed in this way by all persons; but he recognizes that the effects of synderesis – occurrent awareness of practical principles, which can be put to work in practical reasoning – can be blocked either by mental defect, vice, or even powerful emotion. See *Summa Theologiae,* IaIIae 94, 4.

13 The *ergon* argument is controversial in a number of respects: there is controversy over what it means (see, e.g., Gomez-Lobo 1989); there is controversy over how successful it is (see, for example, Whiting 1988 for a pretty full endorsement; Nagel 1980 for a qualified endorsement, and Finnis 1983, pp. 12–23, for a rejection); and there is controversy over whether it is an important part of the overall argument of the *Nicomachean Ethics* (see, for example, Achtenberg 1989 for the view that it is central to that theory; see Austin 1967 for the view that it is a sheer metaphysical add-on). I need not enter into such controversies here.

14 At least for those who admit the existence of such things as ears, eyes, hearts, etc.; but see van Inwagen 1990. While van Inwagen would reject almost all of the positive claims that I make in this section, the force of his criticisms of rival accounts of how complex objects can be constituted is mostly assumed throughout this section.

15 For an analogous use of the language of 'dominant' and 'inclusive,' see Rawls 1971, p. 552. Rawls takes these notions from Hardie 1965, though Hardie's use of them seems to be slightly different from Rawls's.

16 What of Aristotle's other set of examples invoked in the function argument, that is, the carpenter and the tanner? How might the argument that relies on these examples be stated? Without entering into a debate over what Aristotle, in fact, had in mind, we might say that just as one can argue that the existence of a human function is necessary to preserve the unity of the human being vis-à-vis the distinct functions of its parts, one might argue for the existence of a human function as necessary to preserve the unity of a human life vis-à-vis the diverse pursuits that humans engage in. One could, without too much distortion, read Alasdair MacIntyre's discussion of the narrative unity of human life as a version of this sort of argument. See his 1981, pp. 204–220.

17 It might be thought that the fact that natural selection causes it to be the case that the heart pumps blood makes the relevant difference. But as Bedau notes, there are cases in which the necessary and sufficient conditions for natural selection – reproduction, random variation, heredity, and adaptivity – are realized, yet with respect to which we have no inclination whatever to think that there are any true 'in order to' propositions that describe them. He mentions, as an instance of this phenomenon, Richard Dawkins's example of the forces of natural selection favoring the proliferation of certain forms of clay crystals. Clay crystals with certain structures may come to be predominant in a particular environment due to their damming effects, but no one is inclined to say that the clay crystals have those structures *in order to* produce those effects. See Bedau 1991, pp. 650–655, citing Dawkins 1986, p. 153.

18 It might be objected that even if there are grounds to hold that the goodness that is essential to flourishing must be of a variety that is graspable by theoretical reason – if it were not, then there could not be a notion of flourishing univocally applicable to humans and other creatures – all this shows is that there are grounds to worry about the coherence of the concept of flourishing. The judgments affirmed by theoretical reason are not essentially action guiding; judgments of goodness are essentially action guiding. If both of these claims were true, then the coherence of the concept of flourishing is undercut. But the latter claim is false: judgments of goodness are not all essentially action guiding. The judgment that this is a good vacuum cleaner or that that dog is in good condition are not essentially action guiding; whether they are relevant to the guidance of conduct will depend on other practical judgments that one has reached. All judgments of goodness are, indeed, evaluative: but the standards for evaluating a vacuum cleaner as good or a dog as in good condition are all plainly factual, and there seems to be no basis to suppose that these sorts of judgments could not be grasped as true by theoretical reason.

19 It is important to see how this view bypasses what Searle takes to be the crucial objection to any account of teleology in nature. Searle suggests that any such view falls prey to a dilemma: "Either 'function' is defined in terms of causes, in which case there is nothing intrinsically functional about functions, they are just causes like any others. Or functions are defined in terms of the furtherance of a set of values that we hold – life, survival, reproduction, health – in which case they are observer relative" (1995, p. 16). Bedau and I would agree with Searle that the former sort of definition inevitably fails to get at what is 'functional' about functions. But, of course, the falseness of this dilemma rests in the possibility that there could be such a thing as a set of values that are not just values that we hold, but which are further natural facts – such as that there is such a thing as a rat's being in good condition.

20 One might suggest as a modification of this view that the human interests in question must be genuine human goods, not the satisfaction of strange desires like that of using dogs as paperweights. But this still is a highly implausible view. Suppose that a certain plant is overrunning one's garden, harming the produce that is growing there. (See, for example, Judith Thomson's discussion of the 'Son of Kudzu' vine, an extraordinarily aggressive plant with "no apparent redeeming economic or social value"; see her 1996, pp. 142–143.) Are we to say that the weeds are failing to flourish beause they are not fulfilling a human interest? That it would be an aspect of their flourishing to wither and die?

21 Another problem with the normalcy view is that it is incapable of making the following distinctions: (i) the distinction between what constitutes flourishing and what is statistically normal but only coincidentally coexisting with flourishing; (ii) the distinction betwen what constitutes flourishing and what is statistically normal but only a means to flourishing; and (iii) the distinction between what constitutes flourishing and what is statistically normal but a mere side effect of flourishing.

22 Thus, the method of providing an account of human flourishing provided here differs markedly from that offered by Thomas Hurka in his 1993. Hurka's method is to try to determine what the human essence is – those properties that are necessary to humanity – and then, after narrowing this set of properties down by appeal both to moral and nonmoral intuitions, to assert that to possess these properties to a high degree is to achieve perfection. My method is quite different: it presupposes that we have some grasp of what it is for a human to be flourishing, a grasp that is manifested in our views about particular human functions. Hurka's method is bottom up, relying on a least common denominator; my method is top down, relying on an implicit understanding of overall flourishing to which no human may ever have attained, but which nonetheless guides our judgments about the extent to which any particular human is functioning well. Hurka's view strikes me as a concession to the sort of epistemological overscrupulousness that produces stripped-down accounts of how human flourishing is known and, in consequence, stripped-down accounts of the human good. Compare his thin account of the human good (1993, p. 37–44) with the goods affirmed in this section and 1.4, as well as with the full catalog of goods presented in Chapter 3.

23 Why does this method focus on the brain? Why not the heart, or the kidneys . . . ? First, it is easier, even in a thought experiment, to isolate malfunctions in the brain. Secondly, the notion that the rest of the organs contribute to aspects of flourishing mainly by contributing to the good of life does have some plausibility to it. And, finally, the brain is the natural place to focus because it seems to be the locus for the variety of aspects of flourishing that are open to humans, yet not to some lower animals.

24 Philip Kitcher has recently attempted to foist a dilemma on those who are objectivists about the human good. Suppose that one is, as Kitcher puts it, an "explanatory objectivist," one who offers not only a list of the basic aspects of human good but also an account of why those items are included in the roll. An explanatory objectivist would have more hope to provide an account of well-being that can resolve disagreements among adherents of divergent lists of human goods than would a "bare objectivist," one who offers merely a list of constituents of the good. But, Kitcher argues, "If explanatory objectivists are to avoid a similar impasse . . . then it appears that their explanation and justification must take a very particular form.

For suppose that the contents of the list are to be grounded in two principles, one that identifies human lives as going well insofar as they exhibit a certain generic property and one that connects the items alleged to be valuable with the favored property. If the property in question can only be attributed by already making a judgment about what is valuable, then just the controversies that were supposed to be avoided will recur at the higher level" (Kitcher 1999, p. 60). Thus, Kitcher supposes that any plausible explanatory objectivism will have to be reductionist, understanding the human good in terms of entirely nonevaluative properties. But Kitcher falsely assumes either that any explanatory objectivism that appeals to value will appeal to the same sort of value that occurs in the explanandum or that all forms of value are equally subject to dispute. In the explanatorily objectivist view I propose, what is worth having in a life is grounded in the idea of human flourishing – a notion that appeals to value concepts, but not the *same* value concepts that appear in the *explanandum*. And even if it were true that biological conceptions of flourishing were as much in dispute as concepts of well-being – which I doubt – the existence of an independent value notion makes possible the appeal to coherence; on the proposed view, one would have to achieve coherence between what one counts as a human's flourishing qua biological object and what makes a human life go well.

25 It might appear that by making the claim that a creature that has achieved complete actuality has achieved its good, we are begging the question against inclinationism; it might be objected that an inclinationist should deny that we could know by way of speculative reason that this creature has achieved its good. This appearance is misleading, though, for by asserting that a creature that has actualized its potentialities has achieved its good, we do not yet make any practical judgment. Indeed, even Finnis affirms this: he accepts the view that theoretical reason can comprehend this process by which a creature moves from potency to act, and that this movement constitutes the movement toward the good condition of the creature. We can understand what the rat's good is in this sense; we can understand what the angel's good is in this sense; we can understand what the human's good is in this sense. The inclinationist point that Finnis makes is that an understanding of the good for humans, in the sense comprehensible by theoretical reason, "would have no more normative implication . . . for us" than the understanding that we have of the good for angels (Grisez and Finnis 1981, p. 23).

26 That this discussion of Aquinas's is particularly relevant to the grounding thesis was suggested to me by remarks made by Ralph McInerny in his 1980, p. 11.

27 Note that these distinctions correspond to the material, formal, and final causes of knowledge, respectively. It would seem that the reason that there is no distinction that corresponds to the efficient cause is that 'practical' and 'speculative' refer only to different functions of a single intellect, not to different intellects.

28 As an illustration of this schema, consider the knowledge that one might have about stereos. All knowledge of stereos is knowledge that is practical with respect to its object: for stereos are objects producible by human action. Of this knowledge of stereos that is practical with respect to the object, some is speculative with regard to the manner of knowing, some other is practical: for I may know where stereos fit in the classification of all man-made objects (this is speculative with respect to the manner of knowing), and I may know how to construct a stereo, what parts will be required, what steps will need to be taken, in order to produce a well-functioning piece

of equipment (this is practical with regard to the manner of knowing). Of this knowledge that I have that is practical with respect to the manner of knowing, it may be considered either by speculative or by practical reason: for I may know how to put stereos together in the manner of one who merely 'has an interest' in stereos, that is, he or she reads books about stereo construction but never has nor ever will put one together (this is speculative with respect to the end); or I may know how to put stereos together in the way that a stereo repairperson does, that is, by putting that knowing into action for the sake of putting together a stereo (this is practical with respect to the end).

29 Hurka treats the sort of grounding thesis defended in this book as an "accretion" to perfectionism, a thesis that need not be added to the theory and that invites pointless criticism. One example of this is his treatment of Aquinas's view that "goodness and being are really the same, and differ only in idea." Regarding this claim, Hurka writes:

> It is hard to see what, aside from rhetorical flourish, [the claim that goodness and being are really identical] adds to perfectionism considered as a morality. Does any new moral guidance follow from the idea that in developing our natures we gain reality as well as do what we ought? Does the theory acquire new foundations? If not, this strange doctrine should be discarded. (Hurka 1993, p. 23)

Presumably, Hurka would say the same thing about the view that I have presented, the real identity thesis.

Hurka's criticism of Aquinas's view, and by implication of the real identity thesis, is unpersuasive; it reflects more the limited ambitions of Hurka's perfectionism than it does Aquinas's and my own accounts of the relationship between goodness and being. Both Aquinas's and my natural law theories attempt to provide a unified account of the practical and theoretical orders: while these orders are distinguishable, both Aquinas and I hold that there is, at a deeper level, a unity between them. And this attempt to unify the normative and nonnormative orders is not without practical implication. First, accepting the particular accounts offered by either Aquinas or me may have, as I argued in this chapter and will try to illustrate further in Chapter 3, implications about what states of affairs we do hold to be reasons for action. And, secondly, many philosophers have taken the distinction between the normative and nonnormative orders to be an invitation to skepticism in practical matters; to tie them more closely together is to help cut off this type of skepticism. Hurka may not be interested in attempting a deeper account of morality and practical reasonableness, but that does not make the real identity thesis a mere accretion to any perfectionist theory of practical reasonableness.

Chapter 2. Well-Being

1 Contrary to this line of natural law thinking is the Stoic view, which viewed the natural law as simply the product of divine reason, without any attempt to ground it in the nature of the human good. Unlike on the Aristotelian view, there is an unproblematic sense on the Stoic conception of natural law on which the right is prior to the good. See, for thoughts along these lines, Striker 1986, esp. pp. 90–93.

2 It is a matter of some dispute within natural law theory whether it is the agent's good

or the good impartially considered that serves as the starting point for correct practical reasoning. For an identification of this issue, see Veatch and Rautenberg 1991; for
my response to Veatch and Rautenberg, see Murphy 1996a. I lay out a response to this
issue – one that differs from the account suggested in Murphy 1996a – in 5.3.

3 Contrary to this line of natural law thinking is the Hobbesian view, which affirms both
a subjectivist account of the good and the key natural law thesis that the natural law
is rooted in human nature. The way that Hobbes manages to affirm both of these
claims is that he held that there is an end that is universally desired due to basic similarities in the structure of our desire-forming mechanisms: self-preservation. For further discussion, see Murphy 1995b and Murphy 2000.

4 This argument has a familiar air: it is akin to the argument that Moore presses against
Sidgwick's account of why the egoist can consistently reject the claims of utilitarianism (*Principia*, §60). Recall Sidgwick's account: he holds that the egoist's supreme
practical principle employs the fundamental normative notion of 'good for me' (*Methods*, pp. 420–421); since the egoist decides how to act in terms of what is good for
him or her, the utilitarian's appeal to the greater overall good can gain no foothold in
the egoist's practical reasoning. Moore's response was to hold that Sidgwick erred in
thinking that the notion of 'good for x' was intelligible in itself; there is, as Moore
might have put it, no conceptual room for any notion of 'good for' suitable for egoistic purposes: for 'x is good for me' either means that x is good *simpliciter* and happens to be instantiated in me, or that my having x is good simpliciter, or it has no intelligible meaning at all. But for reasons that I mention with regard to Hurka's view,
Moore is wrong: the notion of 'good for' can be stated in a way that is intelligible and
does not collapse into the notion of goodness simpliciter. (See also Mack 1993, pp.
214–217.)

5 One more remark, perhaps slightly polemical, can be made here with regard to
Hurka's dismissal of perfectionism as a theory of well-being. It strikes me that part of
the appeal of perfectionism resides in its being welfarist – in its idea that we are making ourselves better off when we perfect our natures. If this idea is rejected, the perfection of one's nature becomes alien to one: perfecting yourself is really just a kind
of monument building, where you happen to be the monument. This is not, *pace*
Hurka, an Aristotelian perfectionism.

6 I employ the concept of 'desire' here, rather than some other subjectivist notion like
'pro-attitude,' because it seems to me that both the most plausible and the most common subjectivist theories of welfare use it. For a rejection of the view that the best
subjectivist theory of welfare would employ the concept of desire as central, see Sumner 1996, pp. 122–137. For the most part, the arguments that I use against subjectivist
theses are independent of whether the subjectivist view is cashed out in terms of desires or pro-attitudes.

7 First baseman, San Francisco Giants, Texas Rangers, Baltimore Orioles, and St. Louis
Cardinals. Lifetime batting agverage: .303.

8 A DF theorist might offer a different conception of desire, on which to have a desire
is merely to have a pro-attitude toward some state of affairs, rather than to be motivated to pursue it. Nothing essential to my argument assumes the latter conception of
desire. If one inclines toward accepting the pro-attitude conception of desire, one may
make the following substitutions: in place of the idea that desires are ascribed to
agents as explaining why the agents act as they do, say that desires are ascribed to

agents as explaining why they approve of what they do; and in place of a principle of individuation for desires that appeals to motivational force, assume a principle of individuation that appeals to commendatory force. The persuasiveness of the argument, whatever it is, should be unaffected by these changes.

9 There is one other important distinctive feature of Railton's view: technically it counts (according to the classifications set up in 2.1) as a version of formal objectivism, rather than formal subjectivism. Railton wants to say that the satisfaction of an agent's desires is not what constitutes that agent's good; rather, the agent's good is determined by what Railton calls his or her "objective interests" (1986b, p. 175). Terminologically, at least, it seems that Railton is far from DF theory's guiding idea, but the account of objective interests offered by Railton makes clear that a tight connection between the agent's well-being and the agent's desires is preserved. As we have already seen, Railton finds the agent's actual desires – his or her "subjective interests" (1986b, p. 173) – an inadequate starting point for an account of the agent's good: we should, rather, appeal to the agent's "objectified subjective interests," that is, what the agent would want him- or herself to want if he or she had "unqualified cognitive and imaginative powers, and full factual and nomological information about his [or her] physical and psychological constitution, capacities, circumstances, history, and so on" (1986b, pp. 173–174). If Railton held that the agent's well-being were constituted by the satisfaction of his or her objectified subjective interests, his view would be straightforwardly a version of the standard Knowledge-Modified DF theory. But Railton holds that it is the *reduction basis* for the agent's objectified subjective interests, rather than those interests themselves, that is the truth-maker for correct claims of the form 'such-and-such is an aspect of this agent's well-being.' The reduction basis for the agent's objectified subjective interests – roughly, those facts about the actual agent that the idealized agent would employ to determine what the idealized agent would want the actual agent to want – determines what the agent's objective interests are, and the obtaining of the ends of these objective interests Railton identifies with the agent's good (1986b, p. 176).

But the same arguments that I have offered against the move from a Simple to a Knowledge-Modified version of the standard DF theory can be employed against the move from a Simple to a Knowledge-Modified version of Railton's objective interest account: for Railton to motivate adequately the locating of the agent's objective interests with reference to the reduction basis of the agent's objectified subjective interests, rather than with reference to the reduction basis of the agent's subjective interests, he must provide some rationale for doing so. But it seems that the argument thus far has cut off the most straightforward route: that the full information stipulated in the case of objectified subjective interests, yet possibly not present in the case of subjective interests, might cause an agent either to lose desires irrelevant to well-being that he or she otherwise would have had or to have desires relevant to well-being that he or she otherwise would have lacked. While Railton's take on the relationship between well-being and desire clearly makes his view a distinctive version of DF theory, the fact that his Knowledge-Modified view offers the same rationale for rejecting the Simple view that is offered by more standard conceptions of Knowledge-Modified DF theory leaves it open to the same line of objection that I have pressed against more standard Knowledge-Modified DF views.

10 Not all 'passing desires' are occasions of being motivated that are resultant upon a

desire proper and some specificatory or instrumental belief. Some are genuine basic desires that are just quite transitory, and these may not be open to criticism on the Simple view. One might say that since a Simple view must allow these ephemeral desires to determine in some way the content of the agent's well-being, this constitutes an objection to that view. I doubt, though, that a Knowledge-Modified view would provide any way to eliminate such desires. Do we have any reason to think that improvements in information would have any effect on an agent's tendency to form ephemeral desires?

11 This is true with respect to desires also: just because something would satisfy a desire doesn't mean that one has a desire for that something. This follows from the principle of individuation for desires and is also intuitively plausible. I may have a desire for something to quench my thirst, and a bottle of an obscure Lithuanian mineral water might satisfy this desire, but it would be strange to hold that I had a desire for a bottle of that brand of mineral water.

12 Parfit remarks in his survey of different accounts of well-being that "[i]n choosing between these theories, we must decide how much weight to give to imagined cases in which someone's fully informed preferences are bizarre" (Parfit 1984, p. 499). He does not reach a definite answer here, and I will not attempt to pronounce on the relevance of all imagined cases. But it seems that one could have such a desire as described in my text, and such a desire could survive any full-information conditions that are placed on desires if their fulfillment is to count as contributing to one's well-being.

13 It might be responded that since I admit that in this case one who avoids touching a brown box acts intelligibly, and the minimal conception of 'reason for action' that I am working with (0.1) is one in which one acts intelligibly if and only if one has a reason for acting, I am committed to the view that one who avoids touching the brown box in this case has a reason to avoid touching the brown box. But I am not committed to this; I would deny that the fact one acts intelligibly in ϕ-ing implies that one has a reason to ϕ. All it implies, rather, is that one has a reason for action that is satisfied by one's ϕ-ing. And I do not deny that there is such a reason in this case: if one has a desire to avoid touching brown boxes, then one has a reason either to avoid touching brown boxes, or to rid oneself of the desire to avoid touching brown boxes. This reason is satisfied by not touching brown boxes, just as the act of putting the quarter in my left pocket into the machine satisfies the reason to put a quarter into the machine.

14 More exactly: prudential value for humans just is perfectionist value with regard to humans.

15 One might be unmoved by this argument if one thinks that a life could not have gone well if much of it was spent having con-attitudes toward the states of affairs that obtained in it. But this sort of consideration can be incorporated within a formally objectivist theory that is substantively a mixed position (2.1), for such a view could hold that there is a basic good that can only be realized by lacking con-attitudes toward one's own life. Indeed, I think that the good of inner peace as described in 3.3 might be the sort of good in question here.

16 For a different view of why internalism and externalism collapse into one thesis, see Schueler 1995, pp. 57–77. He argues that on the only sense of 'desire' in which it is at all plausible that all reasons for action are rooted in one's desires, the internalist thesis rules out nothing that is allowed by the externalist.

17 Parfit goes on to say: "Nor should we expect our knowledge of such truths, if we have any, to be like our knowledge of the world around us" (1997, p. 121). I return to this worry about the epistemology of practical knowledge on a substantive conception of practical rationality later in this section.

Chapter 3. The Reasons That Make Action Intelligible

1 This list has marked similarities to that presented in Finnis 1980; and indeed my method has been to start with Finnis's mostly adequate list and to modify it where I thought necessary. The main differences between my list and Finnis's are (i) the addition of the goods of inner peace and happiness, (ii) the name and treatment of the good of excellence in agency (which Finnis calls "practical reasonableness"), (iii) the addition of 'excellence in work' within the same category of basic good as play, and (iv) the attempt to provide a dialectical defense of each of these goods by reliance on the method discussed in 1.3.

2 I adapt this account of pain from Shelly Kagan's analysis of pleasure. On Kagan's view, "An experience E that occurs at time t to a person P is pleasant if and only if: (1) P has a desire at t that E occur at t, [and] (2) P's desire is an immediate response to E's occurrent phenomenal qualities (i.e., its qualia)" (Kagan 1992, p. 173). This definition can obviously be transformed into an analysis of pain merely by modifying condition (1) so that P has a desire at t that E not occur at t.

3 I put to the side arguments that move straightaway from the premise "in certain situations, one would prefer being dead to being alive" to the conclusion "life is not an intrinsic good." Even assuming one's preferences to be reasonable, it is consistent with preferring death to life in some case to hold that life is an intrinsic good the goodness of which might be outweighed by the evils attendant on staying alive. While I will later call into question the notion of outweighing presupposed by this argument, that does not affect the point that to say that something is intrinsically good obviously does not imply that there are no situations in which one would prefer not to have that good.

4 Both theists and nontheists characteristically agree that the concept of God, as most perfect being, includes omniscience – not simply knowledge of what is really important in the universe, where what is really important is specified either in some formal or in some substantive way. It would be a deficiency in God as a cognizer not to know everything. Similarly, I say, it seems to me to be a deprivation in us humans qua cognizers to have false views even on matters that are of little importance, however one specifies 'importance.'

5 For MacIntyre, a practice is "any coherent and complex form of socially established cooperative human activity through which goods internal to that activity are realized in the course of trying to achieve those standards of excellence which are appropriate to, and partially definitive of, that form of activity, with the result that human powers to achieve excellence, and human conceptions of the ends and goods involved, are systematically extended" (1981, p. 187).

6 Consider the remarks of Sissela Bok in her book *Lying:* "Those who learn they have been lied to in an important matter – say, the identity of their parents, the affection of their spouse, or the integrity of their government – are resentful, disappointed, and suspicious. They feel wronged; they are wary of new overtures. And they look back

on their past beliefs and actions in the new light of the discovered lies. They see that they were manipulated, that the deceit made them unable to make choices for themselves according to the most adequate information available, unable to act as they would have wanted to act had they known all along." See Bok 1978, pp. 31–32.

7 Parfit thus concludes that subjectivist theories would have to restrict the relevant desires in some way (1984, p. 494). James Griffin carries out the task of narrowing the theory so that only those desires that become part of our aims count (1986, pp. 21–22).

Chapter 4. Welfarism and Its Discontents

1 For a similar consequentialist stratagem and anti-consequentialist rejoinder, see the exchange between Sturgeon and Anderson (Sturgeon 1996 and Anderson 1996). Sturgeon argues that the consequentialist can understand the point of justice, and promise keeping, in terms of the intrinsic value of such states of affairs (1996, pp. 511–514); Anderson replies, rightly in my view, that even if consequentialism can get the right results in this way, it "fails to articulate an adequate rationale for the ends it recommends" (1996, pp. 539–540).

2 For one attempt to work out an account of practical rationality entirely in terms of the expression of appropriate attitudes toward values, see Anderson 1993, esp. pp. 17–43. For some reflections on the point of expressive action, see Adams 1997.

Chapter 5. The Principles That Make Choice Reasonable

1 Why are plans of action the *primary* object of assessment by principles of practical reasonableness, rather than the *only* object of assessment by principles of practical reasonableness? Plans of action are not the only things that are deemed reasonable or unreasonable; agents are deemed reasonable or unreasonable also. In some cases, an agent's reasonableness can be assessed by reference to that agent's plans of action. But, as I will show, principles of reasonableness for plans of action are unable to account for an agent's reasonableness or unreasonableness in forming, revising, and following plans of action. Thus, we will have to formulate principles of practical reasonableness that apply directly to agents. See 5.6.

2 This is the role that Onora O'Neill ascribes to the Categorical Imperative: "The Categorical Imperative provides a way of testing the moral acceptability of what we propose to do. It does not aim to generate plans of action for those who have none" (1989b, p. 84).

3 To offer an example that will foreshadow the later discussion: I shall argue that all distinct instances of basic goods are incommensurable (5.3). To say that a certain plan of action presupposes commensurability and is, therefore, unreasonable is not to say that any agent that forms that plan of action in fact believes in commensurability. It is to say that one's selecting this plan of action makes sense only given this assumption about commensurability.

4 There is, however, a negative feature of this framework that should be mentioned. For, as I conceded, by taking plans of action to be the appropriate object of assessment, one precludes the possibility that failing to act for any good is to be counted unreasonable. But egoism and consequentialism do not state merely that if one acts

for a good, one should maximize the good (whether of oneself or overall); they state that one should maximize the good. This framework, then, is unable to capture this feature of egoist and consequentialist views. But I do not take this to be a great loss, for I think that egoists and consequentialists should, and can easily, divide their view into a principle of intelligibility and a principle of reasonableness: that good is to be pursued and that all those plans of action formulated in order to pursue the good should be ruled out except those that maximize the good.

5 Perhaps we need also to add, in order to get the standard egoistic theory of practical rationality, the thesis of promotionism: that the only reasonable response to goods is that of promotion (4.4). Otherwise, there might be egoistically justified expressive action, the performance of which might conflict with what is required in order to maximize one's own good.

6 If there are any consequentialists that hold that they are not bound to provide a specification of the good, I would respond that they are betraying the consequentialist aim of characterizing the right in terms of the good. For without *some* specification of the good, we have no reason to think that the good provides an independent standard for the right. (In fact, I think a lot of consequentialists do betray the consequentialist project in this way, turning consequentialism into a kind of intuitionism by refusing to commit themselves to a theory of the good.)

7 Again, it seems that, just as in the case of egoism, we also need to assume the promotionist thesis in order to seal the case for consequentialism. See note 5.

8 I imagine that some utilitarians might deny this characterization, affirming instead an account of well-being framed in terms of an agent-neutral notion of goodness. Sumner criticizes this quasi-Moorean view in his 1996, pp. 46–53. Since I agree with Sumner that any account of well-being must do justice to subject-relativity, and no agent-neutral account of the good can pull this off, I shall suppose that the utilitarian does not make this move.

9 The paradox of deontology is that the deontologist holds that "some acts are so objectionable that one ought not to perform them even if this means that more equally weighty acts of the very same kind . . . will ensue, and even if there are no other morally relevant consequences to be considered" (Scheffler 1994, p. 82). For a discussion of the difficulties in providing a rationale for moral restrictions of this sort, see Scheffler 1994, pp. 80–114.

10 It is clear that this is not any kind of a priori argument for the impossibility of there being an adequate explication of agent-neutral goodness. I am just claiming that at present, we lack any such plausible explications. If such plausible explications were forthcoming, I would then have to defend my allegiance to welfarism wholly from within the natural law view by bringing the natural law theory's account of the good in contention with rival accounts that countenance agent-neutral goods.

11 Scott MacDonald also seems to employ this strategy in MacDonald 1990. While affirming that, on Aquinas's view, the rational agent seeks his or her own good, MacDonald points out that each person's interests are "not narrowly individualistic. One might hold that by virtue of their possessing intellect human beings have an interest in a good that includes, perhaps even predominantly, the good of others. Hence, when human beings seek the good of the family or the city they seek it as part of their own good" (1990, p. 339). MacDonald holds that other-regarding concerns can be explained in these terms (1990, p. 340).

12 The reason that 'agent-relative' and 'agent-neutral' are in brackets is that Nagel's text uses the terms "subjective" and "objective" in place of "agent-relative" and "agent-neutral," respectively. Nagel has since used the language of agent-neutrality and agent-relativity, following Parfit, who introduced these terms in his 1984.

13 Slote's satisficing consequentialism notwithstanding; see his 1985, pp. 35–59.

14 Finnis provides a helpfully pedestrian example of how an apparent choice might fail with regard to practical significance. Suppose that one is house hunting, and is interested in only three factors: price, size, and proximity to work. If one is considering two houses, and one of the houses is cheaper, larger, and closer to work than the other, then there is no practically significant choice between them: one who was interested only in those factors, yet insisted on choosing the more expensive, smaller, and more remotely located house, would be acting unintelligibly. See Finnis, Boyle, and Grisez 1987, p. 258.

15 One issue that requires further exploration is that of specifying in a tolerably detailed way precisely how much is included in a state of affairs that is an instance of basic good.

16 Such as Finnis's house-hunting example described in note 14; one who really is interested wholly in size, price, and location, and regrets missing out on the house that is smaller, more expensive, and further from work, is completely unreasonable, perhaps even unintelligible.

17 To claim that they are producible ends is not to claim that they are only reasons when they can be produced; to affirm this is to affirm promotionism (4.4), which I claim that the welfarist can plausibly deny. Rather, it is to claim that reasons are the kinds of thing that at some time or other might be made to obtain.

18 It might be the case that it is peculiar to hold that there are certain requirements that *follow* from placing the goods in a personal hierarchy: it could be just that for the goods to be in a personal hierarchy is for the agent to treat them in accordance with certain fixed rules. But, once again, the defender of the hierarchy view could hold that what it is for the basic goods to form a hierarchy is that it is appropriate to treat them in accordance with those principles.

19 Some agent-neutral predicates can: 'is an instance of Murphy's living' is agent-neutral, and of course, an appeal to identity is relevant. But this is not the type of agent-neutral reason, I have suggested, that arises from agent-relative ones.

20 Compare this way of arguing for the Pauline principle with Scheffler's argument for the need to recognize an "agent-centered prerogative" in order to respond appropriately to the "personal point of view": see Scheffler 1994, pp. 41–79.

21 I am, of course, not claiming that to be adequately cognizant of the other goods that one is forgoing in forming such a plan of action need involve enumerating all such goods, or anything of the kind. I take it that one could reasonably form a commitment 'come what may.' One understanding of Christian marriage would involve just such a commitment; it could be made reasonable in part by the sort of goods that are available only through such a thoroughgoing commitment.

22 In his commentary on the *Nicomachean Ethics,* Aquinas writes: "There is still more uncertainty if one wishes to descend further to the resolution of particular cases. For this subject is not subsumed under art or tradition, because the causes of particular actions are infinitely diversified. Hence, the judgment of particular cases is left to each person's prudence. One who employs prudence aims to consider the things that

should be done at the present time, having considered all the particular circumstances" (II, Lectio 2, 259).

Chapter 6. What Ought to Be Done

1 Hare's view does not. What Hare's view of moral thinking is intended to capture is not why a moral judgment is both impartial and overriding but, rather, what it is to form a judgment that is both impartial and overriding. This leaves to the side whether there is anything uniquely reasonable about engaging in this kind of thinking. Hare's remarks on this subject seem to indicate that there are simply various forms of rationality; the most that he does to unify them is to try to show that sound prudential thinking suggests it would be best for one to adopt dispositions that would also be endorsed by moral thinking (Hare 1981, pp. 190–205).

2 One's decision could go afoul of the nature of the reasons for action without violating a natural law principle if, as the weak version of the epistemological reading of virtue ethics suggests (see 5.7), there are some responses to the basic goods that rest on false presuppositions about the nature of those goods, yet which are not such that principles can be adequately formulated that rule them out.

3 The clearest formulation of Finnis's argument is from an early paper: "To choose directly against [any basic value] in favour of some other basic value is arbitrary, for each of the basic values is equally basic, equally irreducibly and self-evidently attractive. . . . So: . . . *no lying, for truth is a basic value and can be directly at stake in communication*" (Finnis 1970, pp. 375–376). But see also Finnis 1980, p. 124, and Finnis 1991, p. 63. To say that there is a moral absolute against lying is not, of course, to say that one is always bound to tell the truth. It is to say that *if* one asserts something, one must assert only what is true.

4 I grant, of course, that not all instances of intentional deception are attacks on the good of excellence in agency. Some are simply unintelligible: but the unintelligible is not the subject matter of principles of practical reasonableness governing choice (5.1). Some may just be acts of cruelty, made intelligible only by their status as harmful acts somehow bringing inner peace to the agent. But these are clearly not typical cases of lying.

5 Hume's point in describing this case of course concerns motivation: that even the most self-seeking of us are motivated not to walk on the other's gouty toes if it is all the same to us which side of the path we walk on. If psychological egoism were true, however, the fact that continuing over the person's toes would cause him pain and damage would not motivate us in the least. But it does move us: therefore, psychological egoism is false. Similarly, we could say that if ethical egoism were true, the fact that continuing over the other's toes causes the beggar pain and damage would not give us reason to walk on the other side of the path. But we do have a reason to walk on the other side: therefore, ethical egoism is false.

6 Of course, the mere fact that one's judgment about some matter might change and thus remove the dilemma does not show that there is no dilemma. Consider the (alleged) dilemma generated by a person's knowingly making two incompatible promises. The fact that one of the parties might drop dead, thus nullifying the promisor's obligation, has never been thought to cast doubt on the dilemmatic nature of that situation.

7 I am indebted to Henry Richardson for this way of putting the point.

Works Cited

Works are cited in my text by the author's last name and the year the work was published. Exceptions include classic works by Aristotle, Aquinas, Hobbes, Hume, Kant, Mill, Sidgwick, and Moore: all of these texts are cited by abbreviated title. References are given by page number in the cited edition, unless otherwise indicated in the bibliographical entry.

Achtenberg, Deborah. 1989. "The Role of the *Ergon* Argument in Aristotle's *Nicomachean Ethics*." *Ancient Philosophy* 9, pp. 37–47.

Adams, Robert Merrihew. 1997. "Symbolic Value." *Midwest Studies in Philosophy* 21 (1997), pp. 1–15.

Altham, J., and R. Harrison, eds. 1995. *World, Mind, and Ethics*. Cambridge University Press.

Anderson, Elizabeth. 1993. *Value in Ethics and Economics*. Harvard University Press.

Anderson, Elizabeth. 1996. "Reasons, Attitudes, and Values: Replies to Sturgeon and Piper." *Ethics* 106, pp. 538–554.

Anscombe, G. E. M. 1957. *Intention*. Blackwell.

Anscombe, G. E. M. 1958. "Modern Moral Philosophy." *Philosophy* 33, pp. 1–19.

Aquinas, Thomas. 1964. *Commentary on the* Nicomachean Ethics, trans. C. I. Litzinger. Regnery. References given by book, lectio, and section number.

Aquinas, Thomas. 1979. *On Kingship, to the King of Cyprus (De Regno)*, trans. Gerald Phelan. Hyperion.

Aquinas, Thomas. 1981. *Summa Theologiae,* trans. Fathers of the English Dominican Province. Christian Classics. References given by part, question, and article number.

Aristotle. 1960. *Metaphysics,* trans. Richard Hope. University of Michigan Press. References given by Bekker numbers.

Aristotle. 1985. *Nicomachean Ethics,* trans. Terence Irwin. Hackett. References given by Bekker numbers.

Austin, J. L. 1967. "ΑΓΑΘΟΝ and ΕΥΔΑΙΜΟΝΙΑ in the Ethics of Aristotle." In Moravcsik 1967, pp. 261–296.

Ayala, Francisco J. 1972. "The Autonomy of Biology as a Natural Science." In Breck and Yourgrau 1972, pp. 1–16.

Beaty, Michael. 1990. *Christian Theism and the Problems of Philosophy*. University of Notre Dame Press.

Bedau, Mark. 1991. "Can Biological Teleology be Naturalized?" *Journal of Philosophy* 88, pp. 647–655.

Bedau, Mark. 1992a. "Where's the Good in Teleology?" *Philosophy and Phenomenological Research* 52, pp. 781–806.

Bedau, Mark. 1992b. "Goal-Directed Systems and the Good." *Monist* 75, pp. 34–51.

Bergson, Henri. 1911. *Creative Evolution,* trans. Arthur Mitchell. Holt.

Bok, Sissela. 1978. *Lying: Moral Choice in Private and Public Life.* Random House.

Boyle, Jr., Joseph M. 1984. "Aquinas, Kant, and Donagan on Moral Principles." *New Scholasticism* 58, pp. 391–408.

Bradley, Denis J. M. 1997. *Aquinas on the Twofold Human Good: Reason and Human Happiness in Aquinas's Moral Science.* Catholic University of America Press.

Brandt, Richard. 1979. *A Theory of the Good and the Right.* Oxford University Press.

Breck, Allen D., and Wolfgang Yourgrau, eds. 1972. *Biology, History, and Natural Philosophy.* Plenum Press.

Chisholm, Roderick. 1977. *Theory of Knowledge,* 2nd. ed. Prentice-Hall.

Crowe, M. B. 1977. *The Changing Profile of the Natural Law.* Martinus Nijhoff.

Dancy, Jonathan. 1993. *Moral Reasons.* Blackwell.

Darwall, Stephen, Alan Gibbard, and Peter Railton. 1992. "Toward *Fin de siècle* Ethics: Some Trends." *Philosophical Review* 101, pp. 115–189.

Dawkins, Richard. 1986. *The Blind Watchmaker: Why the Evidence of Evolution Reveals a Universe without Design.* Norton.

Dennett, Daniel C. 1981a. *Brainstorms: Philosophical Essays on Mind and Psychology.* MIT Press.

Dennett, Daniel C. 1981b. "Why You Can't Make a Computer that Feels Pain." In Dennett 1981a, pp. 190–229.

Donagan, Alan. 1977. *The Theory of Morality.* University of Chicago Press.

Dworkin, Gerald. 1982. "Is More Choice Better than Less?" *Midwest Studies in Philosophy* 7, pp. 47–61.

Edgley, Roy. 1969. *Reason in Theory and Practice.* Hutchinson.

Feinberg, Joel. 1965. "The Expressive Function of Punishment." *Monist* 49, pp. 397–423.

Finnis, John. 1970. "Natural Law and Unnatural Acts." *Heythrop Journal* 11, pp. 365–387.

Finnis, John. 1977. "Scepticism, Self-Refutation, and the Good of Truth." In Hacker and Raz 1977, pp. 247–267.

Finnis, John. 1980. *Natural Law and Natural Rights.* Oxford University Press.

Finnis, John. 1981. "Natural Law and the 'Is'–'Ought' Question: An Invitation to Professor Veatch." *Catholic Lawyer* 81, pp. 266–277.

Finnis, John. 1983. *Fundamentals of Ethics.* Oxford University Press.

Finnis, John. 1984. "The Authority of Law in the Predicament of Contemporary Social Theory." *Notre Dame Journal of Law, Ethics, and Public Policy* 1, pp. 114–137.

Finnis, John. 1989. "Law as Coordination." *Ratio Juris* 2, pp. 97–104.

Finnis, John. 1991. *Moral Absolutes.* Catholic University of America Press.

Finnis, John. 1992. "Natural Law and Legal Reasoning." In George 1992b, pp. 134–157.

Finnis, John. 1998. *Aquinas: Moral, Political, and Legal Theory.* Oxford University Press.

Finnis, John, Joseph Boyle, and Germain Grisez. 1987. *Nuclear Deterrence, Morality, and Realism.* Oxford University Press.

Frey, R. G., and Christopher Morris, eds. 1993. *Value, Welfare, and Morality.* Cambridge University Press.

Froelich, Gregory. 1989. "The Equivocal Status of *Bonum Commune.*" *New Scholasticism* 63, pp. 37–58.

Gauthier, David. 1986. *Morals by Agreement.* Oxford University Press.

George, Robert P. 1988. "Recent Criticism of Natural Law Theory." *University of Chicago Law Review* 55, pp. 1371–1429.

George, Robert P. 1992a. "Natural Law Theory and Human Nature." In George 1992b, pp. 31–41.

George, Robert P., ed. 1992b. *Natural Law Theory: Contemporary Essays.* Oxford University Press.

Glover, Jonathan. 1977. *Causing Deaths and Saving Lives.* Penguin Books.

Goerner, E. A. 1983. "On Thomistic Natural Right: The Good Man's View of Thomistic Natural Law." *Political Theory* 11, pp. 393–418.

Goldstein, Irwin. 1980. "Why People Prefer Pleasure to Pain." *Philosophy* 55, pp. 349–362.

Goldstein, Irwin. 1989. "Pleasure and Pain: Unconditional, Intrinsic Values." *Philosophy and Phenomenological Research* 50, pp. 255–275.

Gomez-Lobo, Alfonso. 1989. "The *Ergon* Inference." *Phronesis* 34, pp. 170–184.

Gowans, Christopher W. 1994. *Innocence Lost: An Examination of Inescapable Moral Wrongdoing.* Oxford University Press.

Granrose, John. 1970. "The Authority of Conscience." *Southern Journal of Philosophy* 8, pp. 205–213.

Griffin, James. 1986. *Well-Being: Its Meaning, Measurement, and Moral Importance.* Oxford University Press.

Grisez, Germain. 1965. "The First Principle of Practical Reason: A Commentary on the *Summa Theologiae,* 1–2, Question 94, Article 2." *Natural Law Forum* 10, pp. 168–201.

Grisez, Germain. 1978. "Against Consequentialism." *American Journal of Jurisprudence* 23, pp. 21–72.

Grisez, Germain, and John Finnis. 1981. "The Basic Principles of the Natural Law: A Reply to Ralph McInerny." *American Journal of Jurisprudence* 26, pp. 21–31.

Grisez, Germain, John Finnis, and Joseph Boyle. 1987. "Practical Principles, Moral Truth, and Ultimate Ends." *American Journal of Jurisprudence* 32, pp. 99–151.

Haakonssen, Knud. 1996. *Natural Law and Moral Philosophy: From Grotius to the Scottish Enlightenment.* Cambridge University Press.

Hacker, P. M. S., and Joseph Raz, eds. 1977. *Law, Morality, and Society: Essays in Honour of H. L. A. Hart.* Oxford University Press.

Hall, Pamela M. 1994. *Narrative and the Natural Law: An Interpretation of Thomistic Ethics.* University of Notre Dame Press.

Hardie, W. F. R. 1965. "The Final Good in Aristotle's Ethics." *Philosophy* 40, pp. 277–295.

Hare, R. M. 1981. *Moral Thinking.* Oxford University Press.

Harman, Gilbert, and Judith Jarvis Thomson. 1996. *Moral Relativism and Moral Objectivity.* Blackwell.

Hill, Jr., Thomas E. 1992. *Dignity and Practical Reason in Kant's Moral Theory.* Cornell University Press.

Hittinger, Russell. 1987. *A Critique of the New Natural Law Theory.* University of Notre Dame Press.

Hobbes, Thomas. 1993. *Leviathan,* ed. Edwin Curley. Hackett.

Hooker, Brad, and Margaret Little, eds. 2000. *Moral Particularism.* Oxford.

Horton, John, and Susan Mendus, eds. 1994. *After MacIntyre: Critical Perspectives on the Work of Alasdair MacIntyre.* University of Notre Dame Press.

Huizinga, Johan. 1955. *Homo Ludens: A Study of the Play Element in Culture.* Beacon Press.

Hume, David. 1972. *Enquiry Concerning the Principles of Morals,* ed. L. A. Selby-Bigge. Oxford University Press.

Hume, David. 1978. *Treatise of Human Nature,* ed. L. A. Selby-Bigge. Oxford University Press.

Hurka, Thomas. 1987. "Why Value Autonomy?" *Social Theory and Practice* 13, pp. 361–382.

Hurka, Thomas. 1993. *Perfectionism.* Oxford University Press.

Jackson, Frank. 1982. "Epiphenomenal Qualia." *Philosophical Quarterly* 32, pp. 127–136.

Kagan, Shelly. 1987. "Donagan on the Sins of Consequentialism." *Canadian Journal of Philosophy* 17, pp. 643–654.

Kagan, Shelly. 1989. *The Limits of Morality.* Oxford University Press.

Kagan, Shelly. 1992. "The Limits of Well-Being." *Social Philosophy & Policy* 9, pp. 169–189.

Kant, Immanuel. 1956. *Critique of Practical Reason,* trans. Lewis White Beck. Bobbs-Merrill. References given by Academy numbers.

Kant, Immanuel. 1981. *Metaphysics of Morals,* trans. Mary Gregor. Cambridge University Press. References given by Academy numbers.

Kant, Immanuel. 1993. *Grounding for the Metaphysics of Morals,* 3rd ed., trans. James Ellington. Hackett. References given by Academy numbers.

Kitcher, Philip. 1999. "Essence and Perfection." *Ethics* 110, pp. 59–83.

Knowles, Dudley, and John Skorupski, eds. 1993. *Virtue and Taste: Essays on Politics, Ethics, and Aesthetics.* Blackwell.

Kripke, Saul. 1972. *Naming and Necessity.* Harvard University Press.

Lewis, David. 1973. "Causation." *Journal of Philosophy* 70, pp. 556–567.

Lisska, Anthony J. 1996. *Aquinas's Theory of Natural Law: An Analytic Reconstruction.* Oxford University Press.

Little, Margaret O. 2000. "Moral Generalities Revisited: The Radical Case for a Moderate Moral Particularism." In Hooker and Little 2000, pp. 276–304.

Loeb, Don. 1995. "Full-Information Theories of Individual Good." *Social Theory and Practice* 21, pp. 1–30.

Lomasky, Loren. 1987. *Persons, Rights, and the Moral Community.* Oxford University Press.

MacDonald, Scott. 1990. "Egoistic Rationalism: Aquinas's Basis for Christian Morality." In Beaty 1990, pp. 327–354.

MacIntyre, Alasdair. 1981. *After Virtue,* 2nd ed. University of Notre Dame Press.

MacIntyre, Alasdair. 1988. *Whose Justice? Which Rationality?* University of Notre Dame Press.

MacIntyre, Alasdair. 1990a. *First Principles, Final Ends, and Contemporary Philosophical Issues.* Marquette University Press.

MacIntyre, Alasdair. 1990b. "Moral Dilemmas." *Philosophy and Phenomenological Research* 50 (supplement), pp. 367–382.

MacIntyre, Alasdair. 1994. "A Partial Response to My Critics." In Horton and Mendus 1994, pp. 283–304.

MacIntyre, Alasdair. 1997. "Natural Law Reconsidered" [review of Lisska 1996]. *International Philosophical Quarterly* 37, pp. 95–99.

Mack, Eric. "Agent-Relativity of Value, Deontic Restraints, and Self-Ownership." In Frey and Morris 1993, pp. 209–232.

Mackie, J. L. 1977. *Ethics: Inventing Right and Wrong.* Penguin.

Mackie, J. L. 1982. "Morality and the Retributive Emotions." *Criminal Justice Ethics* 1, pp. 3–10.

May, Larry. 1983. "On Conscience." *American Philosophical Quarterly* 20, pp. 57–67.

McDowell, John. 1978. "Are Moral Requirements Hypothetical Imperatives?" *Proceedings of the Aristotelian Society* 52 (supplement), pp. 13–29.

McInerny, Ralph. 1980. "The Principles of Natural Law." *American Journal of Jurisprudence* 25, pp. 1–15.

McInerny, Ralph. 1982. *Ethica Thomistica.* Catholic University of America Press.

McNaughton, David. 1988. *Moral Vision.* Blackwell.

Mill, John Stuart. 1979. *Utilitarianism,* ed. George Sher. Hackett.

Millgram, Elijah. 1996. "Williams' Argument Against External Reasons." *Noûs* 30, pp. 197–220.

Millikan, Ruth. 1984. *Language, Thought, and Other Biological Categories.* MIT Press.

Moore, Andrew, and Roger Crisp. 1996. "Welfarism in Moral Theory." *Australasian Journal of Philosophy* 74, pp. 598–613.

Moore, G. E. 1993. *Principia Ethica,* ed. Thomas Baldwin. Cambridge University Press. References given by section numbers.

Moravcsik, J. M. E., ed. 1967. *Aristotle: A Collection of Critical Essays.* University of Notre Dame Press.

Murphy, Mark C. 1995a. "Self-Evidence, Human Nature, and Natural Law." *American Catholic Philosophical Quarterly* 69, pp. 471–484.

Murphy, Mark C. 1995b. "Was Hobbes a Legal Positivist?" *Ethics* 105, pp. 846–873.

Murphy, Mark C. 1996a. "Natural Law, Impartiality, and Others' Good." *Thomist* 60, pp. 53–80.

Murphy, Mark C. 1996b. "Natural Law and the Moral Absolute against Lying." *American Journal of Jurisprudence* 41, pp. 81–101.

Murphy, Mark C. 1997a. "The Conscience Principle." *Journal of Philosophical Research* 22, pp. 387–407.

Murphy, Mark C. 1997b. "Consent, Custom, and the Common Good in Aquinas's Account of Political Authority." *Review of Politics* 59, pp. 323–350.

Murphy, Mark C. 1997c. "Surrender of Judgment and the Consent Theory of Political Authority." *Law and Philosophy* 16, pp. 115–143.

Murphy, Mark C. 1998. "Natural Law Reconstructed" [review of Lisska 1996]. *Review of Politics* 60, pp. 189–192.

Murphy, Mark C. 1999. "The Simple Desire-Fulfillment Theory." *Noûs* 33, pp. 247–272.

Murphy, Mark C. 2000. "Hobbes on the Evil of Death." *Archiv für Geschichte der Philosophie* 82, pp. 36–61.

Murphy, Mark C. 2001. "Natural Law, Consent, and Political Obligation." *Social Philosophy & Policy,* pp. 70–92.

Nagel, Thomas. 1970. *The Possibility of Altruism.* Princeton University Press.

Nagel, Thomas. 1979a. *Mortal Questions.* Cambridge University Press.

Nagel, Thomas. 1979b. "Death." In Nagel 1979a, pp. 1–10.

Nagel, Thomas. 1979c. "The Fragmentation of Value." In Nagel 1979a, pp. 128–141.

Nagel, Thomas. 1980. "Aristotle on Eudaimonia." In Rorty 1980, pp. 7–14.

Nagel, Thomas. 1986. *The View from Nowhere.* Oxford University Press.

Neander, Karen. 1991. "The Teleological Notion of 'Function.'" *Australasian Journal of Philosophy* 69, pp. 454–468.

Nelson, Daniel Mark. 1992. *The Priority of Prudence.* Pennsylvania State University Press.

Norman, Richard. 1971. *Reasons for Actions: A Critique of Utilitarian Rationality.* Blackwell.

Nozick, Robert. 1974. *Anarchy, State, and Utopia.* Basic Books.

Nozick, Robert. 1981. *Philosophical Explanations.* Harvard University Press.

Nussbaum, Martha. 1988. "Non-Relative Virtues: An Aristotelian Approach." *Midwest Studies in Philosophy* 13, pp. 32–53.

Nussbaum, Martha. 1990a. *Love's Knowledge.* Oxford University Press.

Nussbaum, Martha. 1990b. "The Discernment of Perception: An Aristotelian Conception of Private and Public Rationality." In Nussbaum 1990a, pp. 54–105.

Nussbaum, Martha. 1995. "Aristotle on Human Nature and the Foundations of Ethics." In Altham and Harrison 1995, pp. 87–131.

Nussbaum, Martha, and Amartya Sen, eds. 1993. *The Quality of Life.* Oxford University Press.

O'Neill, Onora. 1989a. *Constructions of Reason: Explorations of Kant's Practical Philosophy.* Cambridge University Press.

O'Neill, Onora. 1989b. "Consistency in Action." In O'Neill 1989a, pp. 81–104.

Parfit, Derek. 1984. *Reasons and Persons.* Oxford University Press.

Parfit, Derek. 1997. "Reasons and Motivation." *Proceedings of the Aristotelian Society* (supplement) 71, pp. 99–130.

Perry, John. 1993a. *The Problem of the Essential Indexical and Other Essays.* Oxford University Press.

Perry, John. 1993b. "Perception, Action, and the Structure of Believing." In Perry 1993a, pp. 121–149.

Perry, John. 1993c. "The Problem of the Essential Indexical." In Perry 1993a, pp. 33–52.

Plantinga, Alvin. 1993. *Warrant and Proper Function.* Oxford University Press.

Potts, Timothy. 1980. *Conscience in Medieval Philosophy.* Cambridge University Press.

Quinn, Warren. 1993a. *Morality and Action.* Cambridge University Press.

Quinn, Warren. 1993b. "Putting Rationality in Its Place." In Quinn 1993a, pp. 228–255.

Rachels, James. 1999. *The Elements of Moral Philosophy,* 3d ed. McGraw-Hill.

Railton, Peter. 1986a. "Facts and Values." *Philosophical Topics* 14, pp. 5–31.

Railton, Peter. 1986b. "Moral Realism." *Philosophical Review* 95, pp. 163–207.

Railton, Peter. 1989. "Naturalism and Prescriptivity." *Social Philosophy & Policy* 7, pp. 151–174.

Rasmussen, Douglas B. 1999. "Human Flourishing and the Appeal to Human Nature." *Social Philosophy & Policy* 16, pp. 1–43.

Rawls, John. 1955. "Two Concepts of Rules." *Philosophical Review* 64, pp. 3–32.

Rawls, John. 1971. *A Theory of Justice.* Harvard University Press.

Rawls, John. 1993. *Political Liberalism.* Columbia University Press.

Raz, Joseph. 1979. *The Authority of Law.* Oxford University Press.

Richardson, Henry S. 1994. *Practical Reasoning about Final Ends.* Cambridge University Press.

Rorty, Amelie Oksenberg, ed. 1980. *Essays on Aristotle's Ethics.* University of California Press.

Sartwell, Crispin. 1992. "Why Knowledge Is Merely True Belief." *Journal of Philosophy* 89, pp. 167–180.

Sayre-McCord, Geoffrey, ed. 1988. *Essays on Moral Realism.* Cornell University Press.

Scanlon, Thomas. 1973. "Rawls's Theory of Justice." *University of Pennsylvania Law Review* 121, pp. 1020–1069.

Scanlon, Thomas. 1993. "Value, Desire, and Quality of Life." In Nussbaum and Sen 1993, pp. 185–200.

Scheffler, Samuel. 1994. *The Rejection of Consequentialism,* 2nd ed. Oxford University Press.

Schmidtz, David. 1994. "Choosing Ends." *Ethics* 104, pp. 226–251.

Schueler, G. F. 1995. *Desire: Its Role in Practical Reason and the Explanation of Action.* MIT Press.

Searle, John. 1995. *The Construction of Social Reality.* The Free Press.

Sen, Amartya. 1982a. *Choice, Welfare, and Measurement.* Blackwell.

Sen, Amartya. 1982b. "Equality of What?" In Sen 1982a, pp. 353–369.

Sidgwick, Henry. 1981. *The Methods of Ethics,* 7th ed. Hackett.

Slote, Michael. 1985. *Common-Sense Morality and Consequentialism.* Routledge & Kegan Paul.

Slote, Michael. 1996. "Agent-Based Virtue Ethics." *Midwest Studies in Philosophy* 20, pp. 83–101.

Sobel, David. 1997. "On the Subjectivity of Welfare." *Ethics* 107, pp. 501–508.

Sorabji, Richard. 1964. "Function." *Philosophical Quarterly* 14, pp. 289–302.

Stocker, Michael. 1976. "The Schizophrenia of Modern Ethical Theories." *Journal of Philosophy* 73, pp. 453–466.

Striker, Gisela. 1986. "Origins of the Concept of Natural Law." *Proceedings of the Boston Area Colloquium in Ancient Philosophy* 2, pp. 79–94.

Sturgeon, Nicholas. 1996. "Anderson on Reason and Value." *Ethics* 106, pp. 509–524.

Sumner, L. W. 1996. *Welfare, Happiness, and Ethics.* Oxford University Press.

Telfer, Elizabeth. 1993. "The Pleasures of Eating and Drinking." In Knowles and Skorupski 1993, pp. 98–110.

Thomson, Judith Jarvis. 1996. "Moral Objectivity." In Harman and Thomson 1996, pp. 65–154.

van Inwagen, Peter. 1990. *Material Beings.* Cornell University Press.

Veatch, Henry. 1981. "Natural Law and the 'Is'–'Ought' Question." *Catholic Lawyer* 81, pp. 251–265.

Veatch, Henry, and Joseph Rautenberg. 1991. "Does the Grisez-Finnis-Boyle Moral Philosophy Rest on a Mistake?" *Review of Metaphysics* 44, pp. 807–830.

Velleman, J. David. 1988. "Brandt's Definition of 'Good'." *Philosophical Review* 97, pp. 353–371.

Weinreb, Lloyd. 1987. *Natural Law and Justice.* Harvard University Press.

Whiting, Jennifer. 1988. "Aristotle's Function Argument: A Defense." *Ancient Philosophy* 8, pp. 33–48.

Wiggins, David. 1988. "Truth, Invention, and the Meaning of Life." In Sayre-McCord 1988, pp. 127–165.

Williams, Bernard. 1973a. *Problems of the Self.* Cambridge University Press.

Williams, Bernard. 1973b. "Ethical Consistency." In Williams 1973a, pp. 166–186.

Williams, Bernard. 1981a. *Moral Luck.* Cambridge University Press.

Williams, Bernard. 1981b. "Internal and External Reasons." In Williams 1981a, pp. 101–113.

Williams, Bernard. 1995a. *Making Sense of Humanity.* Cambridge University Press.

Williams, Bernard. 1995b. "Internal Reasons and the Obscurity of Blame." In Williams 1995a, pp. 35–45.

Williams, Bernard. 1995c. "Replies." In Altham and Harrison 1995, pp. 185–224.

Wright, Larry. 1973. "Functions." *Philosophical Review* 82, pp. 139–168.

Zagzebski, Linda. 1996. *Virtues of the Mind: An Inquiry into the Nature of Virtue and the Ethical Foundations of Knowledge.* Cambridge University Press.

Index

goods
  agent-neutral, *see* agent-neutrality: of
    goods
  agent-relative, *see* agent-relativity: of
    goods
  basic, *see* basic goods
goodwill, 130
Gowans, Christopher W., 209, 244–246
Granrose, John, 241–242
Griffin, James, 46, 67, 69–71, 93,
    100–101, 266n7
Grisez, Germain, 2, 11, 131, 176–177,
    190, 256n7, 256n9, 260n25, 268n14
  on incommensurability, 182–184, 186
grounding thesis, 2, 6, 14–17, 137–138,
    260n26, 261n29
  strong version of, 16–17, 256n9
  weak version of, 15–16, 256n7

Haakonssen, Knud, 4
habituation, 218–219
happiness, good of, 133–135, 135–136,
    197, 265n1
  reductionist understanding of, 134
  unificationist understanding of, 134, 135
Hardie, W. F. R., 257n15
Hare, R. M., 145, 148–149, 269n1
Hill, Thomas E., Jr., 183
Hittinger, Russell, 14, 132
Hobbes, Thomas, 101, 126–127, 175,
    253–254, 262n3
Huizinga, Johan, 114
Hume, David, 13, 182, 239, 256n5,
    269n5
Hume's law (no 'ought' from 'is'),
    13–14, 17
Hurka, Thomas, 48–50, 117, 259n22,
    261n29, 262n5
hybrid theory of nature of well-being, 47,
    92–94, 135–137
hypothetical desire situations, 51–52, 62,
    65–66

impartiality, 202–204, 225–227, 269n1
inclinationism, 6, 8–13, 255n1, 260n25
  in Aquinas, 9–10
  defined, 6–8, 9
  difficulties with, 13, 14–17
  in Finnis, 8–10
incommensurability, *see also*
  commensurability

among agent-relative and agent-neutral
    reasons, 186
  among categories of basic good, 184
  among distinct instances of basic
    good, 185–186, 205–207
  general thesis about, 182–184
  and indifference with respect to
    options, 247–248
indexical judgments, 18–19
indifference objection, 102–105
inner peace, good of, 76, 118–125,
    135–136, 265n1
  and desires, 118
  and pleasure and pain, 120, 122,
    124–125
in-order-to judgments, 26–28, 31
intelligibility, 1–2, 10–12, 150–151,
    158–160, 160–161
intended/foreseen distinction, 165–166,
    168
intention-prescriptivism, 244–245
internalism, 80–90, 264n16
  and well-being, 80–81

Jackson, Frank, 33
Jordan, Michael, 108

Kagan, Shelly, 122, 145, 171, 226, 265n2
Kant, Immanuel, 118–119, 169–171,
    182–183, 184, 187–189
Kantianism
  on the nature of reasons for action,
    169–170
  on the principles of practical
    reasonableness, 170–171
Kitcher, Philip, 259–260n24
knowledge, good of, 38–40, 106–108,
    234–235
Kripke, Saul, 79

Lewis, David, 229
life, good of, 101–105, 265n3
life plans, 133–135, 157, 199–201, 210,
    248–249
Lisska, Anthony J., 4, 5, 8, 13–14, 17,
    43, 256n6
Little, Margaret O., 216
Loeb, Don, 69
Lomasky, Loren, 74
lying, moral rule against, 234–238,
    265–266n6